# AWS Cloud Computing Concepts and Tech Analogies

A guide to understand AWS services using easy-to-follow analogies from real life

**Ashish Prajapati**

**Juan Carlos Ruiz**

**Marco Tamassia**

<packt>

BIRMINGHAM—MUMBAI

# AWS Cloud Computing Concepts and Tech Analogies

**Group Product Manager**: Mohd Riyan Khan

**Publishing Product Manager**: Niranjan Naikwadi

**Senior Editor**: Runcil Rebello

**Technical Editor**: Rajat Sharma

**Copy Editor**: Safis Editing

**Project Coordinator**: Ashwin Kharwa

**Proofreader**: Safis Editing

**Indexer**: Sejal Dsilva

**Production Designers**: Alishon Mendonca, Joshua Misquitta

**Marketing Coordinator**: Agnes D'souza

First published: April 2023

Production reference: 1070423

Published by Packt Publishing Ltd.

Livery Place

35 Livery Street

Birmingham

B3 2PB, UK.

ISBN 978-1-80461-142-5

www.packtpub.com

*To my son Pradhyumn, who endured my occasional (read: always) bad mood; to my mother, Meenaxi and father, Praveen, who have supported me constantly; and to all my friends and family members, whom I treasure as my proudest possession.*

*– Ashish Prajapati*

*To all the people who made this possible (family, friends, and colleagues)… and to these interesting times in which semiconductors, computers, networks, and clouds exist together. And especially to Tobias Weltner, Jeffrey Snover, Bruce Payette, Raimund Andrée, and their related teams. They will probably know why.*

*– Juan Carlos Ruiz*

*To everyone who shares their knowledge for the sake of passion.*

*– Marco Tamassia*

# Contributors

## About the authors

**Ashish Prajapati** is a technical professional currently based in London, UK. He is passionate about helping individuals and enterprises learn cloud skills in an easy and fun way.

His deep background as a virtualization and cloud migration expert allows him to leverage his field knowledge into the classroom by bringing real-world examples to learners.

His work has helped many cloud enthusiasts get started with the cloud, learn the fundamentals, and achieve cloud certifications.

Ask him about the free training program he runs with his awesome colleagues, to help aspiring candidates learn technical as well as behavioral skills, and become solutions architects (#besaprogram).

**Juan Carlos Ruiz** is a technical instructor based in Barcelona, Spain. He has worked in the IT industry for a long time, in top companies such as DEC, Compaq, Microsoft, and AWS, and in multiple roles, such as tech support, development, and operations. He was doing DevOps tasks long before the term was coined.

He's an especially great fan of two activities. The first one is teaching (making sure students understand the basic concepts and relationships). The second one is automation (making IT work for humans, and not the other way around).

**Marco Tamassia** is a technical instructor based in Milan, Italy. He delivers a wide range of technical training to **Amazon Web Services** (**AWS**) customers across the EMEA region. He also collaborates in the creation of new courses such as *Planning & Designing Databases on AWS* and *Exam Readiness: AWS Certified Database - Specialty*. Marco has a deep background as a **Database Administrator** (**DBA**) for companies of all sizes (including AWS) and he's a public speaker. Through the use of public speaking techniques, Marco enriches the lessons and the events he delivers every day.

# About the reviewers

**Allen Thomas Varghese** has been a software engineer for more than 12 years, working on web applications at different levels: frontend, backend, and infrastructure in both cloud and data centers. At the age of 10, he was first introduced to computers, which required floppy disks to boot up at the time, and has not looked back since then. He has a bachelor's in mechanical engineering and a master's in computer science. Currently employed at Squarespace (Unfold) as a lead backend engineer, he is responsible for all its cloud infrastructure.

**Andres Damian Sacco** has been a developer since 2007 in different languages, including Java, PHP, and Node.js. His background is mainly in Java and the libraries or frameworks of that language. In most of the companies he worked for, he has researched new technologies to improve the applications' performance, stability, and quality.

He also participates as a technical reviewer for books from the following publishers: Manning, Apress, and Packt.

**Martin Nanchev** is a huge AWS and automation enthusiast. He is an SME for the AWS SysOp/SA Associate program and holds 12 AWS certificates. Martin is also an AWS Authorized Instructor and helps people become cloud experts. At his current company, Martin is part of the team building a next-generation data platform with the goal of the platform being secure, reliable, performant, scalable, and cost-efficient.

# Table of Contents

# Part 2: Platform Services

## 6

# Part 3: Application Services

# 11

## Decoupled Architectures – in Space and Time    221

# 12

## Containers – Contain Yourself and Ship Some Containers    241

# 13

## Serverless – So, Where Are My Servers?    267

# 14

## Caching – Microseconds Latency: Why Are We Always in a Rush?    285

# 15

# 16

# Preface

This book offers a quick and fun way to learn about the cloud, relating technical concepts to real-life analogies. We will be describing common issues and doubts through real enterprise scenarios, characters, and dialogs.

## Who this book is for

This book is targeted toward anyone who wants to learn about AWS cloud computing and to be able to explain its foundational concepts and mechanisms. You are expected to have a basic knowledge of IT systems.

## What this book covers

*Chapter 1, Understanding Cloud Computing – Demystifying the Cloud*, explains basic concepts related to cloud computing. These concepts will serve as the strong foundation for the whole book. You will learn about various components and service models of cloud computing and how they relate to each other. This chapter will also explore the benefits of using managed services versus unmanaged services.

*Chapter 2, Global Infrastructure behind Cloud Platforms – What Is the Cloud Made Of?*, explores the global infrastructure powering the cloud. Cloud service providers maintain data centers and related infrastructure all over the world to deliver services to their customers spread across the globe. After going through this chapter, you will have a better understanding of which factors to consider while selecting a location to host your application and services.

*Chapter 3, Computing – In Cloud We Trust, Everything Else We Compute*, explains how the cloud is all about virtualization and automation. In this chapter, you will learn about virtualization basics and how AWS offers virtual servers in the cloud. You could get started quickly by using preconfigured images and customize the configuration to suit your application or business need.

*Chapter 4, Storage – Where should I keep My Data and Maybe Publish It?*, looks at how the cloud offers multiple storage options, with different approaches and functionalities. We'll cover block storage (to provide our virtual servers with the disks they need) and other options, such as file storage, which can be simultaneously accessed from many computers. We'll also look at object storage, which is a simpler way to store just objects without the need for a full filesystem… but with the ability to publish those files to the internet without needing a server.

*Chapter 5, Networking – So, How Do I Get Inside, Outside, and Across the Cloud?*, details how most services in the cloud will be located inside networks managed by the cloud provider, and we'll probably keep some other networks on our on-premises locations. So, how can we connect and access cloud services? How do we get inside, outside, or maybe across the cloud network? Can we connect several networks together, even if some are on-premises? We'll cover some of these options and introduce the security aspects, which will be fully covered in subsequent chapters.

*Chapter 6, Databases – To SQL or Not to SQL for So Many Records...*, explains that a database is another fundamental service in IT. The cloud offers multiple database types (relational and non-relational), and for generic or specialized purposes (documents, graphs, in memory, ledger, etc.). This chapter will cover how using a database as a managed service allows the user to concentrate only on the data – no need to worry about hardware, operating systems, or any other unneeded aspect.

*Chapter 7, Identity and Access Management – Who Am I and What Can I Do?*, looks at how cloud computing provides flexible ways for authentication and authorization of users and applications. This chapter will explain the security controls around identity and access management. These controls can be applied at various levels and allow/deny service access based on different criteria defined in the security policy. Cloud security is based on the principle of least privilege and role-based access.

*Chapter 8, Monitoring – Is Big Brother Watching?*, shows that once the services are configured to run in the cloud, we have to monitor them. This way, we can see whether they are properly designed, and also anticipate changes. This chapter will focus on how monitoring allows us to decide whether we're providing the right level of service according to the demand, and see whether all the components behave in the expected way.

*Chapter 9, Scalability – I Scale to the Moon and Back*, discusses how most services in the cloud provide an inherent level of scalability. This is defined as the ability of a service to adapt automatically to the changing load. This way, the service will add resources to guarantee stable performance, even when the demand grows, and reduce resource consumption when the demand decreases, to save costs. Scalability is especially useful when it is automatic, with no human intervention. This chapter will cover how you define some rules, and the cloud scales the resources for you.

*Chapter 10, Automation – Look, My Infrastructure Is in Code!*, uses the definition of IT as "the technology that makes computers work for humans, and not the opposite." Following that definition, we'll try to create and operate all the services in an automated way, not depending on risky and costly human interaction. In the cloud, there are multiple options, based on writing code, scripts, or declaring tasks in a declarative language. The management of the infrastructure using these techniques is often referred to as "Infrastructure as Code." This chapter will cover some of the most used ones.

*Chapter 11, Decoupled Architectures – in Space and Time*, focuses on the concept of removing tight coupling in IT. You will understand the related definition of decoupled architecture and when to use it. Then, you will learn how to use it and its benefits in the cloud. This chapter will also focus on synchronous and asynchronous ways of communication between different services.

*Chapter 12, Containers – Contain Yourself and Ship Some Containers*, offers an overview of the container world in IT, starting with the basics (web services and microservices concepts) and ending with the benefits that IT architectures based on containers can provide. You will also understand the impact that containers have on the way development teams operate and are organized. You will also learn about various ways to run containerized workloads.

*Chapter 13, Serverless – So, Where Are My Servers?*, offers an explanation of what the serverless concept means in IT and what a serverless architecture looks like. You will learn when it's better to go for a serverless strategy compared to a server-based one, but also when the opposite is true. In this chapter, we also clarify how the pay-as-you-go pricing model works and why it is considered one of the main benefits of serverless architectures.

*Chapter 14, Caching – Microseconds Latency: Why Are We Always in a Rush?*, explains what caching means in IT, and why and when architects and developers would need it for their architectures and applications. You will also learn about the most popular caching strategies.

*Chapter 15, Blockchain – Who Watches the Watchmen?*, explores the blockchain world and all the concepts around it, including hash chains and properties such as the immutability and verifiability of a ledger database. You will learn about using a blockchain platform over a ledger database, as well as how these technologies could be used in today's world.

*Chapter 16, What the Future Holds*, focuses on the advantages of the cloud. The previous chapters have described a good number of services, technologies, and analogies, but this chapter proposes some new paths to continue exploring.

## To get the most out of this book

The entire story represents a *journey to the cloud*, and the order of the chapters is based on this journey. Even if each chapter talks about a specific area in cloud computing and IT in general, we strongly recommend you read the book chapter by chapter in the proposed order. Only in this way can you fully get all the concepts and the challenges that companies usually face during the cloud journey.

At the end of every chapter, we provide a list of links that we highly recommend you look at, to integrate the concepts explained with additional information. Some of the links point to the official AWS documentation, others to third-party sources.

To do your own testing, you need an AWS account. Go to https://aws.amazon.com/free/, where you can register for an account from where some services can be tested for free for a limited time (typically, a full year). Read the conditions carefully so you don't incur any charges.

Once you have it, you only need internet access, and one supported browser (Chrome, Firefox, Edge, or Safari). Check out https://aws.amazon.com/console/features/.

# Download the color images

We also provide a PDF file that has color images of the screenshots and diagrams used in this book. You can download it here: `https://packt.link/YC7LL`

# Conventions used

This book is mostly written in the form of dialog. Every time there is a person who is directly speaking with someone else, you will see the following format used:

<visual icon of the speaker> <name of the speaker>: <sentence>

Here is an example:

Berta: Oh, that was cool!

When people don't talk to each other directly, it is the author that is speaking to you as a voiceover/narration. This is simply represented by a paragraph without any visual next to it.

Here is an example:

When Berta heard what Alex said, she was very excited.

There are also a number of text conventions used throughout this book.

`Code in text`: Indicates code words in text, database table names, folder names, filenames, file extensions, pathnames, dummy URLs, user input, and Twitter handles. Here is an example: "Notice the `Get-RedisKey` or `Add-RedisKey` commands."

A block of code is set as follows:

```
SELECT
    VIN,
    Specs.EngSize,
    Specs.HP
FROM vehicles
WHERE type = 'Truck'
```

When we wish to draw your attention to a particular part of a code block, the relevant lines or items are set in bold:

```
Function BackupTheFiles
{
    $SourceB="SourceBucket"; $DestB="DestBucket"
    $Files = Get-S3Object -BucketName $SourceB
    Foreach ($File in $Files)
    {
```

```
        Copy-S3Object -BucketName $SourceB          `
                      -Key $File.Key                `
                      -DestinationKey $File.Key     `
                      -DestinationBucket $DestB
    }
    Publish-SNSMessage -Message "Finished" -TopicARN $SomeTopic
}
```

Any command-line input or output is written as follows:

```
aws s3api list-objects --bucket jcanalytics
```

**Bold**: Indicates a new term, an important word, or words that you see onscreen. For instance, words in menus or dialog boxes appear in **bold**. Here is an example: "The container image we have built can now be tagged and, finally, pushed to a location called a **container registry**."

> **Tips or important notes**
> Appear like this.

# Get in touch

Feedback from our readers is always welcome.

**General feedback**: If you have questions about any aspect of this book, email us at customercare@packtpub.com and mention the book title in the subject of your message.

**Errata**: Although we have taken every care to ensure the accuracy of our content, mistakes do happen. If you have found a mistake in this book, we would be grateful if you would report this to us. Please visit www.packtpub.com/support/errata and fill in the form.

**Piracy**: If you come across any illegal copies of our works in any form on the internet, we would be grateful if you would provide us with the location address or website name. Please contact us at copyright@packt.com with a link to the material.

**If you are interested in becoming an author**: If there is a topic that you have expertise in and you are interested in either writing or contributing to a book, please visit authors.packtpub.com

# Share your thoughts

Once you've read *AWS Cloud Computing Concepts and Tech Analogies*, we'd love to hear your thoughts! Scan the QR code below to go straight to the Amazon review page for this book and share your feedback.

https://packt.link/r/1804611425

Your review is important to us and the tech community and will help us make sure we're delivering excellent quality content.

# Download a free PDF copy of this book

Thanks for purchasing this book!

Do you like to read on the go but are unable to carry your print books everywhere?

Is your eBook purchase not compatible with the device of your choice?

Don't worry, now with every Packt book you get a DRM-free PDF version of that book at no cost.

Read anywhere, any place, on any device. Search, copy, and paste code from your favorite technical books directly into your application.

The perks don't stop there, you can get exclusive access to discounts, newsletters, and great free content in your inbox daily

Follow these simple steps to get the benefits:

1.  Scan the QR code or visit the link below

https://packt.link/free-ebook/9781804611425

2.  Submit your proof of purchase
3.  That's it! We'll send your free PDF and other benefits to your email directly

# Part 1: Cloud Infrastructure and Core Services

After completing this part, you will know all about the cloud infrastructure, operating models, and methods of leveraging the cloud platform. You will also have a detailed understanding of the core services that serve as the foundation for platform, application, and data services.

This part has the following chapters:

- *Chapter 1, Understanding Cloud Computing – Demystifying the Cloud*
- *Chapter 2, Global Infrastructure behind Cloud Platforms – What Is the Cloud Made of?*
- *Chapter 3, Computing – In Cloud We Trust, Everything Else We Compute*
- *Chapter 4, Storage – Where Should I Keep My Data and Maybe Publish It?*
- *Chapter 5, Networking – So, How Do I Get Inside, Outside, and Across the Cloud?*

# 1
# Understanding Cloud Computing – Demystifying the Cloud

The alarm clock goes off… and Alex prepares for a new day. A special, different day, as he is starting his first job as a cloud engineer at **TRENDYCORP**.

As he's riding his bike to the main office, he feels a strong rush of memories from the last few years. Four courses at university learning about computer science, a short course on programming macros in Excel, some months looking for a first job, mixed with several crazy parties and holidays, and finally, this offer from TRENDYCORP. He honestly couldn't figure out why he was hired. He has no experience with the cloud, but this company seemed really interested in it.

The usual first-day steps are taken: signing in at reception, security guards taking a picture for the ID badge, taking the picture again because he doesn't like how it looks, getting a new laptop with all the software preinstalled, connecting to the intranet, and waiting for the initial meeting.

Finally, Alex is pushed into a small room, where some other people are already gathered around a big table. Yes, these tables always seem bigger than the room. While Alex finds the only empty seat, a serious-looking woman stands up and begins to talk:

Figure 1.1 – The meeting room
(Source: Photo by Amanda Mills, USCDCP, at https://pixnio.com/people/seven-
people-at-meeting-on-office#, used under Free to use CC0 license.)

*Eva*: Welcome to TRENDYCORP. My name is Eva and I'm the HR manager who hired most of you. Alex, please sit down immediately. TRENDYCORP, as you all should know by now, wants to continue to be the leader in the Filiburths market – and for that, we have to modernize most of our old-fashioned processes, change most of our technology, and move to the cloud. That is the key – the **cloud**. To be honest, all I know about the cloud is... well, that's where rain is produced, but as all our competitors have decided to go for it, we'll do the same. And that's why many of you were hired; we have to move to the cloud, and I want it yesterday!

She makes a sign to the young woman sitting beside her, who stands up.

*Gloria*: Welcome, all of you. I hope you'll feel comfortable here. My name is Gloria, and I'm the manager of this IT team. First, I'd like to welcome Alex, Berta, and Raj, who are joining the team today. As it is their first day, I'll ask everybody to introduce themselves – but first of all, some technical context for all of you. As Eva said, we have to migrate all our servers to the cloud. I've recently taken some training from our cloud provider, something called **Cloud Essentials**, and I think I have an initial idea of how we should proceed – but of course, I'll need all your collective experience to help us move our projects to the cloud. That said, let's go with your introductions.

*Alex*: I'm Alex. It's my first day here. I've just finished my IT studies at university. Lots of theoretical things, but I have no real working experience. As for this cloud thing, I imagine it's that place where you store your personal photos.

*Berta*: Hello, this is Berta. Like Alex, it's also my first day. I've worked in several companies, some of them our competitors, as a developer and database administrator, for more than 7 years. I can query you using different SQL dialects, in multiple languages. I have also done some basic training on the cloud and read some documents, but I hope I can learn more and be useful to the team.

*Raj*: I'm Raj. Like Alex and Berta, it's my first day here. I know a bit about networking, protocols… in general, communicating between multiple networks no matter where they are. As for the cloud, I've got a collection of scripts to download files; I hope they can be useful.

*Charles*: I'm Charles. I've been in TRENDYCORP for many years, maybe more than 10, and am in charge of network security. Other employees call me *Change-No-Rules Charly*. I'll, of course, help you with every technical aspect you might encounter, but it has to be related to cables, routers, and firewalls. I'll probably ask you lots of questions about that cloud thing. I imagine you studied it at university, didn't you?

*David*: My name is David. I don't work directly for TRENDYCORP; I'm your technical contact for my company **BrandXCloud**. We are specialized in cloud migrations. We have a team of cloud experts working for you, so if you need any technical help, please describe your issue accurately, send it to me, and I'll forward it to the right person.

*Harold*: I'm Harold. I've been in this company for more than 20 years, in all of the important projects. If you need help, tell me, but only if I'm not busy with some tasks. I like discussing solutions, not problems. Over.

After the introduction, Gloria presents a list of applications they run at TRENDYCORP, and it mostly devolves into a conversation between David and her. Everyone slowly fades away, and soon the meeting ends.

# What is cloud computing?

Alex and Berta return to their desks after the meeting. They see Gloria rushing to the meeting room. Gloria is nervous, as it is her first presentation to the TRENDYCORP board about the cloud. Most of the board members are traditional businessmen and have very little to do with technology. She has rehearsed the presentation but still has butterflies in her stomach. She is expecting a lot of *WHY* and *WHAT* questions. Finally, everyone arrives on time and the presentation starts.

*Gloria*: Thank you everyone for making the time to be here. I am happy to walk you through the benefits we plan to achieve by migrating to the cloud. First, I will walk you through the current model of IT at TRENDYCORP, and later, I will talk about how cloud technologies can help us.

Gloria moves to the first slide on the screen:

Figure 1.2 – Server room

(Source: Photo by Indrajit Das, at https://commons.wikimedia.org/wiki/File:139_Server_Room_01.
jpg, used under Creative Commons Attribution-Share Alike 3.0 Unported license.)

*Gloria*: So currently, we are running some of our IT and business applications from this room. It is our data center and…

Before she can finish her sentence, a question is raised.

*Board Member 2*: Which applications?

*Gloria*: We have around 20 applications running here; some notable ones are our internal website, the invoicing system, inventory management system, payroll application, email servers, and some monitoring applications.

*Board Member 2*: Where are the rest?

She moves to the next slide and the picture looks similar but much bigger and tidier:

Figure 1.3 – The shared data center

(Source: Photo by BalticServers.com, at https://commons.wikimedia.org/wiki/File:BalticServers_
data_center.jpg, used under Creative Commons Attribution-Share Alike 3.0 Unported license.)

*Gloria* Those are being run from a shared data center we have on the outskirts of the town.

*Board Member 1*: I didn't know that… but anyway, please proceed.

*Gloria*: So, currently, our applications are split across three locations; one is our own server room, the second is the third-party data center on the city outskirts, and the third is the leased data center near our manufacturing plant in Asia. We have a leased line network connection connecting these three locations so that our developers, who work from this office, can access and connect to the remote locations. As our business is growing at a rapid pace, the need to scale and operate our applications at the same pace is becoming a challenge. Over the past three years, our online business has surpassed traditional methods, and we have a growing customer base that is keeping our software development team busier than ever. I have put together some data points related to growth, budget, and estimations for the next two years in a printed report, which is in front of you.

All the board members open their folders and start browsing through them. Gloria takes a deep breath and drinks some water to soothe her nerves. As everyone is checking the report, the room is filled with an awkward silence. This goes on for a few minutes.

*Board Member 3*: If I read your estimates correctly, you are saying that we are already running 120% of the planned capacity for our IT needs.

*Gloria*: Yes, that's true, and that is adding pressure to our overall online portfolio. On the one hand, we are running at a higher-than-estimated consumption of our applications, and on the other hand, our incident response time and the number of major incidents are increasing.

*Board Member 3*: Major incidents?

*Gloria*: A major incident is a highest-impact, highest-urgency incident. It affects a large number of users, depriving the business of one or more crucial services.

*Board Member 3*: Obviously, this is not good for business. Do we lose business when this happens?

*Gloria*: Yes, we do. Those numbers are on page 5.

*Board Member 3*: That's alarming – and you mean to say we can address this by using the cloud?

*Gloria*: It may not happen overnight, but surely, it will be the right step – because if we keep going with the current model, we will be adding to the problem rather than solving it.

*Board Member 3*: So, this cloud will only solve current problems, or do we need to find some other solution for forthcoming problems?

*Gloria*: There are some additional advantages of using the cloud, and that's what I want to discuss next.

Board Member 3 nods his head.

*Gloria*: Okay, so if there aren't any further questions, I want to present the six major benefits of moving to the cloud.

She moves on to the next slide:

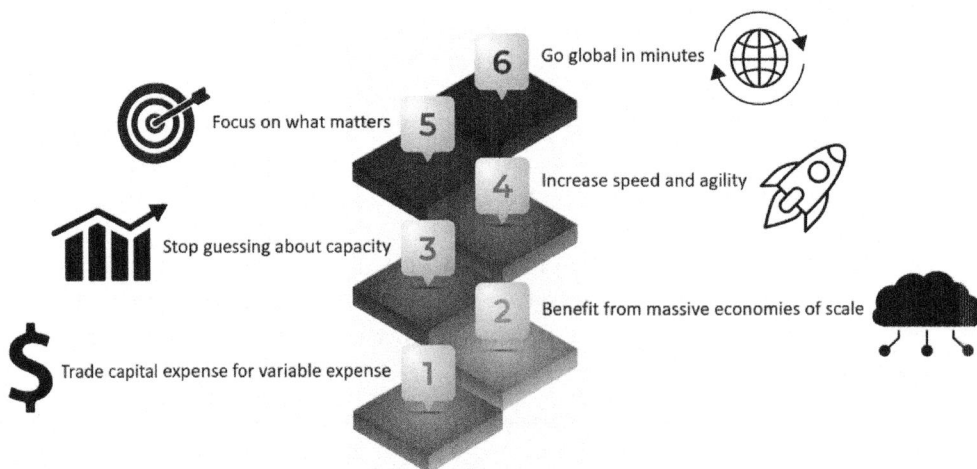

Figure 1.4 – Benefits of the cloud

*Gloria*: Currently, for every new project or capacity expansion in an existing project, we have to make a large capital expense. This includes an expense in terms of buying new servers, adding more storage, upgrading our internet, and more. Whereas with the cloud, we don't have to make any capital expenses, we can use the cloud like a utility, as with electricity, and we pay only the usage charges, which are based on what we use. This model will allow us to trade capital expenses for variable expenses.

*Board Member 2*: Will it result in cost savings or just the same capital expense spread over in shorter chunks?

*Gloria*: We plan to achieve cost savings. I have added that estimation on page 8.

*Board Member 2*: A quick question: won't these services be at a higher cost? Don't we need to take the profit for the cloud provider into account? When I make a meal at home, it is obviously cheaper than having a meal in a restaurant.

*Gloria*: In the case of cookery, that is true, but in the case of cloud services, the answer is different. That's the second benefit.

She moves to the next slide and explains:

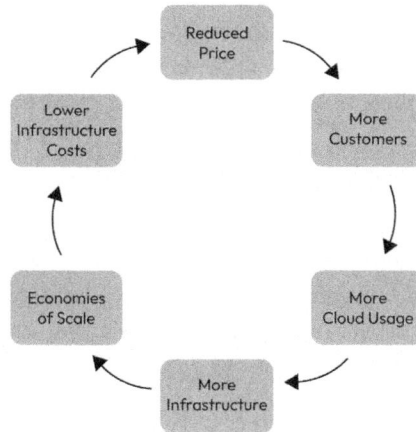

Figure 1.5 – Economies of scale

*Gloria*: Cloud providers benefit from economies of scale. As an example, when one of our customers buys one product, they pay X amount, but when our dealers place an order of the same product in bulk quantity, they get a volume discount. Similarly, cloud providers buy in bulk, negotiate better contracts from hardware manufacturers, power providers, and real-estate companies, and keep their own cost low. This is translated into lower costs for the customer, and if the costs are lower, more customers will use their services, which results in the overall cost of services becoming lower. Some cloud providers get their hardware highly customized as per their requirements and cut down on the cost of things that they do not need. This results in a much lower price for customers.

*Board Member 1*: That's an interesting way of doing business.

*Gloria*: As another benefit, we, as the customer, don't have to worry about capacity. Currently, for every project, we launch or expand; we make a capacity estimation and buy resources based on these estimates – and if these estimates are wrong, we lose money or lose customers.

*Board Member 1*: Can you explain this?

*Gloria*: Let's say our team estimates that for project X, we will need 10 resources. This is based on an estimation of 1,000 customers using that application. If the application is popular and we have more customers than estimated, then the 10 resources may not have enough capacity to handle the increased load and our customers will get a slower response from the application, which results in unsatisfied customers, and we may lose them if this is persistent. Conversely, if the utilization of resources is lower than the estimation, let's say only 4 resources are being used because of less customer demand or a slow sales quarter, we are keeping those extra 6 resources running – and it costs us money to keep those unused resources running.

*Board Member 2*: Can somebody not shut down those resources?

*Gloria*: Yes, we do so, but that only saves the running cost, as with electricity and cooling, but the capital expense of buying that resource is not reversible. And after a finite lifetime—in most cases, it is 2 or 3 years—the resource will no longer be supported and we will have to buy support plans separately, which leads to the maintenance cost of older resources increasing. It is similar to how maintaining a very old car can become expensive as those parts are not in production anymore.

*Board Member 2*: So, we call the cloud provider to shut down those resources and start them again when we need them?

*Gloria*: Not exactly. We don't need any human intervention for it. It is all programmable and sometimes built into the offering of the cloud provider, so we no longer have to guess the capacity for every project. We can start small and then shrink or expand the resources as needed.

*Board Member 2*: Okay.

*Gloria*: Also, since these resources are available on demand, we don't have to go through lengthy procurement cycles, which sometimes take months. We can roll out new features more quickly, run multiple campaigns in parallel, compare their performance, and respond quickly to changing demands. This will increase the speed and agility of our IT team. We will be able to experiment more often, run more proofs-of-concept, and never worry about the high cost of failure, as in traditional systems.

*Board Member 2*: So, what will happen to the engineers we have on 24/7 support? Will this cloud leave them without a job?

*Gloria*: No. It will just change their focus. Currently, they are mostly in fire-fighting mode. They are always busy with undifferentiated heavy-lifting tasks, such as troubleshooting, capacity expansion, backups, or patching activities, and rarely get any time to add value. These activities don't differentiate our business from our competition, as everyone has to do this – but once we start using the cloud, our support team will have more time to focus on things that add value to the business and differentiate us from the competition. They have shared lots of ideas and some of the ideas are pretty interesting. I am sure it can add a lot of value to our business. We can focus on what matters to our business.

*Board Member 2*: So, we won't be needing backups or patching anymore?

*Gloria*: We will still need that, but it just becomes a checkbox activity with the cloud. We select a maintenance window for our workloads and the cloud provider will automate the process of backup, patching, and capacity expansion for us.

*Board Member 3*: That's interesting – but what about our third location in Asia? Will it remain as it is or also go the cloud way? I don't want to renegotiate the lease every time we expand our manufacturing units.

*Gloria*: We don't have to. Cloud providers have facilities all over the globe and we plan to move supporting applications closer to the manufacturing plant in Asia – and we will be able to leverage other global locations too as we expand our manufacturing units. We can go global in minutes.

*Board Member 3*: That's good. Do we need to hire local teams in those areas?

*Gloria*: No, our team from here can perform remote maintenance – and we hope to get a better connectivity speed and performance because of the cloud provider's high-speed network.

*Board Member 2*: Much better. I am fully convinced after hearing you and seeing all the data you presented. Can you also send this report in an email?

*Gloria*: Yes, I will email you just after this meeting.

*Board Member 1*: I am convinced too – and we want to move faster, don't we? I have heard that our competition is already doing so. We don't want to be left behind.

*Gloria*: Thanks for your support on this. We have a few new team members who have joined us this week to accelerate our project.

*Board Member 1*: Keep us posted. And all the best. Thanks.

*Gloria*: Thank you.

The board members leave the meeting room. Gloria heaves a sigh of relief. She has achieved a milestone, *Get buy-in from management*, for the cloud project. As she exits the meeting room, she finds Alex and Berta heading toward the coffee machine.

*Berta*: You seem happy. I am sure the presentation went very well.

*Gloria*: Indeed.

*Berta*: Nice. Want to join us for a coffee?

*Gloria*: A little later. I have to send an important email. Enjoy your coffee.

Gloria dashes over to her desk. Berta and Alex casually walk toward the coffee machine.

## Providing IT as a utility service

After getting their coffee from the vending machine, Berta and Alex return to their desk.

*Alex*: We should talk a bit more with our colleague, Harold. From what I've understood from our meeting, Harold is part of the project, even if he seems a bit reluctant to do it. Seems like he's free now – why don't we talk with him a bit?

*Berta*: I had to deal with this kind of person in my previous job. I really don't like how they behave with new hires, considering them more as a threat than an asset to the company. He probably thinks that he is going to lose his job because of us; that's the reason he hasn't talked with us at all.

*Alex*: Oh, come on! Let's talk with him a bit, and I'll show you that you're wrong!

Harold is focused on a long, complex report when the two young colleagues approach him. Alex addresses him first.

*Alex*: Hey, Harold, how is it going? Are you working on something interesting?

Harold doesn't say a word. Alex, trying again, points at Harold's desktop, a black-and-white picture of an old, huge machine.

*Alex*: Oh, you have a cool wallpaper! What is it supposed to be?

*Harold*: I'm not surprised you don't recognize it; you are too young. In the old days, this kind of machine was used in factories to generate electricity.

Figure 1.6 – Machines generating electricity

(Source: Photo by 継之助, at https://commons.wikimedia.org/wiki/File:Generator_of_Yaotsu_Old_Power_Plant.jpg, used under Creative Commons Attribution-Share Alike 4.0 International license.)

*Alex*: No way! Why would someone have a machine like this when electricity is available at the push of a button? This looks so big – it obviously required a lot of space, lots of maintenance, and tons of money to own.

*Harold*: That's why not every factory could afford it. Let me take you a little back in history. In the early days—I guess about a hundred years ago—there was no central way of producing electricity. Every factory used to set up these types of giant machines to produce their own electricity. Obviously, this was a challenge for small businesses, because of the initial cost and ongoing maintenance.

*Alex*: Wow. I didn't know that.

*Harold*: Sometimes, a big industrial unit needed two or three of these machines to address the growing demands of electricity, and obviously, a dedicated team would maintain and run it. The whole production process would stop if this machine failed, so it was a very critical piece of machinery – but now, electricity production and distribution have become so much simpler and that's why this machine is in a museum. When energy companies started producing electricity centrally and began distributing it, the whole scenario changed. Some energy companies used hydropower or coal power, and nowadays, it can be nuclear or solar power. Companies that operated these power stations started setting up a grid of cables all over the place so that they could distribute electricity to consumers. Consumers could be big industries or small households who would just pay for what they use and never pay for the infrastructure cost of setting up the whole power station.

*Alex*: Wow! I did not know that electricity production has come such a long way. I never think about all this when I consume energy at home or in the office. We just press a button to light a bulb and only pay for what we use.

In the meantime, Berta, who was listening to the whole story, considered the challenges that factories had to face in the old days. Suddenly, she realized that Harold's story was related to their project and to cloud computing in general.

*Berta*: Hey, Harold, sorry to interrupt you. You are basically talking about the same relationship between how companies manage their on-premises IT infrastructure and how they manage their cloud-based IT infrastructure.

*Harold*: What?

*Berta*: Well, as you know for sure, in the early days of computing when companies started to use computers, they started by maintaining a data center—a place to keep, or host, all their applications, servers, networks, and storage. Compare a data center to this giant machine.

*Harold*: You don't have to explain what a data center is to me, young lady!

*Berta*: I'm sure, Harold, but just let me finish. Data centers require a huge amount of capital expenses, and companies such as ours have to keep them running smoothly so that business can run smoothly, and because of that, they hire a team of professionals such as you to maintain and operate them. With business growth, companies may need to add more capacity to their data centers or add more data centers to increase the availability of their applications. This puts an extra burden on companies financially, and they have to focus their time and energy on keeping these data centers running.

*Harold*: Yes, sometimes we call this activity **keeping the lights on**.

*Berta*: Oh, cool – I didn't know that! This is where the interesting part of the story comes in: with cloud computing, companies don't have to worry about all of this. They can choose a cloud provider in the same way we choose an electricity provider for our office or house, and they can start by using the resources hosted in the cloud provider's data centers. These data centers may host ready-to-use applications or the building blocks to build your own custom application. Cloud providers maintain and run data centers all over the world to provide services to their customers, who will pay only for what resources they use – or to use cloud computing terminology, they **pay as they go**, in the same way that we pay only for the electricity we consume.

*Harold*: Hmm…

*Berta*: Cloud providers keep thousands of servers running at scale, so multiple customers can start using it without worrying about setting up their own data centers. This allows their customers to focus on their core activities, usually the development of their applications, and save them from undifferentiated heavy lifting, such as server provisioning, storage expansion, backups, security... Cloud providers provide their resources through the internet; in a similar way, electricity producers distribute their energy through a network of electric wires, grid stations, and other similar components. In both cases, we are still talking about **networks**:

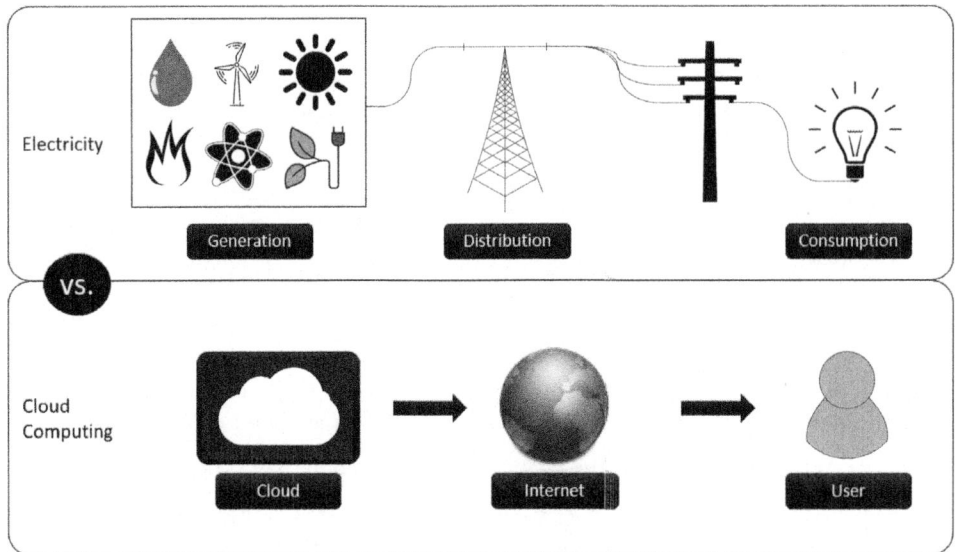

Figure 1.7 – Comparison between electricity and cloud computing

In summary, if we need some electricity, we just have to sign a contract with an electricity provider and then press a button. In the same way, if companies need IT resources, they sign a contract with a cloud provider and just… press a button! Or maybe I should say… call an API! Hahaha!

*Alex*: Berta, you are amazing! What an excellent way to explain cloud computing to everyone. Let's use this explanation in next week's presentation that we have to deliver. Thank you.

*Harold*: Ah! I'm not sure about all that… Please leave and let me work now! I have stuff to do!

Alex and Berta, convinced about what they've said, leave Harold and come back to their desk happier than before. They have just completed one step in their cloud journey and still have a long way to go!

# Differentiating between private, public, and hybrid cloud

Alex is getting ready to leave the office at the end of the day when Raj walks up to him. He notices the gym bag Alex is holding.

*Raj*: So, are you planning on going to the gym after work?

*Alex*: Oh, yes. I am on a hybrid exercise plan this week.

*Raj*: Hybrid?

*Alex*: Yes. I do cardio exercises at home and for weight exercises, I go to the gym.

*Raj*: Nice, that doesn't sound too different from hybrid cloud.

*Alex*: What's that?

*Raj*: So, when you exercise at home, you use the private cardio equipment that you have bought, and it is used only by you. You maintain it and get more equipment if you need it. That's a private gym. Similarly, companies may invest in hardware and software – that is, capital expenditure – to set up a **private cloud**, which gives them a higher degree of customization, and is fully controlled by an internal team. A private cloud may still host public-facing applications, but the companies get full autonomy in setting and maintaining them. Companies follow this path if they have some stringent latency or compliance requirements for their applications.

*Alex*: Ah, I get it – and when I go to the gym, it's a public place. Anyone can pay a fee and use the equipment there. Isn't that like a **public cloud**?

*Raj*: In a way, yes. The gym company sets up a location, maintains an energetic ambiance, hires trainers, puts in equipment, and may have other facilities too, such as lockers, a swimming pool, a sauna bath, and so on. If its pool of members keeps on growing, it will probably also expand its operations to scale its gym facilities. The gym will maintain security, follow local regulations, and a member just pays a monthly fee to use those facilities.

*Alex*: Interesting. Tell me more.

*Raj*: Now, sometimes, a company may not want to fully operate its applications from the cloud – or if they are in the midst of migration, they may end up with a **hybrid model**. Like when you want to exercise, you use your cardio equipment at home, and to use a sauna, you can go to the gym afterward. Similarly, a company may host a latency-sensitive or highly customized application on-premises in their private cloud, such as a custom database, and use a frontend, such as a web server, hosted on the public cloud. This sometimes gives them greater flexibility. Some companies also use the cloud as their failover mechanism – so if they have any issues with their private cloud, they may set up failover to the public cloud and return operations back to the private cloud once the problem is fixed. Another use case could be to launch a new project for which the private cloud may not have enough resources; then they can use the public and private cloud at the same time.

*Alex*: Does this not create connectivity issues?

*Raj*: Yes, but there are ways around it. In my last job, I was helping customers establish these network connectivity options – and believe me, these networks are much easier to establish now and are evolving at a rapid pace. Some of the options are almost 10 times higher in speed than our current network here.

*Alex*: Wow – but what about compatibility issues? I guess it won't be as easy as drag-and-drop from on-premises to the cloud.

*Raj*: In fact, it is like drag-and-drop in some scenarios. Private and public cloud vendors are working together to create solutions that provide a way to migrate your applications seamlessly – and there is a plethora of third-party solutions available to facilitate this hybrid approach. I was amazed when I saw an application being migrated from a private to a public cloud without any downtime.

*Alex*: Without downtime? You must be kidding!

*Raj*: No, I am not. Yes, it requires some very specific networking configurations, but it is completely possible… and in a reverse direction too. Suppose after running a global campaign for millions of users on the public cloud, you want to bring your applications back to the private cloud; that is possible too.

*Alex*: Amazing. I am starting to understand it… but this is enough exercise for my brain today. I don't think I can handle any more at this point. I'm going to go and do some physical exercise too. Do you want to join me on my walk up to the bus stop?

*Raj*: Thanks, but you carry on. Maybe some other time. I am going out for a pizza party with my ex-colleagues today.

*Alex*: Okay. Enjoy the party! See you tomorrow.

*Raj*: See you tomorrow.

## Understanding IaaS, PaaS, and SaaS

Raj has no difficulty locating the pizza place. He has been there before. It is not a lavish place, but its pizza could compete with any Michelin-star restaurant's pizza. Raj's ex-colleagues are all gathered to celebrate Ahmad's new job at a renowned software company. Ahmad is always in learning mode. He has also completed some training and certifications regarding a popular cloud vendor.

Raj knows that it will soon be his turn to throw a party the following month. This small group has, after all, developed a tradition of gathering and celebrating when people start a new job and get their first salary.

*Ahmad*: Thanks for coming, Raj.

*Raj*: I wouldn't have missed the chance to catch up with all of you – or the pizza, of course.

*Ahmad*: Yes, their pizzas are awesome. Much better than PaaS pizza.

*Raj*: PaaS Pizza? Is that some new place you have recently been to?

*Ahmad*: Oh, no. It is the way I describe pizza options. They are not very different from cloud technology.

*Raj*: Wait a minute, are you saying that eating a pizza is similar to cloud technology?

*Ahmad*: In some aspects, yes. Let me tell you how I interpret these different cloud models. We always hear the words IaaS, PaaS, and SaaS, and to explain it, I found that pizzas are the best examples.

*Raj*: I am all ears – and I guess everyone else here is too.

*Ahmad*: Okay. Let's assume you have a craving for pizza. There are different ways of having a pizza. You can make it yourself, buy a frozen pizza from the supermarket and cook it at home, order in and get it delivered to your place, or come to a restaurant such as this and have it:

| Make at home | Take and bake | Pizza delivery | Eat out |

Figure 1.8 – Different ways of eating pizza

*Raj*: Agreed.

*Ahmad*: When you make a pizza at home, you have to take care of having cheese, tomato sauce, toppings, dough, fire – an oven, electricity or gas – soda, and a dining table to eat at. For a person who loves cooking, this is the best option, but it involves a lot of steps. The second option is to buy a frozen pizza from a supermarket, which has already been prepared, and the supermarket or the vendor has taken care of the cheese, tomato sauce, toppings, and dough. You just take it and make it at home. In this case, you only need to take care of the fire, oven – electricity or gas, and have soda and the dining table to eat at on hand. The third option is to get your pizza delivered as per your choice, so you just need to get soda and have your dining table, and the rest is managed by the pizza company. And as the final option, you can just eat out. Walk into a place such as this, pick and order, enjoy your pizza, pay for it, and that's all. Mind you, the paying part is mandatory:

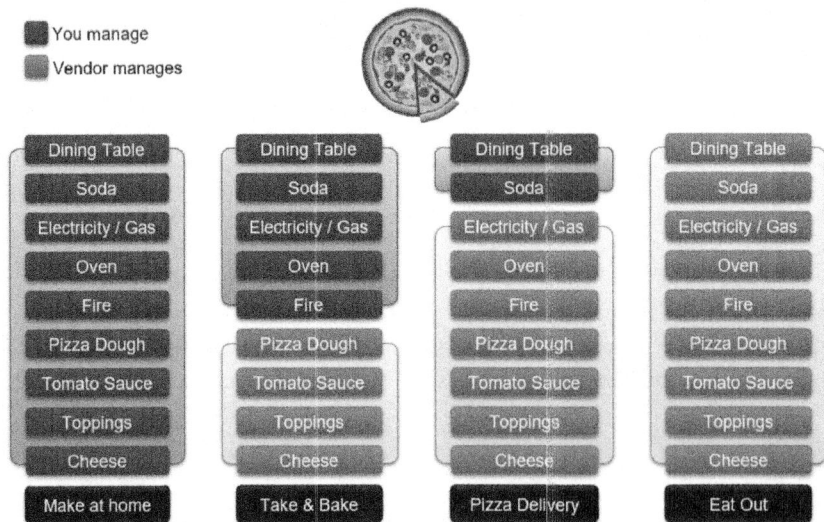

Figure 1.9 – Responsibilities when having pizza

*Raj*: Understood – but this time you are paying, right? I didn't bring my credit card.

Everyone laughs.

*Raj*: I still don't quite get the cloud connection though.

Ahmad notices that everyone at the table is glued to his explanation.

*Ahmad*: Let's consider you want to run an application – so what are your options?

*Raj*: I could run it on a server in my data center.

*Ahmad*: Yes, you could, and who manages it?

*Raj*: It's my application in my data center – so obviously, I have to manage it.

*Ahmad*: Exactly! You take care of the infrastructure – that is, networking, storage, the server, and virtualization; platform – that is, the operating system, middleware, and runtime; and software – that is, the data and application. That is a traditional approach to running an application on-premises. Now, consider if a service provider gives you a ready-to-use server and takes care of the infrastructure, and you connect to it remotely and install the required platform and software. In this way, you have saved a lot of effort and time. This is a way of getting your **infrastructure as a service**, commonly known as **IaaS**.

*Raj*: I understand – so if I am an administrator, I don't have to worry about racking-stacking of servers, cabling, storage, power, or cooling. That surely will save a lot of time.

*Ahmad*: Yes, exactly, and if you are a developer, a cloud provider may offer you **Platform as a Service (PaaS)**, where they give you a ready-to-use system with the required platform pre-configured, so you can just deploy your application and take care of your data storage requirement. Your exposure is reduced and you can focus more on something that makes your application unique rather than focusing on undifferentiated activities, such as installation, patching, updates, and so on.

*Raj*: That can save a lot of time for admins and developers.

*Ahmad*: Yes, true – and then there's the final offering, known as **Software as a Service (SaaS)**, where you have almost zero management responsibility. When you use an online email platform or an online meeting system, the vendor has already set up all the required components. They take care of everything and keep your data safe as per the settings you have configured. So, you can focus on the business rather than maintaining and running the systems:

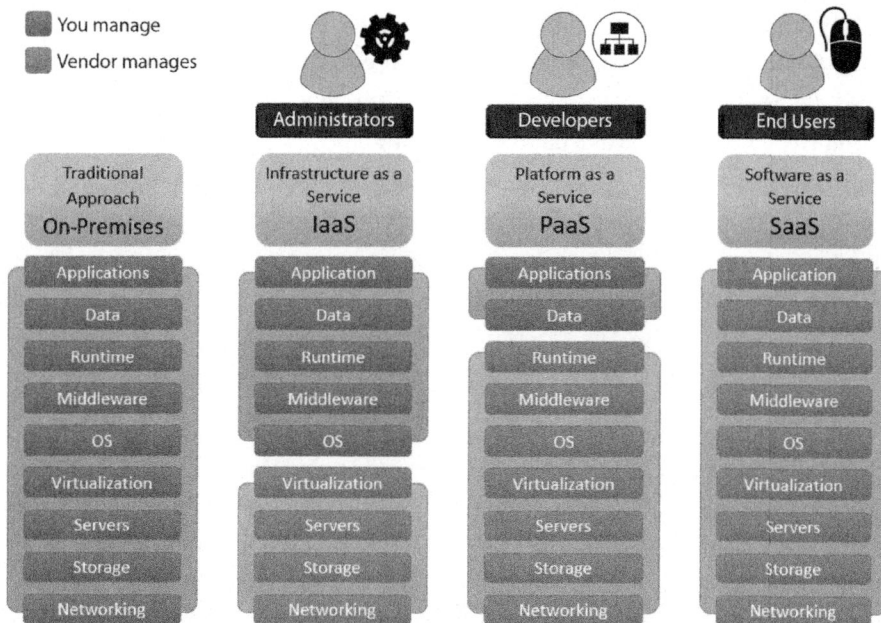

Figure 1.10 – Benefits of the different services

*Raj*: That's so relevant and quite an interesting way to understand these concepts.

*Ahmad*: Yes. Some vendors expand these models and offer various services in this way and sometimes name them differently – such as **Database as a Service (DBaaS)**, **Disaster Recovery as a Service (DRaaS)**, and **Function as a Service (FaaS)**, to name a few.

*Raj*: Interesting. Thanks for explaining this to me, Ahmad. I can't wait to explain this to my colleagues tomorrow. I will probably bring them here one day if they agree to take care of the mandatory pay part of it.

*Ahmad*: Of course. For the time being, let me take care of the mandatory pay part.

Everybody at the table is laughing.

# Distinguishing between managed and unmanaged services

Berta walks into the office and overhears Gloria talking to someone on the phone.

*Gloria*: Thank you so much.

She ends the call and finds Berta facing her.

*Berta*: Good morning, Gloria. How are you?

*Gloria*: Good morning. I am okay, but I'd be better if I could get a cup of coffee.

*Berta*: Can I get you a coffee from the machine?

*Gloria*: The machine is showing **not in service** on its display. I was on the phone with the company that is managing it for us. Glad that it was open early and is sending someone to fix it soon.

*Berta*: Wow, a coffee mechanic on call. Interesting.

*Gloria*: Their contact number is on the **Managed by** sticker on the coffee machine, in case you need to call them sometime. Let's get some coffee from the shop downstairs. I hope they are in service.

*Berta*: Let's go. I need a coffee too.

The downstairs coffee shop is not crowded and service is quick. Gloria knows the barista and introduces Berta to him. Afterward, they find a secluded corner and settle there, sipping their coffee.

*Berta*: I like their service. Fast, easy, and cheap. It won't burn a hole in my wallet if I get my coffee from here every day.

*Gloria*: It's much better now; previously, they didn't have enough staff, and customers had to wait a long time to get their coffee. Luckily, they realized it and fixed the problem.

*Berta*: That's the best thing about a managed service.

*Gloria*: Wait. What? Managed service? I heard that word in the cloud training I attended, but I was so distracted I couldn't focus.

As Berta is about to speak, Alex walks in, looking like he too needs a coffee before starting his day.

*Alex*: Hello! Sometimes, a broken coffee machine leads to a good conversation. Hope I am not interrupting.

*Gloria*: Not at all. We were talking about managed services in the cloud. Join us.

Alex pulls up a nearby chair and settles down as Berta starts explaining.

*Berta*: What happens when you'd like to drink some coffee? Maybe you do this at home… you have bought a coffee machine and probably some coffee. Then, you connect it to the power, pour in water and coffee grounds, and press the buttons. You have to do all the work. You also pay for the electricity, and you need some space at home to keep the machine. Finally, after using it, you have to clean it.

But there are other options. Now, consider the coffee machine in our office. You just press a button, and you get your cup of coffee. Someone does the maintenance, adds water and coffee, and cleans it.

*Gloria*: Not as frequently as I'd like.

*Berta*: That is a service. A service means someone is doing tasks for you, hiding the complexity from you, so you have more time for other things. You can be more creative, instead of spending your time doing routine tasks such as cleaning the machine – and when, like today, the machine is *not in service*, Gloria calls the company responsible for it, and someone visits to fix it. Then, there are also smart coffee machines that can automatically inform the maintenance company if there is any problem via the internet.

*Alex*: I prefer to come here, request my coffee, grab it, and that's all…

*Berta*: Yes, that is an even better example of a service – or maybe of a better service. Of course, someone is doing the work for you; in this case, you don't even see the details. Which coffee machine are they using? How many of them do they have? How much electricity is used? You don't need those details; you just want a cup of good coffee, reasonably fast and reasonably cheap. That's a service. You get what you need and nothing else, and you don't worry about the nitty-gritty of the implementation details.

*Gloria*: And every service in the cloud is built this way? This seems like a completely new way of working!

*Berta*: Well, it depends on what you need. If you just need to store files or a table in a database, you just provide the data—you don't need to see the physical servers. The service provides access to the data, not to the infrastructure needed – but if, for some reason, you need a server with RAM and CPUs, there are services that can provide these to you. Each service can be different, but the idea is the same for all.

*Gloria*: Interesting, so does that mean that all services are managed by the cloud provider?

*Berta*: The level of *managed* may vary. Let me give you one more example.

Berta addresses Alex.

*Berta*: Alex, look at yourself. You wear nice, trendy, and clean shirts – but what do you do when you want your clothes clean? You have multiple options: you can build your own washing machine. Completely DIY, you buy the parts, you assemble it, but very few people do this. Let's assume instead that you have bought or rented it. Now, you have your own washing machine at home. You own the machine. Now, you also need two supplier companies for electricity and water, and, of course, pay for them. Energy is not particularly cheap now. Then, you provide the space for it; it must fit into your house, as well as your house's weird plumbing. You also buy soap, and you take care of any cleaning and repairs when needed. You also assume full responsibility for it: if there's a leak, you need to fix it or get it fixed.

*Alex*: I agree. I have some memories of busted pipes.

*Berta*: There's an easier option. You may find a common place where washing machines are available. Maybe they are in your cellar, belonging to the community and shared with other tenants – or maybe you take your basket to a launderette you find on your street. You go there, choose an available machine, insert the coins, stuff your clothes into it, close the door, push the button, and wait until it's finished. You don't worry about the water supply, electricity, plumbing, and so on:

Figure 1.11 – Cleaning as a service

Some people prefer to use an even more elaborate service. You just take your dirty clothes to a specific place, usually a counter. Some places will even pick your clothes up directly from your home. I've even seen some hotels with a hole in the wall, where clothes seem to disappear, but after some time, they are returned to you, completely clean. Magic? No, just a more elaborate service model. You don't see how it is done, you don't see any washing machine, and you don't care. You only get what you need, that is, your clean clothes.

*Gloria*: Agreed. During my last business trip, I stayed in a hotel where they had laundry bags in the room. You put your clothes into it, housekeeping collected them when they came to clean the rooms, and the next day, you found them in your closet, neatly folded and ironed. They even had a 2-hour turnaround service for urgent cleaning.

*Alex*: Yes, I used a washing machine at home when I lived with my parents. We had 3 leaks in 2 years, and 3 not-so-happy neighbors. Now, I go to a launderette. I don't have the space in my small flat for a washing machine, nor the required power. And the place I go to provides additional amenities: I have my shirts cleaned and ironed too.

*Berta*: Similarly, in the cloud, **managed services** mean that someone does all the configuration, maintenance, and monitoring for you, and you only worry about requesting the service and using it. For example, for all the databases we want to move to the cloud, we just have to migrate the data, and our cloud provider will take care of the hardware and software that might be needed. They will do the backups, updates, and monitoring; they will even update everything to the latest version based on the maintenance window we define.

*Gloria*: So the remaining option is **unmanaged services**, which means we have to do all these tasks?

*Berta*: You're right. It's like having your own washing machine. You have to maintain it, connect it to the electricity and water supply, and pay for it even if you don't use it.

*Alex*: Who would use this then?

*Berta*: Well, you may want to use it if you need a high degree of customization or controls. Sometimes, there may not be a ready-to-use service for a specific task, and you may want to build it from the ground up. That's where an unmanaged service can be helpful.

*Alex*: By the way, the expression *managed services versus unmanaged services* implies a point of view. The service still has to be managed by someone; in the case of managed services, the provider manages it, and in the case of unmanaged services, the user manages it.

*Berta*: Exactly.

*Gloria*: Thanks, Berta. That was very insightful. Let's head back to office; I have quite a busy day today. Now that I have had my coffee, I can take anything head-on.

They enter the office and find a coffee mechanic fixing the coffee machine. Berta and Gloria smile and get busy with their day jobs. After a while, the coffee machine starts showing **in service**.

## Summary

Our new hires have had their first contact with the cloud; now, they begin to understand the service model, its advantages, and some possible options.

The details of how all of this is achieved continue to be magic for them. Over the next few days, they'll dig into the details of how their provider manages (pun intended) to supply these services to TRENDYCORP and the rest of the world.

They'll face the infrastructure being used, the network topology, and how everything is put together to provide a fast and reliable collection of services.

# Further reading

- Cloud computing: `https://docs.aws.amazon.com/whitepapers/latest/aws-overview/what-is-cloud-computing.html`

- Cloud benefits: `https://docs.aws.amazon.com/whitepapers/latest/aws-overview/six-advantages-of-cloud-computing.html`

- Services: `https://aws.amazon.com/products`

- Managed Services: `https://serviceproviderslist.com/what-are-aws-managed-services/`

- Electricity generation: `https://en.wikipedia.org/wiki/Electricity_generation#History`

# 2
# Global Infrastructure behind Cloud Platforms – What Is the Cloud Made of?

Gloria checks the email she has typed out and clicks the send button:

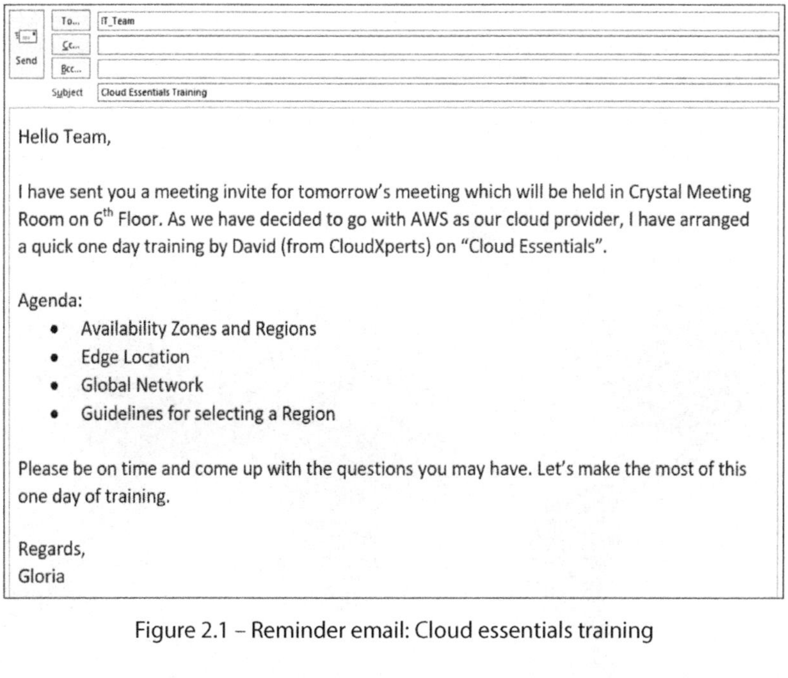

| Send | To... | IT_Team |
|------|-------|---------|
|      | Cc... |         |
|      | Bcc... |        |
|      | Subject | Cloud Essentials Training |

Hello Team,

I have sent you a meeting invite for tomorrow's meeting which will be held in Crystal Meeting Room on 6th Floor. As we have decided to go with AWS as our cloud provider, I have arranged a quick one day training by David (from CloudXperts) on "Cloud Essentials".

Agenda:
- Availability Zones and Regions
- Edge Location
- Global Network
- Guidelines for selecting a Region

Please be on time and come up with the questions you may have. Let's make the most of this one day of training.

Regards,
Gloria

Figure 2.1 – Reminder email: Cloud essentials training

After a while, Gloria checks who has accepted the meeting invite she sent the previous day. Everyone has accepted, even Harold. She has been hoping that this training will help bring everyone to the same level of understanding about cloud technologies and accelerate TRENDYCORP's migration to the cloud.

## Availability Zones and Regions

The following morning, everyone is present in the meeting room and enjoying the catered breakfast. David is busy adjusting the projector screen.

*Gloria*: Good morning, David.

*David*: Good morning, Gloria.

*Gloria*: All set? Do you need anything?

*David*: Yes, all set, except that we have run out of pastries, and I wanted to have a second go at them. Never mind. Just kidding.

*Gloria*: Keep providing us with more free training, and I will ensure a constant supply of pastries for you.

*David*: That's an interesting proposition. I will think about it. By the way, do you want to address the attendees before I start my session?

*Gloria*: I already explained the context to the team yesterday. You can start directly.

As the clock strikes 9, David asks everyone to settle down. It takes a little while for everyone to take their seats. After a formal introduction about his company and himself, he presents the agenda, which is customized for TRENDYCORP. David is a seasoned presenter and loses no time in getting the audience's attention. After going through the history of AWS, he also explains the benefits and shares some data about the benefits that companies get because of the cloud. In due time, he reaches a slide that is basically a world map with a few locations represented using dots, which are spread across multiple geographical areas:

Figure 2.2 – AWS Regions map

*David*: These dots represent the **Regions** that AWS can offer to customers. AWS has the largest global infrastructure footprint of any provider, and it is constantly increasing at a significant rate. As you can see, Regions are spread across the globe. A Region is a physical location, anywhere in the world, where data centers are clustered. Customers don't directly see the data centers, but they work with the building blocks called **Availability Zones**, or in short, **AZs**. Each AWS Region consists of multiple isolated and physically separate AZs within a geographic area. These AZs may have one or more than one data center grouped together.

*Alex*: Can I ask a question?

*David*: Sure, go ahead.

*Alex*: Why do the AZs have multiple data centers? Won't it make sense to keep everything in one data center?

*David*: Good question. A single data center may have between 50,000 and 80,000 servers and the required components such as storage, load balancers, and networking. If there was a huge single data center containing everything, and if it failed or got disconnected, the impact of it would be big. Moreover, a single data center might soon hit the physical limits of expansion, such as in the case of adding more power or cooling. So, instead, multiple data centers are grouped together to form an AZ.

AWS is always monitoring these data centers to ensure they are operating efficiently and providing customers with the required availability. Part of this monitoring also includes capacity planning, checking the customer usage demand on a monthly basis, and ascertaining that the demand is fulfilled.

*Alex*: But if there are multiple data centers, then connecting them can be an issue. What if one of the network links goes down?

*David*: These data centers are not connected over a single link; they use fully redundant and isolated metro fibers. This redundant network ensures that there are no bottlenecks and no single point of failure for the network. This diagram is an illustration of their connectivity:

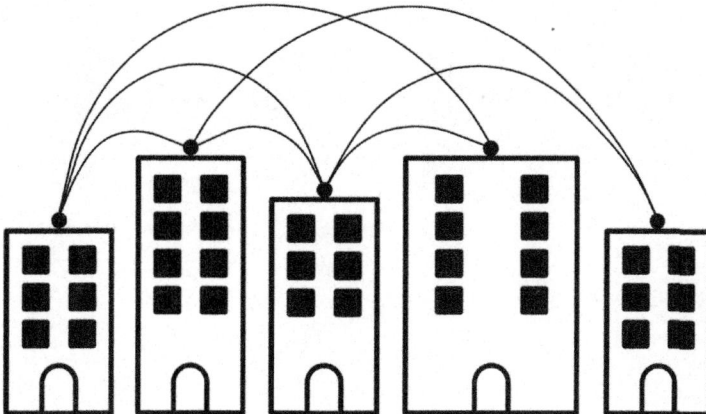

Figure 2.3 – Multiple connectivity paths

Each of these AZs is designed to be completely isolated, and they are sometimes placed miles apart. To achieve this isolation, each AZ has its independent supply of electricity, its own cooling arrangements, and also its own physical security mechanism. This design ensures that it can operate as independently as possible and probably not all of the AZs will be impacted by any outages.

The choice of locations is also influenced by environmental and geographical factors. Probably no two AZs will be in the same floodplain, in the same seismic activity belt, or in the same area of possible extreme weather. This careful consideration of location choice avoids the possibility of multiple AZs being affected at the same time by any environmental factors.

A single data center will always reach a limit in terms of availability, and scalability, and probably would not be fault tolerant. But having your applications distributed and spread across multiple AZs will help you in achieving high availability, fault tolerance, and scalability.

AWS connects these AZs using multiple high-bandwidth and low-latency metro fiber connections. Multiple redundant connections help in avoiding bottlenecks and network availability issues. Even if some of the links are disconnected or operating at lower performance, the overall connectivity will still not be lost.

*Alex*: So, if I understand it correctly, every AWS Region is made up of multiple AZs, and an AZ can have one or more than one data center in it?

*David*: Exactly:

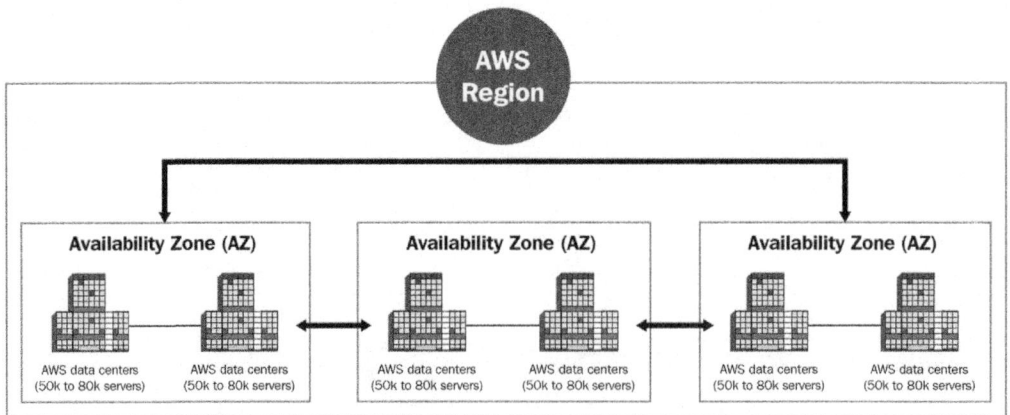

Figure 2.4 – AWS Region and AZs

*Harold*: And every AWS Region has the same number of AZs?

Everyone is surprised to see Harold also taking an interest and even asking a question rather than forming an opinion.

*David*: It depends, and it depends on a number of factors, such as capacity requirements. For example, the North Virginia Region has six AZs, whereas London has three AZs. AWS may add more capacity depending on a specific feature or to address increasing demand. For example, initially, the Beijing Region had two AZs, but later, a third AZ was also added. Because of the AWS global infrastructure, companies can leverage the virtually unlimited scalability of the cloud and be very flexible in the way they operate.

*Harold*: And can I keep my data and applications in any of these Regions?

*David*: Technically, yes. But some AWS Regions, such as AWS GovCloud Regions, are specifically designed to be used by US government entities. There are some stringent regulatory compliance requirements for the US government's use of cloud services. AWS addressed this by building and operating two Regions called AWS GovCloud US-East and US-West, only accessible to US government customers. Only employees who are US citizens are allowed to operate and maintain these Regions. This flexibility and customization allows lots of US government entities to use the AWS cloud for their workloads.

A similar arrangement exists for the AWS Region in China. AWS China Regions (Beijing and Ningxia) are only accessible to customers who have a valid Chinese business license and valid contact information. In accordance with Chinese laws and regulations, you have to fulfill these two requirements before you can use those Regions. You would need a separate set of credentials to access Beijing and Ningxia Regions.

*Alex*: And can we use multiple AWS Regions?

*David*: Absolutely. I will talk more about the Region selection later. But let's now have a quick break for 10 minutes. Get yourself some coffee or tea, and we will talk again.

The break is a welcome event. Some of the attendees use this time to check on their emails, make a phone call, or grab some more coffee.

David can clearly sense that attendees are comfortable with concepts of Regions and AZs, and some are even amazed by the sheer scale of the AWS Global Infrastructure. He is hoping that the next section, where he will talk about Edge Locations and Region selection guidelines, will solidify their understanding further.

David makes himself a cup of tea; he likes the cardamom flavor, which he finds is a unique offering in the TRENDYCORP pantry. After the break, everyone returns to their seats except Gloria. David looks around and finds her giving some instructions to a pantry staff member. He waits for a minute, and that is enough time for Gloria to return to her seat. David now feels recharged for another round of training.

# Edge locations

*David*: Welcome back, everyone. I hope everyone is enjoying the training and learning something new. Let me get started again by asking a question. Where do you do your grocery shopping?

Everyone in the room feels a little confused by the question about groceries in cloud training. After a slight hesitation, Berta answers.

*Berta*: Mostly, I go to the city mall weekly or fortnightly to get groceries from there.

*David*: Nice. And may I ask why you prefer that place?

*Berta*: I can get everything under one roof, groceries, gardening supplies, electronics, magazines, clothes, and more.

*David*: And if you just need a bottle of milk, do you still prefer to go there?

*Berta*: Probably not. It's far from my home, and a bottle of milk doesn't justify the fuel cost. I prefer to get it from a nearby shop in my area, as it is much faster.

*David*: Exactly. So, AWS also apply this logic and have expanded their global infrastructure for some types of services that may need a highly distributed architecture or require a much faster performance at a global scale. That is where **Edge locations** are useful. Besides operating from Regions, your applications (or some of them) can be delivered to your customers from a nearby location, called an Edge Location or **Point of Presence (PoP)**:

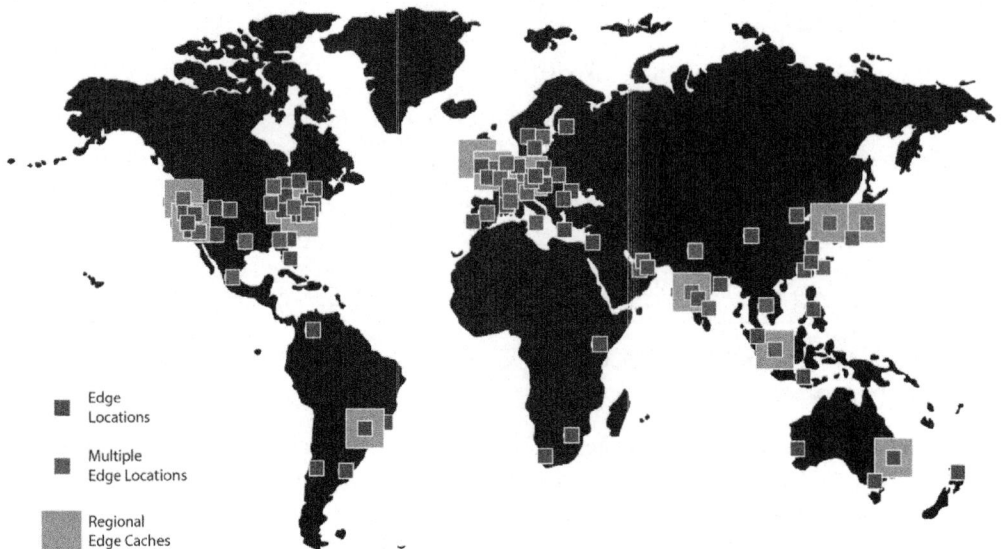

Figure 2.5 – Edge locations

*David*: These dots represent the Edge locations. Currently, there are 300-plus locations all over the world. If you look closely at them, they are near cities that are populous. So, you can serve your content from a nearby location to your customer, and this will improve your application's performance. These locations provide reliable low-latency and high-throughput network connectivity.

*Berta*: It seems there are many of them. So why do we need Regions then? Can't we run everything from these Edge locations?

*David*: Okay. Let me help you in answering your question by asking another question. Does the nearby shop in your area sell everything, such as furniture, shoes, and clothes?

*Berta*: No. Just groceries, because it's a small shop.

*David*: Similarly, consider Regions as your city mall, where you can get almost everything, I mean, most services. But some of the services may require applications to be served from a nearby location to the user, and that's where Edge locations can be useful.

*Berta*: Okay. So, like my nearby shop, Edge locations serve a limited number of services.

*David*: Yes. Some of these services are related to security, content distribution, and DNS resolution. These types of services are well suited to a global architecture.

*Berta*: So, this means that in my application, I can design to use both types of services?

*David*: Yes, absolutely. Based on your application architecture, you may only use the regional service or augment it with services running on Edge locations.

*Berta*: I can understand the content distribution part, but why would someone want to run security components in an Edge location?

*David*: These Edge locations can help you stop most attacks on your application, as they are near the source of the attack. If the attack was not stopped at the Edge location, it would then target your application in the Region, and the impact would be much larger.

*Berta*: And just to confirm, the usage of these Edge locations is not mandatory, right?

*David*: Not at all mandatory. Application architects have full control over which components and services to use or not use. If you have an application that you know is only going to be used in a single location, you may not use Edge locations for it. Some services such as Amazon Route 53, Amazon CloudFront, and Lambda@Edge run through Edge locations. Don't worry about understanding all these services now. We will talk about them at the right time.

*Berta*: And are these locations also hidden?

*David*: Yes. All this infrastructure is running in undisclosed and unmarked buildings. AWS restricts physical access to people who need to be at a location for a justified business reason. Employees and vendors who need to be present at a data center must first apply for access and provide a valid business justification. The request is reviewed by specially designated personnel, including an area access manager. If access is granted, it is revoked once necessary work is completed.

*Berta*: Top-notch security.

*David*: Yes. AWS regularly achieves third-party validation for thousands of global compliance requirements, which they continually monitor to help their customers meet security and compliance standards for finance, retail, healthcare, government, and beyond.

AWS operates globally, and in different geographies, there are different compliance standards. To achieve these compliance requirements, AWS goes through third-party validations. Also, AWS has customers from different verticals, such as finance, retail, government, and healthcare, among others, and these third-party validations ensure that all the required compliance standards are followed and adhered to.

*Raj*: Running this big infrastructure surely requires an immense amount of power and cooling capabilities. How does AWS take care of sustainability in the cloud?

*David*: I appreciate your concern. Let me try to answer it. AWS has set itself on a path to operate with 100% renewable energy by 2025. And for AWS, it is not only about achieving technical outcomes but also about energy efficiency. In some of the AWS data centers, direct evaporative technology is used for cooling, which reduces energy and water consumption. AWS has also started using reclaimed or recycled water for its cooling system in some of the data centers. A novel project in Ireland is recycling heat from an AWS data center for local community buildings.

*Raj*: Interesting. Thanks.

Gloria seems happy as everyone is actively participating in the training. She is certain that this will clear up some confusion that the IT team may have during the migration to the cloud. She now understands the flexibility that the cloud offers for building and running applications without the challenge of maintaining their own data centers. All the compliance and security standards the cloud offers would certainly let her team focus on adding value to the business rather than doing the undifferentiated heavy lifting. She gets busy taking some notes.

# A global network

David moves to the next slide and shows a picture. This time, the dots on the world map are connected using dotted lines:

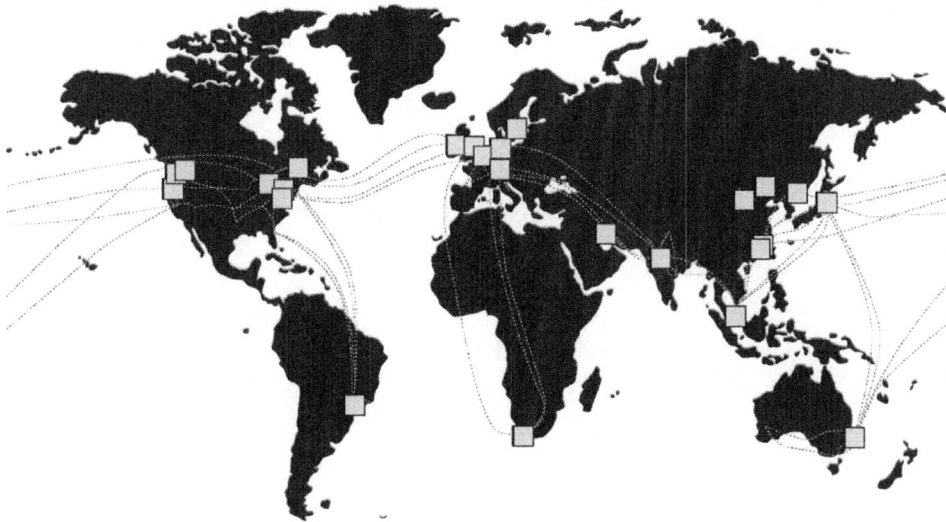

Figure 2.6 – A global network

*David*: Can anyone guess what this graphic represents?

*Charles*: The circles represent the AWS Regions, and the dotted lines probably represent network connectivity.

*David*: You are right. The dotted lines are the AWS global network backbone. AWS very early realized the importance of having a steady and performant network for customers. AWS built a global network infrastructure connecting every data center, AZ, and AWS Region. The purpose-built private, highly available, low-latency, fully redundant global network infrastructure operates using 100 GbE metro fiber cable. These trans-oceanic cables are spread across the oceans.

*Charles*: You mean AWS owns this network? That's a huge project.

*David*: I would say this network is controlled and managed by AWS. The AWS network backbone circles the globe and is linked with tens of thousands of networks and delivers consistently high performance. Customers can design their workload to use this purpose-built, low-latency network. As this network has a global footprint and it is expanding rapidly, you can offer your applications to end users in virtually any country.

*Charles*: And it is redundant.

*David*: Yes. And encrypted too. Security is the most important principle at AWS. The AWS global network is encrypted at the physical layer. All the data flowing through it automatically gets encrypted. Customers can also add additional layers of encryption depending on the services they plan to use.

*Charles*: Are Edge locations connected to this global network?

*David*: Yes. And you can use this global network for multiple services to provide a faster upload or download for your global customers or provide connectivity to your branch offices.

*Charles*: Does this network use networking equipment from any specific vendor?

*David*: No. It uses custom-built hardware and software fine-tuned for AWS's specific use cases.

Charles seems amazed. He has been in the networking field for as long as he can remember. Just the sheer thought of building and operating a network at this scale feels overwhelming to him.

*Harold*: But why not use globally existing internet connections rather than building a whole backbone network?

*David*: There are multiple reasons behind it. The first reason is security. Traffic traverses AWS infrastructure rather than the public internet and is end-to-end encrypted.

Second is the availability of the network. As this global network is maintained and run by a single entity, it gives AWS better control over scaling and redundancy. Most **internet service providers** (**ISPs**) scale their networks based on the traffic patterns they observe over a period of time. If you launch a workload with sudden peaks of traffic that may congest something in their network, they would probably drop it or give it a very low priority. As AWS can observe and monitor the whole network traffic, they can respond quickly to any outages or traffic congestions.

The third reason is performance. Internet connections traverse multiple ISPs, and all of them may have different ways of forwarding or prioritizing the traffic flow. There may be potential of traffic getting diverted or black holed or anything like that, but by having their own backbone network, AWS can deliver reliable and consistent performance.

The final reason is to connect closer to the customer. This private network avoids internet hotspots or sub-optimal external connectivity. So, customers are able to leverage the global backbone and get connected through the optimal path near their locations.

*Harold*: Hmm. I would think all these investments in a global backbone, multiple AZs, and backup power increase the cost of the service. In the end, it will be the customer who is paying for all of these. And when AWS is maintaining most of the services for the customers, that cost will also add up. I guess maintaining and running our own data center will be much cheaper. The cost of a cup of coffee in a café will always be higher than preparing it by yourself at the office or at home.

At this point, Gloria realizes it is the same question she had answered in the board meeting. She is interested to see how David answers it.

*David*: Yes, you are right, Harold. Sometimes, this is true. But when it comes to the scope of IT services in the cloud, there are some new, interesting advantages we never considered before. The first one is automation. The service will be provided automatically; that means there's no need to have a human performing the required tasks, as they can be executed by scripts or code. Every cloud service is created and controlled by code, which is constantly reused, so the cost can be lower. The second advantage is economies of scale.

*Harold*: Economies of scale?

*David*: Let me use a simple example to explain it. Here's a question: have you ever used a shuttle bus service, the one that is usually provided by a hotel to pick up and drop off passengers from an airport or tourist spots?

Figure 2.7 – Shuttle service

*Harold*: Yes. And most hotels operate it too. It is much cheaper than taking a taxi.

*David*: Exactly. Imagine you are the owner and the driver of a shuttle like this, which provides a transportation service from one place to the other—in our case, from the hotel to the airport.

You start your business by purchasing the bus; from that moment, it needs to be maintained. In the beginning, you will sell your tickets at an initial price that you think is reasonable, considering how much the bus is costing you. You don't have many customers initially, and you need to dedicate some of your time to advertising the service and its quality.

After some time, you start to get more customers. Because of the way you work and the energy you have put into the business a very popular hotel asks for your service, and the number of customers keeps increasing. Now the shuttle performs more runs per day, bringing more people to the places they need to go. The interesting thing here is that the shuttle is costing you the same; it's still the same bus, but now you have more customers, and so you can earn more money.

At this point, you can decide to continue in this way, or maybe, you consider getting benefits from economies of scale and start reducing the ticket fare. This is something that customers will appreciate a lot, and, for sure, this will increase the popularity of your service to the point you will get more and more customers. If the number of customers further increases, well, you will probably start thinking about substituting the shuttle for a larger one. And this is the fantastic thing: as you charge less for the service, you get more customers! In the end, the total income is much bigger! And everyone benefits from it.

*Harold*: Interesting. Does this mean that AWS lowers the prices of existing services?

*David*: Oh yes. And several times. It's a strategy of the company: as more customers use their cloud services, the price of those services will be lower, because, from AWS' point of view, the underlying infrastructural cost is divided among all the customers.

*Harold*: That's smart! So, one day you wake up and realize that you have got the same service at a lower price by doing nothing?

*David*: Yes. And that is announced publicly in AWS's *What's New* blog post. I will send you this link, too, in the follow-up email.

Gloria likes the shuttle example and it seems like Harold has understood it too. She is pondering whether Harold is changing his perception of the cloud.

*David*: Now, let me expand on that shuttle example to explain one more thing. Let's imagine you have to buy a shuttle for your business. What will be the crucial points you will consider before deciding? Let's talk about factors other than the brand name or the look of the vehicle.

*Alex*: Can I think about a car rather than a shuttle? I don't want to compete with Harold's business.

Many people giggle across the room. Harold smiles too for a moment but then returns to his serious posture.

*Raj*: I will first think about the emission standards of the vehicle. I don't want to contribute to more pollution. Glaciers are already melting.

*David*: That's a good point. Some countries are very strict about emission standards. If a vehicle is over the approved limits, it will be non-compliant with the basic requirement of getting registered. So, obviously, it is one of the first things that you should check; whatever you are planning to buy should be compliant with the local regulations. I can give you one example from my last visit to the Taj Mahal in India. Only battery-operated coaches are allowed near the heritage monument. Petrol or diesel vehicles are not allowed. And that is the law. These compliance standards are not something that you can overlook or bypass. What else does one need to consider?

*Berta*: Speed, or should I say performance?

*David*: Yes, that makes sense. Should I say the *need for speed*?

*Berta*: Well, in a way, yes. I don't want to race on a track, but speed matters.

*David*: Agree. What else should you be considering before deciding to buy a car?

Charles and Gloria speak at the same time.

*Gloria*: Features…

*Charles*: Cost…

*David*: You both are right. Features and cost are important factors too. Gloria, can you think about a feature you may be looking for?

*Gloria*: Well…a sunroof, cruise control, and a navigation system, to name a few.

*David*: Yes, I would like these features too. So, the availability of a service is a consideration. And Charles, you are right too. Cost is an important factor to consider.

*Charles*: Just to clarify, I am considering the purchase cost and maintenance cost afterward.

*David*: Absolutely, we should consider **capital expenditure (CapEx)** and **operational expenditure (OpEx)** . So, if I try to summarize, I would say that we identified four major factors: compliance, performance, features, and cost.

Now, compliance will be a factor that can't be compromised. It is not a choice. It's a basic requirement to legitimately own a car. For other factors, such as speed, features, or cost, everyone's priority may be different. Agree?

Everyone in the room nods a yes. Gloria begins to realize why David is talking about these factors. David moves to the next slide:

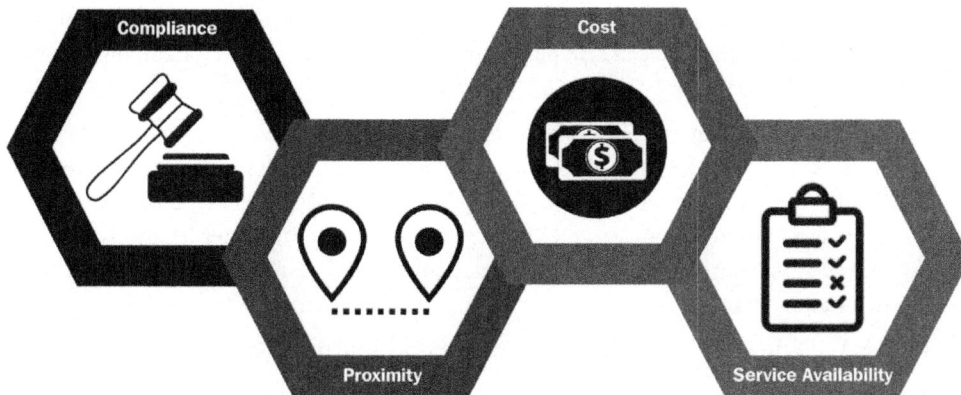

Figure 2.8 – Consideration for selecting a Region

*David*: In the same way you have considered some regulations to select a car or a shuttle bus, similarly, when you want to decide about selecting an AWS Region for your application, you have to consider some factors. First and foremost is compliance. For example, if you are storing some personal data about the citizens of a country, there will likely be some rules to force you to keep that data within the political boundaries of that country.

*Charles*: Like the **General Data Protection Regulation (GDPR)** compliance.

*David*: Yes, and other countries may have their own laws. So, if your business is subject to those laws, you have to comply with them. The second factor is proximity to the user. I will call it speed for the sake of this discussion. No one likes a slow application. So, if you host an application in Singapore for customers in the US, they may perceive a higher latency in accessing that application. Therefore, proximity to your users also matters.

*Alex*: Are there any tools available to check the latency to an AWS Region?

*David*: Yes, there are some. Let me show one to you.

David shows an online tool to check HTTP latency for different AWS Regions from the browser.

*David*: Now, another factor you should consider is cost. Instead of having a flat rate for a service in every AWS Region, the price may be different across different Regions.

*Alex*: But why should the cost be different? Isn't there a similar infrastructure in every Region?

*David*: Yes, it is similar, but the cost also depends on some additional local factors. As in our shuttle example, maybe in one country, taxes and fuel costs are different than in another country. One country may have higher import duties than others. That is also considered when AWS decides on service costs.

If AWS is able to get a better price for power, cooling, and real estate, that may result in a lower cost to customers. The cost can also be affected by taxes in that country, manpower costs, and many more factors.

Also, the supply and demand of AWS services capacity may result in different prices. For example, if you check the costs using the AWS pricing calculator, you will find that most of the prices in the North Virginia Region are cheaper than other Regions. If there are no compliance issues, you may decide to host your production systems near your customer locations, and maybe for backup storage or for recovery from large-scale events, you may choose a Region such as North Virginia where the cost is lower.

*Gloria*: And is the cost in North Virginia cheaper because there are six AZs there?

*David*: That could be a factor. As AWS may have a lot of capacity there, that would mean more supply could result in cheaper prices.

*Berta*: If I remember correctly, North Virginia was the first Region in AWS's global infrastructure.

*David*: Yes, you are right. Now, an interesting question. Why do you think AWS has selected North Virginia as its first Region?

Everyone starts thinking, but they remain clueless.

*David*: Let me not trouble your brain further.

He shows a web page displaying a map with lots of submarine cables, concentrated on the East Coast of the US, near North Virginia:

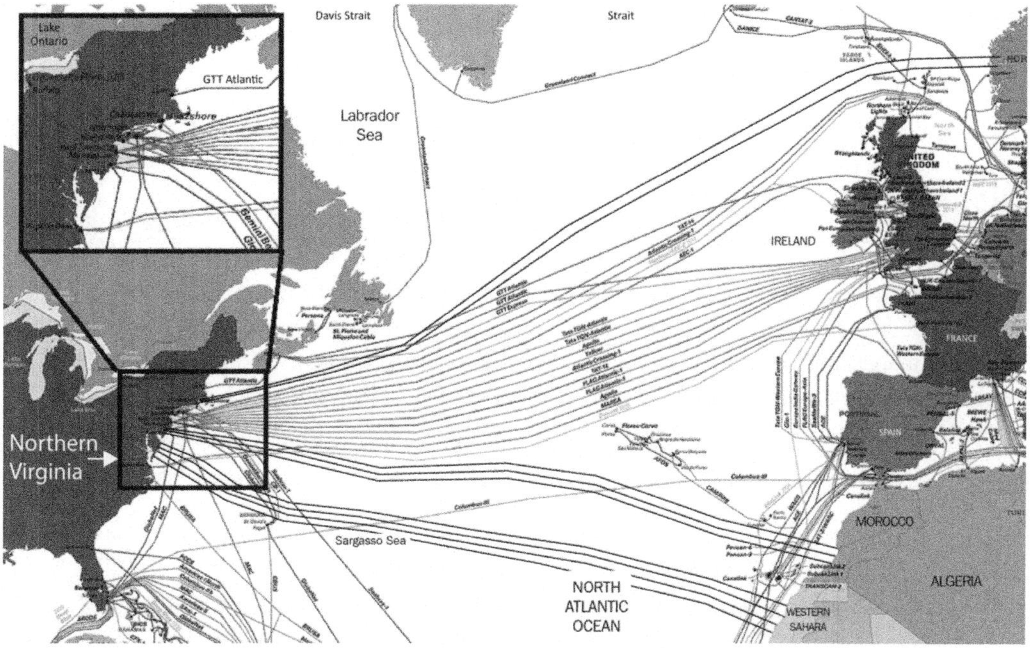

Figure 2.9 – Submarine cable map

🧑 *David*: What you see on the map are the submarine cables that carry internet traffic across continents. As you can see, there is a high concentration of cables on the East Coast of the US, connecting it to mainland Europe and other places. So, if the services are hosted in North Virginia, not only will the customers in the US be able to access them at low latency but also the customers in Europe will not perceive a large latency. So, North Virginia became a logical choice.

🧑 *Charles*: That is interesting. I never thought about that.

🧑 *David*: Yes, that's interesting. And the last factor you may want to consider for selecting an AWS Region is service availability in the Region. Compare it to the features you are looking for in your car or shuttle. Some of the AWS services may not be available in every Region, and you may need to avail of a specific AWS Region to use it. For example, the Amazon Connect service is only available in some AWS Regions.

🧑 *Raj*: And why is that?

🧑 *David*: I don't know the exact logic behind it, but most of these services are created based on customer demand. Or if it is a newly launched service, it may take some time to be available in every AWS Region. But a Region only goes live when core services are available, so core services such as Amazon EC2 and Amazon S3 will be available in all AWS Regions.

🧑 *Raj*: Do we have a list of these services per Region so we can compare?

*David*: Yes, there is. Let me quickly show it here, and I will share the link in the follow-up email.

*Raj*: Thank you.

After showing the services and Regions table, David summarizes the discussion and calls for another break.

# Disaster recovery

As David checks the remaining content to cover as part of this training, he realizes that the next topic of **disaster recovery** (**DR**) would attract lots of questions. TRENDYCORP has struggled in the past with its inability to failover to a stand-by location. This is one of the factors that got them looking for a solution in the cloud. He checks the time and realizes that even with additional questions, he should be able to finish training on time. As everyone returns to their seats after the break, he starts again.

*David*: Okay, folks. We're almost done for today. The last topic I would like to cover will complete this overview of the AWS Global Infrastructure: disaster recovery or, simply, DR. Does anyone already know what DR means?

*Harold*: Yes, of course! This is not something that cloud vendors invented; it has existed for ages!

*David*: Absolutely, Harold, but it's important that all of you understand, as a company that is moving to the cloud, what the benefits are that AWS gives you when it comes to defining a DR plan, or strategy, for your applications. Alex, Berta, before talking about DR on AWS, do you need clarifications about DR in general?

*Alex*: If you have time, why not?

*Berta*: Yes, please.

*David*: Perfect. First of all, let's clarify what a disaster is. Generally speaking, it's any kind of event that can disrupt a service. We are not talking about a simple downtime but an event that can potentially destroy or make completely unavailable the infrastructure of that service for hours, days, and, sometimes, weeks. A disaster can have an impact on a specific component of an infrastructure; a typical example is the complete loss of a large production database. But a disaster can also impact an area within a data center—think about a fire in a data center's room—or an entire data center—because of a lack of electricity in its area or because of a natural disaster such as earthquakes or typhoons. It's obviously important to recover from those disasters, and this is done through a proper DR strategy.

Based on how critical an application is, especially for the business, a company has two main metrics to consider when it comes to defining a DR strategy: the **recovery time objective**, or **RTO**, and the **recovery point objective**, or **RPO**. The RTO identifies for how long an application, or the service it provides, can stay unavailable; a very critical application may have an RTO of seconds. The RPO identifies how much data the company can afford to lose after the recovery; a very critical application may have an RPO of seconds, too. I hope everything is clear so far.

*Alex*: Yes, at least for me.

*Berta*: Almost. I have a question: if I have to define and implement a backup-and-restore policy for the resources of my application, is my backup-and-restore policy my DR strategy?

*David*: This is a good question, Berta, and the short answer here is yes, but it's also true that a company can implement different types of DR strategies, more or less sophisticated. The scenario you just described, Berta, is usually called **backup and restore**. In case of a disaster, backups are used to restore resources and data, and then the related service is up and running again. In this case, the RTO is determined by the time taken to perform the backup and restore operations. The more data involved, the larger the backup and the longer the restoration will be. Meanwhile, the RPO is determined by the frequency with which you perform the backups. If you take a full backup of your infrastructure per day, after the recovery, you may lose one day of transactions in the worst case.

Berta, imagine you are working remotely from home.

*Berta*: Okay…

*David*: You are working on an important deployment that can't be postponed for any reason. You have your laptop with all your code in there and…you have backups. Every day you perform a backup of your working directory to an external USB drive. If, for any reason, you lose the code you are working on, you can restore the copy from your external drive. This is your current DR strategy, but what if you have problems with your laptop?

*Berta*: I guess I should have another laptop with me?

*David*: Only if you think that is worth it, based on what you are working on and how much is critical. If you do that, your DR strategy will be a bit more sophisticated, and you have to manage two laptops instead of one, plus the backup of your code. Let me ask another question, Berta: what about if your internet connection goes down for many hours?

*Berta*: Oh, that would be bad! But I guess I have a solution here as well; I can go to my parents' house and work from there; I still have my bedroom.

*David*: Nice! As you can see, your DR strategy is now further sophisticated! If you lose something in your working directory, you can restore it from a backup—let's imagine you take these backups every hour, automatically by a script. If you lose your computer, you have another one ready. If you lose your internet connection, you can temporarily change houses. If you put in place a strategy like that, it means that your project is important and that your RTO and RPO are pretty low—you can't stay without working for more than a couple of hours and you can't lose more than 1 hour of work. Your computer is an important resource you have, the copies of your working directories are your backups, your house is your **primary site**, and, lastly, your parents' house is your DR or **secondary site**. Technically, the process that takes place when you switch from your primary site to your secondary site, in your case, Berta, when you move from your house to your parents', is called **failover**.

*Berta*: Amazing, now everything is clear, David.

*Alex*: For me too, thanks!

*David*: Now that we have defined the main concepts, you can easily understand what the possibilities are that the AWS cloud can offer you, folks.

In the same way, the infrastructure of your applications can be built within a single AZ, can span multiple AZs, or can be multi-Region—your DR strategy could allow your applications to quickly recover from downtime that could take place at the AZ or at the Region level. AWS services provide many different features that help you implement the DR strategy that perfectly fits your needs: cross-Region backups and cross-AZ or cross-Region data replication mechanisms are just two examples. In the next months, you will get the chance to learn everything you need.

Before we finish, another important aspect to remember about DR on AWS is that on the DR site, you can build infrastructures whose complexity depends on how critical applications are as well: if an application is very critical, that is, the RTO and RPO are close to 0 seconds, then you would probably go for a DR site that is almost an exact copy of the primary site. If an application is not critical at all, you may want to store just the backups in your DR site, taking all the time you need to create, configure, and start all the resources you need. About this second option, the point to remember here is that in the cloud, you can save costs by removing idle resources at the DR site. You create them when you need them, and so, you pay for them only when you use them!

*Harold*: This is really useful. We don't have to spend a lot of money just to keep a DR environment running. With automation and cross-Region copies of data, we can quickly recover from any disaster. We probably won't need regional disaster recovery too often, but we should surely design for cross-AZ capabilities.

*David*: I agree. Though AWS designs its services with redundancy in mind, it is always better to design your applications with the same approach too. It is always better to consider all the what-if scenarios, such as what if an AZ goes down? If an AZ runs out of capacity for a specific resource, can my application automatically use another AZ and provision the resource? If there is a regional outage, can our application dynamically redirect traffic to another Region? These questions can help you decide on the type of redundancy you should implement at your application level.

# Summary

The training lasts the whole day, and all of them go through the various services AWS has to offer. Everyone is astonished by the depth and breadth of the available services.

David engages the audience through different activities, demos, and questions. At the end of the training session, he thanks everyone and collects their feedback. Gloria stands to address the team before leaving.

*Gloria*: Thank you, David, for this insightful training. I am sure everyone has now got answers to lots of questions they had in mind at the start of the training. I was personally amazed by the sheer scale of the AWS Global Infrastructure. It has been built with a great level of redundancy and security by running data centers in unmarked buildings, keeping them connected through multiple redundant links, and following all the compliance policies. Also, the design itself is highly available as we can use multiple AZs in a Region. And our customers will surely benefit when we start using those Edge locations to serve the content from locations near them. We have to keep in mind the compliance, proximity, cost, and service availability criteria for selecting a Region for our workloads. But don't feel confused if you still have lots of new unanswered questions. We will address them internally and through more training sessions from David. Soon, we are launching a project to start building some test servers in the AWS cloud, which will surely help you to learn more and be more confident in your use of the available services. Thanks, everyone, enjoy your weekend, and we will meet on Monday.

Everyone starts leaving slowly. David starts to pack his laptop in his backpack. He notices a big paper box with his name on it near his backpack. He is a little confused and opens it. There is a note that says *Your supply of pastries* and a dozen pastries. He remembers his conversation in the morning with Gloria and remembers that she was giving some instructions to a pantry staff member. He now realizes what the conversation might have been about. He searches for Gloria and finds her catching the elevator. He waves, and Gloria waves back as the elevator door closes.

# Further reading

- Cloud infrastructure:

  - `https://docs.aws.amazon.com/whitepapers/latest/aws-overview/global-infrastructure.html`

  - `https://aws.amazon.com/about-aws/global-infrastructure/`

- Datacenters:

  - `https://aws.amazon.com/compliance/data-center/`

  - `https://aws.amazon.com/compliance/uptimeinstitute/`

  - `https://aws.amazon.com/compliance/data-center/data-centers/`

  - `https://aws.amazon.com/blogs/security/take-a-digital-tour-of-an-aws-data-center-to-see-how-aws-secures-data-centers-around-the-world/`

- Security and Compliance:

  - `https://docs.aws.amazon.com/whitepapers/latest/aws-overview/security-and-compliance.html`

- What's New Blog:

  - `https://aws.amazon.com/new/`
  - `https://aws.amazon.com/blogs/`, then filter by the **News** category.
  - `https://aws.amazon.com/blogs/aws/`

- GDPR:

  - `https://aws.amazon.com/compliance/gdpr-center/`

- Disaster Recovery:

  - `https://aws.amazon.com/what-is/disaster-recovery/`

# Computing – In Cloud We Trust, Everything Else We Compute

Harold is at his desk when he hears an email notification on his laptop:

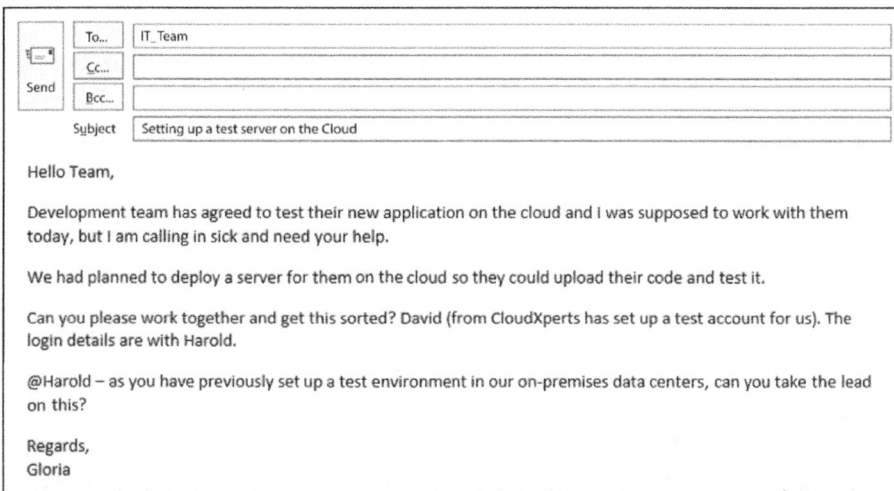

| Send | To... | IT_Team |
|---|---|---|
|  | Cc... |  |
|  | Bcc... |  |
|  | Subject | Setting up a test server on the Cloud |

Hello Team,

Development team has agreed to test their new application on the cloud and I was supposed to work with them today, but I am calling in sick and need your help.

We had planned to deploy a server for them on the cloud so they could upload their code and test it.

Can you please work together and get this sorted? David (from CloudXperts has set up a test account for us). The login details are with Harold.

@Harold – as you have previously set up a test environment in our on-premises data centers, can you take the lead on this?

Regards,
Gloria

Figure 3.1 — Setting up a test server on the cloud

Harold is a little confused after reading this mail from Gloria. He has certainly set up a lot of test environments in the past, but never on the cloud. He tries to figure out how to address this when Alex walks up to his desk. Seems like Alex has also read Gloria's email.

*Alex*: Good morning, Harold. Seems like we are going to see some action today on the cloud.

*Harold*: Well, I hope so too. It would be better if we brainstormed a bit before randomly trying our luck with the cloud. I was told by Gloria that we have to watch out for the cost too, as there's a pay-as-you-go approach with the cloud and we may easily go overboard if we are not careful. Let's gather in the meeting room in 10 minutes and call the others too.

*Alex*: Sure.

# Understanding virtualization and hypervisors

After 10 minutes, Alex calls Berta, Raj, and Charles into the meeting room. Harold is already there and is standing next to a whiteboard. Alex feels like he is entering a classroom and Harold is going to deliver a very complex lecture.

*Harold*: So, you all have read the email, and I assume you are clear on the task.

*Berta*: I understand what is expected, but I am not really sure how to achieve it.

*Harold*: And that's why we are having this meeting. I am sure that everyone understands that running a server on the cloud is not going to involve any physical racking, stacking of servers, or laying out network cables. As per the little knowledge I have gained in the last few days, it is all going to be virtual—virtual servers, virtual networks, virtual storage, and so on.

*Alex*: Can you explain a bit about virtualization so that we all are on the same page? My understanding of virtualization is from my college days when my professors explained **Java Virtual Machines (JVMs)** to us, which could run Java code in a portable way.

*Harold*: Well, that's not very different from it. Let me explain it to you by giving you an example.

The others in the room are all ears. They have mostly seen Harold asking questions; this time, he is providing answers.

*Harold*: Do you live in a multi-storey building or an independent house?

*Alex*: I live in a multi-storey building.

*Berta*: I live in an independent house.

*Raj*: Me too.

*Harold*: Okay. Next question. Let's consider that the multi-storey building and the independent house are constructed on the same size of land, the same square meter area. Which one will accommodate more families or residents?

*Berta*: I guess the multi-storey building would, as it has multiple floors.

*Harold*: Agreed. Virtualization is not so different. I will explain server virtualization to you, which is the most common and most popular form of virtualization. Consider that the piece of land where the multi-storey building or the independent house is constructed is like a physical server. On that physical server, you could install one operating system and let one application run from it, like one independent house and one family living in it. That family has full control of the house; they take care of security, take care of bills; they use the facilities, such as the garage, storeroom, and so on. Similarly, the operating system installed on that server takes control of the whole server and performs tasks such as resource allocation, memory management, network communication, storage connections, and so on. Mostly, it hosts only one application. This is a traditional 1:1 approach of using one server for one application. However, most of the time, using this method, the server will have a lot of resources not in use, such as memory and CPU, which is a waste of money:

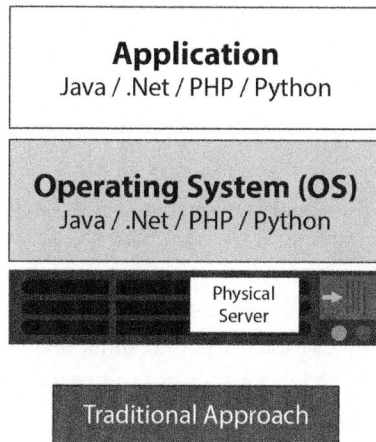

**Application**
Java / .Net / PHP / Python

**Operating System (OS)**
Java / .Net / PHP / Python

Physical
Server

Traditional Approach

Figure 3.2 — Traditional approach for hosting an application

*Alex*: Why don't we install multiple applications on the same server and utilize the server fully?

*Harold*: Technically, it is possible, but it has some challenges. These applications may have some conflicting requirements in terms of the patch level, security settings, or network port, which could result in compatibility issues.

*Berta*: Agreed, and if one application crashes and we need to restart the servers, all the other applications running on that server will also be affected.

*Harold*: Yes, and that's where the virtualization approach helps. Now, Alex, how many floors are in your multi-storey building?

*Alex*: Fourteen.

*Harold*: And does only one family occupy all fourteen floors?

*Alex*: No way. Every floor has a different number of apartments and they are occupied by different families. Some floors have fewer apartments than other floors do, as some apartments are bigger in size. I mean, in terms of the area in square meters.

*Harold*: And who maintains the whole building?

*Alex*: A building management agency takes care of it. They have appointed a caretaker who lives in one of the vacant apartments in the building. He is very nice.

*Harold*: Lucky you. So, a few things are clear here – multiple families live in the building, each in their own apartment, and there is a caretaker. All families most probably share some common facilities, such as escalators, parking spaces, play areas... Right?

*Alex*: Yes, a swimming pool and a gym too.

*Raj*: Wow, you are a lucky man!

*Harold*: Server virtualization is no different. In the case of server virtualization, one physical server runs multiple **virtual machines** (**VMs**), and each VM has its own operating system and runs its own application. These virtual machines are kept isolated by the hypervisor running on the server.

*Alex*: Hypervisor?

*Harold*: Your building management agency manages the whole building and ensures that the common facilities remain in a usable state. Similarly, a hypervisor runs on a physical server and ensures that all of the VMs get the required resources and that they are kept logically isolated. The hypervisor provides the isolation between your VMs and resources on your physical server. An operating system running inside a VM may think that it has direct access to the physical CPU, physical memory, and the other physical resources of the server – but it's actually the hypervisor that virtualizes the physical hardware of the server and presents it to the VM as virtual CPUs, virtual memory, and other virtual resources. It provides a layer of isolation.

*Berta*: It sounds like the hypervisor has now become the primary operating system of the server.

*Harold*: Yes, it is a kind of operating system that is fine-tuned to run on bare-metal servers, but it may not have all the bells and whistles a traditional operating system provides. These hypervisors run very efficiently and mostly don't require a bigger footprint in terms of memory or CPU. They consume very few resources on the physical server and try to make those resources available to the VMs running on that server:

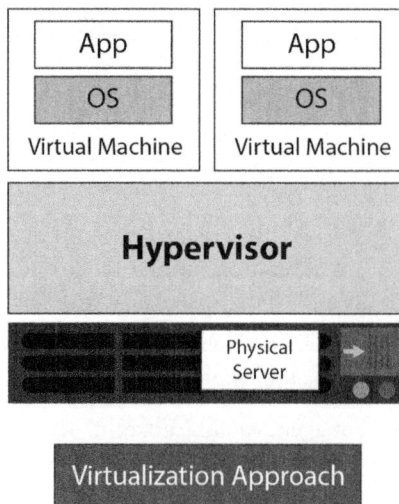

Figure 3.3 — Virtualization-based approach for hosting an application

*Berta*: So, multiple VMs can run on the same physical server and the hypervisor ensures that they all are logically separate from each other. In this way, we could run different operating systems and applications on each server.

*Harold*: Yes, that's the idea. This will also allow the server to be utilized at its max capacity. As the new generation of servers has ample power in terms of CPU and memory, virtualization is the best approach to leverage that power. Just as you may find apartments of different sizes in a multi-storey building, similarly, the VMs running on hypervisors can be configured for different sizes in terms of CPU, memory, or other resources.

*Alex*: Thanks, Harold. This is very clear.

*Harold*: We need to build two servers to test a new application. It is practically finished, and the developers say it works well on their computers… but they'd like to check it in a test environment controlled by us.

*Berta*: Windows or Linux?

*Harold*: Haha, good joke. Both of them, of course.

*Alex*: And I can assume they need us to set up these servers… on the cloud today.

*Harold*: You've got the point… you're learning fast. Maybe I will be considered an experienced communicator soon… Let's take a quick 5-minute coffee break and think about how we can complete the task. I have a meeting with the development team, so I will be gone for a short while, but you can do your research during that time.

*Raj*: Coffee is always welcome.

All of them, except Berta, go to grab some coffee. Berta makes herself busy reading some documentation on the AWS website. Harold heads to his meeting with the developers. Raj and Alex head out for a coffee.

## Distinguishing between the available options

After the break, Raj and Alex return to the meeting room and find Berta poring over the AWS webpage. Alex springs into action mode.

*Alex*: Okay, folks – how do we start with the virtual servers we need to create?

*Berta*: Well, I can see from the AWS documentation that there are many options available; I would suggest learning about them in advance, documenting what we need, and then trying to create these servers based on what we have learned. What do you think?

*Alex*: It works for me.

*Raj*: Same for me.

*Berta*: If it's okay with you, I'll quickly recap what the key points I've learned so far are. First of all, Amazon EC2 supports several operating systems, such as the latest versions of Microsoft Windows Server and the most popular Linux distributions, and they recently announced support for macOS.

*Alex*: EC2? What's that?

*Berta*: Oh, apologies. **EC2** is the service our provider uses to create those virtual servers. It stands for **Elastic Compute Cloud**.

*Raj*: Harold told us we need both Windows and Linux, but for the latter, which distribution of Linux are we going to choose? I think we could go for Amazon Linux, considering we don't have specific requirements here.

*Berta*: Yes, I agree. Perfect. The next point is related to the instance family and the related instance types available.

*Alex*: I'm not 100% sure I understood that point, honestly. Anyone that could clarify it for me?

*Berta*: Sure, Alex. We have all been coming face to face with new concepts every day for the past few days – I totally understand. Let me explain the concept in this way: imagine you have to buy a new pair of shoes… Okay?

*Alex*: Okay…

*Berta*: When you visit a shoe shop and the clerk asks you what you need, you don't just say, "I need a new pair of shoes." That would be obvious, and, more importantly, the clerk would never be able to help you because your request was too generic. The clerk would surely ask you, "Which type of shoes do you need?". Choosing the type of shoes is like choosing an EC2 **instance family**. You may need to buy running shoes, shoes for a ceremony, sneakers, sandals, and so on; in the same way, with Amazon EC2, you may need a General Purpose instance, or a Storage Optimized instance, Compute Optimized, Memory Optimized, and so on. Based on your needs, you can select the instance family that best fits the requirements of your application.

*Alex*: Okay, everything is clear so far except for one thing: what's really different between one instance family and the other? For example, what makes the Accelerated Computing instance family perfect for machine learning workloads? At least, that's what the documentation suggested.

*Raj*: I can help you here, Alex. What is different is the hardware underneath, the hardware of the physical hosts on top of which the virtual server will run. Plus, the operating system of the host will have ad hoc configurations. Based on your example, by choosing the instance family you mentioned, you will get servers with **Graphics Processor Units** (**GPUs**) and with other hardware useful for machine learning stuff. I'm sorry for interrupting you, Berta. Please go ahead with the rest of the explanation.

*Berta*: Thanks, Raj, no problem. So… you, Alex, are in the shoe shop and you just specified which type of shoes you are looking for. The second question that the clerk will ask you will be, "Which size?" In the same way, with Amazon EC2, once you have decided on the instance family, you need to specify the instance type. Every instance family provides a certain number of options in terms of size, represented by the words micro, small, medium, large, extra large…. Meanwhile, with shoes, you just have… a number. Hehehe.

*Alex*: …and every instance type, or I should say size, based on your analogy, determines the number of CPUs and RAM that the EC2 instance will have, am I right?

*Berta*: Yes, you are right, but don't forget other technical aspects associated with a virtual server, which are also determined by the instance type you selected: the type of storage it supports, the network performance, and the support for IPv6, to mention the most important aspects.

*Alex*: Can I change the instance type after I have selected it and the virtual server has been created?

*Berta*: Yes! In the same way that you can change your pair of shoes if you've realized, once you're home, that they are too big or too small. Well, to be more precise, with Amazon EC2, it will take a few seconds to shut down your virtual server, change the instance type, and start the server again. For your shoes, on the contrary, you will have to go out again, return to the shop, and hope that another size will be available! Amazon EC2 is definitely faster in this case! Hahaha!

*Alex*: Haha, that's true, Berta! And thank you again for the explanation, it was super clear!

The meeting is close to the end when Harold suddenly comes in.

*Harold*: Did you finish the meeting? I hope it cleared up any doubts. We need to create those two servers soon, as Gloria asked us to.

*Raj*: Yes, Harold, but before effectively creating the two servers, we need to speak with the developers and ask them a couple of questions.

*Harold*: What questions?

*Raj*: We need to understand which type of application they are building, which features they have, and whether they have specific requirements from the server standpoint that need to be satisfied. Only after that will we be able to create the servers.

*Harold*: And what about if the development team will not be able to provide the information you are looking for, Raj? I don't want to be stuck in the process.

*Raj*: I doubt that will happen, Harold. Amazon EC2 provides an instance family called General Purpose, which is the best for generic standard applications. This instance family, based on what we understood by reading the documentation, represents a good trade-off between performance and costs. And then we can choose a micro or small instance type and see whether it will be sufficient.

*Harold*: Instance family? Instance type? Can anyone explain what Raj is talking about?

*Berta*: Sure! Harold, imagine you have to buy a new pair of shoes…

The team is learning about the immense possibilities and options available in the cloud, which offers them flexibility that was unheard of in the on-premises world.

## Getting the right configuration

As everyone has had enough information to get started, they now want to put their knowledge into action. They have no fear of making huge mistakes either, as the cloud allows them to experiment often without any high cost of failure.

*Alex*: Okay, now we have all the configuration documented. I'd like to see those servers running – let's hurry up and go for it. They will probably be ready in 10 or 15 minutes. How do we start?

*Harold*: Well, not so fast… I'd also like to see them running, but in my experience, I always say that once everything seems decided, take a break. Then sit down, think, brainstorm more possible ideas… and only after that begin to work on it. This might seem a waste of time, but I can assure you it's a time-saver in the long term.

*Berta*: It seems a reasonable idea – but what are you thinking about?

*Harold*: I was thinking about the software configuration of these servers. Yes, virtual servers, I know. We know some of the current needs, but I can imagine there will be new ones in the future. Maybe we'll need different configurations while the developers are introducing changes to the apps, or maybe more environment types. I'm sure you can find some way to configure them later, but maybe we'll have to plan the method in advance.

*Alex*: You mean, we'll probably need a way to run scripts or other configuration tasks on them?

*Harold*: Exactly. And it will have to be done in a safe, quick, and reliable way.

*Raj*: Quick and reliable? That seems like a task for automation. Humans usually make mistakes when under pressure.

Berta goes to the whiteboard, cleans it, and begins to draw.

*Berta*: Well, let's brainstorm the possibilities. I'd like to have all of them discussed and documented, as Harold says; it seems the best way to proceed, especially in this new, unknown environment.

*Harold*: You also seem to be learning fast…

*Raj*: Let's start from the beginning. I can imagine choosing the operating system is the first step. How is this configured in the cloud?

*Alex*: There are not too many options here. We just need to choose one image with the right operating system we need. Looks like there's a menu with many predefined images containing most operating systems, at least supported versions of them. Windows, Linux, even some Macs. So, we need one with Linux and another one with Windows for our applications.

*Berta*: What exactly is an image?

*Alex*: According to the documentation, it is a predefined structure that contains information on how to create the virtual server. The most important information seems to be what you want inside the first hard disk, especially the operating system that comes preinstalled.

*Raj*: And once the server is booted from the image, we have a running instance, where we can install our applications and configuration files.

*Alex*: Exactly… it's your computer, so you install what you need. Even with the cloud, the responsibility for what you run on this computer is the customer's.

*Harold*: Wait. I have an idea. Is it possible to create our own images? We could install a bunch of our business tools and create all the servers already loaded with them. It seems logical, as they will also be on the disks… Something like a **Master Image** that we had on-premises.

*Berta*: That would save lots of time…

*Alex*: Totally possible. The process is clearly documented; first, you create a running instance from a standard image, and then you install all your tools and applications. You test them, and once verified, you create your own custom image from that running server and store it. Then, you can use it to quickly create more servers, as many as needed. And, of course, you can have multiple images with multiple combinations…

*Charles*: Remember to set the right permissions for all of them; we don't want unauthorized users to start or create new computers…

*Raj*: Hello, Charles, welcome to our meeting!

*Charles*: I was listening to your brainstorming session and have decided to join in to collaborate on the security aspects.

*Berta*: Welcome, Charles… Just a second, let me write all of this on the whiteboard. Predefined images, custom images, how to create them, and their permissions.

*Harold*: Nice. Then, I can imagine we'd also need a way to make some changes on these computers while they're booting. Some sort of an initialization script. Maybe we'll have to make some changes we didn't anticipate when the image was created.

*Alex*: The documentation to the rescue again! It seems we have a way to specify an initialization script. It's optional, but if you define it with the creation process, it will be run by the operating system.

*Harold*: What can be done inside this script?

*Alex*: Whatever you need… it's code you have to provide. And it can be written in many scripting languages: Bash, Python, PowerShell…

*Berta*: We could provide a generic script that could call others and change them dynamically, according to our current needs. Again, with the right permissions, I assume. By the way, what is this script called?

*Alex*: It has a funny generic name, it's called **UserData**. It seems it can be used for more things, not only as the initial script.

*Berta*: I'll write it here, but I'll write down **initial script** too. Look, I've found some examples:

```
#!/bin/bash -ex
sudo yum update -y
sudo yum install -y httpd
sudo chkconfig httpd on
sudo service httpd start
echo '<B>TrendyCorp Server</B>' | sudo tee /var/www/html/index.html
<PowerShell>
    mkdir C:\inetpub\wwwroot

    Import-Module ServerManager
    Install-WindowsFeature web-server, web-webserver -IncludeAllSubFeature
    Install-WindowsFeature web-mgmt-tools

    '<B>TrendyCorp Server</B>' | Out-File C:\inetpub\wwwroot\index.html

</PowerShell>
```

Figure 3.4 — UserData scripts

*Raj*: Now that I see these examples, I have one question. You know I don't like to perform any sort of IT task manually. Is there any way to automate the creation process? Setting hardware, images, operating system, initial scripts…

*Harold*: This is the right approach. IT has to work for humans, and not the opposite way around. We don't want it to take hundreds of clicks to create a server when we're in a hurry… or in the middle of our holidays, so a scripted or automated way is mandatory.

*Berta*: I'd like to propose doing the tasks manually on the console while we are learning. And once we understand the process and all dependencies, we'll try to automate it.

*Raj*: Well… I can live with this idea, for a limited time… just a few days.

*Harold*: Agreed. Any other way to configure the servers?

*Alex*: Are we using any kind of configuration tool right now, such as Chef, Puppet, DSC, or System Center?

*Harold*: Yes, all four of them, in fact. We have lots of previous experience with these, and a huge library of scripts and recipes. Can all of them be used in the cloud too?

*Alex*: Yes, why not?

*Raj*: It does not matter if they are virtual; they're just computers with an operating system. Of course, assuming they are reachable from the network.

*Charles*: I like the smell of firewalls in the morning…

*Alex*: Remember our provider offers around 200 different services, and some of them are designed to manage a fleet. For example, they offer OpsWorks, managed servers with Chef or Puppet preinstalled. We can reuse our existing recipes on them.

*Harold*: Sounds nice, all those recipes have been improved for years…

*Alex*: And there are also some serverless services such as Systems Manager, able to run an inventory and generic code on any server.

*Berta*: I've added these to our picture. We have plenty of options!

*Charles*: Yes, it's me again. A final security question: how are we going to patch these servers? You know, against vulnerabilities in the operating system…

*Alex*: That's an easy one. When you launch a new server, the images will be available with the current patches on them. The cloud provider takes care of this.

*Raj*: This is true, but only if you launch a new server from a standard image. What happens after several months? Or if you launch a server using a custom image?

*Alex*: True. In that case, you need a process to update the running server, similar to **Patch Tuesday**. Or we can create a new image with the updated patches. Don't worry, there are also services to help us in this scenario.

*Berta*: Hmm… Please take a picture of the whiteboard. How are we going to remember all these options?

The whiteboard now looks like this:

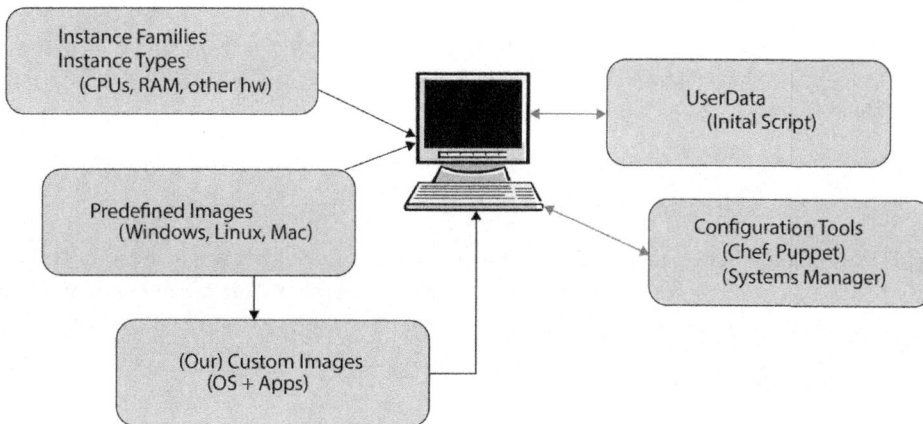

Figure 3.5 — Configuration options

All of them break for lunch. They've agreed to put all the documentation together, study it, and meet again to create the first two servers.

## Running the servers

The team is in the meeting room, sitting around the big table. Alex is projecting his laptop monitor onto the big screen so that everybody can see it.

*Alex*: Well, I think we can start. Let's use a multiple-eyes approach for this. I'll follow our step list to create a server, and please, stop me if something is not clear, or if I'm making a terrible mistake…

*Berta*: Don't worry, I'll document everything… even your minor mistakes. Come on, relax – it seems easy.

Alex connects his browser to the cloud provider console page. He logs in with a username and password provided by TRENDYCORP.

*Alex*: I'm logged in – but what was the name of the service we need?

*Berta*: I think it's written in our files, but there's a faster option. You have a **Search** button there. Search for `virtual servers`.

*Alex*: Here it is: *Virtual Servers in the Cloud*. Here's the option to **Launch Server** and start it.

*Raj*: Wait a minute – don't start yet! You have to select the Region first. Do you remember about Regions and these compliance rules?

*Alex*: Sure, here's the list of all available Regions. We'll choose this one so that all the data will be physically stored there. Berta, please add this to the documentation.

Being carefully supervised by his colleagues, Alex goes through the six steps to create one Linux server. He chooses an image, selects the right instance type and some networking parameters, pastes the contents of a test UserData, and clicks **Done**. Everybody holds their breath for several seconds… and then the server turns green, with a **Running** status.

*Harold*: It only took a few seconds to create a running server! How is that possible?

*Alex*: Just let's do it again… this time, we'll create the Windows Server…

Alex clicks on **Launch Server** again and repeats the same six steps, choosing a Windows image this time, and pastes a UserData script – this time, written in PowerShell. Again, after several seconds, a second server appears, with a green **Running** state on the console.

*Alex*: Can I create several more? This is fun!

*Raj*: I want to try, too! Give me the keyboard!!!

*Harold*: Honestly… May I try too? I've never been able to get a server so quickly! Once, it took me six months for it to be up and running…

Harold connects to the same account with his PC browser. After 10 minutes, he has created several servers… and has destroyed them after some time. A strange smile is now on his face…

*Berta*: Guys, I hate to be the picky one, but how can we check whether these computers are really working? We have to use them – otherwise, they're just some icons on a web page.

*Alex*: Well, technically, you're right. Let's connect to them interactively. Let's start with Linux. I think the setup opened SSH automatically. Raj, do you want to try? You'll need a key; I've stored it in this shared folder.

Raj keys some commands on his own computer. After 10 seconds, he's connected interactively to the Linux server, checked the operating system version, and updated the software repositories.

*Raj*: Great! And quick too. Can you give me the IP address of the one with Windows? I've seen your menus have opened a **Remote Desktop Protocol** (**RDP**) for it, by default. Please get me the administrator password…

Raj types again. Now, he's connected to the Windows Server with a graphical desktop, where he has started to launch some applications and a PowerShell console.

*Raj*: I'm going to create a menu in our Connection Manager to connect to these servers even faster – but remember, I'd like to automate all of this. Is it possible to connect remotely to a specific port, maybe to run a web server on them?

*Alex*: Sure. We created one internet information server and one Apache server earlier, respectively. Can we try them?

*Charles*: Now, I get it – that last communications menu when you created the servers. Something is controlling the traffic to these servers, some sort of firewall. SSH or RDP was opened by default… and that's all. We'll need to provide some more network configuration rules to allow that traffic.

Raj is trying at the same time, but he can't connect.

*Raj*: Hmm… You're right. I can only connect with SSH or RDP.

*Charles*: Secure by default. Those are the only ports you opened.

*Berta*: Well, all of these interactive connections seem to be working; we can consider all this firewalling later. Can anyone monitor the two servers we created?

*Alex*: I'll do it.

*Harold*: One final consideration… I've been thinking since I created those servers…

*Charles*: Harold, you're scaring us… you have a strange smile we've never seen on your face.

*Harold*: Hehe… These servers were created and booted really quickly, and with all the configuration we needed. All tests seem okay – and I've been able to create and destroy other ones in minutes. This is making me consider the possibilities.

*Raj*: What are you thinking about?

*Harold*: If we need a different configuration later, is it better to modify it on a running server? Or maybe is it better to create a new server from scratch, with the new configuration, and destroy the previous one? It's very fast to create a new one.

*Alex*: And if they are destroyed, for example, during the night, you don't pay for them… this could save lots of money. Imagine weekends, holidays, peaks…

*Harold*: Exactly. An interesting approach. I wouldn't dare to do it with our on-premises servers, especially destroying the old server…

*Alex*: …but here in the cloud, you can do it with no problems. Maybe it's the best way.

*Berta*: Now that you mention it, I've read about this in some tech magazine. It's an analogy about how to treat servers. On-premises servers are considered pets; they have a name, you spend a long time choosing one, you take care of them, clean them, and if one is broken, you feel awful.

However, servers in the cloud are treated like cattle. You have a herd, with a number of them; you don't even know their names. If one has a problem, you just replace it – and you exploit them per your business requirements. When you no longer need them, you remove them.

*Charles*: And the cattle are always fenced. Security is important.

Each employee is now flooded with a new bunch of ideas. All of them are excited, each one considering a different point of view.

*Raj*: I'm pretty sure that this full **create-and-destroy** process can be automated, scheduled, triggered by events, or whenever we need it with just a click.

*Berta*: We'll have to plan for different changes. Changing hardware, the instance type, or maybe extending the disk sizes is not the same as changing the software or patching the servers.

*Alex*: What happens if we add or remove servers? Some type of scalability? How are clients going to connect to a variable number of servers? Can we create clusters?

*Harold*: Hey guys, I created a Mac while you were talking!

*Berta*: Feel free to experiment, but remember to destroy all your tests, or Gloria will get to your ears!

## Summary

At the end of the day, everyone except Harold leaves for the day, really excited by their success. Harold, meanwhile, sends a status email to Gloria:

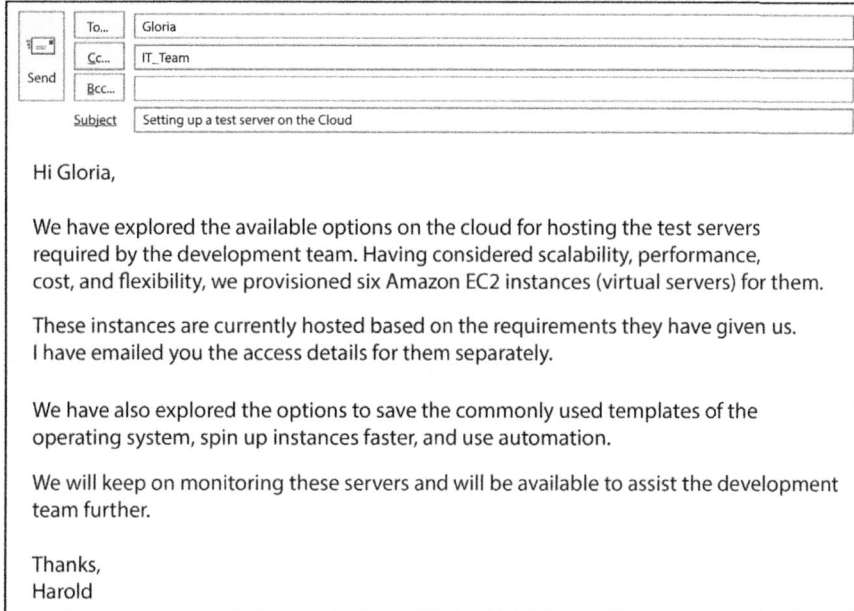

Figure 3.6 — Status email

The day's work done, Harold shuts his laptop and heads home.

# Further reading

- Virtualization: https://aws.amazon.com/what-is/virtualization/

- EC2: https://aws.amazon.com/ec2/

- Instance Types: https://aws.amazon.com/ec2/instance-explorer/

- Images: https://docs.aws.amazon.com/AWSEC2/latest/UserGuide/AMIs. html

- UserData:

  - https://docs.aws.amazon.com/AWSEC2/latest/UserGuide/user-data.html

  - https://docs.aws.amazon.com/AWSEC2/latest/WindowsGuide/ec2-windows-user-data.html

- OpsWorks: https://aws.amazon.com/opsworks/

# 4

# Storage – Where Should I Keep My Data and Maybe Publish It?

Gloria is back at the office and summons the team to the meeting room. She is eager to know about the details of their first task of provisioning test servers in the cloud for the development team. She wants to hear it first-hand.

*Gloria*: Well, everyone, fortunately, I'm back. Did you have any issues with the creation of those servers I requested?

*Alex*: We had a fantastic time working together, learning about the possibilities, and then creating the servers. It was even fun. They are up and running now.

*Harold*: It was great!

*Gloria*: Good, it's very motivating to see you all engaged in these new tasks. Now, I've got the next task for you.

*Berta*: Of course. What do we need now?

*Gloria*: I have received another request from the development team. They want to move their test data to the cloud. And they have sent a list of the different types of data they want to migrate.

She shows them a table on her laptop:

| Dataset no. | Data type | Approximate size | Currently stored in | Use case |
| --- | --- | --- | --- | --- |
| 1 | Old invoices | 2 GB | A Linux server | To be used as test data for our new payment collection system. |
| 2 | Images and JavaScript files | 10 GB | A directory on a Windows-based web server | We plan to redesign our partner website in the cloud. |
| 3 | Product details | 500 GB | A shared storage system | Details about products to be used by a fleet of Linux-based web servers. |
| 4 | Customer database backup | 40 GB | An external hard disk | Not required as of now but just keeping it as we may need it in the future. |
| 5 | Invoices database backups | 15 GB | A Windows file server | To be used for the invoicing system testing. This data will be used on the test server, which is provisioned by the IT team in the cloud. |

Table 4.1 – The dataset to migrate

All of them take some time to read the requirement table. They realize they will be spending their day working on this.

## Enumerating the different types of storage

Some questions arise among the team members, almost simultaneously.

*Berta*: They want to migrate their databases too?

Berta seems excited, as databases belong to her expertise area.

*Gloria*: Not the production databases, at least not yet. But they need to transfer some database backups to the cloud.

*Charles*: I can see there are different use cases, depending on the data types. We need to find out the specific solutions provided. I did some research on storage types, for a different project.

*Gloria*: Great. Do you mind sharing with us the different storage types available in the cloud?

*Charles*: Let me first explain the basic storage types that are used in most computing environments, and then we can discuss the specific solutions provided by the cloud.

*Berta*: That is much better.

*Charles*: There are three primary categories for storage: block storage, file storage, and object storage. I will explain them one by one, using examples. Consider you have bought a piece of land to build a house. You can divide this piece of land as per your own requirement; maybe you need a bigger garage, a smaller outhouse, a big garden, or a swimming pool in the backyard. As you own this piece of land you can divide it as per your own requirements.

Similarly, when you attach a disk to a server, you can divide it as per the application or operating systems requirements and start storing your data. In technical terms, this is called **partitioning the disk**. It is a logical way to divide your storage into different areas and use it for different purposes:

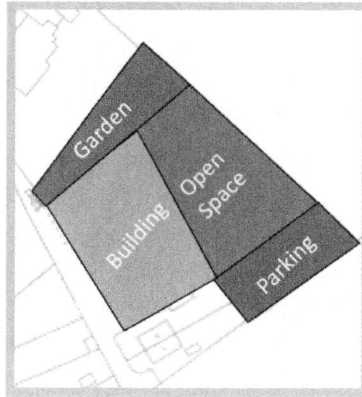

Figure 4.1 – Dividing a piece of land

*Alex*: But why divide it instead of using the whole disk?

*Charles*: That is also possible; consider that you will just have one partition for the whole disk and use it for whatever purpose you have. The operating system of the server can work with multiple disks, partitions, and filesystems on it; it controls the storage space and formats every block of the storage before it can be used. You create partitions to logically isolate your data. For example, one disk may have a partition for the operating system files and another partition to keep data, log files, or database files. The filesystem stores your data spread across multiple blocks of the disk, and that's why it is called **block storage**.

*Berta*: Does my laptop hard disk also use block storage?

*Charles*: Yes. And the USB drive you have connected to your laptop uses block storage too. In this case, the disk is physically inside the laptop, but in the case of servers in a data center, this storage will be presented or assigned from a more complex system as a **Storage Area Network (SAN)**. A SAN offers multiple storage arrays, which are also block storage devices. They connect to the servers using the SAN fabric, which is a powerful dedicated network.

*Berta*: Then the storage may be outside the servers. Would it not make it slower?

*Charles*: SANs are highly optimized and fine-tuned to provide efficient storage to multiple servers. The fabric hardware offers high-speed connectivity and the SAN uses specific protocols, such as **Internet Small Computer Systems Interface (iSCSI)** or **Fiber Channel (FC)**, purposely built to efficiently access the storage. In the end, the operating system receives blocks of persistent storage. And before you ask, **persistent** means data can exist independently; even if no servers are connected, it will be safely stored there. But you still need a server to use this data from your applications.

*Berta*: …in the same way as we need to connect a USB drive to a laptop for accessing the data.

*Charles*: Exactly. So, when you add new data or update existing data on a block storage device, the request goes through the operating system. The operating system creates a filesystem on the storage when it is formatted. It tracks which blocks to read, write, or update for a particular request. The server where the storage is attached owns the data. Of course, you can add permissions for access, but even if the request is coming from another server for the data, the request has to go through the owner server. It is best suited for a one-to-one scenario where you need a server to control the storage.

*Alex*: So, are there cases when you would like multiple servers to access the same data?

*Charles*: Oh, absolutely. That is another type of storage that we call **file storage**. If you have applications running on multiple servers, they might need to access the same data, so you require some shared storage. Instead of one server owning the storage, it is shared. All these servers are allowed to access the files but cannot format the whole filesystem, as they are basically consumers and not the storage owners. Servers are usually given permissions to some files or folders to work with. Think of it like an apartment in a building where you live. You are allowed to make some modifications to your apartment, such as rearranging the furniture, changing the wall color, or maybe hanging some paintings, but you cannot break a wall and create a new entrance to your apartment. So, you can still decide on things within the apartment but not the whole building:

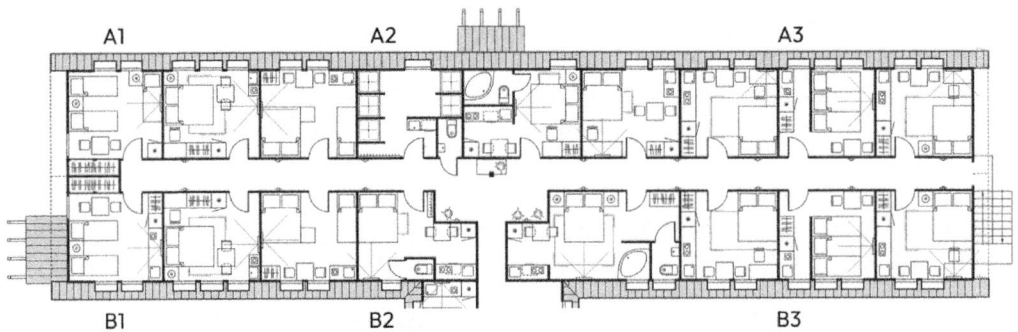

Figure 4.2 – An apartment

*Alex*: So, I am guessing this file storage is also shared and accessed over a network by multiple servers.

*Charles*: You are absolutely right. File storage systems also have specific protocols to use over the network, such as a **Network File System** (**NFS**) or **Server Message Block** (**SMB**). When you want to set up home directories for your users or folders for some common files such as onboarding documents, file servers are great. You can do most filesystem operations, such as create, update, delete, and share…and also set locks over the files.

I've also seen there are dedicated physical devices. They are referred to as **NAS**, short for **network-attached storage**. They are just a type of server with disks, which is fine-tuned to serve files over a network and has some capability for security, durability, redundancy, and scalability. Probably, there will be something similar as a cloud service.

*Alex*: So, file storage can be a good choice for the development team's requirement for keeping the product details data, which will be used by a fleet of web servers.

*Charles*: Probably, but it's too early to jump to conclusions. Could object storage prove to be a better choice for it?

*Harold*: Object storage? This is a little new for me. I have worked with block and file storage systems before, but not object storage systems.

*Charles*: Let me give you an example. You remember that I moved from Dubai 4 years ago?

*Harold*: Yes. I do remember.

*Charles*: So, when I left Dubai to come here and work for TRENDYCORP, I wanted to bring with me some of my stuff, mostly books, computers, and musical instruments. But I still had to find a place to settle down here, and only after that would it have been a good time to shift everything. So, I checked for available options to hold my stuff in Dubai for some time. I found a self-storage company offering this type of service. They were offering that I either rent a whole unit and keep all of my stuff there or rent space per box. I decided to rent the whole unit, which was like a small room and stored all my stuff there. This self-storage unit was reasonably priced and I could go anytime to access my belongings. It was very cheap compared to renting a residential room for just keeping stuff.

Figure 4.3 – Self-storage unit
(Source: Photo by Self Storage, at https://commons.wikimedia.org/wiki/File:Stokado_Self_Storage1.jpg, used under Creative Commons Attribution-Share Alike 3.0 Unported license.)

*Harold*: Yes, self storage has become a nice choice, especially in big cities where houses are becoming smaller and smaller. Some people prefer to use it to keep their house clutter-free.

*Charles*: Agreed, but they are designed for very specific needs. You can't rent a unit and start living there. It may not have a water supply, heating, or electricity, as they are not required for a storage unit. In this way, the service provider keeps the cost low and offers better prices to customers. So, I stored my stuff in one of those units, moved here, and once I moved into my own place sometime after, I hired a courier company to get that stuff shipped to me here.

*Alex*: Interesting.

*Charles*: So, if you look at this example, I basically stored objects. And I could keep any type of object there, provided it fitted in the unit I rented. And I only paid for the duration I kept my objects there, rather than getting into long-term rental agreements or complex leasing processes. I wanted my stuff to be safely stored and accessible whenever I needed it. That's exactly what they provided. Similarly, you can also keep your data in the form of objects.

*Harold*: How is an object different from a file?

*Charles*: In a way, they are the same, but objects have additional attributes, such as metadata—data about the data.

*Alex*: Can you please explain this?

*Charles*: Let's refer to the same example of the storage unit. All the stuff I kept there, I stored in boxes. And on top of the boxes, I added extra information on a sticky note, which had words such as cables, musical instruments, and drum parts. So, this extra information helped me find stuff without opening the whole box.

*Berta*: This is like when I add labels on my jars of spices. Before that, I had made some stupid mistakes while preparing dinner. I don't want to talk more about it, though.

*Charles*: So, this metadata is basically additional information that you can add to facilitate identification of the data inside the object.

*Harold*: Yes, but a filesystem also maintains additional information. For example, for a file, it may store date created, type of file, size, content, and the last accessed time.

*Charles*: Agreed, but I'd call these **filesystem attributes**. It is a form of metadata. Depending on the operating system, you might even add your own attributes to each file, for example, author, department, and expiration dates.

*Harold*: Of course, I could also use folders to separate the files…

*Charles*: Yes, you could. And object storage supports them too, in addition to metadata. If we look at object storage from the outside, it is similar in structure in terms of folders and subfolders, but internally, everything is stored in a flat structure. The folder or subfolders are added as a part of the whole path, which makes the object name.

*Harold*: That's interesting. And how do I access these objects? I guess not the same protocols as for block and file storage.

*Charles*: Yes, you are right. You can access it using **Representational State Transfer (REST)** or using **Simple Object Access Protocol (SOAP)** requests over HTTP/HTTPS.

*Harold*: That means we don't require a specific client-side component or an agent, as most applications can make REST/SOAP calls over HTTP/HTTPS.

*Charles*: Exactly, and that makes it easy to access without requiring a lot of complex dependencies. Different vendors name it differently, but the concept remains the same. If you have ever used Dropbox, Google Drive, or Microsoft OneDrive, you have actually used object storage. Be aware that most object storage doesn't allow a direct edit of the object (unlike block and file storage), but rather you have to overwrite an existing object or create a newer version of it.

*Raj*: This is great, and while you were discussing all this, I documented all of it in a tabular format for easy comparison. Check your emails.

Everyone checks their email and finds the following table:

| | Block Storage | File Storage | Objest Storage |
|---|---|---|---|
| Unit of transaction | Blocks | Files | Objects (files with metadata) |
| Example | Laptop disk | Windows share | OneDrive / Google Drive / Dropbox |
| How can you update? | You can directly update the file | You can directly update the file | You cannot update the object directly. Ypu create a new version of the object and replace the existing one or keep multiple versions of the same object. |
| Protocols | SCSI, Fiber Channel, SATA | SMB, CIFS, NFS | REST/SOAP over HTTP/HTTPS |
| Support for metadata | No metadata support. It stores only filesystem attributes. | No metadata support. It stores only filesystem attributes. | Supports custom metadata |
| AWS services | Amazon EBS Amazon Instance Store | Amazon EFS Amazon FSX | Amazon S3 Amazon Glacier |

Figure 4.4 – Storage types

*Alex*: Thanks for documenting it, Raj. This is so useful.

*Raj*: All credit to Charles for explaining it. I am guessing that our cloud vendor, AWS, offers all of these storage types.

*Charles*: Definitely. All of them are well-documented on its web page. And now that you have a better understanding of the different types of storage, let's start looking into the specific solutions or services we might need, on the AWS platform.

*Gloria*: Let's do it as a parallel activity. Why don't each of you pick a type of storage and gather enough information about it? Let's meet tomorrow morning and discuss your findings. We can then think about suitable storage options to migrate the development team's data with.

*Alex*: Okay, I'm preparing object storage, whatever that can be.

*Harold*: May I volunteer for block storage?

*Raj*: Perfect, then I'll prepare shared storage.

*Berta*: Agreed, then. I'll coordinate and document all your findings and I hope tomorrow we'll be able to migrate these huge files to the cloud.

*Charles*: I will work with you on the documentation part.

*Gloria*: It's so great to see a team effort. Let's meet tomorrow and discuss this in detail. I will also reconfirm some priorities of the data transfer with the development team. Also keep in mind that whatever we store in the cloud should be secure, highly available, highly durable, and cost-efficient, too.

The day goes by while everyone gets busy trying to do their research.

Everybody has learned the fundamentals of generic storage technologies, disks, and filesystems, but also about other options such as object storage and file storage. All of them are eager to deep dive into the specific implementation details in the cloud.

## Object storage

The next day, everyone is back in the meeting room and keen to share their findings. Alex volunteers to start first.

*Alex*: Well, I think I know enough about object storage. First, you have to know this is the simplest way to store data. No huge complications or parameters; you just store objects in the cloud, choose an AWS Region, and that's all. AWS calls this service **Amazon Simple Storage Service** or **Amazon S3**…and let's not forget the meaning of the first S.

*Harold*: I imagine you can separate the files somehow, not only by Regions?

*Alex*: True. You keep your objects in separate boxes, but they are called **buckets**. You can have multiple separate buckets with different owners or permissions.

Now, let's go into the definition. Buckets store objects, but what is an object? Many people think it's just a file, but that's only one of the possibilities. An **S3 object** is a sequential stream of consecutive bytes together with a name that is used as a **key** to find and use later:

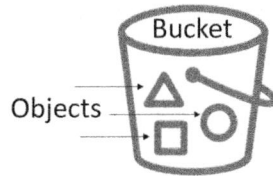

Figure 4.5 – Amazon S3 bucket and objects

*Harold*: But that is the definition of a file, or at least any sequential file you can find on any of our laptops or servers.

*Alex*: Well, a file is a particular case of an object. But there are more: you can also store any sort of stream, maybe one generated in the memory of one of our programs. If you need to permanently store it, it can also be stored in S3. Of course, you have to provide a name, or as you properly said, a key, as this is always mandatory.

*Berta*: Interesting. What about Gloria's requirements?

*Alex*: Well, like many services in the cloud, S3 is not only a single physical device but also a huge bunch of redundant systems. Because of this, S3 can offer *high availability*. Every time you store an object, it's a logical copy. But it is physically stored in multiple redundant subsystems, and at least in three **AZs**, remember, short for **Availability Zones**. Remember what we discussed about the redundant infrastructure and minimizing the effects of a possible disaster. Lastly, hardware is cheap, according to the economies of scale factor we mentioned some days ago.

*Harold*: You mean each file—sorry, each object—is copied onto three disks, one in each AZ?

*Alex*: That is a very simplified view. Objects are copied in multiple subsystems, redundantly, and there could be at least three copies but there could be many more copies as well, depending on the performance required. Having multiple copies can provide much better read performance because all reads can be done in parallel.

Then we have *durability*. Gloria seemed really interested in this. You know, every storage system can lose information through power failures, disk heads falling over the plates, magnetic fields, and so on. However, S3 offers extreme durability, thanks to the way it is designed.

*Berta*: What is the exact definition of durability? We'll have to explain it to Gloria.

*Alex*: Any object in any storage system has to be durably stored; that means not lost in any way. **Durability** is measured as the probability of being able to retrieve the file again. The opposite would be the risk of losing that data.

*Raj*: I've got a nasty idea. I can write a script to store 1 million files in S3, and then another script to read them continuously until I catch a read error. This way, we can calculate how long it takes, which can give us a good estimation of this durability.

*Alex*: It seems like a fantastic idea. Tell me when you get this error. But I have some news for you. According to the documentation, S3 is designed to offer an annual average durability of 99.999999999%. That's eleven 9s.

Raj, your test would take some days. Do the math. If you store 1 million files in S3, statistically you'll lose 1 file every 100,000 years. So, start immediately and tell me whenever you see this error!

*Raj*: It seems durable enough! But I'll do my test anyway…no, I'm joking.

*Alex*: Then we have to consider another important aspect—the cost. S3 is not expensive. Imagine we have lots of large objects. So, S3 provides a reasonable price, but there's not a single option. There are several different options, based on how we are going to access our objects. Depending on the access pattern and how we plan to use our objects, we decide how to store them within S3. These are called **S3 storage classes**.

Imagine you have parked your car at the airport. If you are taking a long holiday abroad, you are not going to need your car for a long time, so you park it in the long-stay parking area. However, if it's a 1 day short flight, you'll return on the same day and you'll want to have your car quickly, so you park it in the short-stay parking section. Of course, depending on your needs, the price will be different.

S3 storage classes offer the same idea, you can choose between *Standard* or *Infrequent Access* storage depending on how frequently you are going to access, which means read, your files. This can be set up separately per file, and of course, the price will be significantly different.

But pay attention here: this is not about performance, the objects will be retrieved at the same speed. And you will have all the benefits of having three copies of each object. In fact, there's an even cheaper option where you just keep one copy, sacrificing some durability.

*Raj*: Is there a long-term layer? I mean, for data that is probably never read…

*Alex*: Yes, this is called *S3 Glacier*. It is used for archived data, where you assume the data will be seldom accessed, or maybe you have to keep it for some years for legal requirements. It is much cheaper but data is not immediately accessible. If you need to retrieve the data, you have to make a request for it. Anyway, many people are substituting their old magnetic tapes for Glacier. It has the same durability as the other storage classes. Can you imagine a magnet deleting your old tapes? This is cheaper and safer.

*Raj*: Are there any tools to automatically change the class of each object to the most cost-efficient class?

*Alex*: Yes, look for *S3 Lifecycle Management* in the console. And now, I have a nice surprise for you. S3 is a storage service…

*Raj*: …a simple storage service…

*Alex*: Yes… but not only for storage, but it is also a publishing service. Every object you store in S3 is automatically served to the network using HTTP.

*Berta*: You mean I could store my personal web pages on it…and that's all, I have a web server with them?

*Alex*: Exactly. Completely serverless. The easiest way to build a web server; you just copy the files onto it. Of course, you have to set the right permissions to decide who can see them.

*Raj*: I assume it has to be a static web server if there is no server behind it that could execute some code, such as a Java or .NET application. You mentioned serverless. I assume there will be no servers to manage or pay for.

*Alex*: Totally right. S3 takes care of all networking and permissions.

*Harold*: What is a **static web server**?

*Alex*: All the web pages are static; they are just copied to the client, to your browser. They can run some code but only inside the browser. That means they won't run code on the server side. But I imagine many applications can benefit from this system, being much simpler, cheaper, and cleaner.

*Berta*: All of this seems amazing, but I can imagine there will be some limitations of S3. Otherwise, there wouldn't be other storage systems…

*Alex*: You hit the bullseye. S3 is designed to easily store and publish files but not as a full filesystem; it's just a flat list of objects with their names. It cannot create a filesystem, folders, locks, or file operations, such as appending or editing the object. It's optimized for readers—objects can be easily read by thousands of readers—but writing on them is not done frequently. And it cannot boot an operating system.

*Harold*: Wait, wait, wait…no folders?

*Alex*: No folders. The bucket just keeps a flat structure internally. But don't worry, all the tools you can use to access S3, including its API, allow the simulation of folders, by cleverly using path separators in the keys, which are used to create the objects. `/folder1/folder2/file3.jpg` would be a perfectly valid object name. This allows you to simulate those folders, for example on your website.

*Berta*: And of course, there will be a maximum number of objects per bucket.

*Alex*: Negative. You can store an unlimited number of objects in a single bucket, assuming their names are different. You'll pay for the bytes stored, and if you feel your bucket is becoming too crowded, you can get more separate buckets. Each one has its own globally unique name.

*Berta*: So, to relate this fantastic investigation you did to Gloria's requirements, in what situations is S3 used?

*Alex*: To name a few, all files, data, and configurations that are not constantly being modified. Also, if we need to publish files using HTTP.

Then, everything which seems like a backup is sent to S3. It's reliable and cheap to use S3 Glacier, which is a tier within S3; it gives us the same durability but at a minimum price. Those backups are not restored daily, hopefully!

Remember the images we used for EC2? Every custom image we create will be in S3 too. It is the perfect use case as they are created once and read many times.

Oh, and I almost forgot. S3 can also be used for big data analytics, as it offers the best price but maybe some data analysts would like to write queries over it. Yes, SQL queries. There are some services that can offer a view of the files stored inside S3 as if they were tables…yes, tables in a database. Much cheaper than a traditional warehouse with expensive disks.

*Harold*: You mean we can perform all of our SQL queries over data stored in S3? And that we can create a data lake using S3?

*Alex*: Yes, but we'll see that after we finish this assignment.

There are many other possibilities, such as object versioning, bucket replication, events, permissions, endpoints, multi-part uploads, and byte-range reads.

*Berta*: That's good, we have enough information to get started with Amazon S3. Once we get to hear about the other options, we will start mapping the right services to migrate the developers' data.

With that, Alex sits down. He's happy to have covered the basic functionality everybody will need: storage, durability, availability, folder structure, storage classes, publishing, permissions, SQL queries, and data lakes. But he also knows they might need more features, such as bucket replication, so he decides to continue his investigation by reading all the documentation pages on the S3 service.

## Block storage

Harold offers to share what he has learned about block storage.

*Harold*: Well, this storage option seems easy. There are several new features we can choose from, but the concepts are very similar to the classical disks we use on-premises. They've done a good job!

Block storage provides a number of fixed-size sectors that are all consecutive, and they form a disk. You can create multiple disks, then connect them to Amazon EC2 instances, and the operating system will see them as raw drives, and format them with any filesystem they need, and that's all, you can create files, folders, read, write, append, lock, and delete them…whatever the filesystem offers.

You can use a service called **Amazon Elastic Block Store** (**Amazon EBS**). This one connects the volumes to the Amazon EC2 instances over the network.

*Berta*: Wait, I'm writing all of this down. You've said blocks and volumes?

*Harold*: Yes, the terminology is really important here. All the storage sectors provided by the service are called **blocks**. All of them have the same size. And all the sectors are offered together in a **volume**, or EBS Volume, similar to **Logical Units** or **LUNs**. Of course, you can have some volumes attached to the same server.

*Alex*: You mentioned more options?

*Harold*: There's another disk option called instance store. It follows the same idea, providing fixed-size blocks to the servers, seen as volume, but, these are provided by the virtualization engine. That means they are directly attached to the Amazon EC2 instance instead of using the network. They will be faster, but they are ephemeral.

*Raj*: What is ephemeral?

*Harold*: **Ephemeral** is the opposite of persistent. The full disk and the data inside are deleted when the Amazon EC2 instance is stopped. For this reason, they are good for some tasks and faster, but the resultant data must be stored outside of them in EBS or maybe a database.

*Alex*: So, in an EBS volume you can have folders, lock files, and append or edit info.

*Harold*: Yes, it's the operating system that finds these virtual drives or logical units and formats them. NTFS, FAT, EXT2…you can choose. But you have to create the volumes, give them the right size, attach them to the Amazon EC2 instances, and ask the operating system to format them. Well, except for the first disk, the root volume, it will be formatted for you. The EC2 launch from its image will install the operating system on them.

*Alex*: I think that a volume is like a parking lot: it has a fixed total area; when it is inaugurated, which means formatted, it gets those white lines painted on the floor, and you have a fixed-size block, a place where you have to park.

*Berta*: Can an EBS volume be expanded? Maybe I chose too small a size.

*Harold*: Yes. Even with the instance running. The maximum size of each separate volume will depend on the different types of volumes Amazon EBS has to offer, but currently, the maximum is 16 tebibytes per volume. You can use **Redundant Array of Independent Disk (RAID)** if you need to create bigger logical volumes.

*Berta*: Tebibytes? What's that?

*Harold*: We have to use the standard units of measurement, as the ISO standard (and all the applications) currently use them. The old joke calling 1,024 bytes a kilobyte is wrong and terribly ambiguous, as the *k* prefix legally means 1,000 in every culture and situation, not 1,024. If you need powers of two, they have to be called **kibibytes**, **mebibytes**, **tebibytes**, and so on. So, please edit your requirement list to use the right prefixes.

*Charles*: What about security copies?

*Harold*: Every volume can have copies, called **snapshots**. They can be done at any time, manually or automatically. They are stored in S3; remember this is a reliable and cheap option and is incremental. You can restore any volume from a snapshot and copy the snapshots to another Region if you wish, as I commented. Snapshots are the way to access the volumes.

*Raj*: Harold, can volumes offer redundancy?

*Harold*: Every EBS volume is replicated three times. If one copy is lost for any reason, it will automatically be rebuilt, the user does not have to do anything. But, for performance reasons, all these copies are restricted to a single AZ, the same one where the EC2 instance is located.

*Raj*: It seems like a strong dependency.

*Harold*: Filesystems have very strict timing constraints for local disks, but you will always be able to copy a volume to another AZ, or even a different Region, by using snapshots.

*Charles*: And what about encryption?

*Harold*: You can choose, for each separate volume, whether it is stored encrypted or not.

*Berta*: What about performance?

*Harold*: You have to choose. Each volume can be based on classical disks, those with cylinders, heads, and magnetic material called **Hard Disk Drives** (**HDDs**), or **Solid State Drives** (**SSDs**). In the end, both types are a collection of blocks that can be seen and mounted as a volume. And once you have selected SSD or HDD, you have even more options for balancing price and performance.

*Alex*: I assume SSD will be faster but more expensive.

*Harold*: Yes, in general, but be careful. There are some scenarios where HDD can be faster than SSD. Sequential operations on long files can be better run on HDD. Remember, an EBS volume is not a single physical disk, so some sequential operations could be parallelized in the underlying system. We'll have to check these cases.

*Raj*: Can volumes be moved from one instance to another?

*Harold*: Each volume is attached to a single instance at a given point in time, and each instance can have multiple volumes if needed. You can detach a volume from an instance and keep it in a *not connected* state with all the data intact; remember, this storage is persistent, not ephemeral. After some time, you can attach the volume to another instance and the data will be there. You can also clone the volumes via snapshots or just remove them.

*Raj*: So, you can't connect one volume to multiple servers at the same time?

*Harold*: Originally no, but now there's a type of volume allowing **Multi-Attach**. These disks can be attached simultaneously to up to 16 instances, so they're ideal to build a shared-disk cluster. But you have to follow the exact installation procedures so that the cluster software protects the integrity of these drives. And the Multi-Attach feature requires the use of specific instance types.

Well, guys, I think that's all. You can read about performance monitoring, **input/output per second** (**IOPS**), automatic snapshots, and many more options in the documentation. Now I need a coffee break.

Everyone breaks for coffee. All of them sit around Harold, who seems to have found lots of similarities between the classical disks and SANs they use on-premises and the AWS EBS service. Berta is asking about the available volume types and the balance between the cost and the needed performance. Alex is commenting on the possibility of storing data in EBS volumes even when they are not attached to servers. Harold comments this is something that could be done on-premises, but it seems much more frequent in the cloud. After some discussion, they decide to continue with Raj's session.

# Shared storage

This time it is Raj's turn to explain file storage.

*Raj*: As Charles mentioned, shared storage systems are designed to be used by multiple clients at the same time. And they operate using some very specific protocols, such as NFS and SMB. Now, these protocols are suitable for a specific operating system type. Most Linux distributions have NFS client software built-in and come with utilities and tools to connect to shared storage systems over a network. On the other hand, Windows-based operating systems favor the SMB protocol. AWS has services to offer both options. When you are looking for NFS-based shared storage, you can leverage Amazon **Elastic File System** (**EFS**). As its name suggests, it is elastic in nature. You don't have to pre-provision a specific size of storage. The storage grows and shrinks with usage. So, you are only charged for the actual storage consumed.

*Charles*: That's interesting. In traditional shared storage, first, we define size, and later we have to keep on adding more capacity, which is really an administrative burden.

*Raj*: Well, Amazon EFS saves you from that. Along with that, it offers different storage classes, which you can choose based on your access frequency or durability requirement. If you have configured your networking, you can also use this shared storage from your on-premises servers too, as it uses the NFS protocol stack, which is widely supported. As it is offered as a managed service, you don't have to worry about patching, updating, or maintenance of the underlying systems. You just create an EFS filesystem and mount it on clients. Those clients can be a mix of on-premises servers or Amazon EC2 instances.

*Harold*: I am guessing once we have the filesystem ready in the cloud, we can use any supported file copy tool to migrate data to it.

*Raj*: Yes, you are right. AWS also provides a service called *AWS DataSync* for this use case, and you can use it to copy data to another EFS filesystem across AWS Regions too.

*Charles*: That will surely come in handy for our migration task.

*Harold*: So, just to confirm, this EFS filesystem exists within a Region, and to connect to it we need mount points?

*Raj*: You are right, and these mount points can be across AZs. So, you can use it for applications where high availability is a requirement. The service also supports automated backup, encryption, and **life cycle management**.

*Alex*: What is life cycle management?

*Raj*: The service automatically achieves the right price and performance for your data by moving it to different tiers within Amazon EFS. So, if the data is not very actively used, it can be moved to a tier called Infrequent Access, and this will cost you less. You can configure the trigger for transition based on the number of days since the last access to the data. It's kind of a set-and-forget mechanism. You just configure a filesystem and the service takes care of scaling, maintenance, transitioning, backup, and encryption.

*Harold*: That's a pretty interesting solution for Linux-based workloads. How about workloads running on Windows-based operating systems?

*Raj*: Glad you asked. There's a similar service family named *Amazon FSx*. It offers different flavors for different use cases. In this family, there's a service called *Amazon FSx for Windows File Server*, which is geared toward Windows-based workloads. It provides a native Windows filesystem for your workloads with full SMB support. At the backend, the storage is built on Windows Server, so if you are migrating your Windows-based application, it will maintain application compatibility and even its existing permissions.

*Charles*: And you don't have to maintain that backend Windows server, right?

*Raj*: Yes correct. It is a managed service, so patching, maintenance, and availability are maintained by the service. You can choose the required performance and durability based on your application requirements. When you create a filesystem, you can specify either a Single-AZ or Multi-AZ deployment and select the required throughput. **Throughput** is basically the sustained speed at which your system can serve data.

*Charles*: Is this filesystem also elastic in nature?

*Raj*: There are some differences here compared to Amazon EFS. For an Amazon FSx filesystem, you have to specify the required capacity. You have to choose a size between the minimum and maximum storage capacity. But you don't have to create a bigger volume initially; you can increase storage capacity as needed. Just be aware that once a filesystem gets created, you can't decrease the storage capacity. There is another requirement, too. As it is a Windows-based filesystem, it is likely you'll connect it to a Microsoft Active Directory to provide user authentication and access control. You can use either an Active Directory hosted in the AWS cloud or connect it to your self-managed Active Directory service, even running on-premises.

*Charles*: That is flexible.

*Alex*: I have one question. What would be the impact of selecting the wrong storage?

*Raj*: The wrong storage type can result in multiple issues related to availability, durability, performance, compatibility, and cost. It's possible the storage you selected is not durable enough to provide the required retention. To maintain the required durability, you may start storing multiple copies of your data, which will result in extra costs. Or maybe the storage you selected is not compatible with your existing applications and you may have to redesign your application. So, the selection of the right storage is a crucial factor for your application.

The team is happy with the explanation. It seems every traditional storage method has an equivalence in the cloud, and the EFS and FSx family also match the functionality they already know. They are beginning to realize that the service model and the myriad of available services provide the exact functionality for any need. So, the main issue is finding the right service; S3, EBS, FSx, and EFS are some names to remember. So, they create a small table on the whiteboard. Once the explanations are finished, everybody wants to start the migration immediately.

# Starting the migration

After a short lunch break, they all gather in the meeting room. With the notes they took previously, Berta tries to coordinate and document all the migration tasks.

*Berta*: I think we now have enough information to get started with the migration task. Let's go over the tasks one by one. I've edited the list to use the right units. Shall we proceed?

Everyone agrees and starts looking at the list sent by the development team:

| 1 | Old invoices | 2 GiB | Linux server | To be used as test data for our new payment collection system. |
|---|---|---|---|---|

Table 4.2 – Dataset no. 1

*Berta*: Any suggestion for dataset no. 1?

*Alex*: Would Amazon S3 be better to store our invoices as objects?

*Raj*: It is possible to use Amazon S3…but then the application using that data needs to be modified to use HTTP or HTTPS.

*Alex*: You are right.

*Raj*: I think Amazon EFS is a better choice. We won't need any application modifications as we can easily mount it on the Linux server. Using the AWS DataSync service, we can easily migrate it to the cloud.

*Berta*: That sounds reasonable, and even if the data grows, we don't need to expand the storage manually.

*Charles*: Let's add a column in the list for possible storage options against each dataset.

*Berta*: Done. What about the next dataset? Let's look at that:

| 2 | Images and JavaScript files | 10 GiB | Stored in a directory on a Windows-based web server | We plan to redesign our partner website on the cloud. |
|---|---|---|---|---|

Table 4.3 – Dataset no. 2

*Alex*: I think this is suitable for storage in Amazon S3. As a web server is involved, we can use Amazon EC2 as a web server and let it fetch the images and JavaScript files from Amazon S3. Anyway, JavaScript doesn't require processing on the server side. Another thing: as the development team is redesigning the website, they could start using some serverless and managed services in AWS.

*Harold*: That's a good idea. In the worst case, if they don't want to redesign their website, we can copy these files on the Amazon EBS volume of the Windows-based web server and still keep a backup copy on Amazon S3.

*Charles*: We can also use the versioning feature of Amazon S3 to keep older versions too.

*Berta*: Okay. Good idea. Next item. Dataset no. 3:

| 3 | Product details | 500 GiB | Shared storage system | Details about products to be used by a fleet of Linux-based web servers. |

Table 4.4 – Dataset no. 3

*Raj*: This dataset is best suited to be hosted on Amazon EFS. We can create a filesystem, and after copying the data, mount it from a fleet of web servers. It is currently stored in a shared storage system, which I guess is an NFS share.

*Harold*: Yes, I can confirm that this is hosted on a NAS storage in our on-premises data center, using NFS.

*Raj*: Then Amazon EFS is perfect for this dataset.

Everyone nods their approval and Berta notes it down on her sheet.

*Berta*: Okay. Moving on to the next dataset. Dataset no. 4:

| 4 | Customer database backup | 40 GiB | On an external hard disk | Not required as of now but just keeping it as we may need it in the future. |

Table 4.5 – Dataset no. 4

*Harold*: This is a single file, 40 GiB in size.

*Charles*: Okay. How about keeping backup files in Amazon S3 Glacier? I guess it would be much cheaper and fits the use case of keeping archival data.

*Harold*: Agreed, we can upload this file to Amazon S3 Glacier, but what would happen if we hit a network issue while uploading it? It is a big file.

*Alex*: We can use the multipart upload feature of Amazon S3 and upload the larger files in smaller chunks, in parallel. If any part fails, we can upload only that part again.

*Harold*: That's nice. So, Amazon S3 Glacier for dataset No. 4.

*Berta*: Noted. Next item. Dataset no. 5:

| 5 | Invoices database backups | 15 GiB | Windows file server | To be used for the invoicing system testing. This data will be used on the test server, which is provisioned by the IT team in the cloud. |

Table 4.6 – Dataset no. 5

*Charles*: I think Amazon FSx will be the best choice for this dataset.

*Raj*: But if we plan to use Amazon FSx for Windows, we will need to connect to Active Directory. And currently, we don't have access to our Active Directory in the cloud.

*Charles*: Oh, I see.

*Berta*: How about mounting an Amazon EBS volume on this instance and copying data to it? This system is already running in the cloud on the instances we created. So, it would be a matter of adding an additional volume with the required size and copying the data from an on-premises server to that Amazon EC2 instance.

*Alex*: Yes, that should work, and we can take a snapshot of the volume after we complete the data transfer.

*Harold*: That would surely tick the checkbox of durability.

*Berta*: Nice. Let me note that too and share the updated sheet with all of you. I have also added a column about ownership.

Berta updates the sheet and shares it with everyone:

| Dataset no. | Data type | Approximate size | Currently stored in | Use case | Proposed storage in AWS cloud | Owner of data migration |
|---|---|---|---|---|---|---|
| 1 | Old invoices | 2 GiB | Linux server | To be used as test data for our new payment collection system. | Amazon EFS | Charles |
| 2 | Images and JavaScript files | 10 GiB | Stored in a directory on a Windows-based web server | We plan to redesign our partner website on the cloud. | Amazon S3 | Alex |
| 3 | Product details | 500 GiB | Shared storage system | Details about products to be used by a fleet of Linux-based web servers. | Amazon EFS | Raj |
| 4 | Customer database backup | 40 GiB | On an external hard disk | Not required as of now but just keeping it if we may need it in the future. | Amazon S3 Glacier | Berta |
| 5 | Invoices database backups | 15 GiB | Windows file server | To be used for the invoicing system testing, which we have deployed on the newly created server you have created for us in the cloud. | Amazon EBS | Harold |

Table 4.7 – Proposed storage for migration

*Raj*: This works for me.

Everyone else nods their approval too.

*Berta*: As everyone is okay with it, I will send the updates to Gloria.

*Harold*: And if we make any mistakes, they will be easy to fix. That's the good thing about the cloud: the freedom to experiment.

Everyone starts working on the tasks at hand. They read the documentation and help each other in completing them. They bond well while completing the tasks and start working as a single unit. Everybody is happy with everything they have decided during the last few days.

However, Charles is not completely sure. In the last few meetings, a doubt has constantly nagged at him: *network security*. He realizes that they have created some servers with their storage, but the network configuration seems to have been too easy, using too many defaults. What are the isolation options to segment or filter the traffic? Are there no firewalls? Who will be able to connect to these servers? Will nasty hackers be able to gain access? And what about connectivity; will they be able to connect their on-premises networks to the cloud in a secure way?

Therefore, Charles plans to take all these networking aspects into consideration in the next meeting.

## Further reading

- REST: https://aws.amazon.com/what-is/restful-api/
- Object Storage:

    - S3: https://aws.amazon.com/s3/

    - S3 Storage Classes: https://aws.amazon.com/s3/storage-classes/

    - S3 Glacier: https://aws.amazon.com/s3/storage-classes/glacier/

    - S3 LifeCycle Management: https://docs.aws.amazon.com/AmazonS3/latest/userguide/object-lifecycle-mgmt.html

- Block Storage:

    - EBS: https://aws.amazon.com/ebs/

    - Instance Store: https://docs.aws.amazon.com/AWSEC2/latest/UserGuide/InstanceStorage.html

    - Multi-Attach Volumes: https://docs.aws.amazon.com/AWSEC2/latest/UserGuide/ebs-volumes-multi.html

- (Shared) File Storage:

    - EFS: https://aws.amazon.com/efs/

    - FSX family: https://aws.amazon.com/fsx/

    - AWS DataSync: https://aws.amazon.com/datasync/

    - Data Lakes: https://aws.amazon.com/big-data/datalakes-and-analytics/what-is-a-data-lake/

# 5

# Networking – So, How Do I Get Inside, Outside, and Across the Cloud?

Raj is heading early to the office. He has been thinking about many things since yesterday. *What about network security? How did they protect the servers they had already created?*

Luckily, for Raj, he was going to learn about the following at the office that day:

- Networking in the cloud
- Defining the right routes
- Filtering traffic with security rules
- Connecting multiple networks

## Networking in the cloud – to isolate and protect

As Raj enters the meeting room, he finds Charles whiteboarding something with Alex.

*Raj*: Good morning, everyone. I hope I haven't missed anything important.

*Charles*: Not at all. I was just explaining to Alex the basics of networking.

*Raj*: Yes, good idea. I was especially thinking about the security of our servers in the cloud. I'm afraid when we created our EC2 servers, we used the default security options for them. Maybe now is the right time to design something better.

*Charles*: Yes, let's do it and propose it to the team before Gloria requests it. This way, she'll realize we're really anticipating the company's needs.

*Alex*: Good plan. So, let me summarize this drawing for you, Raj. I am sure you already know all these concepts, but explaining them will help consolidate what I've learned.

*Raj*: Yes, why not?

Alex starts explaining the diagram on the whiteboard:

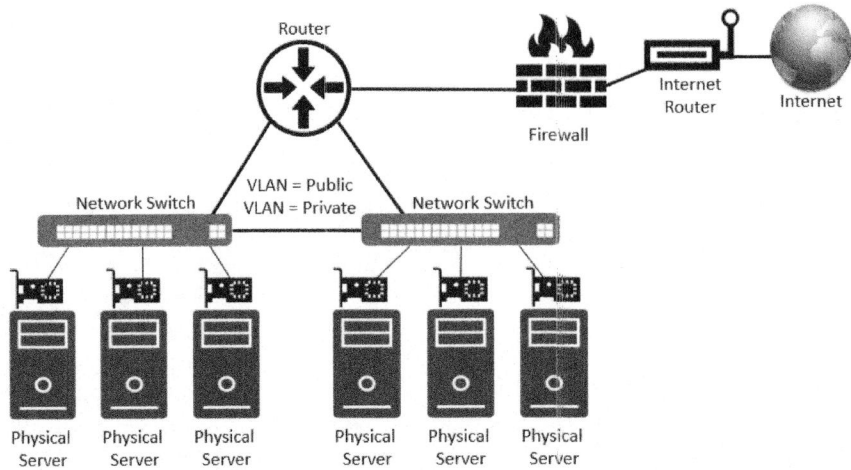

Figure 5.1 – Networking in the physical world

*Alex*: Let me start from the bottom. In a typical network, physical servers are connected using network cards, switches, and cables. As there are a limited number of ports where servers can be connected, multiple switches must be connected together to expand the network. And as the network grows, more security and isolation are needed, so the concept of a **Virtual Local Area Network (VLAN)** is introduced. VLANs ensure the logical separation of servers, even if they are connected on the same physical network. Depending on your needs, you can decide to create multiple VLANs; for example, you can have one for all public-facing servers and another one for all internal servers.

*Charles*: Correct.

*Alex*: And all VLANs are physically connected using routers, so the traffic can reach any desired computer, no matter where it is inside the company, even in different locations. Routers can be hardware devices or can be implemented by software.

*Charles*: What about the internet?

*Alex*: It follows a very similar approach; you physically connect your existing network to the internet by using an internet router, which will forward all the traffic. And most likely, you need to add a firewall, protecting your network from all traffic, maybe malicious, coming from the internet. In a small network – such as a home network – one single device can perform all the functions of routers, internet routers, and firewalls. But in a corporate network, you use separate devices, performing separate roles.

*Raj*: Great explanation, Alex, and a nice diagram, Charles. If you look at the AWS network, the implementation is not very different. Let me try to map these components to the AWS world.

Raj picks up the pen and starts drawing AWS-specific components over the same diagram:

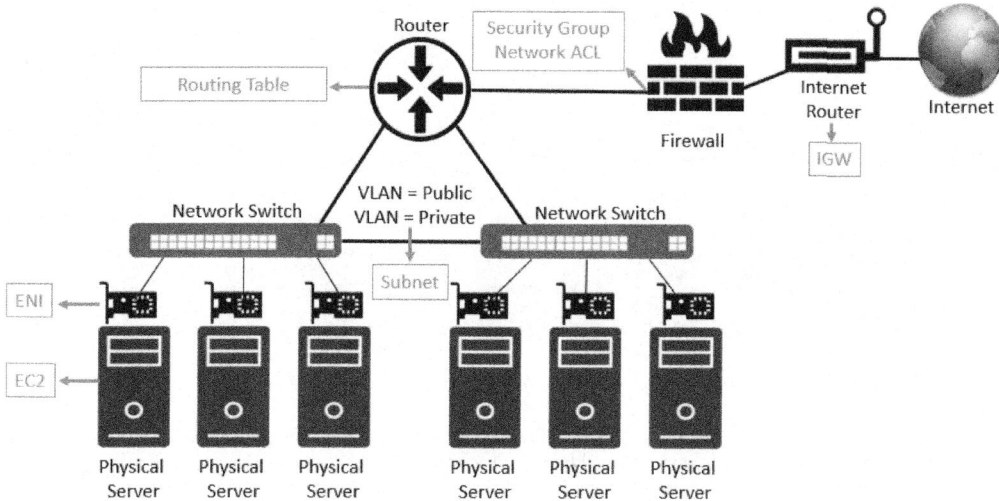

Figure 5.2 – Networking in AWS

*Raj*: In AWS, instead of physical servers, you host your applications on Amazon EC2 instances, as we saw before. These instances have at least one network card for all communications; each card is called an **Elastic Network Interface** (**ENI**). Though these ENIs are virtual, they have the characteristics of a physical network card, such as a **Media Access Control** (**MAC**) address. Of course, they are assigned an IP address for communication. In the AWS network, you won't see or operate a network switch, as all the physical connectivity is done by AWS for you.

Then, for isolation and security, you define multiple **subnets**. Subnets have a similar, but not exactly the same, functionality as a VLAN. You can create subnets to isolate your workload, such as a subnet for public-facing resources and another one for private resources.

*Charles*: You can also add subnets based on departments, environments, and other factors.

*Alex*: This is great, as there are similar components available in AWS to those in a physical network. I didn't find it difficult to understand. What about security?

*Raj*: Now, the first thing we need for security in the cloud is isolation. You probably don't want other companies to reach your business servers. For this isolation purpose, AWS offers a networking construct called a **Virtual Private Cloud** (**VPC**).

Raj draws a box surrounding several of the components and writes **VPC** on top of it:

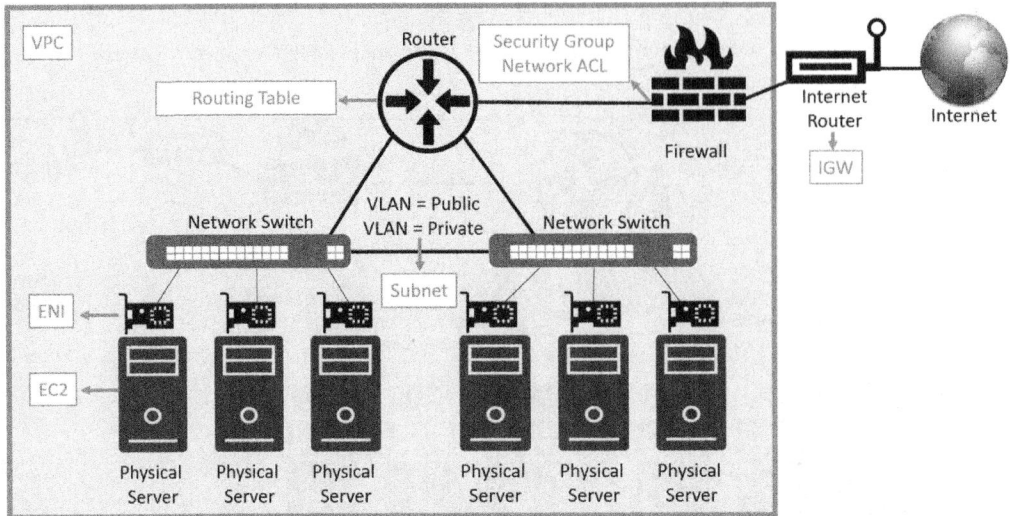

Figure 5.3 – A VPC

*Raj*: A VPC is a logically isolated section of the AWS cloud. You can launch your resources inside a VPC in a way that closely resembles a traditional network in a data center, and you can leverage all the benefits of scalability provided by AWS infrastructure. You can control resource placement, connectivity, and security inside a VPC. It's like your own data centers but in the cloud.

*Alex*: I think it's similar to your house, or rather the wall surrounding it. Inside your house, you have some rooms, and you can move freely among them. But if the external door is closed, no one can go in or out.

*Raj*: Exactly. And that door is always closed by default. But we'll see later how to open it and decide who is allowed to use it.

*Alex*: What is the maximum size of a VPC? Could it be very big – for example, expanding over all of the AWS network?

*Raj*: Inside a VPC, you can create multiple subnets, and each one can be rather big if you wish, holding thousands of computers. Or maybe it can be really small, just a few computers. They can have different sizes. But remember, a VPC is a regional construct. It can use all the **Availability Zones (AZs)** in that region, but only inside the region. Each subnet will reside in the specific AZ you choose, and you can even create several separate subnets in the same AZ. But remember that each subnet will belong to a single AZ.

Raj draws another diagram and highlights some of the IP address ranges in it:

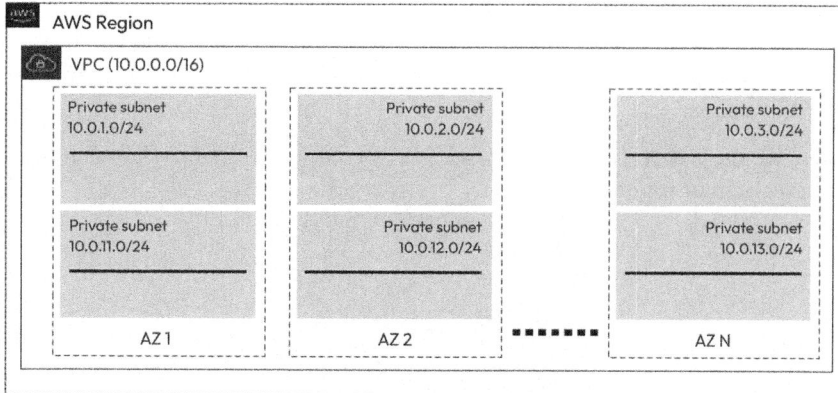

Figure 5.4 – VPC and subnets

*Alex*: That means I can decide where to connect my computers, in which AZ, and also in which subnet?

*Raj*: You have total freedom of choice. Each server – well, their ENIs – can be connected where you want. You choose the region, VPC, and then the subnet, which is associated with an AZ. This way, you can connect several servers grouped together in the same subnet, in separate subnets in different AZs, or any combination, depending on your high availability needs. If one AZ has any issue, you will have servers unaffected in other AZs.

*Charles*: It's like having different rooms in your house. You can decide their sizes and also where you want them physically. But they have to be inside the house.

*Alex*: So, I can decide to create one big VPC or maybe several smaller ones. And also multiple subnets inside each VPC?

*Raj*: Yes, but keep it simple. In the cloud, there's no need to have many subnets and many firewalls between them. We can filter the traffic using other security methods.

By the way, every AWS account has a VPC in each region, preconfigured with some standard settings. This **default VPC** allows customers to launch resources faster. In fact, when we deployed our test EC2 instances for the development team, we used that default VPC. Fortunately, these settings are really restrictive, as it is meant to be *secure by default*. In all probability, they're too tight; we might have to relax the rules a bit. Or maybe we can create other VPCs with our own IP address ranges and custom security.

*Raj*: To summarize – when you create a new VPC, you just have to provide some basic settings, such as the subnets you need, which AZs they are in, and their CIDR range. AWS will automatically create the required components to support all operations inside a VPC. You automatically get an implicit router linking your subnets, and some defaults for a DHCP scope, a default network ACL, a default security group, and a main route table. The default setup allows all devices inside the VPC to communicate with each other, but only if they're inside the VPC.

*Alex*: What is CIDR?

*Raj*: **CIDR** is short for **Classless Inter-Domain Routing**. It is a way to represent IP addresses. An **IP version 4 (IPv4)** address is made up of 32 bits. A portion of that 32 bits (on the left) represents the subnet. The remaining bits (on the right) are used to represent the specific hosts inside that subnet.

*Charles*: Let me give you a simple example of it. In most hotels, your room number represents two pieces of information:

Figure 5.5 – Identifying a room

(Source: Photo by Smooth_O, at https://commons.wikimedia.org/wiki/File:Missing_room_number_413.jpg, used under Creative Commons Attribution-Share Alike 3.0 Unported license.)

Let's assume you have been allocated room number 318; it is very likely that the first digit (3) represents the floor number, and the remaining two digits (18) represent the room on that floor. So, in a three-digit numbering system in a hotel, the first digit is always reserved for the floor, and the remaining two digits are the room number. This three-digit system can be used by a hotel that has a maximum of 9 floors and a maximum of 99 rooms on each floor. But if you want to number the rooms of a skyscraper with 20 floors, each one having 120 rooms, this three-digit system won't work. You will probably look for a five-digit system and reserve the first two digits for the floor and the remaining three digits for rooms on that floor. In a similar way, you can change the bits allocated in IP addresses too. If you need more hosts in a network, you can allocate a smaller portion for the network addresses and a bigger portion to store the specific address. For example, if you have a CIDR range of 192.168.1.0/24, the first 24 bits represent the network address and the remaining 8 bits (32 bits in total, with 24 bits used for the network address) represent the host. In this address space, you can have up to $2 \wedge 8 = 256$ hosts.

*Alex*: And if I use a CIDR of 172.16.0.0/16, does it mean it has the same number of bits (16) for network and host addresses?

*Charles*: Yes, you are right. If you have used 10.0.0.0/8, you will have 8 bits for network addresses and 24 bits (32 bits in total, with 8 bits used for the network address) for host addresses. So, basically, CIDR provides an easier representation of the size of the network.

*Raj*: In AWS, when you create a VPC, you can only use the range from /16 to /28. And once you have allocated the IP address range for the whole VPC, it is to be further divided into logical chunks and allocated to subnets in the VPC.

*Alex*: Can you create a VPC but not create any subnet in it?

*Raj*: Technically, yes, but I don't see a lot of use cases for it. All of your resources such as Amazon EC2 instances, Amazon RDS databases, Amazon ElastiCache clusters, and Elastic Load Balancers have to be inside a VPC. These resources anchor themselves to a subnet within an AZ.

*Alex*: You mentioned all computers inside the VPC can communicate with each other. But what happens if I need some computers inside the VPC to be reachable from the internet – for example, our public web servers? Or, in contrast, they might need to access some configuration files or patches that are on the internet. I assume the internet is outside our VPC.

*Raj*: You are right. Until now, our VPC was fully isolated. This is the default. You have a house with solid walls and no door. All the inhabitants move freely, but only inside the house. But if you need internet access, it's pretty easy. You just request a component called an **internet gateway**, and you attach it to the VPC. That's all; now, the VPC is physically connected to the internet. You have created a door in your house; now, you have to decide who can go in or out.

*Alex*: What are the rules, then, to decide who can go inside or outside the VPC? Or move inside it? I mean, if I have resources inside a VPC, will they be able to communicate with each other?

*Charles*: All communication between resources is decided by **route tables**. All subnets inside a VPC are connected to the VPC router. This router is implicit; you cannot see it, but its route tables can be created and modified. As soon as a VPC gets created, it builds the main route table, as a default. The main route table allows all communication within all subnets inside the VPC.

*Alex*: Do you mind explaining to me in simple terms what a route table is?

*Charles*: Yes, but let's call in Berta too. I can see that she has just arrived.

Now, the Cloud team has got a much better view of the basic networking concepts in the cloud: VPC, subnets, IP addresses, CIDR, and the implicit router. They have realized these are compatible with the classical TCP/IP concepts they already knew, the ones we can find in any network. Anyway, more ideas are needed, so they are waiting eagerly for the next chat.

## Allowing or disabling traffic by defining the right routes

As the explanation goes into more detail, it's evident to all of the team that some more advanced concepts will be needed. Specially, all of them have some doubts about routing tables defining how traffic can flow inside the VPC or move in or out from it. Based on these tables, they'll learn now how to separate different types of subnets (public and private).

*Charles*: Welcome, Berta. We were commenting about route tables. As it is a complex but powerful idea, let me use an example for you. Berta, where did you go on your last holiday?

*Berta*: We rented a small car in southern Europe. We visited Dali's museum, the beaches, the east coast, the south… lots of cities and nature too. But we covered lots of kilometers.

*Charles*: And while driving, did you get lost at some point?

*Berta*: Fortunately, not. We were scared at the beginning, as we didn't have any sort of GPS or map, and the names on those would have been in a different language as well. But most of the road signs were pretty clear. I especially liked this roundabout; I took a picture of it because this one was critical to find the road back to our hotel:

Figure 5.6 – The roundabout

(Source: Photo by Arriva436, at https://commons.wikimedia.org/wiki/File:Gledrid_Roundabout_
sign.JPG, used under Creative Commons Attribution-Share Alike 3.0 Unported license.)

*Charles*: That's exactly the key. When you arrived at this sign, you got a clear indication. It tells you that if you have arrived at this roundabout, find the name of your destination and choose the right exit. It doesn't matter how you arrived here; you just find your destination, follow the right exit, and continue driving. There will be another sign at the next roundabout. You continue driving, following each indication at each roundabout until you arrive at your final destination.

*Alex*: So, this is a route table – just a list of destinations?

*Charles*: Exactly. It is a list of destinations but also how to proceed to them.

In IP terms, each subnet has one route table. All tables are stored within the router configuration. Remember that we don't see the router, but we can create or edit its route tables. There is only one table per subnet, as there's only one per roundabout.

*Alex*: How does the VPC use the route tables?

*Charles*: The VPC has to proceed this way to decide how to send a packet to its final destination. It will simply take the source and destination IP of the packet and then make the decision.

First, if both the source and destination happen to be in the same subnet and the CIDR mask is used to decide, the packet can be sent directly to the destination ENI. No more routing, and no maps – we've arrived at the destination.

Alternatively, they may be in different subnets. It's like you are at one roundabout and have to decide how to leave it, so you use the traffic signs. We need to find the best route, as many subnets can be physically connected in multiple ways. First, we find the right routing table by checking the source subnet from the packet source IP. Now, we know which roundabout we are at. Then, an entry in the table, based on the destination IP, will indicate where to forward the packet.

*Berta*: I get it. The default route table must be empty so that there's no way to go out!

*Charles*: Almost. Remember that we can have multiple subnets inside one VPC. All of them are always interconnected; each route table must specify that. The **main route table**, which is the default, has always a single entry for this. It says, *If you are inside this VPC, you can still go to any other subnet inside the same VPC*. This default entry declares the destination IP as the same CIDR range for the whole VPC. Then, the traffic is sent to a logical name called `local`, which points to the VPC router. This main route table is initially associated with all subnets, who share it. This way, all traffic can be sent internally to any other subnet but only inside the VPC. And this entry cannot be modified or removed:

| rtb-e3b2e69a / Default VPC Default RT | | | | | |
|---|---|---|---|---|---|
| Details | Routes | Subnet associations | Edge associations | Route propagation | Tags |

**Routes** (2)

| Q Filter routes | | | | Both ▼ |
|---|---|---|---|---|

| Destination ▽ | Target ▽ | Status ▽ | Propagated |
|---|---|---|---|
| 172.31.0.0/16 | local | ⊘ Active | No |

Figure 5.7 – The main route table of a VPC

*Berta*: Good idea! If the destination is not an IP address but a name (such as `local`), that means you can specify multiple subnets with just that single entry – no need to know all the router IP addresses in each subnet. And it is great for subnets that could be created in the future, so there are no worries about IP addresses. It's like a theme park we visited; there was an information booth on every street. If a child got lost, they were sent to a place called the *central office*, no matter how far away it was from where the child was found.

*Charles*: And now we have the most interesting usage of route tables. We have to decide who can use the internet… and its internet gateway.

*Alex*: Yes, what we have now means that all the computers inside the VPC will be able to talk to each other, but only inside the VPC. This was the initial isolated situation.

*Charles*: Yes. Some subnets can be labeled as **private subnets**. The internet traffic will never reach them. You usually have on them your databases, business logic, and everything not exposed to the internet. So, these subnets will continue to use the main route table.

*Berta*: I get the point. And you designate only a few subnets to be reachable from the internet; you keep your web servers on them, for example.

*Charles*: Exactly. These subnets are called **public subnets**. It's very easy to configure them; you create a new route table, maybe one for all of them, and you only need to add an extra entry. All traffic going to the VPC will stay local, but now all traffic going elsewhere (destination 0.0.0.0/0) has to be sent to…

*Alex*: … the IP address of the internet gateway!

*Charles*: Hmm… yes, conceptually. But in the cloud, it's even easier. You just add the name and the identifier of the internet gateway. Again, no need to know its address!

*Alex*: Amazing! Simple but powerful! It seems routing tables are a good way to isolate the traffic for security! And routing to names instead of IPs makes things even easier. But of course, it is very important to define all route tables properly.

*Charles*: Sure, but I'm afraid there are more security options. Let's break for lunch; thinking of holidays in the south has made me terribly hungry!

All of them stop for a lunch break. They discuss what they've covered – how a VPC mimics a physical data center, with its subnets, router, and routing tables. During lunch, some more questions arise, especially about security and connecting multiple VPCs.

## Filtering traffic with security rules (stateful and stateless)

After the lunch break, the team continues to discuss the security needs it found. It seems the VPC is isolated using the internet gateway and routing tables, but that may not be secure enough for some scenarios.

*Alex*: I'm thinking about one scenario. What happens if you create a public subnet with several servers – you know, adding an internet gateway and changing the routing table to point to it? Then, will all the hackers on the internet be able to connect to these servers?

*Raj*: I was also thinking about a related scenario. If one team has an application running inside the VPC, it will be able to access all the servers inside that VPC. If they make a mistake, nobody will stop them. Maybe the test environment could delete all the production databases if someone copies the wrong parameters, as a connection string…

*Alex*: There's also the enemy inside, some hacker inside the company, inside the VPC. As all subnets are interconnected, who is going to protect the services from inside the VPC?

*Berta*: Is that where **security groups** and **network ACLs** fit in?

*Charles*: Exactly. These two mechanisms are also provided by the VPC to further filter the traffic according to your needs, or the applications' needs. Both of them do the same, filtering traffic as a firewall does. But security groups are applied at the ENI level, and network ACLs are applied at the subnet level. And security groups are easier to use.

*Raj*: Let me give you an example, Berta. I live in an apartment in a multi-story building that is inside a gated community. We have a cluster of three multi-story buildings, and each building has its own security guard:

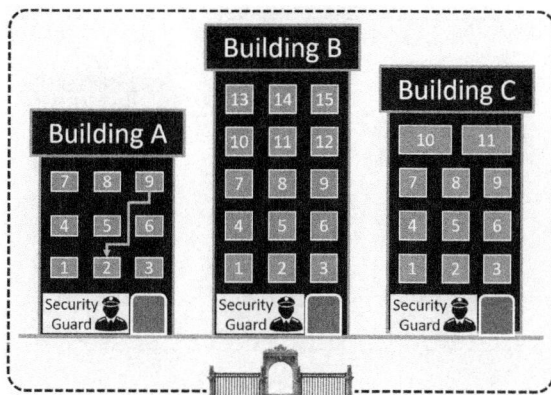

Figure 5.8 – A gated community with a security guard in each building

Raj continues:

> *Raj*: I live in building A in apartment 9. If I have to meet my friend, who lives in apartment 2 in the same building, I have to just walk down to her apartment and knock. If she is in, she will allow me to come inside. Consider the door of the apartment as a security group, which is protecting it. If somebody wants to enter any apartment, they have to be allowed through the door, but if a resident of the apartment wants to go out, they can just open the door and go out. Similarly, a security group is applied on an ENI level and protects the resource. If anybody wants to access the resource, they have to be allowed through security group rules. An inbound security group rule controls the traffic that's allowed to reach the resources that are associated with the security group, whereas an outbound security group rule controls the outbound traffic that is allowed to leave the resource.

> *Alex*: Are there any default rules in a newly created security group?

> *Raj*: Yes. By default, all outbound traffic is allowed. That means if the instance or the resource is communicating with other resources, it will be allowed. But there is no default rule to allow inbound traffic to reach the instance. So, if you host a web server and want to allow only HTTP traffic from outside, you have to create an inbound rule and open port 80. Just be aware that security groups only can have *allow* rules; it's just a list of who's allowed. You cannot create a *deny* rule in a security group. Also, you can associate multiple security groups with an ENI, and all the rules inside those security groups will be additive.

> *Berta*: That means, as there is only an *allow* rule, there will never be any conflicts when you apply multiple security groups.

> *Raj*: Exactly. Now, let me now explain **Network Access Control Lists (NACLs)**. Now, imagine I have to meet a friend who lives in building C, apartment 5. This is in a different building, so I have to come out of my building first, pass through the security guard of building A, pass through the security guard of building C, and then knock on the door of apartment 5. There is one security guard per building; let's consider the building as a subnet, and the security guard who is protecting the whole building is the NACL. NACLs protect the whole subnet, and each subnet needs to be associated with one and only one NACL:

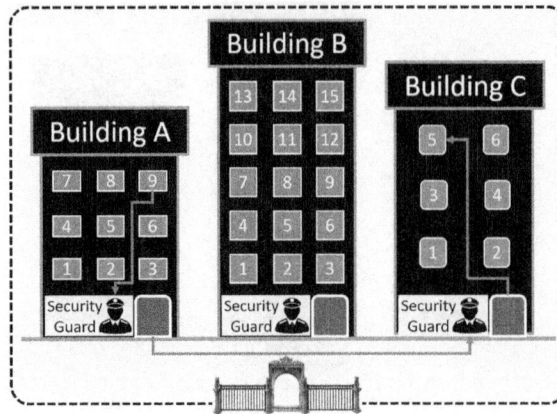

Figure 5.9 – Going between buildings

*Raj*: NACLs also allow *deny* rules. They are very useful to immediately block traffic.

*Berta*: But if NACL supports both *allow* and *deny* rules, there are chances of conflicts. How does an NACL handle them?

*Raj*: NACL rules are numbered and sorted. The rules are evaluated starting with the lowest numbered rule. If a match is found, the corresponding action of *allow* or *deny* is taken. So, if you have set up a rule number, 10, for allowing SSH traffic and another rule number, 20, to deny SSH traffic, rule number 20 won't be processed, as the first match of SSH traffic will trigger the action defined in rule number 10. If no match is found, traffic will be denied, as there is always a last deny-all rule, which cannot be deleted:

Inbound rules control the incoming traffic that's allowed to reach the VPC.

| Rule number Info | Type Info | Protocol Info | Port range Info | Source Info | Allow/Deny Info | |
|---|---|---|---|---|---|---|
| 10 | SSH (22) ▼ | TCP (6) ▼ | 22 | 0.0.0.0/0 | Allow ▼ | Remove |
| 20 | SSH (22) ▼ | TCP (6) ▼ | 22 | 0.0.0.0/0 | Deny ▼ | Remove |
| * | All traffic ▼ | All ▼ | All | 0.0.0.0/0 | Deny ▼ | |

Figure 5.10 – Rules in a NACL

*Berta*: And as there is only NACL per subnet, there will never be conflicts with the same numbered rules. This is interesting.

*Raj*: So, NACLs can protect a whole subnet, whereas security groups protect individual ENIs, or rather the instances attached to those ENIs. Finally, security groups are stateful, whereas network ACLs are stateless.

*Alex*: I always get confused between stateful and stateless. Can you please explain these to me in simple terms?

**Charles**: Let me give you an example of immigration systems in the UK and in India. If you go to India, you have to go through immigration upon arrival and also at departure. In both directions, you get a stamp on your passport. But in the UK, you are subject to immigration only when entering the country. Only at arrival is your immigration status checked; there are no checks performed while departing the country:

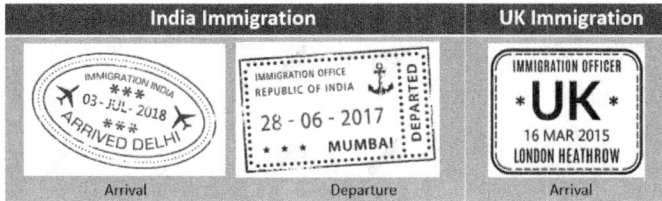

Figure 5.11 – India and UK immigration

The UK system is based on **stateful** filtering; there is no need to check a person while they are departing from the country. If they are departing, it is implicit that they went through immigration upon arrival, and if they were already checked at arrival, then why check again at departure? Similarly, in stateful filtering, as with security groups, every TCP request will be checked, but if it is allowed, the TCP response to it will also be implicitly allowed. With only one rule, you allow all traffic needed for an application protocol; there's no need to create pairs of rules. The security group remembers the state of the traffic and allows it automatically if it is a response to an allowed request. For example, if you have a web server, you just allow HTTP traffic on port 80 in an inbound direction. The response to that HTTP request will automatically be allowed, without explicitly creating a rule.

In the case of **stateless** filtering, you have to explicitly create rules in both directions. In India, you have to go through the immigration desk upon arrival and also upon departure; your documents are checked in both directions. You have to be explicitly allowed to enter and also leave the country. Network ACLs are the same. If you create a rule to allow traffic in an inbound direction, you have to also create an explicit rule to allow the response of that traffic, so you usually end up creating pairs of rules, as with a classic firewall.

**Alex**: That's an interesting way to remember the difference between stateful and stateless. I'm going to create a couple of rules in my test VPC, and the best thing is that they are free!

**Charles**: Think about the possibilities. Now, you can create groups of applications or servers and decide who belongs to them. This means the traffic between applications can be segmented and isolated. This is something we previously had to do with complex firewall configurations; now, it seems much easier. Building a three-tier application with security groups can be done in seconds.

The group is now happy. They have now learned most of the security options provided by a VPC. Using routing tables, security groups, and network ACLs together can be enough to cover all their needs to isolate all traffic inside a VPC. The idea of using security groups to segment the different tiers of an application seems the most powerful one.

# Connecting multiple networks in a safe way

For the Cloud team at TRENDYCORP, it's now time to wrap up what they've learned so far about networking, in particular in AWS. Gloria decided to organize a final meeting in the late afternoon, in order to be updated about the progress so far and to be able to present a report to the company management the following week.

*Gloria*: Okay, folks, how are your network things doing?

*Harold*: We've made lots of progress with network security in the cloud. But we realized something is still missing.

*Alex*: Yes, we've learned we can create multiple VPCs. Maybe we should separate our environments into different VPCs, instead of just using one.

*Charles*: Exactly, we'll have to do this. And I'm afraid we'll also have to connect those separate VPCs to our on-premises networks. But, of course, in a safe way.

*Gloria*: Okay, I'm curious. Let's see what you have in mind.

*Raj*: The first thing we'll need to do is create separate VPCs, but then link them together. For example, the *development* environment might be in a VPC handled by a team, the *test* and *prod* could be two separate VPCs, and maybe the *databases* could be isolated in another one. We can use **VPC peering**.

*Berta*: Wow! Please explain that stuff!

*Raj*: Sure! This is the easiest way to connect VPCs. With VPC peering, one VPC can request a peering relationship with another one. If accepted by the VPC administrator, both will behave as a single VPC. Each computer can now use resources from other VPCs, with all the security levels we saw, of course. And all traffic is sent using the internal AWS network. No traffic goes to the internet.

*Berta*: This brings back a memory of my last trip. We rented two rooms in the hotel for the family, and we had two adjacent rooms. Adjacent but separate. We were initially using our phones to agree on when to go down for breakfast. After some time, we realized there was a door connecting both rooms, so we agreed to keep it open, and now all traffic moved freely. That means my children were constantly in our room, as the TV was bigger. I wish I had had a security group at that time:

Figure 5.12 – Adjacent rooms – VPC peering

(Source: Photo by PortoBay Hotels & Resorts, at https://www.flickr.com/photos/
portobaytrade/36893932826, used under Attribution-NoDerivs 2.0 Generic (CC BY-ND 2.0) license.)

*Raj*: You can even peer together VPCs in different regions or with different accounts.

*Berta*: Seems really powerful, but is there any limitation?

*Raj*: Yes, there are some limitations. Peering has to be properly configured – that is, no overlapping IP ranges. And the route tables must be properly defined, but that is not a limitation, just something we have to design, as we already know how to do it.

*Alex*: Route tables again to the rescue!

*Raj*: The other limitation is stricter. Routing between VPCs is not transitive, as a peer relationship is only defined between two VPCs, and not more. You can create a full mesh between pairs of VPCs, but you cannot peer too many of them; otherwise, you incur very complex management. But there's a solution for both issues called Transit Gateway, which I'll explain later:

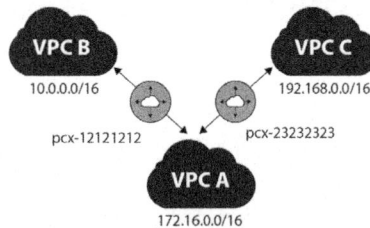

Figure 5.13 – Multiple peerings

*Raj*: The next important topic is how to connect our on-premises networks. We have lots of computers on them, and maybe they'll have to communicate with the ones in the VPCs. The most generic scenario is having multiple networks in the cloud and also on-premises. This has already been considered by AWS and is called a **hybrid cloud**.

One of these days, we will have to migrate our existing on-premises applications to the cloud, not just create new VPCs there directly. We'll need ways to connect all these networks, so let's see them, as there are several options as usual.

The simplest way to connect one VPC to an on-premises network is by using an **Amazon Virtual Private Network** or, simply, **Amazon VPN**. An Amazon VPN is like a standard VPN, a connection that leverages the internet, encrypts the data in transit, and asks for authentication to be used. It's also pretty simple to put in place, and a company doesn't need to coordinate with anyone else to build one:

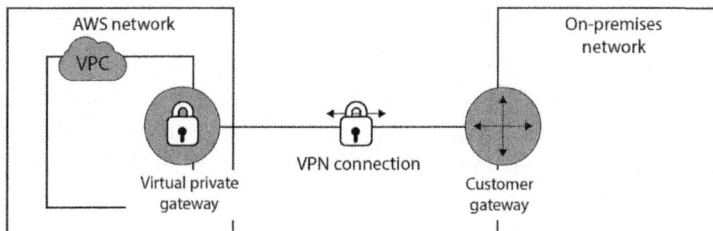

Figure 5.14 – Using a VPN to connect two networks

*Alex:* And what's the name of the service to do all that? There is a service for everything!

*Raj:* You still have to use Amazon VPC for it, Alex.

*Alex:* Okay, got it. One service less to learn about, ha ha!

*Harold:* What performance can you get from an Amazon VPN?

*Raj:* Generally speaking, you get a maximum throughput of 1.25 GB per second.

*Harold:* Hmm, okay, thanks.

*Gloria:* And how much time does it take to put in place a connection like this?

*Raj:* As I said before, there's no need to involve anyone else, so it can take a day, half a day, or a couple of hours. It depends on how much bureaucracy there is in the company for things like that.

*Gloria:* Perfect. Please go ahead with the second option you mentioned.

*Raj:* The other way to connect a VPC to your physical network is through another service, which is called **Amazon Direct Connect**, sometimes referred to by the acronym **DC** or **DX**. It's a totally different type of connection; it's private, dedicated, and physical. Through a DX connection, you can physically connect your on-premises networks to the closest AWS region. This is possible because of an entity in the middle, called a **Direct Connect location**, which is basically a room within someone else's data center, where cables are connected:

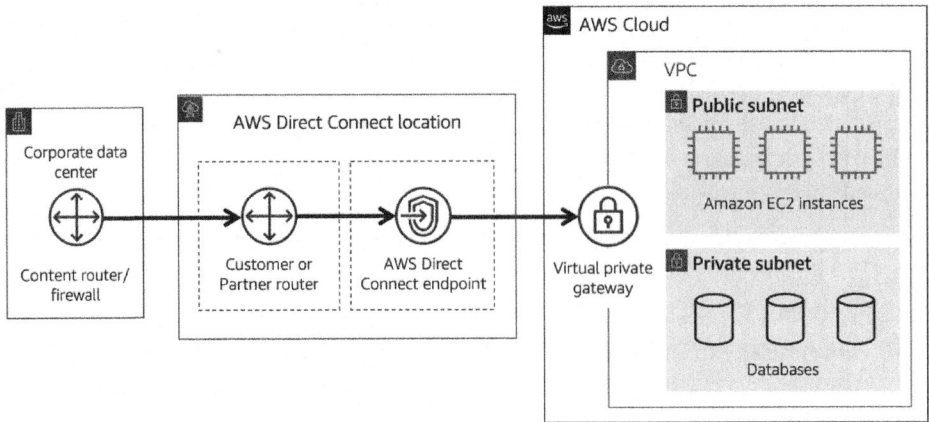

Figure 5.15 – Direct Connect

*Gloria:* Someone else's data center?

*Raj:* Yes, based on where companies' data centers are located, the companies can take a look at a list of possible DC locations that different AWS partners provide. Sometimes, even the company itself can use its own data center as the DC location. As you all have probably understood, this type of connection takes more time to be put in place; in general, AWS needs about 20 working days, so a month more or less.

*Harold*: I suppose that this DC connection provides much more speed, right?

*Raj*: You are absolutely right. Because it is physical, a DC connection can provide a bandwidth of up to 10 Gbps; for the same reason, it is also much more reliable than a standard VPN, whose performance may be impacted by internet fluctuations. The bandwidth you buy is guaranteed. Lastly, because it's private and dedicated, it's also more secure.

Taking a look on the internet at some architectural diagrams of AWS architectures, I've seen the two solutions used together often – DX for urgent or critical traffic and an AWS VPN for the rest. But each one acts as a backup of the other, for maintenance operations or technical issues.

*Gloria*: Amazing, Raj. Thanks for the explanation and the clarity. Is there anything else we need to talk about?

*Harold*: You mentioned some limitations with VPC peering. I suppose that Transit Gateway thing is designed to overcome them, right?

*Raj*: Exactly, Harold. The **VPC Transit Gateway**, referred to by AWS with the acronym **TGW**, can be used instead. It's a fully managed service that allows us to connect *thousands* of networks.

*Harold*: Thousands!?

*Raj*: Yes, Harold, you heard correctly. And you can connect multiple types of connections to it, such as VPCs, but you can also add VPN and DC connections to on-premises networks. It basically provides a *hub-and-spoke* design to connect all of these networks within the same AWS region. Then, you can define the visibility you need between any of the desired networks:

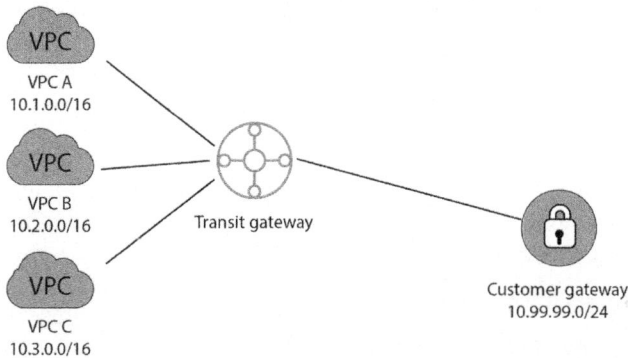

Figure 5.16 – TGW

TGW solves the complexity involved with creating and managing multiple VPC peering connections at scale, and as I said, it allows us to create more complex network configurations because of the ability to connect hybrid connections too.

*Charles*: A question for you, Raj – is VPC peering still a valid option to connect VPCs or everything should be managed by TGW?

*Raj*: That's a very good question, Charles. AWS always gives you different options when it comes to taking an architectural decision, and most of the time, the *best* option is just the one that perfectly fits your requirements; for example, if you are looking to keep costs as low as possible, you don't want to deal with a maximum bandwidth limit, and you don't want any additional latency in the private communication between your servers, VPC peering is the best option.

*Charles*: What about cross-region communications? Do these technologies support them?

*Raj*: Yes, absolutely. As we said, you can peer two VPCs created in two different regions, you can connect them through TGW too, or you can peer two TGWs.

*Alex*: I'm sorry, folks, but I don't think I 100% got how TGW works, to be honest. Raj or Charles, could you please clarify it a bit more?

*Raj*: Sure, let me explain TGW in another way. I don't know if you know this, but all of the biggest airlines have a central hub that they use for specific flight connections:

Figure 5.17 – Traffic hubs

British Airways' hub, for example, is located at London Heathrow, Emirates Airlines has its own in Dubai, and Air India is in New Delhi. For their international flights, they collect passengers in their central hub. Are you following me so far, Alex?

*Alex*: Yes, thanks. Please, go ahead.

*Raj*: British Airways always provides international flights to New York from London Heathrow. They collect passengers from all over the United Kingdom at Heathrow Airport, and then they are sent to major cities all around the world. It's a hub-and-spoke design, like TGW. Once you are connected to an airline's hub, you can fly anywhere, airline routes permitted. In a similar way, TGW connects VPCs, VPNs, and DC connections, so generic traffic that reaches TGW can go anywhere (to your on-premises network, or a specific VPC), based on the routes you specify at the TGW level.

*Alex*: Cool! Now I've got it. Thanks as usual for the clarity of your explanations, Raj.

# Summary

All the team is gathering around the coffee machine. They have enjoyed all the presentations done during the day but are starting to feel tired. Too many concepts packed into a single day. Suddenly, Gloria joins them with a great smile on her face.

*Gloria*: Okay, folks, it seems you have done an amazing job so far – you know now the foundational aspects of cloud computing, you've learned the global infrastructure provided by our cloud vendor, and you demonstrated that you were able to deal with the main compute and storage resources that this cloud provider… er, provides. Am I right? Does anyone want to add something?

*Harold*: We have already studied networking in the AWS cloud as well. I think the team now knows about the networking basics, especially about services, features, configuration, and security. We also know how to secure what we have already built.

*Gloria*: Oh, amazing. You folks are doing a great job by sharing knowledge with each other and, at the same time, learning new things together. I was able to understand the last topic as well, even if I'm for sure the least technical person in this room.

*Alex*: It was great for everyone! I learned a lot about peering, VPNs, DC, and TGW.

*Gloria*: I think we are good to go, so enjoy the weekend. Next week, I will liaise with the management about the current status of the project. I'm satisfied with what you have learned and put into practice so far. What's next, folks? What are you planning to face as the next topic?

*Harold*: I think we need to start talking about databases. Based on some quick research I did on the internet, it seems like another topic with a large number of services involved.

*Berta*: Yeah! And for sure, I will be able to contribute here more than what I have so far, considering my expertise in databases. I'm looking forward to explaining to you folks the basic concepts, and then we can start delving deep into the database services available. Ultimately, we don't have to master all of them; we just need to understand which ones we can use for our purposes!

The meeting ends, and all the members of the Cloud team leave the office happy, especially because of the good feedback given to them by their manager. Now, it's time to take some rest before they begin to learn about databases.

# Further reading

- VPC: `https://aws.amazon.com/vpc/`

  - `https://docs.aws.amazon.com/vpc/latest/userguide/how-it-works.html`

- CIDR: `https://docs.aws.amazon.com/vpc/latest/userguide/how-it-works.html#vpc-ip-addressing`

- Subnets: `https://docs.aws.amazon.com/vpc/latest/userguide/configure-subnets.html`

- Route Tables: `https://docs.aws.amazon.com/vpc/latest/userguide/VPC_Route_Tables.html`

- Internet Gateway: `https://docs.aws.amazon.com/vpc/latest/userguide/VPC_Internet_Gateway.html`

- Security Groups: `https://docs.aws.amazon.com/vpc/latest/userguide/VPC_SecurityGroups.html`

- Network ACLs: `https://docs.aws.amazon.com/vpc/latest/userguide/vpc-network-acls.html`

- VPC Peering: `https://docs.aws.amazon.com/vpc/latest/userguide/vpc-peering.html`

- AWS VPN: `https://docs.aws.amazon.com/vpc/latest/userguide/vpn-connections.html`

- Direct Connect: `https://aws.amazon.com/directconnect/`

- Transit Gateway: `https://docs.aws.amazon.com/vpc/latest/userguide/extend-tgw.html`

# Part 2:
# Platform Services

In this part, you will discover the most basic services in the cloud – the foundational ones that can be used to build upon, including virtual servers and their storage, networking, and databases. Security at all levels will also be introduced here. Related tasks such as monitoring and automation will also be covered. Finally, one analogy will describe the common terminology used in most of them.

These services and components will be likely understood by all audiences, as they have their equivalents in classical, on-premises systems.

This part has the following chapters:

- *Chapter 6, Databases – To SQL or Not To SQL for So Many Records…*
- *Chapter 7, Identity and Access Management – Who Am I and What Can I Do?*
- *Chapter 8, Monitoring – Is Big Brother Watching?*
- *Chapter 9, Scalability – I Scale To the Moon and Back*

# 6

# Databases – To SQL or Not to SQL for So Many Records...

Gloria has summoned the team to her office urgently. The team feels a bit odd, as this feeling of urgency is new for them.

*Gloria*: Hello again… I know you're busy, but there's something important and urgent that I need to communicate…

*Charles*: Now you'll make us choose what comes first, the good or the bad news?

*Gloria*: Ha ha… It's important, urgent, and… good news for all of us. We have been allocated some budget for training… that is, for your training in the cloud. As you're currently doing, self-training is fine, but a more formal approach will save time and possible misunderstandings.

*Alex*: Fantastic! What's the schedule?

*Gloria*: I told you it was urgent. All of you are enrolled tomorrow for a foundational class, which is called *Essentials*. It's just one day, but a really concentrated class. All the main cloud concepts are covered there.

*Raj*: I hope it's a technical course, not one of those boring marketing sessions.

*Gloria*: No marketing at all. I attended a similar course some months ago; but this one is even more technical, considering your skills. You have probably already discovered some of the concepts covered in your investigations: Regions, EC2, VPCs, all the storage options, and databases, to name a few.

*Raj*: Great!

*Gloria*: And there's even more! For the moment, we've also decided to enroll Berta in an additional course about databases in the cloud. Berta already knows some database concepts, so we thought she'll formally improve her knowledge with this three-day course. By the way, Berta, you'll start the database course immediately after the *Essentials* one.

*Berta*: Okay, I'll be ready. I've already received my enrollment email; I'll check if there are any prerequisites.

*Gloria*: Just an important point for all of you: in my previous job, everybody considered training as a prize – a week with no work…

*Alex*: You mean we don't deserve a prize for all our self-training efforts?

*Gloria*: No, that's not what I said. Of course, you deserve a prize. But at TRENDYCORP, training is not considered a prize; it's a tool, a valuable tool that will help us achieve our objectives faster, better, and more safely. And that brings responsibility for all of us. If you attend a training session, we assume you'll be able to use that knowledge later and help your colleagues with it.

*Berta*: Got it. Maybe we can formalize a way to share what we learn after the courses?

*Gloria*: Yes, think about how to do it. And, talking about prizes, I'm talking with Human Resources about your compensation salary. It's too early to speak about it, but if the databases get migrated in time, with the right security, there could be another nice surprise for you. Please concentrate on your training sessions and, next week, we can begin to decide on the plan needed for all our databases.

Everybody is excited. The plan seems a good one – formal training has suddenly appeared in their lives… and the promise of a prize if everything works well is really motivating. Over the next few days, all of them attend their courses.

## Purpose-built databases: using the right tool for the right job

After an intense week, all the members of the cloud team have finished their courses. They then meet at the office to share what they have learned. As all of them have arrived pretty early, they decide to have their usual pre-work coffee in the cafe in front of the office. All of them seem really excited, trying to speak at the same time.

*Alex*: I've learned a lot about identity and permissions. That's something we'll have to understand in depth in all of our projects.

*Raj*: Yes, there were many concepts in this *Essentials* course. I'd like to learn more. They mentioned an *Architecting* course, where you learn how to build solutions.

*Harold*: I particularly enjoyed the labs. We were given a real environment where we could play with the services. Berta, how was your course? I assume it was longer than ours.

*Berta*: Fantastic. Three intense days, with lots of theory and labs. Do you know how many database services are available? I thought there were two of them, *relational* and *non-relational*, but our provider offers around 10 different types.

*Charles*: Well, first things first… I think we should start with Gloria's ideas about databases. After that, I'm afraid we'll have some tasks to perform.

*Harold*: Yes, I agree, considering all the challenges we are facing with the current databases we are managing on-premises.

*Alex*: Wait, wait, folks! If databases are going to be our first topic, then I'm afraid I have to ask you for some help to keep me aligned on the theory. I know it's a shame, but I barely know what a database is.

*Raj*: Come on, Alex, it's not a problem at all. We still have some time, and I can clarify the concept in minutes.

*Alex*: Thank you, Raj!

*Raj*: You're welcome. So, the concept of the database in IT started more or less around the 1960s, when physicists and mathematicians—I don't think the term **computer scientist** was used at that time—were looking for an efficient way to store their data. It had to be safely stored on storage devices that were terribly expensive at the time. The **database** concept was then created; it provided a new way to organize, manage, and store data—more efficient and cost-optimized. The end user does not see the files – just the data in an organized way.

At that time, several implementation models were created. For example, the **Hierarchical Database**. But then the **Relational Model** appeared and was widely accepted.

*Alex*: But this was more than 40 years ago!

*Raj*: Yes, the first formal definitions date from the 1970s. It's impressive, I agree, and we are still using them; everything in IT changes quickly but relational databases and **Structured Query Language** (**SQL**) seem to stick around.

*Alex*: What's the relational model?

*Raj*: Let's imagine a generic database. Think of a filing cabinet:

Figure 6.1 – Filing cabinet as a database

(Source: Photo by rrafson, at https://commons.wikimedia.org/wiki/File:File_Cabinet.
jpg, used under Creative Commons Attribution-Share Alike 3.0 Unported license.)

This is your database, a place where you store your data. Your data is not just thrown in there without any logic or order; it must be properly organized. In fact, in the same way that data is organized into drawers in a filing cabinet, in a database, data is organized into *tables*. Generally speaking, drawers contain documents of any kind; meanwhile, tables contain *rows* (technically, they should be called *tuples*, but we can stick to rows):

| EmployeeID | FirstName | LastName | Title | DeptCode | Email | Extension | Joined |
|---|---|---|---|---|---|---|---|
| 1 | Mary | Smith | HR Manager | 1 | msmith@company.com | x5001 | 2008-06-01 |
| 2 | Albert | Gordon | Engineer | 2 | agordon@company.com | x5032 | 2010-06-05 |
| 3 | Eva | Rodriquez | Engineer | 6 | erodriquez@company.com | x5321 | 2011-04-08 |
| 4 | Retta | Gotz | Manger | 2 | rgotz@company.com | x6000 | 2017-07-01 |
| 5 | Martin | Castro | Trainee | 2 | mcastro@company.com | N/A | 2022-05-01 |

Figure 6.2 – Table with rows

*Alex*: Can we have multiple tables?

*Raj*: Yes, with the relational model, a single database usually contains multiple tables. The nice thing is that all tables can have relationships between them. That's why the model is called relational:

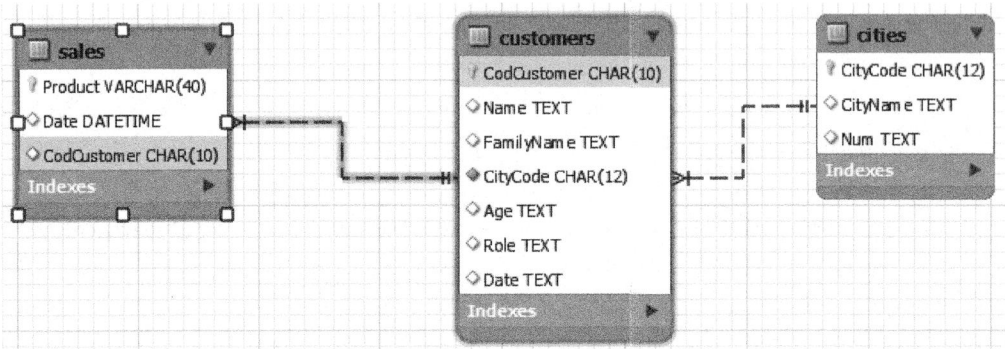

Figure 6.3 – Tables and relationships

*Alex*: Okay, I'm following you. From what I know, it's with the SQL language that you retrieve rows, right?

*Raj*: Exactly! Together with the relational model and the database concept, a language was invented, SQL, which allows you to *query* your data. It is basically like the way you get exactly the document or the documents you are looking for from a filing cabinet. You can also use the same language to create tables and insert or delete data. Practically all relational databases use SQL, which hides the implementation details. You just describe which data and tables to use in your operations, and the database engine will process them. Maybe the data comes from multiple tables; the SQL engine will take care of that.

*Alex*: Nice, I'll start learning this SQL language:

```
1 •  SELECT CodCustomer,CityName,Name,FamilyName,Role FROM trendycorp.customers
2    INNER JOIN trendycorp.cities ON customers.CityCode = cities.Citycode
3    WHERE trendycorp.customers.CityCode IN ("CIT_00001","CIT_00005")
4    AND trendycorp.customers.Name LIKE 'A%'
```

| CodCustomer | CityName | Name | FamilyName | Role |
| --- | --- | --- | --- | --- |
| CUS_000540 | Lisboa | Andrés | Pellegrino | Investor Paradigm Planner |
| CUS_001119 | Lisboa | Ashley | Olson | Dynamic Assurance Technician |
| CUS_001232 | Lisboa | Ana María | Ibars | Future Identity Supervisor |
| CUS_001390 | Lisboa | Alessio | Clark | Regional Paradigm Developer |
| CUS_002920 | Lisboa | Aina | Haywood | National Solutions Technician |
| CUS_003856 | Lisboa | Arnold | Aguirre | Central Web Coordinator |
| CUS_003965 | Lisboa | Ann | Nogales | Internal Solutions Strategist |
| CUS_004473 | Lisboa | Ariadna | González | Internal Intranet Administrator |
| CUS_005077 | Lisboa | Anne | Higgins | Dynamic Mobility Coordinator |
| CUS_005531 | Lisboa | Alex | Aguirre | District Tactics Representative |
| CUS_005774 | Lisboa | Armando | de Santana | Regional Accountability Strate… |

Figure 6.4 – SQL query

*Berta*: You forgot to talk about indexes, Raj. In a filing cabinet, an **index** is the way people store documents in a drawer, so they can be easily retrieved. Usually, they use labels to indicate the category of each document or maybe divide the documents by letter. When you are looking for the employee *Berta*, you quickly go to label *B*, and then you can quickly find all the employees whose names start with that letter. In general, an index is built with a structure to leverage that principle. Indexes are a way to get your data much faster from tables in databases.

*Raj*: True. Then we have something newer, which is the **non-relational model**. These databases are logically simpler, as each database has only a single table. Many companies have started to use these in the last decade as well. But this is a separate topic that Berta will clarify for us. Am I right, Berta?

*Berta*: Yes, exactly!

*Harold*: So, in the end, a database is a process, the database engine, and some tables and indexes on disk. With what we've learned, I think we could easily deploy this in the cloud. We need an Amazon EC2 instance with the right OS, and then we will install our database software on it, create the tables, store data in them, and start querying the data.

*Berta*: Well, yes and no…

*Harold*: What's this "yes and no" answer in binary logic?

*Berta*: I mean it can be done, but maybe it's not the best idea. Of course, you can use EC2 or any other sort of virtual server. Then you can install whatever you want on it, and, of course, that can be database software. Our cloud provider does not care about what we install inside our servers; it's our responsibility. But we don't need a full server with its OS to have a database.

*Harold*: Come on, you're joking. To have a database, you need a server, then the right OS, and then you need to install the database software on it. We already mentioned that, in the end, a database is a process running on some system.

*Berta*: This is true, but only if you are using a traditional database set up on premises. You needed a server—physical or virtual—and on that, you had to install the OS and the database, configure networking, exclude the database files from your antivirus, plan for maintenance, apply patches, maintain high availability, do backups… Lots of tasks needed to be done for sure, but they provided no creativity, and no competitive difference to your business.

*Harold*: That's how it has always been done. Do you mean there's a different way in the cloud?

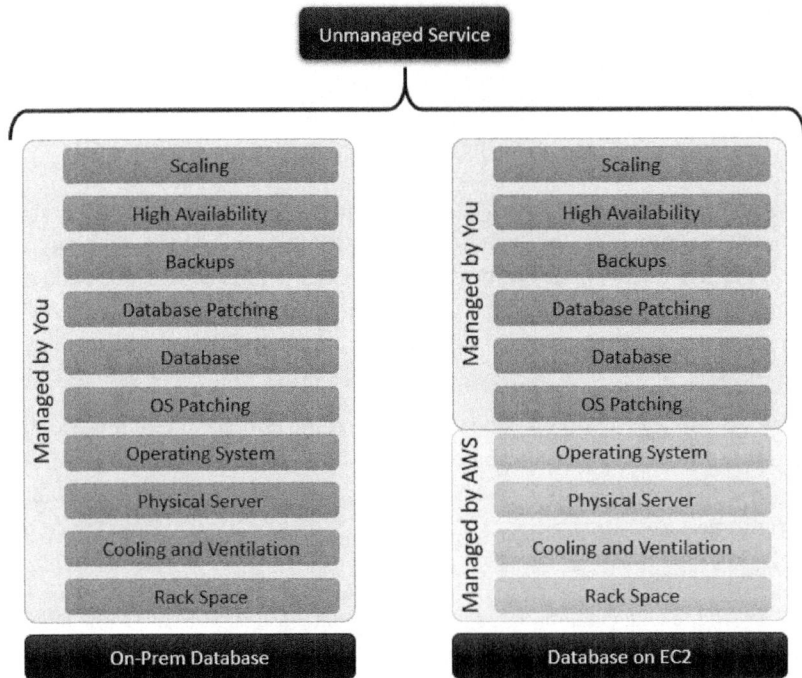

Figure 6.5 – Unmanaged databases

*Berta*: Yes. Now we have **Fully Managed Databases**. You just request the type of database you need, and that's all; the cloud provider will do all that is needed for you. It will provision the hardware, allocate storage, and will give you an endpoint where the database engine will be available. Then you can make your queries to this endpoint – no server, no OS, no management. And you can even select to perform backups on a schedule, make the database highly available, perform auto patch-updates, and more, in an automated fashion. Rather than you taking care of all this heavy lifting, you can just select some options and let your cloud provider take care of it.

*Charles*: I assume the endpoint is just an IP address, maybe with a DNS name pointing to it?

*Berta*: Exactly. You send your queries to the endpoint, the engine processes them, and you get the results. The provider will handle disk space, monitor performance, decide on high availability, and make the needed backups. Of course, you have to define how you want all of these to be, but it will be automatically done. There's no need to dedicate time to tedious tasks; you can then concentrate on your table design and the application itself, which provides value to your company, not spending hours doing backups and restores:

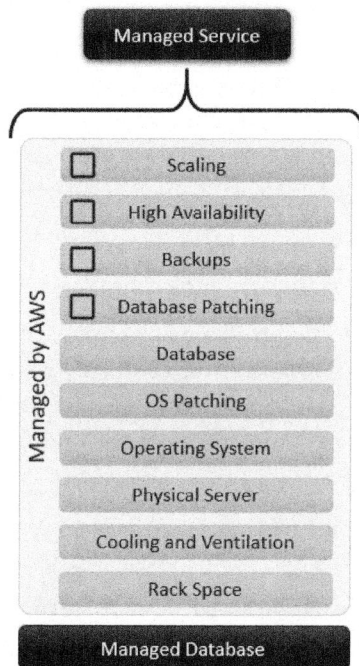

Figure 6.6 – Managed databases

*Harold*: Seems powerful, and also a completely different way to work.

*Berta*: Imagine you're an architect. You spend your time designing new buildings. But you have a team to save you time. You won't be mixing concrete or cutting the wood for the doors. Someone does this work for you. It's the same with these databases. And the best thing is it will be cheaper compared to the operational costs involved when you manage your database.

*Harold*: You mean the cloud provider does some extra tasks for you, such as the backups, and it's not more expensive?

*Berta*: These tasks are not performed by humans; they are automated. Remember, again, the economies of scale cloud advantages (as explained in *Chapter 1, Understanding Cloud Computing – Demystifying the Cloud*). The cost is divided among all customers.

*Alex*: And you mentioned our provider offers 10 different databases? I'm curious – I can't imagine what all the options might be.

*Berta*: Yes, this will be our first topic during our meeting.

*Harold*: That's a meeting that will never take place if we keep talking. Your coffee is getting cold. Let's drink it and go to the office.

The cloud team has moved to its usual meeting room. Gloria starts to share her learning from the database training she attended.

*Gloria:* Good morning, everyone. I'm glad you are all here already. I'm pretty sure you are going to tell me what you've learned last week and I'm super excited about it, but…

I would suggest that you focus from the very beginning on the database topic because my managers started to ask about our migration plan for our on-premises databases. So, Berta, I think you should step in here. We obviously don't have time to get a full training session from you, but I'm sure you can give us an overview of databases in the AWS cloud.

*Berta*: Sure, Gloria. I've just prepared a short presentation with a few slides about that topic.

Berta is now next to the projector, sharing her presentation supported by some slides.

*Berta*: The AWS cloud platform provides many services, including some under the category *Databases*. In particular, AWS has released eleven different database services so far.

*Charles*: Eleven!?

*Berta*: Yes, eleven. AWS calls them **purpose-built databases** because each of them is supposed to be used for a specific purpose. In other words, for a specific set of use cases. During the three-day training I attended, the instructor told us many times that AWS is against the traditional *one-size-fits-all* approach of using a relational database for every possible use case.

*Alex* What's this one-size-fits-all approach?

*Berta*: Many companies use a single database for all their projects. It may have been a good idea in the past when you had to negotiate the price of licenses, but it imposed lots of limitations on projects, in terms of design and scalability. Apart from that, a single maintenance operation affected all the applications at the same time. Fortunately, this is no longer needed.

*Gloria*: Sorry to interrupt you, Berta. I have a question about our current on-premises databases, the ones we use at TRENDYCORP. Are all of them relational?

*Harold*: I can answer that question, Gloria. Yes, they are.

*Gloria*: Okay, thanks. Berta, please go ahead.

*Berta*: As I was saying, the one-size-fits-all approach doesn't work anymore. AWS provides three different database services that follow the relational model. Apart from these, in the last few years, they've developed and released eight different non-relational database services.

We will talk about the difference between relational and non-relational databases later, but now let's focus on the database offering AWS provides to its customers. Let me tell you a short story from my past. I still remember when I was a child, it was summer, and I really wanted to have a bird. I asked my father, and he told me that before buying a bird, we had to buy a birdhouse. I was so happy about it that I asked my father if we could build it by ourselves, and he agreed.

Figure 6.7 – A birdhouse

(Source: Photo by Santeri Viinamäki, at https://commons.wikimedia.org/wiki/File:Birdhouse_in_
thuja_tree.jpg, used under Creative Commons Attribution-Share Alike 4.0 International license.)

The problem was that my father realized that in his old toolbox, he had only a hammer. We immediately realized that we could start to build the birdhouse and that we might be able to build some form of construction, but obviously, the odds were that we might end up with something that was less than ideal. We then decided to buy a new shiny toolbox, with all the tools we needed at our disposal.

Figure 6.8 – A toolbox

(Source: Photo by Daren, at https://commons.wikimedia.org/wiki/File:Toolbox_%28226362564%29.
jpg, used under Creative Commons Attribution 2.0 Generic license.)

For every single part of the birdhouse, with its own characteristics, we used a specific tool. Obviously, there were some tools that were used more often than others, but we ended up with a birdhouse built by using many of the different tools we found in the toolbox.

In the cloud, you don't build birdboxes, but architectures that support your applications. As some of you already know, modern applications are built by following the **microservice approach**, so these applications are made up of smaller parts usually called **services**. Just like a birdbox is made of different pieces (the roof, the walls, the interiors, the base, etc.), an IT architecture has load balancers, servers, and many other resources, including databases. Services that are a part of an application could potentially have different characteristics from each other, and so different *requirements*. In the same way that me and my father used specific tools to build specific pieces of the birdhouse, IT architects use specific database services to store the data of specific services.

*Charles*: And what about if our applications are not *modern* like the ones you mentioned?

*Berta*: It's not a problem, we always need to start from the requirements. Each of our applications has specific requirements about how they store their data, so we will find the *right tool for the right job* for sure, using the motto of the trainer who delivered the database course.

The following is a list of the 11 database services that AWS provides. Our task is to have high-level knowledge of each of them, analyze the data requirements that our applications have, and then decide which database service we want to use for each use case we identify:

| Database type | AWS service |
|---|---|
| Relational | Amazon Aurora  Amazon RDS  Amazon Redshift |
| Key-value | Amazon DynamoDB |
| In-memory | Amazon ElastiCache  Amazon MemoryDB for Redis |
| Document | Amazon DocumentDB (with MongoDB compatibility) |
| Wide column | Amazon Keyspaces |
| Graph | Amazon Neptune |
| Time series | Amazon Timestream |
| Ledger | Amazon Ledger Database Services (QLDB) |

Figure 6.9 – Current database offerings by AWS

Berta now sits down – her presentation has ended.

*Gloria*: Amazing, Berta! Thank you so much for the presentation. Let's have a quick break, to digest all this information. Let's come back in 10 minutes because we need to talk about the differences between relational and non-relational databases next. I've heard amazing things about the latter, and most of them are pretty new by the way.

The 10-minute break begins. After it, everyone is back in the meeting room.

*Berta*: Okay, everyone, let me try to explain to you the difference between relational and non-relational databases.

*Harold*: I'd like to first ask if we should call them SQL versus NoSQL databases, or relational versus non-relational databases?

*Berta*: People use them interchangeably, but I think relational versus non-relational is the right term. I will soon explain why calling them SQL versus NoSQL may not be appropriate.

*Harold*: Okay.

*Berta*: Think about a relational database as like living in a house. Every room in the house has a different purpose and you keep different types of stuff in it. You would keep all the food items in the kitchen, you may have all your washing powder in the laundry room, and maybe you keep all the tools in the garage. Now, if you need something from a room, you just walk into it and grab what you need. You don't have to leave the house; you just use the corridors. Consider the house as a database, rooms as tables, and corridors as your SQL query. Through a SQL query, you can get whatever data you need, from the different tables that are inside a database. You don't have to leave the house. Your data may be stored across different tables, but it is still within a single database. You need to write your query in such a way that you could traverse through different tables, perform some operations across tables, and get the result.

*Alex*: I get the idea. But can you explain to me what a transaction is?

*Berta*: Let me give you an example; let's suppose you are doing an online money transfer from one of your bank accounts to another account. If you have initiated a transfer of, let's say, $100, then this request may be broken down into some smaller steps. First, and on a very high level, $100 will be deducted from your source account. Then the source bank will transfer that amount to the destination bank, which will deposit it in your account. But what happens if there's a problem in any part of the whole process? For example, your destination account details might be wrong or not be in an operating state. Then, the whole $100 will be deposited back into your source account; the money won't be lost. This is a transaction.

There is always a sequence of operations in every transaction. Here, the money has to be first deducted from your source account, and only after that will it be deposited in the destination account. A transaction is a unit of work that is always treated as a whole. It has to either happen in full or fail, but it will never leave you in a partial state. Like in your bank transfer, either the whole $100 will be deposited in your destination account or it will be reverted to your source account.

*Alex*: I get it now. And probably every transaction will be treated in isolation. For example, I may have started an online transfer from my source account to multiple destination accounts and every transaction will be carried out independently.

*Berta*: Yes, that's true. Or maybe there are many customers doing transactions at the same time. No matter how many transactions succeed or fail, your data will always be in a consistent state in a relational database.

A transaction is something similar to cooking your favorite dish. You find all the ingredients needed in a recipe book. Then you go shopping for all those ingredients. If you can buy all of them, you go back home and follow the recipe until the end. But if some of the ingredients were missing, you can't prepare the dish. You don't create half a dish; it's all or nothing.

*Harold*: To get data from relational databases, we use SQL queries, but how do we get data from non-relational databases?

*Berta*: Generally speaking, these non-relational databases will have their own way to query data – probably an API call sent to an endpoint. But nowadays, some non-relational databases also support the SQL language. And that's why I don't like to call them NoSQL databases, as SQL support may be there.

*Harold*: Got it. And to clarify: only relational databases support transactions; non-relational databases do not support transactions.

*Berta*: That is another misconception. Non-relational databases have evolved and some of them do support transactions, like traditional relational databases.

*Harold*: That's interesting.

*Berta*: Another major difference between these databases is how scaling works for each of them. In relational databases, scaling is vertical, which is called **scale-up**. When you need better performance, you keep on running the same database, but on a bigger server. You just replace the existing server with a bigger one, with more memory, CPUs, or faster disks.

But growing this way has some limits. Sooner or later, you may hit a limit that is not economically or physically viable. Non-relational databases use a different approach: most are scaled horizontally, which can be called **scale-out**. You will be adding more nodes to your databases and that will increase the performance of the database:

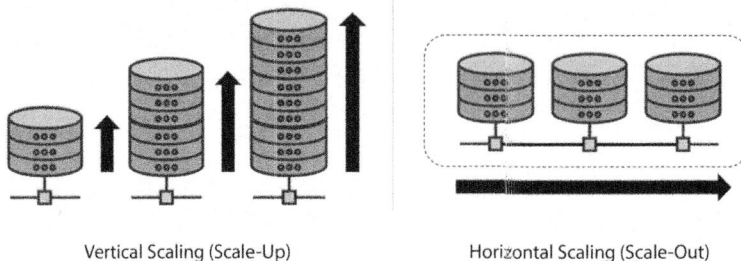

Vertical Scaling (Scale-Up)          Horizontal Scaling (Scale-Out)

Figure 6.10 – Vertical versus horizontal scaling

*Berta*: Let me share these details in a table format, so we can use it in the future.

Berta sends an email to everyone containing the following table:

|  | **Relational Databases** | **Non-Relational Databases** |
|---|---|---|
| **Optimized for** | Storage | Performance |
| **Data Storage** | Rows and Columns | Key-value, document, Wide-column, graph |
| **Schema** | Fixed | Dynamic |
| **Querying** | Using SQL | Proprietary method and/or SQL |
| **Scaling** | Vertical | Horizontal |
| **Transactions** | Supported | Support varies |

Table 6.1 – Relational versus non-relational databases

Berta lets everyone browse the email. After a short while, she refreshes the main concepts she mentioned: managed databases, purpose-built databases, and the 11 different available types, and finally, the concepts of tables, relationships, transactions, and the SQL language.

## Relational databases

After a short break, Berta continues her presentation, now focusing on relational databases.

*Berta*: Now, let's discuss relational databases in depth. Depending on your requirements, you may have databases for **Online Transaction Processing (OLTP)** or for **Online Analytical Processing (OLAP)**. Both of them are relational but fine-tuned for different purposes.

OLTP systems are a great choice where short, rapid, high-volume transactions such as insert, update, or delete are required. Think about a database for any e-commerce platform, where lots of users are buying products, returning products, adding products to their shopping carts, writing reviews for a product, rating a product, and so on. In these situations, an OLTP system will be useful. Some of the common databases in this category are MySQL, Microsoft SQL Server, Oracle databases, MariaDB, and PostgreSQL.

*Charles*: They seem to be the classical databases everybody knows. Then, where are OLAP systems useful? Let me guess: when you need to analyze a huge volume of data, right?

*Berta*: Yes, OLAP systems are the right choice for a data warehouse requirement. In case you don't know, a **data warehouse** is also a relational database, but optimized for a specific type of task. Every time you have to analyze existing data, looking for trends, reports, or any sort of complex analysis, it's much better to use an OLAP system. These operations are read-only queries, maybe with complex joins. By separating them into a different system, they will be performed much faster, and they will not affect the performance of the transactional system, which is usually much more critical. And you can also store lots of historical data for your analysis, so that means they tend to be bigger.

To summarize, our cloud provider offers solutions to address the need for both types of relational systems, OLTP and OLAP, all of them as managed offerings.

*Charles*: So, you just request what you need, and AWS manages every detail for you?

*Berta*: Yes. Let me explain **Amazon Relational Database Service** (**Amazon RDS**). Amazon RDS allows customers to select a specific database engine (out of six available options) and the required configuration, such as performance, high availability, maintenance schedule, and so on, and a database instance will be provisioned for you. Your database instance will get an endpoint (like a traditional database) for connecting through applications or any management applications. You can also choose to place your database on private subnets based on your security requirement and control the network access of it using security groups:

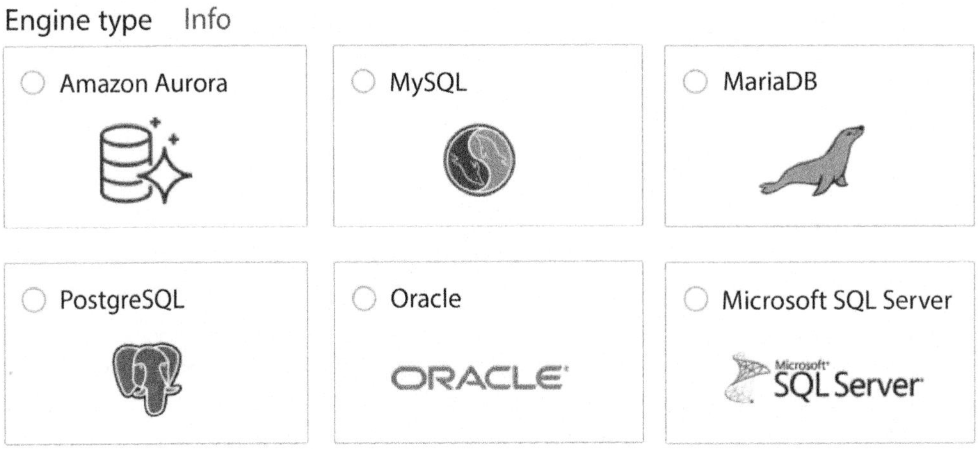

Figure 6.11 – Engine choice for Amazon RDS

*Alex*: How does Amazon RDS achieve high availability?

*Berta*: Amazon RDS supports a feature called **Multi-AZ Instance**. Once you enable this feature, a synchronous standby database is automatically created in a different availability zone. In case of any planned or unplanned outage of the primary instance, Amazon RDS will automatically fail over to the standby instance. Your application won't need any modification to use the failed-over instance, as the same connection string will point automatically to the standby endpoint.

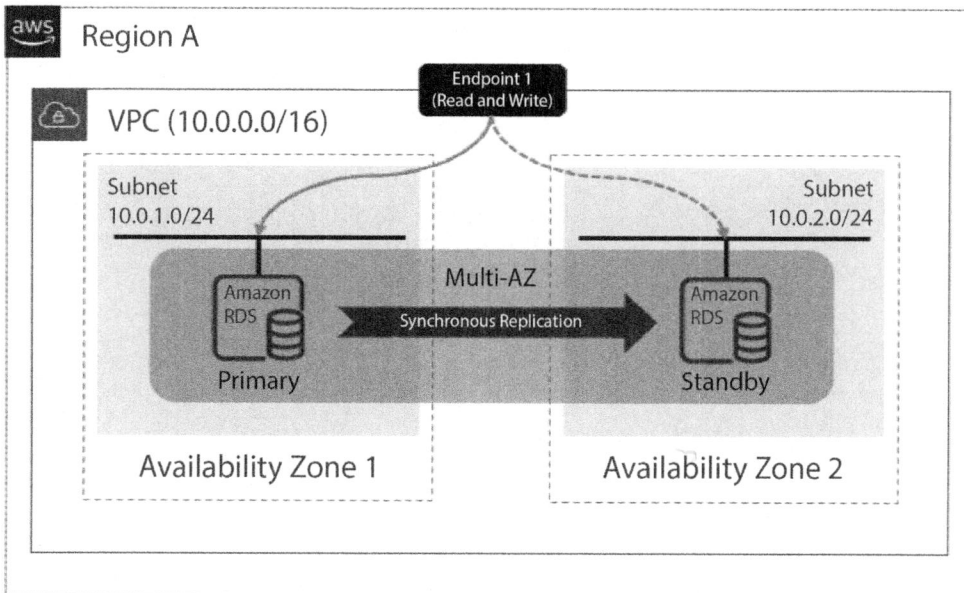

Figure 6.12 – Amazon RDS Multi-AZ

*Charles*: Can we connect to the standby instance, for example, to run some reports?

*Berta*: Originally, no. The standby instance is only active if the primary instance has an outage. Both instances share an endpoint, but only the primary instance will handle any read or write requests, remember, using SQL. AWS takes care of keeping both instances identical, by using synchronous replication from the primary instance to the standby instance. But nobody can use the standby, apart from the replication process, until there's a failover.

But this technology is evolving very fast. As I was told on the course, there's now a new option called **Multi-AZ DB Clusters**. The idea is similar; there's one primary instance, but now we have two more instances, called reader instances, located in two different AZs. That makes a total of three copies of the database across the Region. In this scenario, both reader instances also hold a synchronous copy of the database, as before, but now you can also make read queries on them. There's an extra endpoint for this purpose, so we could get our reports from there, without disturbing the transactions in the primary instance, especially its performance:

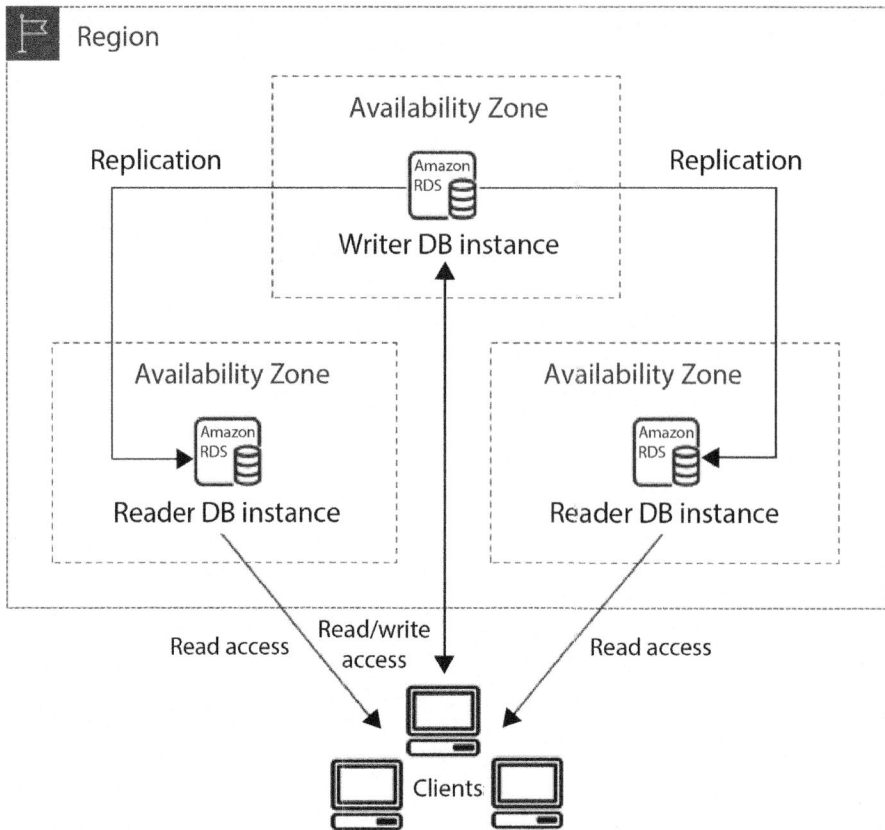

Figure 6.13 – Amazon RDS Multi-AZ DB cluster

*Charles*: Nice! And if we can't use this Multi-AZ cluster for some reason?

*Berta*: In RDS, we have another option for all these frequent read-only operations. If you want to run reports or want to use the data for maybe a dashboard, you can use **Read Replicas** (**RRs**).

*Charles*: Read replicas?

*Berta*: Yes, a read replica is another database instance with a full copy of the data. You just configure it and AWS will replicate all data from the primary instance to it automatically. But this is different from Multi-AZ; you can have multiple read replicas, and they could even be in different regions. Every read replica gets a new endpoint, so you can point your reporting or dashboard applications to it, and it will provide data, without impacting your primary database instance.

All data replication will use the internal AWS network, and in this case, it will be asynchronous. Read Replicas may not be immediately updated, but based on different factors, they may observe some data lag, so the application has to handle it:

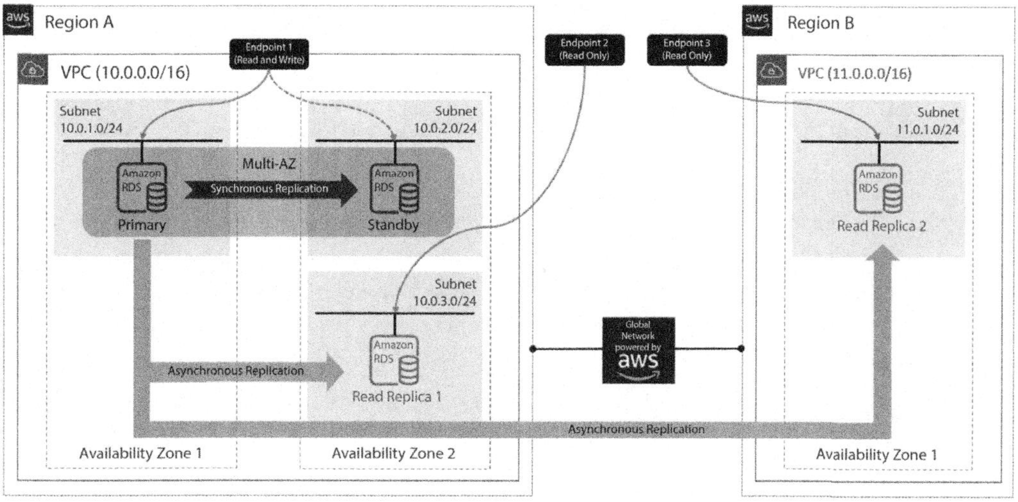

Figure 6.14 – Amazon RDS read replica

*Charles*: That's interesting. This saves the headache of manually copying data from one AWS region to another region.

*Berta*: Yes. One thing to be aware of here is that read replicas are not writable. Read replicas are not used for automatic failover. All write requests from your application must be handled by the primary database instance. If you have configured Multi-AZ and the primary database is down, a standby will automatically be made the primary. In case the region in which your Multi-AZ database is running is down, both the primary database and the standby will be down. If you happen to have a read replica in another region, you can promote it to become a read/write copy and then point your application to the read replica endpoint. The business keeps running!

*Charles*: But can we automate this process somehow?

*Berta*: Yes. Everything can be automated; although, in this case, we have to write the logic we need in a script. I still have not researched the multiple automation options available, but it's fully possible.

*Charles*: Great. We'll have to prepare for these automation possibilities too.

*Alex*: Berta, what is the **Amazon Aurora** engine? I have been reading the documentation regarding RDS and there are many references to it.

*Berta*: Amazon Aurora is Amazon's brainchild. If a customer chooses a commercial database vendor such as Microsoft or Oracle, these provide best-in-class features and performance but come with a heavy price tag. On the other hand, if a customer chooses open source databases such as MySQL, MariaDB, or PostgreSQL, these are comparatively economical, but may not have all the bells and whistles a customer may want. The key point is that all of these databases were not originally designed to use cloud advantages; RDS makes a good effort to add some features, but the underlying SQL engine does not know anything about the cloud.

Amazon realized these limitations and created its own Amazon Aurora database. Aurora is available as part of RDS. It is a cloud-based relational database, compatible with MySQL and PostgreSQL. So, if you use Aurora, you can maintain your application compatibility for existing applications, get cloud-scale performance, and not pay a hefty price.

*Alex*: Okay. But what are the cloud advantages Aurora has?

*Berta*: To keep it simple, the storage is separated from the compute part. The storage system uses three AZs in a region, and makes six copies of everything, using a quorum algorithm. That gives high availability and much better performance. And everything is transparent; there's no need, for example, to allocate enough space. There's even a serverless option where you just make your queries!

*Harold*: Hmmm… I configured quorum, or consensus, algorithms on some on-premises clusters. I'm afraid I'll have to reread my documentation.

*Berta*: Do it to satisfy your learning curiosity needs, but again, this is fully transparent to the user.

*Harold*: Good. Another question: why can't we use Amazon RDS for OLAP operations? Why do we need a separate database for it?

*Berta*: Technically, you can, but it is not very efficient. OLAP systems store data mostly in a columnar format (rather than a row format). The columnar format is well suited to complex analysis, long-running queries, and reporting. Also, it is expected that OLAP systems will not be modified as often as OLTP systems. They are designed to respond to read queries much more efficiently than write queries and their transactional approach. In the end, it is still a relational database but organized to favor analytical operations such as financial analysis, budgeting, and sales forecasting.

*Harold*: Okay. And does AWS offer a database solution for these use cases?

*Berta*: Yes, **Amazon Redshift** is the data warehousing solution from Amazon. With Amazon Redshift, you get all the flexibility to use SQL to analyze your structured or semi-structured data across different sources. It is offered as a managed service, so customers don't have to worry about managing data warehouse infrastructure. I hope everyone has got some clarity on the relational databases. Let's now focus on non-relational databases.

*Harold*: Sure.

After the explanation, a short break is taken. Berta has covered the main distinction between OLTP and OLAP, related products (RDS, Aurora, Redshift) they can use for those purposes, and the options available to make these systems more highly available, such as read replicas or Aurora distributed mechanisms.

## Non-relational databases

After the break, Berta wants to finish her explanation with non-relational databases. As there are several types that she wants to talk about, she starts as soon as possible.

*Berta*: AWS also offers different non-relational databases, and there are many of them. Each one of them is suited to a specific use case, for example, graph databases.

*Alex*: These are for graphics?

*Berta*: No, *graph*, not graphics. You can store different entities and the relationships between them, building a complex graph. They can be used in recommendation engines, fraud detection, identity graphs, and similar applications. For that purpose, **Amazon Neptune** would be the right choice.

You can also have databases in RAM, for extreme performance, or databases that are time-based, where you analyze time series, such as for the Internet of Things, stock prices, measurements such as temperature or pressure, or anything where the time sequence is important. You can use **ElastiCache** as a memory cache, and **TimeStream** for time-series storage and analysis.

*Harold*: I think I have read something about an immutable database?

*Berta*: Yes, that is **QLDB**, Amazon **Quantum Ledger Database**. It is a database where the change log cannot be modified or tampered with. It's very useful for legal proof, or just to maintain the sequence of changes as a fully historical log of all activity that can be verified.

*Alex*: This is great. I like the idea of having purpose-built databases, rather than trying to use only one type of database. But these databases seem too specialized. Is there any generic-purpose database that is also non-relational?

*Berta*: Sure. There is one is called **Amazon DynamoDB**. It is a non-relational database, supporting both key-value and document data models. Being non-relational, nobody enforces a fixed schema. So, each row in DynamoDB—called an **Item**—can have any number of columns at any moment. That means your tables can adapt to your changing business requirements, without having to stop the database to modify the previous schema:

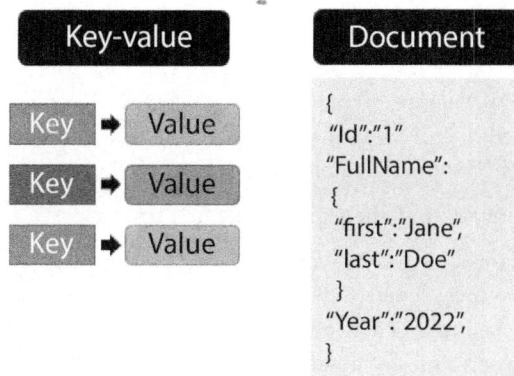

| Key-value | Document |
|-----------|----------|
| Key ➡ Value | { |
| Key ➡ Value | "Id":"1" |
| Key ➡ Value | "FullName": |
| | { |
| | "first":"Jane", |
| | "last":"Doe" |
| | } |
| | "Year":"2022", |
| | } |

Figure 6.15 — Key-value and document model

*Harold*: So, if the data is stored as tables, how is it different from relational databases?

*Berta*: The key here is that there's only one table, without any relationships. If your application requires them, you can surely create multiple tables, but they will be completely independent, in separate databases. The application will have to perform the joining logic. You usually have to design the table for all the queries you might anticipate, including all the data and possible indexes.

Also, traditional relational databases have separate endpoints for control operations to create and manage the tables, and a separate endpoint for data operations to **create, read, update, and delete** (also called **CRUD**) actions on the data in a table. DynamoDB simplifies this: it offers a single endpoint that can accept all types of requests. Amazon DynamoDB is serverless; so, you don't worry about any of the operational overhead. Also, DynamoDB supports eventual and strong consistency.

*Harold*: Could you please explain it?

*Berta*: Sure. A **database consistency model** defines the mode and timing in which a successful write or update is reflected in a later read operation of that same value. Let us consider an example to explain it. Do you use a credit or debit card?

*Harold*: I use both. For cash withdrawals, I use a debit card, and for purchases, a credit card.

*Berta*: Good. So, if you have withdrawn some money using your debit card and you immediately check your account balance again, will the recent withdrawal reflect in the account statement?

*Harold*: Yes. It will.

*Berta*: And if you made a purchase with your credit card, will it also reflect it at the same time?

*Harold*: I think it shows the transaction in a *pending* state; it doesn't show as *completed* immediately.

*Berta*: Correct. Credit card processing works slightly differently. The vendor from whom you have purchased the product has to claim a settlement of the transaction. Eventually—by that, I mean after some time—the transaction will show as *completed* in your account.

DynamoDB always stores multiple copies of your data. Let's assume it keeps three copies. At any time, one of the copies is chosen as a **Leader**. Every time a write or update request is initiated, DynamoDB will ensure that at least two copies (the leader and one more copy) are immediately updated to reflect the change. The third copy will have stale data for some time, but finally, it will also be updated to reflect the change.

*Harold*: But why not update all the copies in the first place?

*Berta*: The performance impact. If DynamoDB had to wait for all three copies to confirm the write, the application that requested to write would have to wait longer, waiting for the slowest node. Imagine you want to host a meeting with three people in different time zones; you would have to find a common timeslot that suits all three participants. This problem is somewhat simpler when the meeting requires only two people to attend.

*Harold*: Oh, I get it now. It's another quorum algorithm, similar to the one used in Aurora. A majority of storage nodes take the decision. So, the third copy is still waiting to be updated, but the acknowledgment of the write has already been sent to the application. This means my data in different copies is not consistent, but at least two copies will have the latest data.

*Berta*: Yes, for some time. This is sometimes referred to as data being in a **soft state**. But there are options available in DynamoDB if you want to always read the most up-to-date data.

*Alex*: But why would someone be interested in reading stale data in the first place?

*Berta*: For better performance. Let me give you an example. Let's say you have stored stock prices for a company in DynamoDB. Consider the price of the stock to be $100, and all three copies currently have the same value of $100. Now, you read this data in two different applications. Application one, which is a news scroll, displays the current price of the stock, and application two, is a financial application with which you can buy or sell stocks.

*Alex*: Okay.

*Berta*: If you have a news scroll application, you could add a disclaimer such as *This data is delayed by 15 minutes* and display the data from DynamoDB. In this case, accuracy is not that important, as you are okay with having data delayed by 15 minutes. DynamoDB will never supply you with wrong data or random data, but it might give you data that is stale. It was accurate a while ago, but currently, it may or may not be accurate. As there are three copies, and your read request can land on any copy, there is a one-in-three chance that you may get stale data. But this method will always return the data with the lowest latency. This is called **eventual consistency**.

*Alex*: Agreed – if you don't specify the node, your query might end up in any of them.

*Berta*: Now, if you want to use the same stock data for a financial application – this means your priority is accuracy rather than speed. You always need to get the most up-to-date data for any financial transaction. In DynamoDB, you can indicate—by using a parameter in your query—that the reader needs the most recent, accurate data. This time, DynamoDB will find out which is the leader and will deliver data from it; this way, you'll get the most up-to-date data. This is called **strong consistency**.

*Alex*: That's nice. Based on your read requirement you can choose to have eventually consistent data or strongly consistent data. I like the flexibility it offers.

*Berta*: Eventual consistency is the default mechanism. If a requester doesn't specify any parameter and just issues a request to read, DynamoDB interprets it as an eventual read request.

*Harold*: So, all write requests are always consistent; it's when you read that you select eventual consistency or strong consistency.

*Berta*: That's correct.

*Charles*: In the traditional world, the performance of a database is based on the server it is running. How is the performance of DynamoDB controlled?

*Berta*: In the case of DynamoDB, you have to configure **Read Capacity Units** (**RCUs**) and **Write Capacity Units** (**WCUs**) to achieve specific performance. These are table-level settings. An RCU defines the number of strongly consistent reads per second of items up to 4 KB in size. Eventually consistent reads use half the provisioned read capacity. So, if you configured your table for 10 RCU, you could perform 10 strongly consistent read operations, or 20 eventual read operations (double the amount of strongly consistent reads) of 4 KB each. A WCU is the number of 1 KB writes per second.

*Charles*: Okay. What I don't understand exactly is how many RCUs or WCUs are required for a new application, or for an application that has spiky or unpredictable access?

*Berta*: Amazon DynamoDB has got you covered. It has two capacity modes for processing, on-demand and provisioned. In the **on-demand** mode, DynamoDB instantly accommodates your workloads as they ramp up or down. So, if you have a new table with an unknown workload, an application with unpredictable traffic, or you want to pay only for what you actually use, on-demand mode is a great option. If you choose **provisioned** mode, you have to specify the number of reads and writes per second needed for your application. So, if your application has predictable and consistent traffic, you want to control costs, and only pay a specific amount, the provisioned mode is better.

*Charles*: And this mode has to be selected at table creation time or can it be modified later?

*Berta*: You can set the read/write capacity mode at table creation, or you can change it later too, either manually or programmatically.

*Harold*: By the way, you mentioned some non-relational databases also support querying through SQL?

*Berta*: Yes. DynamoDB supports PartiQL, an open source, SQL-compatible query language. Furthermore, you can use a client-side GUI tool called NoSQL Workbench for Amazon DynamoDB, which provides data modeling, data visualization, and query development features for DynamoDB tables.

I think we now have enough information to map our existing databases to AWS services. Let's start listing all the databases that we plan to migrate to AWS and work as a team to identify possible migration methods.

## Summary

Gloria has been checking the progress of all conversations. She is really happy with how the team is advancing in their learning and using that knowledge for the assigned tasks. She also feels lucky about how the team is collaborating, and how the new members are integrating with the older ones, especially as she had anticipated potential problems among them. Now she realizes that learning about all these new cloud technologies is a challenge that is uniting the team.

Now they've analyzed some of the database types offered by the cloud provider in depth – RDS, Aurora, and DynamoDB, the challenge is mastering all of them, as there are 11 types in the end – some relational, some non-relational. They've also taken a look at the **Database Migration Service (DMS)**, which allows them to migrate a full database into the cloud.

Once all databases and migration tools had been considered, the whole team started a **Proof of Concept (POC)** migration, which ended successfully. So, after a nice celebration party, they migrated some other production databases.

But now it's time to start diving deeper into security. So, the next step in Gloria's plan is asking the team about identity and access management, including identities as users, groups, or roles, and also the permissions that can be granted to those identities. She is also considering the topic of data encryption.

But besides asking the team about self-training, Gloria begins to think about other practical ways to improve their knowledge and performance. There will be a huge event organized by the cloud provider in a couple of months. She feels the entire team could attend it. She'll discuss this with Eva but won't tell her team until it is approved.

## Further reading

- On quorum or consensus algorithms:

    - `https://en.wikipedia.org/wiki/Consensus_(computer_science)`

    - `https://aws.amazon.com/es/blogs/database/amazon-aurora-under-the-hood-quorum-and-correlated-failure/`

    - `https://aws.amazon.com/es/blogs/database/amazon-aurora-under-the-hood-quorum-reads-and-mutating-state/`

    - `https://aws.amazon.com/es/blogs/database/amazon-aurora-under-the-hood-reducing-costs-using-quorum-sets/`

- On cloud-based databases:

    - `https://aws.amazon.com/products/databases/`

# 7

# Identity and Access Management – Who Am I and What Can I Do?

There's now some tranquility floating in the air. Many services are already running in the cloud like a charm. There are instances with Windows and Linux, many applications and web servers created in seconds are running on them, and some databases have already migrated to the cloud.

Our IT team is more confident about the process they're following. They know they've still got lots of things to learn, but they feel the core services are already in place.

During this relatively calm period, Gloria has organized a small visit to the software team area. It is intended as a social event so that both teams can get to know each other.

## Visiting the software team

Gloria greets everyone present as they prepare to meet the software team:

*Gloria*: Good morning, all. I have a small surprise for you. I'd like to invite you for some pastries, those ones you seem to love. But this time, it will be in a different room, as I'm going to introduce you to our software team.

*Charles*: Who is attending? I mean, I'd like to…. *(Whispers)* Yum… those pastries…

*Harold*: I already know most of the software team, but I'd also like to participate. Maybe we can share our recent knowledge of the cloud and also learn from what they're doing. We can start a more DevOps-like approach…

*Alex*: I like DevOps but prefer Pastry-Ops…

*Gloria*: I'm beginning to know all of you better, especially about your serious pastry addiction. Yes, all of you are invited, and there are lots of pastries for everyone. Let's go then.

All of them (Gloria, Alex, Berta, Charles, Raj, and Harold) go into the software department. It is a relatively large room, with several cubicles, lots of monitors, a huge pile of pastries on the table, and a fun atmosphere:

*Frank*: Hello, I'm Frank. I'm the manager of the software department. Welcome to our den. Here, you can see where we build all the magic of this business. As you can see, we are a team of 80 people, mostly developers, and we are in charge of more than 40 critical business applications, in many different environments and languages. We build them, then test, improve, fix…

*Alex*: Hello all! But do you have any modern applications?

Everybody in the meeting begins to exchange strange looks, and then all the developers start laughing like crazy.

*Alex*: Was it something I said?

*Frank*: Well, yes. In fact, this is one of our major discussion points. Some of our apps were written in COBOL in the 1980s and can only run on this mainframe. So, you get the idea. Of course, we're starting to break some of them into microservices, and we're also learning about containers, Docker, and Kubernetes, but it will take some time.

Currently, we're just considering building a small three-tier application as a test in the cloud, with some simple logic and a small database. We've heard you have some experience with this.

*Berta*: I thought several of us came here only to help devastate your pastry stock, but yes, this is a topic where we can also offer some help. For example, we were discussing the different types of purpose-built databases in the cloud, and yes, we currently have some of the migrated applications using them.

*Frank*: Fantastic! Do you think we could use one of your environments for our testing? Maybe you can create one for us while we decide whether we need a separate account?

*Gloria*: Of course, we can. In fact, we all work for the same company and have the same goals. And, by the way, we have a separate account for testing.

*Raj*: But it would be extremely important to keep these environments somehow isolated, to be able to update them separately, and to avoid possible mistakes in production.

*Berta*: Maybe we can create a separate VPC where you can have your test databases and set up a peering relationship.

*Raj*: No, I'm not talking about separating traffic. I'm thinking about responsibilities; each environment has to have clear life cycles, owners, and permissions.

*Frank*: What you are referring to is **Identity**, to have all the actors clearly defined, and of course, this goes together with their associated permissions – who is allowed to use the service and what can be done on it. I assume this can be done in the cloud.

I will send you an email to get some test accounts created for my team. For now, enjoy the pastries. Nice meeting you all.

Frank leaves the Cloud team and goes back to his cubicle. But he has given enough food for thought to the team about the accounts and access requirements:

*Raj*: We could separate the traffic using security groups and network ACLs, but TCP/IP does not know about users or identities, only about network traffic. Something else is needed.

*Charles*: This is bringing a strange thought to my mind. Guys, how are our recently migrated services running? I mean, who has permission to, for example, delete a full table, or stop an EC2 instance?

*Berta*: I think we have set up all of our services with a single user, who is an administrator.

*Charles*: So that means everything runs smoothly, as all our services have no restrictions, but…

The Cloud team realizes what this means and all of them turn red in their faces.

*Raj*: But is not the best practice in security. We have to follow the **principle of least privilege**, which means that every actor in IT has to have the minimum permissions to do a task, but just those and no more.

*Charles*: Sure. And that requires maintaining separate identities, for different processes, environments, users, or departments. We cannot run the whole IT shop as a single environment, and with just a single administrator with no limits. Hackers would eat us in seconds if they knew…

*Berta*: Yes, we are following the *worst practice*, if that term exists. Normally, you grant only the minimum set of permissions that is required. If someone complains about a missing permission, you can add it later. We did the opposite, giving all permissions by default, and probably never thought of removing the unnecessary ones.

*Raj*: Yes, I'm afraid we skipped that step. When we created some EC2 instances, and also some RDS databases, there was a field about permissions or roles. I started investigating but didn't have the time. There's a service called **Identity and Access Management (IAM)**. It takes the responsibility for all **identity** (that means **the users**) but also for **access**, which I can imagine is the **permissions**.

*Gloria*: Well, things are clear. I'm happy we had this chat, as now we know more about our current risks, and of course, this leads to the next steps for you. I've written a list on this dirty napkin, but I'll copy them into our task system. They are:

| Tasks |
| --- |
| 1. Study IAM, including its purpose, details, possibilities, quirks, philosophy, and price. |
| 2. Define the separate actors we might need, currently and in the future. |
| 3. Provide the minimum privileges and no more. |
| 4. Reconfigure all our running systems to use only these minimum privileges. |
| 5. Create some test accounts for Frank, based on his email. |
| 6. Maybe there's a way to get audit reports or logging? |

Table 7.1 — Security – the proposed task list

*Gloria*: Please organize them as you feel convenient and tell me when you have some conclusions. And Alex, please, stop devouring the remaining pastries.

The Cloud team goes back to its office with a clear challenge. It will prioritize the list, divide the tasks, study all the topics, and for sure, it will come up with a satisfactory security environment for everybody.

## Methods for accessing cloud services

After a couple of days, the Cloud team meets again around the coffee machine.

*Berta*: What a shame. We completely forgot about securing our services.

*Charles*: I think it is a serious mistake. Fortunately, we discovered it pretty soon. What do we have as a start?

*Raj*: I've been reading lots of documentation about IAM – remember, access and management. The service takes care of **identity**, which means proving who you are. And then it takes care of **access**, which is what you can do once you are identified – that is, your permissions.

*Charles*: I'm taking note of this important difference:

| Identity | Who you are | Authentication, Identification |
|----------|-------------|-------------------------------|
| Access | What can you do | Authorization, Permissions |

Table 7.2 — Authentication versus authorization

*Raj*: I have an example to remember this. If you are traveling to or from the USA, you need a passport with your identification. This is used for authentication, so you can prove it's you to the authorities. But that's not enough; once you are authenticated, you need a permit, such as a visa or a work permit. This is access, defining what you are authorized to do.

*Alex*: But won't a single service offer both functionalities, identity and access?

*Raj*: Yes, it makes sense to simplify both of them in a single service, as they are highly related. In the end, it is a database with defined users, groups, and permissions.

*Alex*: I've also continued to dive deeper into IAM and also the encryption possibilities the cloud provides, which in this case are found in a different service.

*Charles*: And I've been learning the generic way to access services securely. Let me start with it.

*Alex*: Please tell us. IAM seems to be an important part of security, but I'm lacking a broader vision about when it is used.

*Charles*: Yes. Well, every time you do any sort of request in the cloud (for example, to create a database, create an S3 bucket, or shut down an EC2 instance), you request it in the console, maybe on that tiny console application running on your smartphone, or even by code, in one script. No matter how you make your requests, all of them are translated to calls; every service defines an API for each operation.

These requests are sent from the client (maybe your laptop) to the service endpoint. For that purpose, we use a well-known protocol; remember, we use the internet as the way to reach the cloud, so this protocol is usually *HTTPS*, although *HTTP* can also be used in some situations.

*Alex*: Another endpoint?

*Charles*: Lots of them. We used endpoints, for example, to add data to the database, but we also have endpoints to control each one of the services. You send your request to the right endpoint, in the right region, and to the right service.

*Alex*: It seems complex.

*Charles*: Not at all. All of this is handled by AWS. You have only to select the right region and service, maybe in the console. All the translations to HTTPS will be hidden.

Now, every time you start any operation, maybe just by clicking on the console, it will be packed into a series of HTTPS requests. They will contain your identity in a structure called a **token**. And all this traffic is encrypted. It's like sending a letter with instructions, saying, *I am this person, and I would like you to perform these steps. Please answer, and tell me what you did.*

The service will receive these requests and use IAM to check the identity of the user. And then it will check whether that user has the needed permissions to do the requested operation. This is done on every attempt to perform any action.

You can also log all attempts, successful or failing, to access any service. All calls to the API are logged with a service called **CloudTrail**. It creates audit logs you can analyze later.

I think someone will be able to explain later the details of how IAM works, but that is the general idea. Any questions?

*Alex*: A more generic one. All this security seems complex, as many layers are involved. A hacker could interfere with the cables connecting the AZs, inject a virus into an EC2 image. Or maybe someone has set up their password to be as complex as my credit card pin, *1234*. To avoid any security incidents, who is responsible for the configuration? The cloud provider?

*Charles*: This is called **the shared responsibility model**. That means the responsibility related to security is shared. Let's have a short break, after which I'll explain it.

The team has discussed the important difference between authentication and authorization, and how requests arrive in the cloud and are evaluated. Anyway, the members have yet to understand the shared responsibility model and how the IAM service fits in with it.

# The shared responsibility model

After this short break, the team gathers again in the meeting room:

*Charles*: Let me give you an example to explain the shared responsibility model.

*Alex*: I am all ears.

*Charles*: You live in an apartment building, right? Can you tell me whether there are any security controls in your building?

*Alex*: Yes. We have cameras in the common areas, access cards to operate elevators, and videophones at the building entrance.

*Charles*: Great. And have you installed all these security controls?

*Alex*: Nope. They were already there. I guess when the building was constructed, the builder might have added all these things.

*Charles*: And you also have a lock and key for your apartment.

*Alex*: Definitely.

*Charles*: So, in this situation, there are some security-related responsibilities that are shared. The builder is responsible for providing the basic security controls, such as the security cameras in common areas, a secure lock for your apartment, a door videophone, and an access card for the elevator. And it is your responsibility as a resident of the building to ensure that you use these security controls to your advantage, right?

*Alex*: Can you please explain?

*Charles*: As a resident, you should ensure that you always check the door videophone before letting someone into the building. You have to ensure that you do not lose your access card, or if there is an entry code for the elevator or entrance, you should not be sharing it with others. Also, you need to ensure that security cameras are operational or pointing in the right direction, and of course, you have to lock your apartment and keep your key safe. Maybe you also enhance your apartment security by installing an additional pair of locks or a wireless alarm system, or maybe getting a dog.

*Alex*: I get it now – so the builder has taken care of providing the basic security devices and we, as residents, should not worry about getting those things installed, but we have to use those security controls to our advantage. This way, we don't have the operational burden of all the infrastructure required for security.

*Charles*: Exactly – and security responsibility in the cloud is no different. Your cloud provider takes care of the **security of the cloud**. The cloud provider ensures that customers don't suffer the operational burden of components such as the host operating system, virtualization layer, or the physical security of the facilities where the service runs. The cloud provider is responsible for protecting the infrastructure powering the services. This infrastructure is largely composed of the physical hardware, software running on that hardware, networking equipment, and the locations where these data center facilities are hosted.

*Alex*: This will surely save customers a lot of time. But then, what are the responsibilities of a customer?

*Charles*: A customer is responsible for **security in the cloud**. Let's take an Amazon EC2 instance as an example. AWS will ensure that the infrastructure required to run this instance is secure; the customer will manage the security inside it. The customer will manage operating system updates, security patches, application software security, domain join, operating system-level firewall settings, and so on. AWS provides security controls to help customers do these activities. For example, you could use the AWS Systems Manager service to apply patches, add security to your Amazon EC2 instances using network access control lists and security groups, and run your application inside an Auto Scaling group for high availability.

*Alex*: I understand. So, the security of the cloud is managed by AWS, and the security in the cloud is managed by the customer:

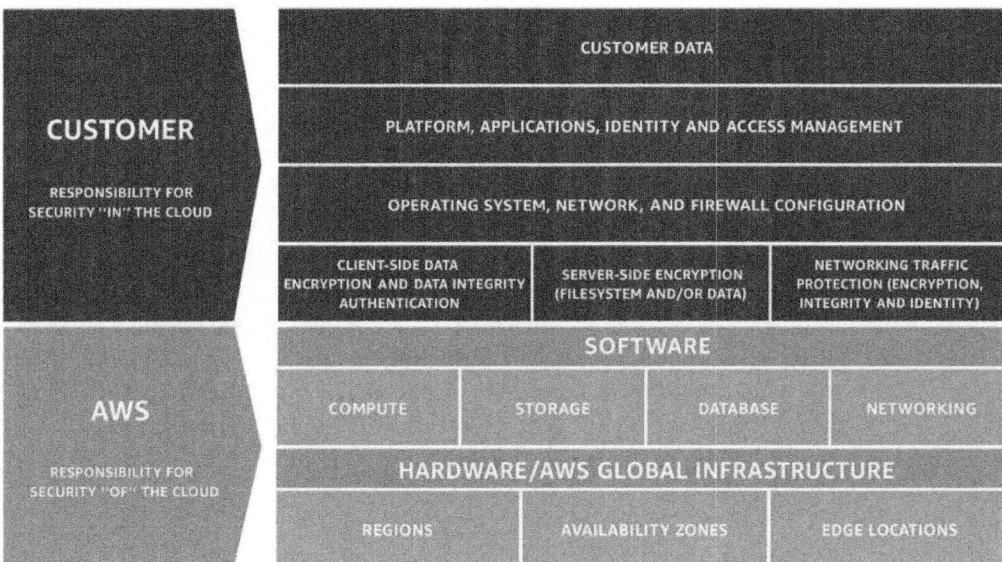

Figure 7.1 – The shared responsibility model

*Charles*: Exactly. But for some higher-level services, also called **abstracted services**, such as Amazon S3 or Amazon DynamoDB, AWS manages the required infrastructure layer, the platform, and the operating system. These abstracted services just provide an endpoint to customers for storing or retrieving data. Customers then manage encryption, classification, retention, and appropriate permissions.

*Alex*: This is very clear now. You just mentioned permission management. I had a hard time understanding the AWS IAM service, and I think Berta was also struggling with it. Can you explain how permissions work in AWS?

*Charles*: I can try, but the best bet would be to learn it from Raj. In fact, he is about to set up some new accounts for the developers and QA team. Let's see whether he is available, and we can also include Berta in our discussion.

*Alex*: Great. Let's go and check whether they are available.

This has been a nice explanation of the shared responsibility model, especially regarding the difference between *security of the cloud* and *security in the cloud*, but the team realizes a more technical approach will soon be needed.

# Authentication and authorization in the cloud

Later, all of the team are gathered around Raj's desk so that he can walk them through the IAM service:

*Raj*: Okay. Let me first explain some basic concepts first, and then we will address the requirements of the software engineering team.

An account in AWS is a fundamental part of accessing AWS services. Every account has a unique 12-digit number, such as *123456789012*, to identify it. This number is randomly assigned by AWS when you sign up for a new account. An AWS account serves two basic functions. First, it acts as a container for the resource you create. When you create an Amazon S3 bucket or an Amazon EC2 instance, you are creating a resource in your AWS account. Every resource gets a unique identifier for itself called an **Amazon Resource Name** (**ARN**). Second, it also acts as a security boundary for your AWS resources. Any resource you create is available only to users who have credentials for that same account. The email address that is used to register the AWS account is called a **root user**. And inside an AWS account, you can use the AWS IAM service to further create users, user groups, policies, roles, and so on:

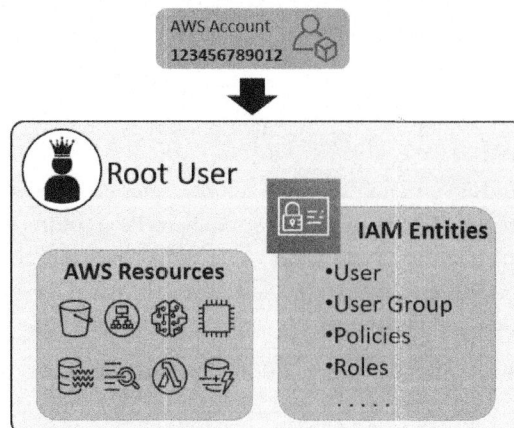

Figure 7.2 – An AWS account

*Berta*: And I guess this root user has all the privileges in this account. Right?

*Raj*: Absolutely correct. I call this user a **superuser**, who has all the power over this AWS account. They can create resources, change billing information, update contact information, and add more users if needed. In a single-account scenario, there is no way you can restrict a root user.

*Harold*: If this account has ultimate privileges, surely it's better we don't use it for day-to-day tasks.

Everyone realized that Harold had also joined them and was listening attentively:

*Raj*: Yes. It is a highly recommended best practice to not use this account for daily activities. A better approach is to create other separate users with only the required privileges and use them for each specific purpose. And that's why we need a service such as AWS IAM to manage these users.

*Alex*: Do we also get some additional user accounts by default in a new AWS account – like in some operating systems, where we have a guest account?

*Raj*: Nope. Only the root user. So, the first thing you should do after logging in as a root user is to create an administrator account for performing administration tasks within your AWS account. In the AWS Management Console, you can identify a user by checking the details in the top-right corner. Like currently, I am logged in as a user called `admin_raj`. The account I'm using is only dedicated to **Proof of Concepts** (**POCs**) by the software engineering team. It is always better to have separate AWS accounts to segregate workloads, business units, environment, geography, and billing entities:

Figure 7.3 – An AWS IAM user

*Alex*: If we have many AWS accounts, wouldn't managing them be complex?

*Raj*: There is an AWS service called **AWS Organizations** that can help you to manage multiple accounts. That is a separate discussion we can have some other day; for now, let's focus on the basics to achieve our business requirements.

*Berta*: Yes, all clear.

*Raj*: There are many different terms in AWS IAM. I won't confuse you by talking about all of them at the same time but rather show you how they all work together. AWS IAM stores IAM resources for you. The user, group, role, policy, and identity provider objects are called **IAM resources** and are stored in IAM. AWS IAM helps you securely control access to AWS resources. As Berta commented this morning, you use IAM to control who is authenticated (signed in) and authorized (has permissions) to use the resources. Or, in simple English, it controls *who can access what*.

Now, let me show the request we have received from the engineering team manager, Frank, to get a few accounts created.

Raj shows them the email:

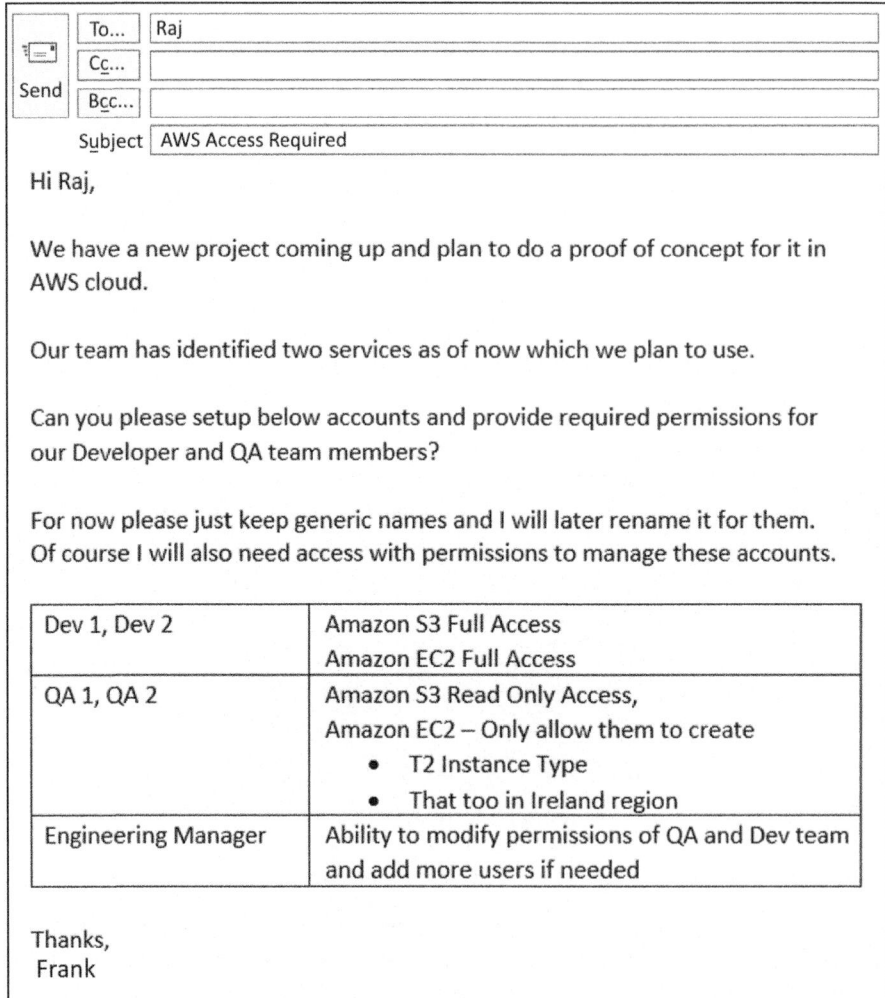

| Send | To... | Raj |
| --- | --- | --- |
| | Cc... | |
| | Bcc... | |
| | Subject | AWS Access Required |

Hi Raj,

We have a new project coming up and plan to do a proof of concept for it in AWS cloud.

Our team has identified two services as of now which we plan to use.

Can you please setup below accounts and provide required permissions for our Developer and QA team members?

For now please just keep generic names and I will later rename it for them. Of course I will also need access with permissions to manage these accounts.

| Dev 1, Dev 2 | Amazon S3 Full Access<br>Amazon EC2 Full Access |
| --- | --- |
| QA 1, QA 2 | Amazon S3 Read Only Access,<br>Amazon EC2 – Only allow them to create<br>• T2 Instance Type<br>• That too in Ireland region |
| Engineering Manager | Ability to modify permissions of QA and Dev team and add more users if needed |

Thanks,
Frank

Figure 7.4 – A request for AWS access

Once everyone has read the mail, Alex speaks first:

*Alex*: I guess we need to create five users here and assign them the requested permissions: Dev1, Dev2, QA1, QA2, and Engineering Manager.

*Raj*: I agree. But instead of literally just following the request, let's think a little bit more about it. Do you think there might be more requests to add more developers and QA users in the future?

*Alex*: Probably yes, as the request is just for two developer accounts, but we actually have dozens of developers in the software engineering team, and this is similar for QAs.

*Raj*: Right, and if we have multiple accounts with similar access required, should we keep on assigning permissions to them individually, or is there a better way?

*Berta*: We should group them together for better administration.

*Raj*: Exactly. That's where the IAM resource **user groups** can be helpful. We can create one group for developers and another one for QAs to get started. Should we also create a group for the engineering manager?

*Berta*: Probably not, as this may be an individual user. But we can have a group called Admins, and maybe in the future, if we need more admin-level users, we can add them to the group.

*Raj*: That's correct. One thing to be aware of here is that these groups are called *user groups* for a reason. They can only have users inside them. You cannot add a group to another group. Nesting of groups is not currently possible in AWS IAM. *A user can be a member of multiple groups, but a group cannot be a member of another group.*

*Harold*: Ah. Good to know. Different from other systems.

*Alex*: Just a query. I assume if you configure the permissions for a user or a group and make a mistake, you can edit them later.

*Raj*: Of course. For example, if you forgot to add a user to a group, then they do not have the right permissions. You just have to add the user to the group.

*Alex*: But, as in other systems, the user has to log off and log on again to become part of the group and then receive those permissions.

*Raj*: Not with IAM. It does this dynamically. The user just has to retry the operation. No need to log off.

*Alex*: This is nice to know. Please, Raj, go on.

*Raj*: I can first create users or groups in any order and add users later to their respective groups. For now, I am assigning them only privileges to log in through the management console. If they need command-line access or want to use scripts, or even **Software Development Kits** (**SDKs**), I could create an access key and secret access key for them.

Raj creates five users (Dev1, Dev2, QA1, QA2, and SWMgr (for the software team manager)) and two user groups (Dev and QA). Then, he adds Dev1 and Dev2 to the Dev group, followed by QA1 and QA2 as members of the QA group.

*Raj*: So, a part of the request is complete. In this AWS account, I had previously created a group called Admin, and I'd prefer to add SWMgr to that group. This way, SWMgr will inherit the policies I have applied to the Admin group. As for the other users and groups that I just created, they can log in or get authenticated but can't perform any other operation until you give them explicit permissions.

*Berta*: Are policies and permissions two different things or just the same?

*Raj*: In simple terms, a policy defines a set of permissions. A **policy** is an object, containing a list with multiple permissions. Any **IAM identity** (IAM users, IAM user groups, and IAM roles) can be assigned one or multiple policies, assigning all the permissions specified to them. AWS first uses your IAM identity for authentication – that is, identifying who is making the request. After that, the list of **permissions** will provide either *allow* or *deny* access to perform an action on a specific resource, controlling which actions will be possible. And you can also assign policies to several resource types, so the resource owner can restrict access even more.

Policies are stored in AWS as **JavaScript Object Notation (JSON)** documents. I just gave you an example of a policy being assigned to a user, but you can assign policies to IAM user groups and also to IAM roles:

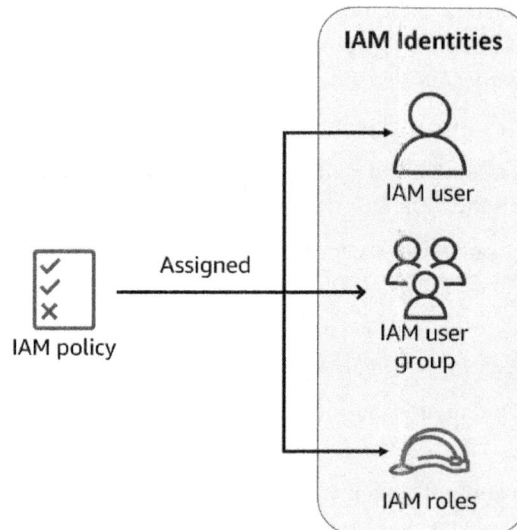

Figure 7.5 – IAM policy assignment to IAM identities

*Charles*: And you can have the same policy assigned to multiple identities, and an identity can have multiple policies. Right?

*Raj*: In the case of IAM policies, your understanding is correct. But there are other policies in AWS that may have a different implementation. For our current requirement, we are focusing on IAM policies only.

*Charles*: Okay. You said policies are JSON documents, so do I have to write the whole JSON document myself?

*Raj*: If you like doing it yourself, yes, you can. But AWS offers a visual policy editor in which you can select the services, required permissions, specific resources, and conditions to build a JSON document, and this is automatically created for you. AWS also offers you lots of managed policies that are prebuilt, based on common use cases and job functions. Let me show you an AWS-managed job function policy called **Administrator Access**:

```
1 ▾ {
2       "Version": "2012-10-17",
3 ▾     "Statement": [
4 ▾         {
5               "Effect": "Allow",
6               "Action": "*",
7               "Resource": "*"
8           }
9       ]
10  }
```

Figure 7.6 – An AWS-managed job function policy, Administrator Access

*Alex*: Wow! This looks like a very old policy, created in 2012.

*Raj*: Ha ha! It is not the policy creation date; it is the current version of the policy language. The version policy element specifies the language syntax rules that are to be used to process a policy.

*Alex*: Got it. And if I interpret this policy, it allows every action on every resource. Right?

*Raj*: Yes, you are correct. You can specify **wildcards** in policies in multiple situations – for example, when specifying resources or actions. It is very convenient, as this makes the language simpler, especially when you want to provide access to multiple resources with a single line.

*Berta*: Looks like it is a suitable policy for the SWMgr user.

*Raj*: It is too powerful and very broad, but just to explain the concept to you, let's use it instead. Actually, I have assigned this policy to the Admin group and also added SWMgr to it, so this policy automatically applies to that user. Let me show you another policy that can be useful for our requirements:

```
1 ▾ {
2       "Version": "2012-10-17",
3 ▾     "Statement": [
4 ▾         {
5               "Effect": "Allow",
6 ▾             "Action": [
7                   "s3:*",
8                   "s3-object-lambda:*"
9               ],
10              "Resource": "*"
11          }
12      ]
13  }
```

Figure 7.7 – An AWS-managed policy, AmazonS3FullAccess

*Berta*: This policy allows only S3 and S3 Object Lambda permissions on every resource. So, it is basically providing full access to the Amazon S3 service.

*Harold*: A good fit for the developers' group, I guess.

*Raj*: Yes, you are right. We can attach this policy to the group, and they will have full S3 access. The only thing that will be missing will be providing them with full Amazon EC2 access. There is a managed policy for that too, but let me create a single policy in which I will add both permissions – Amazon S3 full access and Amazon EC2 full access.

Raj uses the Policy Editor and creates a policy that looks like this:

```
 1 ▾ {
 2        "Version": "2012-10-17",
 3 ▾      "Statement": [
 4 ▾          {
 5                  "Sid": "VisualEditor0",
 6                  "Effect": "Allow",
 7 ▾                "Action": [
 8                      "s3:*",
 9                      "ec2:*"
10                  ],
11                  "Resource": "*"
12              }
13          ]
14    }
```

Figure 7.8 – A customer-managed policy

*Harold*: So, this will allow every S3- and EC2-related action. But I think you forgot to add S3 Object Lambda permission.

*Raj*: Oh yes. You are right. Good spot! As this is a policy that we created in our account, this is referred to as a customer-managed policy. And as it is managed by the customer, they can modify it anytime. Policies support versioning, so we will now have two versions of this policy. The latest version is automatically set as default, which can be changed if needed. Remember that you cannot modify an AWS-managed policy. AWS manages it for you. You can attach both types of policies to an AWS identity.

Raj uses the Policy Editor and edits the policy, which now looks like this:

```
1  {
2      "Version": "2012-10-17",
3      "Statement": [
4          {
5              "Sid": "VisualEditor0",
6              "Effect": "Allow",
7              "Action": [
8                  "s3:*",
9                  "ec2:*",
10                 "s3-object-lambda:*"
11             ],
12             "Resource": "*"
13         }
14     ]
15 }
```

Figure 7.9 – A customer-managed policy – version 2

Raj attaches this policy to the developer user group.

*Raj*: Let's now focus on the requirements of the QA group. I plan to use an AWS-managed policy, which is called **AmazonS3ReadOnlyAccess**. I guess the name is self-explanatory. Let me show it to you.

Raj shows the AmazonS3ReadOnlyAccess policy, which looks like this:

```
1  {
2      "Version": "2012-10-17",
3      "Statement": [
4          {
5              "Effect": "Allow",
6              "Action": [
7                  "s3:Get*",
8                  "s3:List*",
9                  "s3-object-lambda:Get*",
10                 "s3-object-lambda:List*"
11             ],
12             "Resource": "*"
13         }
14     ]
15 }
```

Figure 7.10 – The AmazonS3ReadOnlyAccess policy

*Berta*: I like the granularity and level of detail that we can go into.

*Raj*: Yes, you can be as specific as possible or as generic as you want. You can control permissions for every single API call through IAM. Now, I am going to focus on the remaining policies for the QA group. To fulfill this requirement, we will use a **condition element**. It is optional and lets you specify conditions to filter when a policy is in effect. The condition key that you specify can be a global condition key (such as `aws:SourceIP`, `aws:CurrentTime`, and `aws:MultifactorAuthPresent`) or a service-specific condition key (such as `ec2:ImageID`, `ec2:KeyPairName`, and `ec2:Region`).

*Charles*: Looks like for the QA group, we will use service-specific conditions to restrict the launch of Amazon EC2 instances only in a specific region, and only using a specific instance family.

*Raj*: Yes. And instead of allowing all EC2-related actions, I will only allow the `ec2:RunInstance` action, which grants permission to launch one or more instances. Let me create this policy and show it to you.

Raj creates the policy and shows it to everyone. He also attaches the required policies to the QA group:

```
1  {
2      "Version": "2012-10-17",
3      "Statement": [
4          {
5              "Sid": "VisualEditor0",
6              "Effect": "Allow",
7              "Action": "ec2:RunInstances",
8              "Resource": "*",
9              "Condition": {
10                 "StringEquals": {
11                     "ec2:Region": "eu-west-1"
12                 },
13                 "StringLike": {
14                     "ec2:InstanceType": "t2.*"
15                 }
16             }
17         }
18     ]
19 }
```

Figure 7.11 – A customized policy for the QA group

*Alex*: This is amazing. You can control various aspects of a request and be very specific in granting permissions.

*Raj*: Yes, and on top of that, it is not complex. I am not sure if you realized it or not, but we have achieved all the requirements outlined in the mail.

*Charles*: That's superb.

*Harold*: Will we be able to audit this access?

*Raj*: Absolutely. All these requests, whether allowed or denied, get captured by a service called AWS CloudTrail. It captures all the aspects of a request, such as who, when, what, where, and which, for every request. It is like a camera running in your AWS account that captures every API call. So, for every API call to an AWS resource, AWS IAM controls the access, allows or denies the request based on the policies, and AWS CloudTrail captures that information, whether the request was allowed or denied:

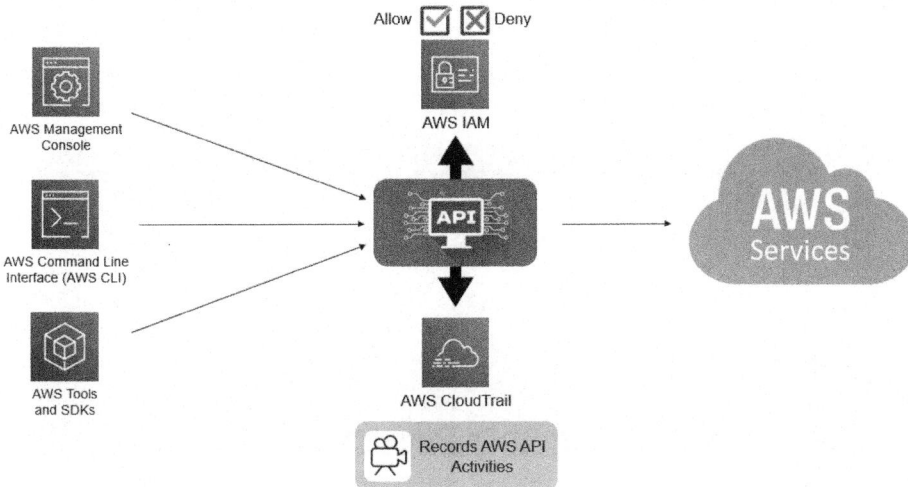

Figure 7.12 – Accessing an AWS service

*Harold*: That's nice. We haven't discussed roles. I guess we don't need roles for the engineering team requirement. But I still want to know.

*Raj*: Sure. Let me explain it to you by giving an example. Everyone! Think about any movie star you like. And don't tell me who they are; otherwise, I will start judging you.

Everyone laughs:

*Raj*: Now. Think about the different roles they have played in different movies. The actor is the same person, but depending on the movie script, they may have played a role of a different character. The character role they performed is temporary. They may be in that role for a given period of time and may perform some other role later, in another movie.

*Harold*: Do you mean to say that you can log in to a role?

*Raj*: More or less. An IAM role is similar to an IAM user, but there are some important differences. Roles and users are both AWS identities. Can anyone tell me what AWS identities are?

*Alex*: IAM identities identify who is making a request.

*Raj*: Correct. An IAM user account is also an identity, but it is uniquely associated with one specific person. Roles are also identities, but they are intended to be assumable by anyone who needs them. You do not log in to a role; you **assume a role**.

*Harold*: I am still confused.

*Raj*: Okay, let me give you another example. In most Linux systems, if you log in as a user, you get a $ prompt. Can you run every command from the $ prompt successfully?

*Harold*: Not every command. Some commands may require you to have a higher-level privilege, such as a superuser. We can use a sudo command to run programs with the security privileges of another user (by default, as the superuser). **Sudo** stands for **superuser do**:

```
$ yum install httpd
Loaded plugins: extras_suggestions, langpacks, priorities,
You need to be root to perform this command.
$
$ sudo yum install httpd
Loaded plugins: extras_suggestions, langpacks, priorities,
Resolving Dependencies
--> Running transaction check
---> Package httpd.x86_64 0:2.4.54-1.amzn2 will be install
--> Processing Dependency: httpd-tools = 2.4.54-1.amzn2 fo
4-1.amzn2.x86_64
```

Figure 7.13 – The sudo command in Linux

*Alex*: This is very similar to **User Account Control** (**UAC**) in Microsoft Windows and the RunAs tool.

*Raj*: So, let's summarize it – you assumed the role of superuser by the sudo or RunAs command, executed the command with higher privileges, and after the execution, you returned to the standard user privileges. Is this correct?

*Harold*: Yes, that's correct.

*Raj*: IAM roles are similar. For example, you can first log in as a developer user in the AWS account. Later, you have to check some of the QA resources, so you can assume a QA role, check those resources, and return to your developer role. You just temporarily assumed a role for a specific task and returned to your developer session.

*Alex*: Similarly, a movie star assumes a role, and after the shoot is finished, they return to their own persona.

*Raj*: Yes. Another way of putting it is that you wear different hats at different times. IAM roles are similar. If you look at the icon of an IAM role, it is actually represented as a hat:

**IAM Role**

**Trust**
Who can
assume this
role

Defined by the role
trust policy

**Permissions**
What you can
do after
assuming a role

Defined by IAM
permissions policies

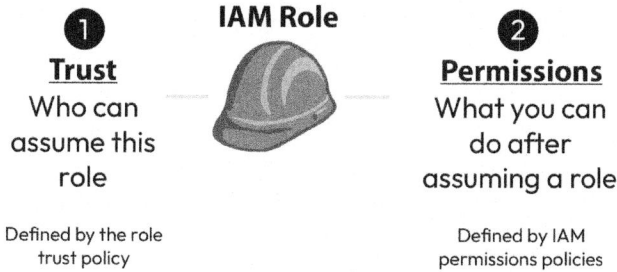

Figure 7.14 – The icon for an AWS IAM role

You can wear different hats depending on the need. If you visit a construction site, you may wear a hard hat; if it's summer, you may wear a Panama hat; in winter, you may wear a different hat.

*Harold*: But why not add all required permissions to the user or group? Why would we want to actually switch roles?

*Raj*: For multiple reasons. Maybe there are some conflicting policies on the groups you belong to. Also, you may not want to always have the highest level of access for regular tasks. As a best practice, I always log in as a read-only user in the AWS account, and only when I have to modify something do I assume the admin role and perform my task. Once done, I return to my read-only user persona.

*Harold*: That's a better approach. You are basically avoiding any mistakes that may happen unknowingly.

*Charles*: Or running any malicious code that would try to make use of your current permissions.

*Raj*: Also, IAM roles give you short-term access. It does not have standard long-term credentials, such as access keys or passwords. When you assume a role, you always get temporary security credentials for your role session. A role can be assumed by an IAM user in the same AWS account as the role, by an IAM user in a different AWS account than the role, or by an external user authenticated by a supported identity provider such as Microsoft Active Directory. Also, an AWS service such as Amazon EC2 or Lambda can assume a role.

*Alex*: I just want to confirm that there is some mechanism by which we can control who can assume which role.

*Raj*: Yes. That is called a **trust policy**. It is a JSON document in which you define the principals (users, roles, accounts, and services) that you trust to assume the role. Roles are just authentication; you will also need to attach policies to roles if you want to give them permissions:

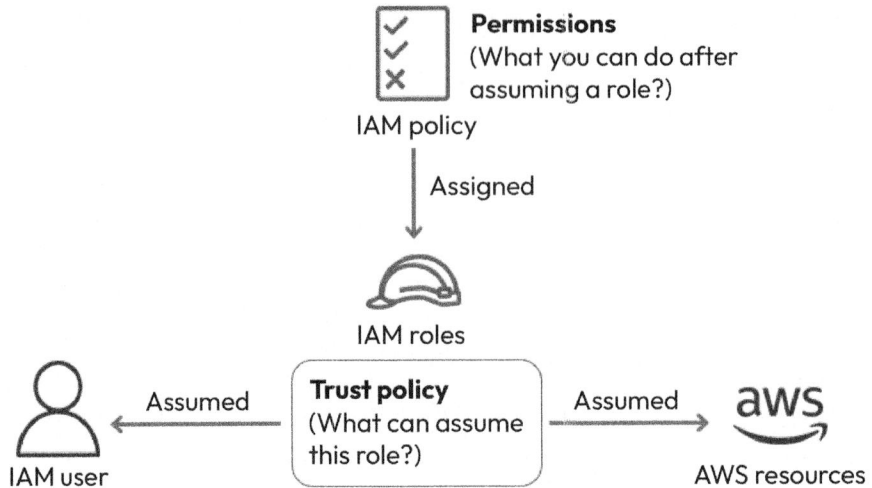

Figure 7.15 – A trust policy and IAM policies for an IAM role

*Harold*: What happens if there are conflicting policies applied to an IAM Identity?

*Raj*: There is a policy evaluation logic that comes into play. Let me first give you an example so that it is easier to understand. Let's say you are boarding a flight. Just before boarding an airline, the staff will scan your boarding pass and may ask you to show valid travel documents (maybe a passport or visa for the destination, maybe a hotel booking, or maybe a return ticket). These requirements are enforced by the destination, and airlines have to check all these before allowing someone to get on board. Besides, there may also be some checks for that individual against a *no fly list*. A no fly list is a list of people who are prohibited from boarding commercial aircraft. There could be various reasons why an individual may end up on that list. I suppose none of us are on that list.

*Harold*: Probably not.

*Raj*: Right. So, the checks performed by airlines may be in the following order. They may first check whether a person is on a no fly list. If the answer is yes, they won't allow them to board. This check is performed at the very beginning of the process. If that person is not on the no fly list, they will check whether they have valid travel documents. If this check is passed, they will be allowed to board. If they are neither on a no fly list nor have a valid travel document, what should the airline do? Should they allow them to board?

*Alex*: No. As that individual is not fulfilling the entry requirements for the destination, they should not be allowed to board:

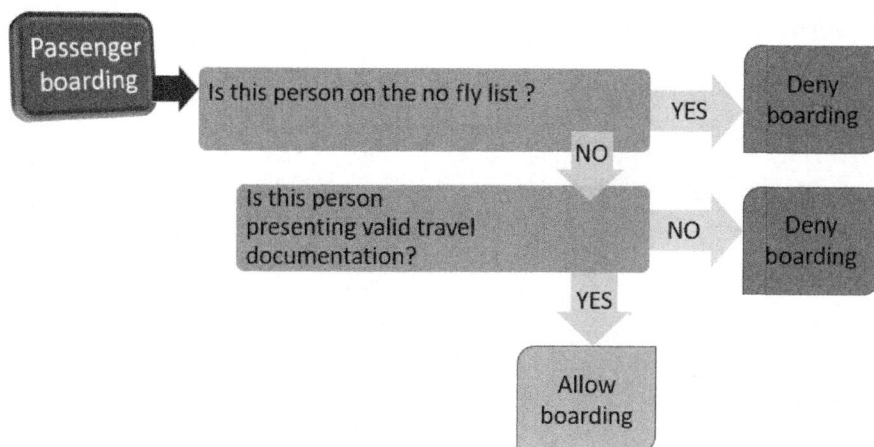

Figure 7.16 – A passenger boarding a commercial flight

*Raj*: Yes, you are correct. Policy evaluation logic in AWS is also not very different. Now, I want to clarify one thing here; although we have only talked about IAM policies (also referred to as identity-based policies), there are other policies that are also evaluated before a request is allowed or denied. You can use **resource-based policies**, **permission boundaries**, **access control lists (ACLs)**, and **session policies** to control access. And there's also another level provided by another service called **AWS Organizations**, which groups multiple accounts, and provides more policies called **Service Control Policies (SCPs)**.

*Berta*: Wow, there are so many ways to control access.

*Raj*: Yes, but the policy evaluation logic remains the same. Every API call starts by evaluating all applicable policies, merged together. If a deny statement is present for the request, the decision is made to deny the request, and no further processing is required. This is called an **explicit deny**. Somewhere in some policy, your request was explicitly denied.

If no deny statement is found, then a check is performed for a matching **allow** statement for the request. It is like verifying whether the request was explicitly allowed. If a matching allow statement is found, the request is allowed.

If there is neither a matching deny statement nor a matching allow statement, the request is denied. This is called an **implicit deny**:

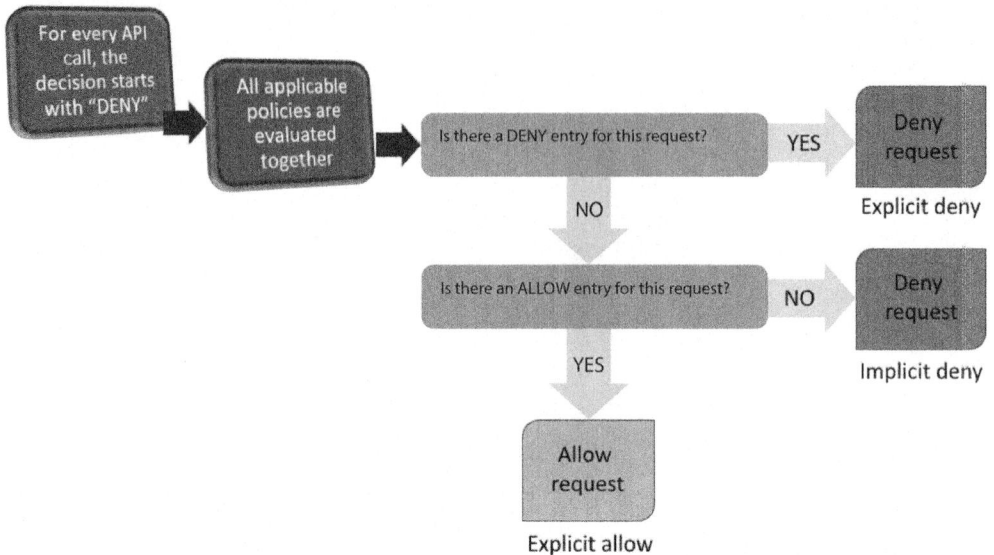

Figure 7.17 – High-level policy evaluation logic

*Harold*: I get it now. Thanks for explaining.

*Raj*: No problem at all. Let me do a modification before replying to Frank. I will modify the policy for SWMgr, as I don't feel comfortable with admin-level access permissions. I will create a new policy to meet the requirements and reply to the email.

Raj removes the SWMgr user from the Admin group and creates and attaches a new policy satisfying the requirements. The new policy looks like this:

```
1  {
2      "Version": "2012-10-17",
3      "Statement": [
4          {
5              "Sid": "VisualEditor0",
6              "Effect": "Allow",
7              "Action": [
8                  "iam:UpdateUser",
9                  "iam:UpdateGroup",
10                 "iam:CreateUser"
11             ],
12             "Resource": "*"
13         }
14     ]
15 }
```

Figure 7.18 – The policy for the SWMgr IAM user

Once he's finished, everyone thanks Raj for his exhaustive research on IAM and his explanations. They've seen IAM identities, IAM policies, and most importantly, the algorithm used to determine whether access is granted or not. Of course, there are more aspects to learn, but these are the ones that will be initially needed.

# Encryption and decryption

The team has now acquired a more complete knowledge of IAM, their identities, their policies, and how they can be used to grant or deny permissions to diverse resources. But a final consideration has to be made – encryption, which is not done by IAM:

*Alex*: I'd like to end the day with a very short description of encryption. Most data can be encrypted; sometimes, it is even mandatory, but it will be performed automatically, without you noticing it.

*Harold*: Are you talking about **encryption in transit** or **encryption at rest**?

*Alex*: With many of the services in AWS, you can choose both.

*Raj*: I assume encryption is not provided by IAM. I didn't see that on the documentation, and it seems a different feature. Probably a separate service?

*Alex*: It is called **KMS**, short for **Key Management Service**.

*Raj*: Keys?

*Alex*: Yes. The main purpose of KMS is encryption and, of course, other related tasks, such as decryption, signing, and verifying documents. All of them are provided as separate APIs, but in this case, these actions are not visible in the console.

*Raj*: How can they be used then?

*Alex*: When you configure at-rest encryption – for example, for an EBS volume, or a database – the service itself will request KMS to encrypt or decrypt. You don't see the process; it's done automatically for you. And it's very fast, by the way. You don't perceive any reduction in performance.

*Raj*: So, why is it called KMS again? For keys?

*Alex*: To encrypt or decrypt, AWS uses well-known algorithms, using symmetrical encryption, where both parts share one single key, or asymmetrical encryption, where a key pairs with a private and a public key. You have to decide who generates those keys, who stores them, and their possible renewal. KMS can also take care of your keys, so that's the reason the service is named so. Encryption relies heavily on these keys. KMS can generate them, store them, and provide the API for the services to encrypt or decrypt using the right key.

*Harold*: I assume you can also create your own keys and then store them on KMS?

*Alex*: Correct. Some companies have security standards where the keys must be generated by a team with specific tools and constraints, and then you import them into KMS. You can even ask KMS to use a hardware security module to store the really critical keys. If you use this feature, KMS will use another service, called CloudHSM, to provide the hardware needed.

*Harold*: This was for encryption at rest. What about encryption in transit?

*Alex*: In this case, you configure HTTPS or a similar protocol in the specific service – for example, a web server. All traffic will be encrypted. But these protocols need the encryption keys packed into a digital certificate. Certificates are provided by a different service called **AWS Certificate Manager** (**ACM**). We won't go into this now, but it's a similar idea; it can generate and store certificates for your services.

*Raj*: Thanks, Alex. Now, this is clear.

After a much-needed break, the team goes back to its work, thinking about how easy and robust the AWS IAM service is. The team has also had a look at encryption using KMS, and the relationships to other related but different services, such as ACM or CloudHSM.

One important thing everybody has quickly discovered is that filtering traffic in a VPC uses ports and protocols, but that does not involve user identities, so it's not considered *permissions* but instead *traffic filtering*.

While having a cup of tea, Raj realizes that it would be better if the team started focusing on monitoring, as it would be an activity that they may perform on a regular basis.

## Summary

The team has learned about the IAM concepts (users, user groups, roles, and policies) but is now facing some practical work ahead. With all they know now, they have to decide which IAM entities to create.

After that, they will create the right permissions grouped inside policies, assign them as needed, and test them exhaustively. Only then will they begin to create more users for other departments.

Gloria also wants to help the team more practically. She's planning to request an audit log after all those permissions are in place, to see whether everything is running as expected or not.

# 8

# Monitoring – Is Big Brother Watching?

Gloria has received a mail from her boss, with just a single *?* in the subject line. She checks the thread of related emails and finds out that it has something to do with an AWS notification. She reads the full thread with a worried look:

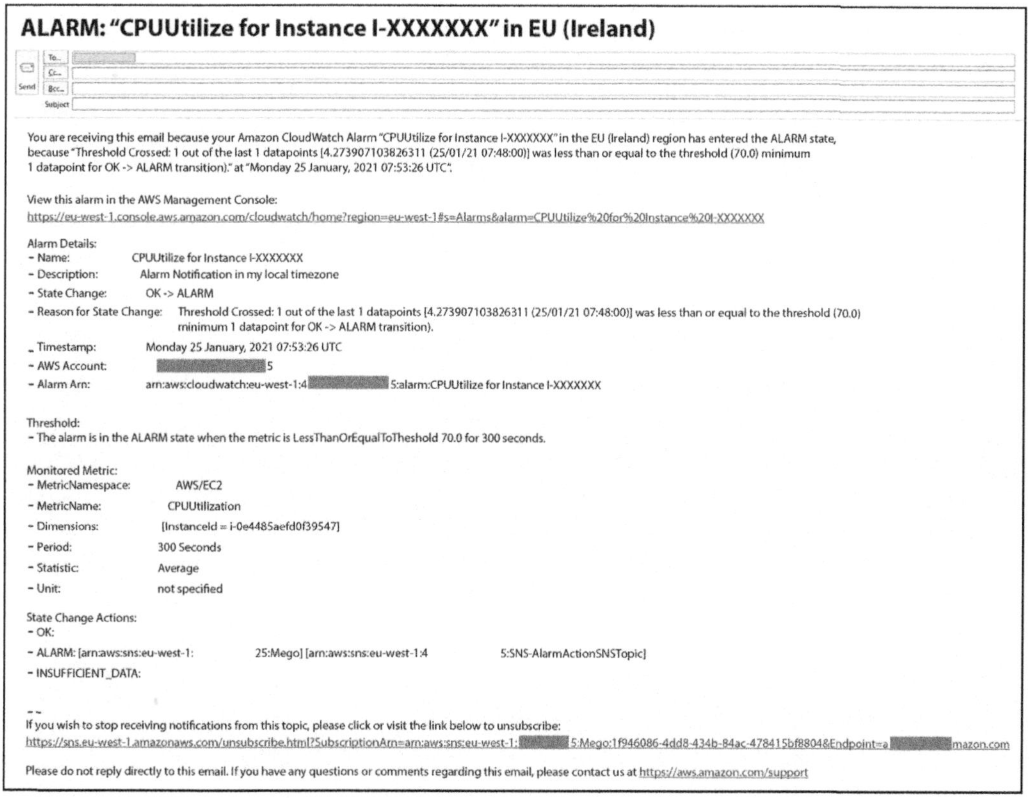

Figure 8.1 – Notification email

She realizes that these notifications are being sent to her boss's email inbox. She needs to make the IT team aware of it, to fix the possible issue soon. She replies to the last email, forwards it to the IT team, and quickly goes to the IT block.

## The notification emails

In the IT block, only Harold is at his desk.

*Gloria*: Good morning, Harold.

*Harold*: Good morning, Gloria. I've already read your email; I can explain it.

First, it is not a critical error. It is just a notification about a specific version of a runtime being deprecated. Second, let's make sure that your boss doesn't get worried about it, only us.

*Gloria*: That's nice. Where did you learn to read minds?

She chuckles. Before Harold can reply, the gang returns from their coffee break. They exchange greetings.

*Gloria*: It looks like I have got a new task for you today, and this one has taken on a higher priority. It's already in your inbox; Harold can also brief you about the issue.

*Alex*: I prefer live conversations rather than emails.

*Raj*: Me too.

As Gloria leaves, they all gather around Harold's desk.

*Berta*: What's all this about? Something critical?

*Harold*: Not at the moment, but it could become a very critical issue if we do not pay attention. It is about monitoring. We can't just deploy resources and forget about them. We also have to monitor them.

*Raj*: I was exploring this topic just yesterday.

*Alex*: Can we discuss the usefulness and importance of monitoring? Why should someone monitor their resources? Why is it so important?

*Raj*: The first thing that comes to my mind is knowing about the *performance* of all services. If you don't monitor, and this is valid for any system, you don't know whether your users are getting the expected performance. The user experience is critical; if the system is not fast enough, they'll file lots of complaints, or worse, they'll go to our competitors. You might think that a login request is fulfilled by your application in 2 seconds, but is it really happening in that time? We need to collect data to see how our resources are performing.

*Alex*: Agreed.

*Raj*: Another benefit of monitoring is checking the *utilization* of your resources. You have to know whether they are underutilized or overutilized. Underutilized resources mean you are basically wasting money. For example, if your application just requires an EC2 instance with 4 CPUs and 16 GiB of RAM most of the time, and you are using a 16 CPU, 64 GiB RAM instance for it, you are basically wasting your resources and paying extra for something that is not needed. On the other hand, if you have under-provisioned your resources, maybe you chose a very small-size database instance for a heavy-traffic application, your database will always be running at peak utilization and may not deliver the expected performance to your users. Eventually, they will start complaining about it.

*Harold*: And maybe they will even start using your competitor's application.

*Raj*: Yes, that's true. Utilization and performance are highly related.

*Charles*: I can also think of two more reasons to monitor, based on my experience as a network administrator. First, monitoring gives you data about your *service health*. You can detect when a service has become unhealthy and immediately take some corrective action on it. But if nobody has ever measured what a healthy service looks like, you won't be able to compare, detect the problem, and fix it. For example, the average traffic coming to your application on a normal day: if that traffic drops by a great extent, maybe it is because your system is unhealthy.

*Harold*: Yes, good point. We need to know what a typical usage pattern for our services is like.

*Charles*: The last thing I can think of is monitoring for *security*. Every application, even internal applications, may be a target for a security breach. Monitoring can help you identify these security breaches. Also, if you configure things properly, you can automate immediate responses to these breaches, instead of being paged in the middle of the night in an emergency to fix it.

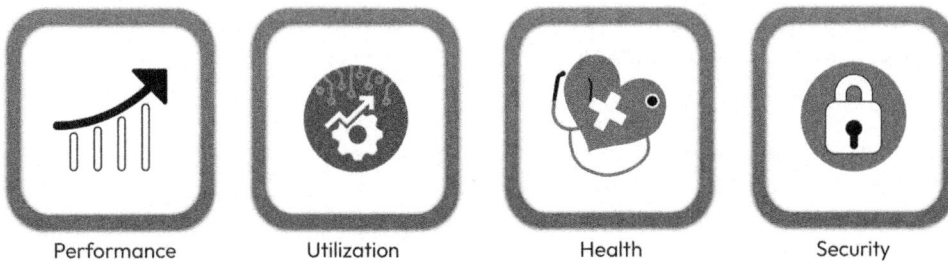

Performance          Utilization          Health          Security

Figure 8.2 – Why monitor?

*Alex*: The four concepts to monitor seem related: *Performance*, *Utilization*, *Health*, and *Security*. In the end, all of them guarantee the service is working in the most effective manner.

Fortunately, I don't have any of those pagers to wake me up at night. Even if I had one, it would make no difference. Every attempt, even the loudest lawn mower or loudest construction work, wouldn't hinder my sleep.

Everyone laughs.

## Monitoring – metrics and tools

Raj has recently been reading a lot about monitoring. He has found lots of documents on the web pages of their cloud provider, and he has also recovered some of his formal documentation from his time at college. Once all these have been processed and merged, he steps forward to provide his expertise to the team.

*Raj*: I've been reading a lot about what can be monitored. While you were explaining the advantages, something came to my mind from my university classes, so I found this in my old notes.

There was a clever guy who said that if something can be expressed in numbers, and that means objective numbers coming from a system, then you can learn about it and improve it. Conversely, what can't be expressed in numbers will not provide any sort of useful or satisfactory help. Or something similar, I don't exactly remember by heart.

*Alex*: Hey, it's like my neighbors! Both of them have laptops and they know I'm an IT guy. The first one always comes to me asking for help and says, "*My computer does not work,*" and that's always the entire problem description I will get. Of course, I just tell him "*Restart your computer.*" The other one says, "*The average latency of my disk today is about 90 ms. What could be happening?*" so he deserves a bit more help, and the solution is easier to find.

*Raj*: A really common scenario. I hate when my neighbors want me to fix their smartphones. Well, going back to what I said earlier, I have some homework for you. If you are curious, investigate the identity of the guy that I mentioned, and what exactly he said, as this is the base of every monitoring system.

*Berta*: Interesting, I'll do it. Well, the internet will help. But please give us a hint.

*Raj*: He is considered to be one of the fathers of the scientific method. He was made a Lord because of his many contributions to science and technology. He was born in Belfast in 1824, and he's buried in the same location as Sir Isaac Newton. And if you work in IT, at least in operations, you should know him.

*Berta*: This should be enough. I like the idea.

*Harold*: In the end, IT is science. We need measures using the scientific method, not just saying "*Reboot to see whether the problem goes away.*"

*Raj*: Fully agreed. Then, following this idea, everything that can be observed, measured, and described with numbers is what will be useful for our systems, and that's what we'll monitor. These concepts are called **metrics**. Of course, we need a monitoring system that captures all these metrics over time, stores them, and can use them.

*Harold*: I can imagine this monitoring principle is used in many daily situations. For example, my car shows lots of data on the dashboard, such as speed, RPM, level of gas in the tank, and temperature; the information is captured by the car sensors, but it has to be displayed properly to become useful.

*Berta*: This is interesting. There's lots of information in my car, but not all of it seems to be important for every purpose. For example, I like to check the RPM when I'm driving, especially fast, on some roads. However, my father drives on the motorway and he only checks the speed indicator, to avoid being fined.

*Raj*: Monitoring frequently offers multiple levels. Maybe you just check the speed, or maybe you also need the RPM and the oil level. And if you take your car for its regular maintenance, you'll see how they connect more sophisticated monitoring devices to display how the engine works internally. More metrics.

![Alex] *Alex*: Or if you are in a hospital room, the amount of monitoring can be astonishing depending on your illness. I assume this medical monitoring will generate alerts too.

![Harold] *Harold*: Coming back to our cloud, can we have something similar to a car dashboard for our services? It is clearly very useful, and I can imagine it's also easy to set up.

![Raj] *Raj*: Yes, very easy. The first thing to know is that all monitoring for all services in the cloud is centralized in a single service called **CloudWatch**. Every other service you use (S3, EC2, RDS, practically all of them) will collect its own important metrics and will send them to CloudWatch. In the end, CloudWatch will keep an internal database with all the metrics being received.

![Alex] *Alex*: So, CloudWatch receives metrics from all services. Once there, what can you do with them?

![Raj] *Raj*: Lots of possibilities. You can simply display them using simple, predefined graphics. Or you can create complex dashboards with much more fancy visual graphics. Or export all metrics to other systems. Or act upon them. This is an example of how these simple visuals might look:

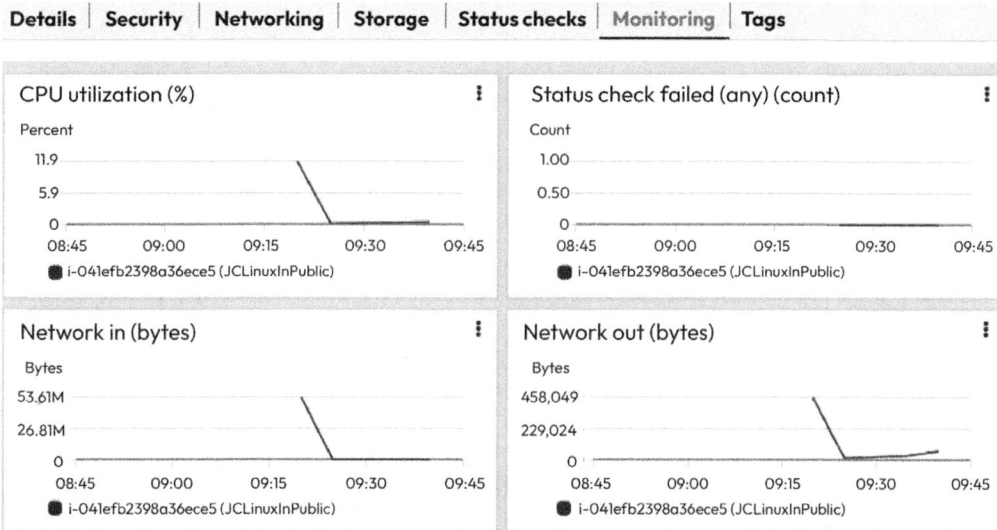

Figure 8.3 – Simple metrics

![Berta] *Berta*: Nice. I assume you can build and configure what and how to display. Are all these graphics in the CloudWatch console?

![Raj] *Raj*: The most common ones are just visible within the console for your service. You have seen some of them in the EC2 or RDS console, in the **Performance** tab. This way, you don't have to navigate between different consoles for common tasks.

But if you are dedicated to monitoring, it's better to build a dashboard with all the metrics you need together, maybe coming from the multiple services forming a solution. For this, you use the CloudWatch console. There are some visual styles you can use and, unlike your car, you can build multiple dashboards with the style and look you want, like these:

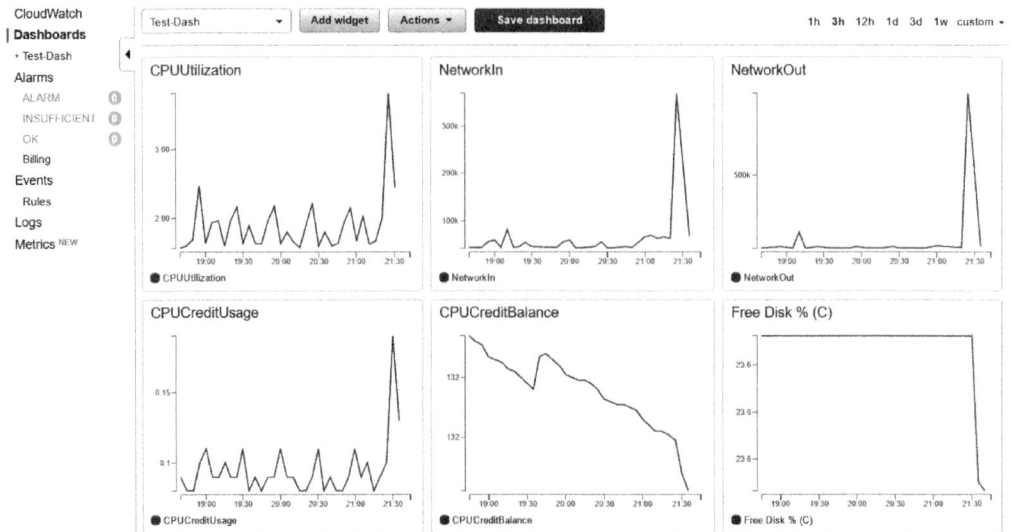

Figure 8.4 – Building your dashboards

Alex: I have a fantastic idea. Let's create separate monitoring dashboards. One of them will show a stable fixed number, or maybe a number that is constantly decreasing. Then, we can label it something like *Errors Today*, and display it as big as possible. Then, we create other dashboards with the real metrics, performance, errors, or whatever we might need for our daily monitoring. Every time Eva or the press visit us, we can show only the first dashboard, on a huge monitor:

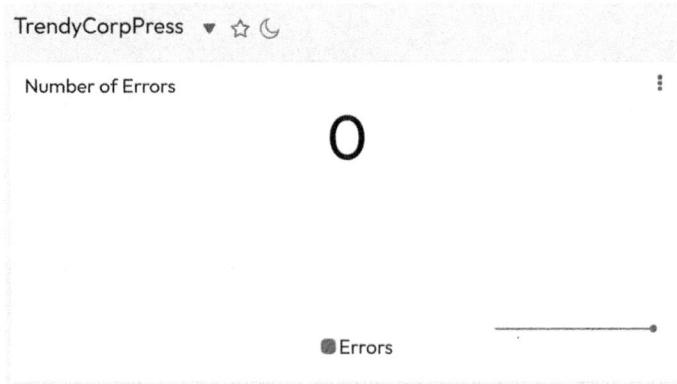

Figure 8.5 – Dashboard for the press

Harold: I'm not sure whether this is a terrible or a fantastic idea. Let me think about it. In the end, it's your own company's data. But maybe it's probably something that doesn't match the company values on transparency.

*Alex*: Noted, Harold. Raj, can we get metrics from every AWS service?

*Raj*: Yes, CloudWatch will automatically receive metrics from most of the AWS services. For example, you can measure how many bytes you are storing in an S3 bucket.

But that's not all. CloudWatch also offers an API where you can provide your own metrics. For example, the number of errors in your application, the number of users who clicked the **I don't like this** button, or even the temperature of the room.

*Alex*: How can you add the temperature of the room? Is there an AWS service for that?

*Raj*: No, but that's a **custom metric**. You just capture it with a sensor, using IoT, a small board computer line, a Raspberry PI device or similar, a laptop, or a server running on-premises. All of them can call the CloudWatch API to store it in the cloud. Remember, it has to be a number, something that can be measured. That's a metric.

*Harold*: You mentioned you can count, for example, the number of errors found in an application?

*Raj*: Yes, that way you can integrate the metrics from AWS services with any metrics provided by your applications, all displayed in a single dashboard per environment if you wish. And you can also build alarms on this data to react automatically to any issue.

*Harold*: But how do you capture the application data? Does the application logic have to be modified to call the CloudWatch API?

*Raj*: That's an option if you want to do it. There's even an easier way: you can download an agent that will monitor the log files you specify. It will check for specific text (for example, error codes) and will count all of them (remember, we only work with metrics). Then, it will send the count to CloudWatch in real time. No need to write any code, and the agent is free.

*Berta*: That means we can choose between **agent-based** and also **agentless** monitoring?

*Raj*: You can have both. Agentless is always running there. Each service will automatically send its "default" metrics to CloudWatch; you don't need to install anything extra. But if you are using EC2, you can optionally install this free monitoring agent, and it will send additional *custom* metrics coming from inside the instance; examples of these custom metrics only available with agent-based monitoring include **virtual memory usage** and **disk utilization**. The monitoring agent is also a logging agent, which allows you to specify a list of logs you might want to send to the cloud too. We need to keep in mind that if we decide to install the monitoring agent, each EC2 instance will need specific IAM permissions to send and store metrics and log entries into CloudWatch; these permissions, as we all know already, need to be specified within one or more IAM policies that need to be assigned to an IAM role; and lastly, the IAM role must be attached to each single EC2 instance.

*Berta*: It seems using agent-based monitoring is like monitoring your house. The building has some fire detectors in the common areas, but you can also add yours inside your apartment. They will provide an extra layer of protection.

*Raj*: Exactly. In the cloud, the service behavior is monitored, but if you wish to monitor what happens inside them, in your applications, you have to use the agent.

*Charles*: But that means you can capture different metrics from multiple applications, multiple services, and multiple instances. You'll get lots of data constantly arriving from many sources. How do you find the problematic issues amongst this mountain of metrics?

*Raj*: First, you have to choose which metrics you want to capture and also which ones to display in dashboards. Of course, you capture only the metrics that are useful to you.

Then, you can choose how frequently to do this capture. For example, checking whether a disk is almost full can be done every 15 minutes, not every second.

Finally, there's a convention to give strict names to the captured metrics. For an AWS service, you specify a namespace, which is formed by the prefix AWS and the service name. If it is a custom metric coming from your applications, you have to provide your own prefix, different from AWS. In both cases, you then provide a **dimension**, specifying, for example, which instance you're referring to and the metric names. The sequence of stored data will have values and also timestamps:

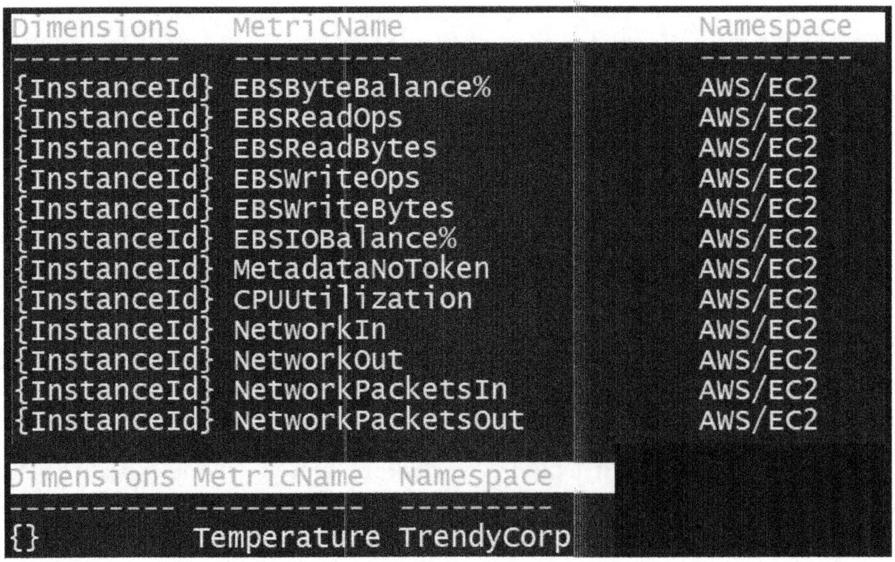

```
Dimensions     MetricName                    Namespace
----------     ----------                    ---------
{InstanceId}   EBSByteBalance%               AWS/EC2
{InstanceId}   EBSReadOps                    AWS/EC2
{InstanceId}   EBSReadBytes                  AWS/EC2
{InstanceId}   EBSWriteOps                   AWS/EC2
{InstanceId}   EBSWriteBytes                 AWS/EC2
{InstanceId}   EBSIOBalance%                 AWS/EC2
{InstanceId}   MetadataNoToken               AWS/EC2
{InstanceId}   CPUUtilization                AWS/EC2
{InstanceId}   NetworkIn                     AWS/EC2
{InstanceId}   NetworkOut                    AWS/EC2
{InstanceId}   NetworkPacketsIn              AWS/EC2
{InstanceId}   NetworkPacketsOut             AWS/EC2

Dimensions MetricName    Namespace
---------- ----------    ---------
{}         Temperature   TrendyCorp
```

Figure 8.6 – AWS and custom namespaces

*Raj*: Anyway, CloudWatch takes care of all these naming conventions. You only need to use them if you plan to use the API to write your own metrics.

Alex: Hey, look what I've found! I'll print this on a big poster under our monitoring system:

*"I often say that when you can measure what you are speaking about and express*
*it in numbers, you know something about it; but when you cannot measure*
*it, when you cannot express it in numbers, your knowledge is of a meager and*
*unsatisfactory kind; it may be the beginning of knowledge, but you have scarcely, in*
*your thoughts, advanced to the stage of science, whatever the matter may be."*

Now the team has learned the monitoring basics. They know where all these ideas come from, and the *meager knowledge* poster has been printed and posted in the middle of the room. They understand what metrics are and how CloudWatch captures these metrics, the possibility to add an extra monitoring agent, their names, and how to display them on fancy dashboards. They take a short break.

## Reacting to events – alarms

The team return from their break, with Alex quite excited to know more about alarms.

Alex: I know an alarm is a self-explanatory word, which I can relate to my morning wake-up alarm, but can you explain to me what alarms are in the AWS context?

Raj: Sure. Let me try. When you set a wake-up alarm on your clock, you set a time for it; as soon as the clock reaches that time, an action is taken. In this case, a sound will be played. Similarly, alarms in Amazon CloudWatch can trigger an action based on the breach of the metrics threshold you have defined. In your alarm clock, the threshold is the time that you have selected. In Amazon CloudWatch, you can select a metric to monitor and define a high or low threshold, and if the metrics fall outside of the defined levels, any action that you have defined as part of the alarm will be executed.

Alex: I get it. I have two questions. First, can we have multiple alarms for the same metrics? Second, can we have multiple actions for an alarm?

Raj: The answer to both of your questions is yes. In your alarm clock, you can obviously set multiple alarms, maybe one for waking up, another for afternoon lunch, and another to remind you to drink water. And within an alarm, you can define multiple actions. You may have a smartwatch, which may allow you to play a sound as a wake-up alarm, and maybe it can hook up to your home automation system and can also take another action to maybe activate your coffee machine and also to open the curtains:

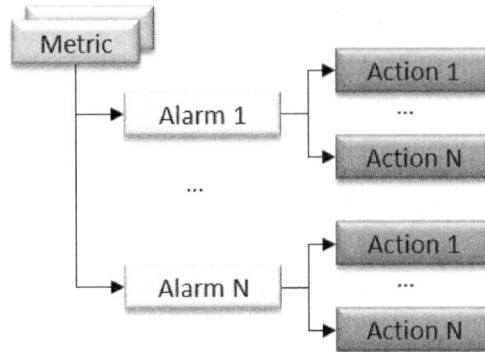

Figure 8.7 – Metrics, alarm, and action

*Alex*: So, maybe I can set an alarm on Amazon EC2 instance CPU utilization metrics and define a threshold of 70%, set up a notification to be sent to the administrator of the system, and also log an incident in a ticketing system.

*Raj*: Yes, you are right. You can do all that.

*Alex*: I don't understand a practical use of a lower threshold breach though.

*Raj*: We discussed custom metrics a few minutes ago. Let's say we have an e-commerce application and the operations team collects custom metrics about the number of orders received per hour. If the system is getting fewer orders than expected, maybe someone should be notified about it, as it may be due to some error in the application.

*Alex*: That makes sense. What are some of the common actions?

*Raj*: the first thing to be aware of regarding an alarm is that there are three states for an alarm—*OK*, *Alarm*, and *Insufficient Data*. See this table I've prepared:

| Alarm State | Description |
| --- | --- |
| OK | Technical meaning = The metrics are within the threshold. |
| | In simpler terms = Everything seems okay. No red lights. |
| ALARM | Technical meaning = The threshold of the metric is breached. |
| | In simpler terms = Something is wrong; better check. |
| INSUFFICIENT_DATA | Technical meaning = The metrics data is not available. |
| | In simpler terms = Give CloudWatch some time to collect the data. If the state persists, it could also indicate that a specific resource is not used at all, that a resource is stopped, or lastly, that there could be a misconfiguration. |

Table 8.1 – Possible alarm states

An action defined in an alarm is only invoked in response to a state transition. So, if an alarm enters the *Alarm* state or returns to the *OK* state, you can tie in actions with it.

*Alex*: Okay.

*Raj*: Let me now explain actions to you. The most common action is to notify someone. For example, in the case of a fire alarm, the action is to warn people about the fire, and this can be done in multiple ways: a loud warning sound, flashing lights for people with hearing difficulties, flashing fire symbols on elevators, and so on. To send notifications, you can use Amazon Simple Notification Service, which allows you to send emails, SMS, integration with a ticketing system, and more.

*Berta*: Any other common actions?

*Raj*: For Amazon EC2 instances, you can also configure an alarm to stop an instance, terminate or reboot it, and also recover it. A very basic rudimentary example could be to monitor the CPU utilization of an Amazon EC2 instance running a batch job, which is using a lot of CPU. And you can set an alarm to stop the instance when CPU utilization is below 10%, hoping that the job has finished and that's why you don't need the instance in a running state. This is a very primitive way, but I hope it gives you an idea. In the real world, I would prefer to have some other metrics or events to verify job completion status.

*Berta*: I have a question. Let's say the job running on the Amazon EC2 instance goes into a state of low CPU utilization for a fraction of a second. Can that result in the instance being stopped?

*Raj*: It depends. When you configure an alarm, you can set up an evaluation period for the state change. So, you may define that if CPU utilization is less than 10% and it stays below 10%, let's say for a time period of 15 minutes, only then trigger the alarm. This way, you can cut down on the noise generated by an alarm.

*Berta*: That's interesting.

*Raj*: Also, if you are using another AWS service called AWS Systems Manager for incident management, you can create incidents in it, which your IT team can look into.

*Charles*: This is nice. Can we also display alarms on a dashboard?

*Raj*: Yes, you can. And it displays different colors also to visually tell you the state of the alarm. For the OK state, it is green; for the Alarm state, it is red; and for the Insufficient Data state, it is gray.

You can also configure cross-region and cross-account alarms. So, in a central dashboard, you get the status of multiple resources from different AWS accounts and different AWS regions. Alarm state change history is retained for 14 days. You can also use the automatic dashboard, which allows you to focus on a single AWS service and displays important metrics. Also, you can share the dashboards with people who do not have AWS access. You can share dashboards with someone's email addresses. One thing to note is that a dashboard cannot display events.

*Alex*: What is an event?

*Raj*: People sometimes get confused with events and metrics. Let me clarify it for you. **Metrics** are data about your system performance. An **event** describes state changes of your AWS resource. While CPU utilization of your Amazon EC2 instance is a metric, when an Amazon EC2 instance is started or stopped, that is an event. Lots of AWS resources automatically emit events when a state change happens. You can use these event changes to trigger actions through the use of rules.

*Alex*: I get it, but this sounds to me like an alarm because it is also based on state change.

*Raj*: Alarms and events are not the same; there are very specific differences. Let me send you more details by email:

| | Alarms | Events |
|---|---|---|
| Usage | Monitor metrics | Monitor actions (changes) |
| Trigger | Metric threshold breach | Rule-based<br><br>Self-trigger at schedule |
| Can be added to CloudWatch Dashboard | Yes | No |
| Customization | Support custom metrics | Support custom events |
| Does it always indicate a problem? | Mostly | Not always |
| Example | Triggering an AutoScaling policy based on some metrics (e.g., sustained CPU usage) | An instance getting launched/terminated because of the AutoScaling policy |
| Allows you to take proactive action | Yes | No |
| Common actions | Message to Amazon SNS topic<br><br>EC2 Actions (start/stop/terminate/recover, etc.)<br><br>Scale and AutoScaling group<br><br>Create incident in AWS Systems Manager<br><br>Create OpsItems in AWS Systems Manager Ops Center | Message to Amazon SNS topic<br><br>Trigger AWS Lambda functions<br><br>Run commands through AWS Systems Manager<br><br>Orchestrate multiple actions using AWS Step functions<br><br>Integrate third-party applications as event targets (using EventBridge, which is the new version of CloudWatch Events) |

Table 8.2 – Differences between alarms and events

The team is busy reading the email. After a while, Charles speaks up.

*Charles*: I hope you can control what functionality is available to different users through AWS **Identity and Access Management (IAM)**.

*Raj*: Absolutely, Amazon CloudWatch integrates well with AWS IAM.

Berta has compiled all information related to metrics, alarms, possible states, and events. She plans to build a short reference document to use in all future projects. But she finds something important is still missing: logging. So, she plans to ask her colleagues some questions about it.

# Logging

Alarms seem to be very useful. But Berta has realized something extra might be needed in their daily operations.

*Berta*: I've got a question for you. How can we store a log of everything that has already happened? Alarms seem very useful to fix a problem in a hurry, but I'd also like a more reflexive point of view. For example, analyzing what happened in the past after some time, or looking for root causes or correlations.

*Charles*: Back to the scientific method again?

*Berta*: Remember, IT involves engineering. So, how can we get audit logs in the cloud?

*Alex*: Is that like the logs they used on ships long ago? Everything considered important had to be logged there. For example, *"03:32, the 1st observer thinks he has seen a mass of ice."*

*Harold*: And not just long ago. Have you seen *Star Trek*? All episodes start with the Captain's log on the Enterprise.

*Charles*: And talking about enterprises, all companies must maintain business logs for all financial operations. Otherwise, they would get into some serious problems with the tax department. Or, in a factory, the traceability of everything that was manufactured. And I imagine modern ships also keep navigation logs.

*Raj*: You can see how important logs are. Everything considered important is stored there, so it can be reviewed later. And it can be as easy as a set of text files.

And, as Berta mentioned, they're extremely useful. You can look later for root causes, correlations of events, and trends. It's a fantastic way to prove something happened, to know when it happened, and analyze and learn about it after some time, maybe not in a hurry, as the issue might have been already fixed.

*Berta*: But are you talking about security logs or operation logs?

*Raj*: In general, both of them. There's not a terrible difference. All these logs keep entries with all the relevant info and a timestamp. Technically, it is not a huge difference if they have to log an IAM access, or maybe a server that ran out of memory. In all cases, the entry is saved in a text file, that is, the log file.

*Harold*: But there's a non-technical difference. A security log will probably contain more sensitive information. So, these logs should be stored separately and protected with more strict permissions.

*Raj*: Agreed. We'll comment on this difference later. But the most important issue is receiving these entries and storing them on the file promptly, so no fact is lost. And, of course, to have enough storage for them, which is not an issue in the cloud.

*Berta*: Okay. So, how is this done in the cloud? I assume it should be really easy, but how is this managed? Is there any new service we have to learn?

*Raj*: AWS takes a nice approach to logging. Let's imagine you need to capture log data quickly and safely to a file. Of course, that is probably needed for every service you're using, such as EC2, S3, EBS, VPC, and databases. Do you think every service provides its own logging?

*Charles*: I imagine not. Otherwise, lots of the code to write in a file would need to be replicated to every service. But, on the other hand, each service needs separate logging.

*Raj*: Exactly. Every service captures the information that has to be logged and sends it to CloudWatch. It uses a very similar approach as when metrics were captured.

Inside CloudWatch, there's a feature called **CloudWatch Logs**. It will receive all logs from all services and will be in charge of storing them in separate log files. These files are stored in S3 storage, for the many advantages we have already discussed. But all access to them is centralized in the CloudWatch Log menu.

Logs can be grouped together into **log groups**, so they can be easily found. For example, all logs related to a full solution involving multiple services will be together, or simply creating a tree based on the service name. Look, these are some of my test log groups:

| | | |
|---|---|---|
| ☐ | /aws/rds/cluster/davinci/error | Never expire |
| ☐ | /aws/rds/cluster/dbauroracluster/error | Never expire |
| ☐ | /aws/sagemaker/studio | Never expire |
| ☐ | /ecs/ConsoleAppNetCoreForContainer/ConsoleAppNetCore… | Never expire |
| ☐ | /ecs/ContainerWithWEB/ContainerWithWEB | Never expire |
| ☐ | /ecs/first-run-task-definition | Never expire |
| ☐ | /ecs/JCDockerLinux/JCDockerLinux | Never expire |
| ☐ | JCTemperature | 1 month |

Figure 8.8 – Some log groups

*Harold*: I see. It's like a corporation; all the tax books will be stored separately, maybe per company and per year. I assume each group can contain multiple files.

*Raj*: Yes. Or any small business. For example, in my car repair shop, they keep a separate log for all operations done on each car, and another one for accounting.

*Alex*: I can assume these logs can become very large. Could they fill the hard disk? It happened to me several times on my home PC.

*Harold*: This is a frequent and serious problem with on-premises servers. The logs fill the system disk and the computer stops completely. To recover the situation, you usually have to delete the logs, so the system starts again, but the logs are usually lost.

*Raj*: Well, first, when you configure the service, you choose only the events you'd like to log, and the rest will be ignored. For example, take a look at the **RDS** menu; you'll be able to choose what gets logged:

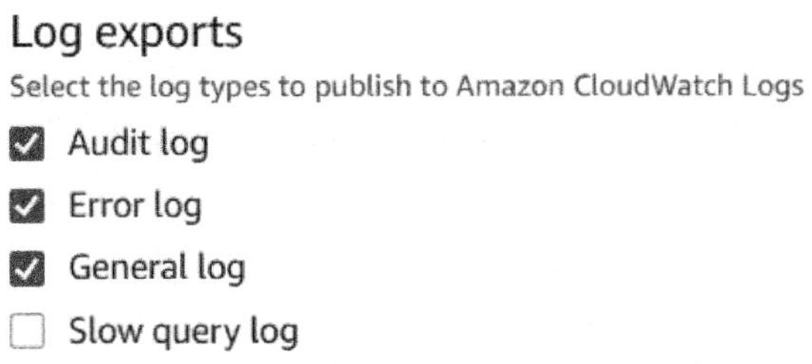

## Log exports
Select the log types to publish to Amazon CloudWatch Logs

☑ Audit log

☑ Error log

☑ General log

☐ Slow query log

Figure 8.9 – Logging options in RDS

*Raj*: Or in VPCs, there are *VPC flow logs* where the selected traffic can be logged:

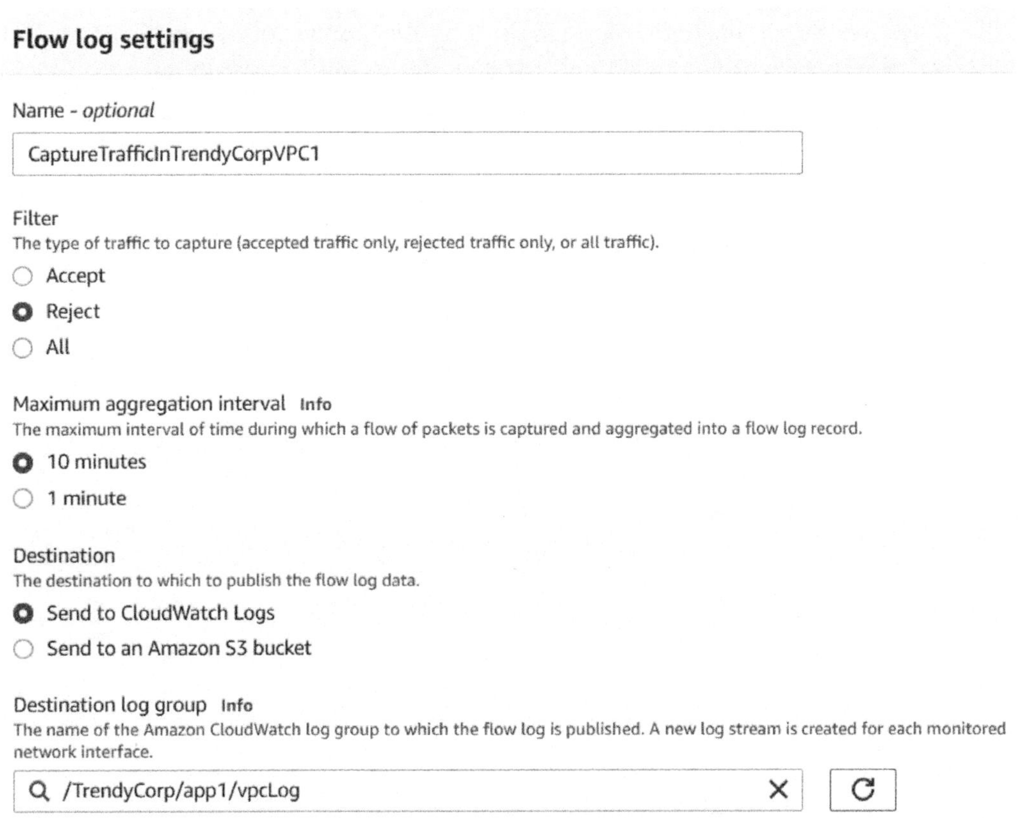

## Flow log settings

Name - *optional*

CaptureTrafficInTrendyCorpVPC1

Filter
The type of traffic to capture (accepted traffic only, rejected traffic only, or all traffic).

○ Accept

⦿ Reject

○ All

Maximum aggregation interval  Info
The maximum interval of time during which a flow of packets is captured and aggregated into a flow log record.

⦿ 10 minutes

○ 1 minute

Destination
The destination to which to publish the flow log data.

⦿ Send to CloudWatch Logs

○ Send to an Amazon S3 bucket

Destination log group  Info
The name of the Amazon CloudWatch log group to which the flow log is published. A new log stream is created for each monitored network interface.

🔍 /TrendyCorp/app1/vpcLog                                    ✕    ⟳

Figure 8.10 – Flow logging options in a VPC

*Raj*: Then, even if many entries are captured, there's no space problem. As they are stored in S3, you'll have the maximum storage defined by S3, which is…

*Berta*: Unlimited! No more *full disk* errors!

*Raj*: And that takes us to the last thing. If you store lots of huge logs for a long time, you'll end up paying some real money, even in S3. For that purpose, you can define a **retention policy**. CloudWatch Logs will remove old logs for you, automatically. Of course, we have to consider the retention time we need for each log, so it can be used during its intended lifespan.

*Harold*: Cool. Can we use any API to write on these logs, let's say, from our own applications?

*Raj*: For sure. It's very similar to the API we used to provide metrics. You can create your own **custom logs**, and even use an agent if you don't want to write the code.

Of course, you need permission to write on any log. You don't want any unauthorized user to add fake entries to the tax log or to any other log.

*Alex*: During my last holiday in Rome, I visited a museum, and at the exit, there was a huge book where every visitor could write something, such as "*Alex and his friends were here.*" Everybody had permission to write or modify other visitors' entries, which was really fun.

*Harold*: I can imagine this visitor log could provide lots of useful business insights to the museum owners.

*Berta*: Talking about this, once the logs are stored, how can we use the data in them?

*Raj*: You have multiple options; you can, for example, read them from your applications, and build your own analysis. Or something simple, such as opening them in a spreadsheet.

You also have a tool called **Log Insights**. You make queries over the logs using something very similar to SQL.

*Berta*: You mean I can do SELECT * FROM LOG WHERE Message = 'Error'?

*Raj*: Something similar. Try it. The tool will help you write the correct query:

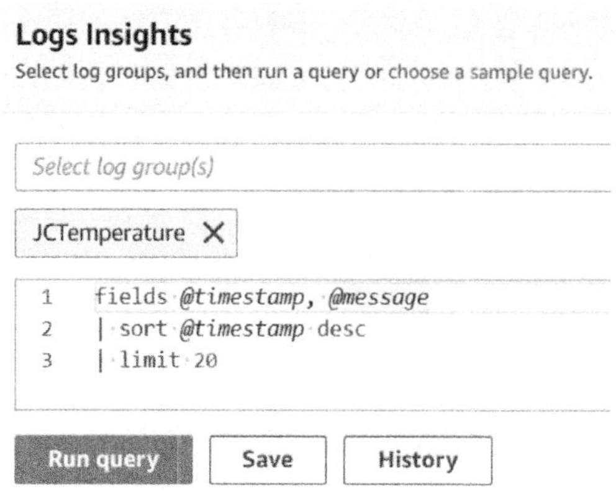

**Logs Insights**

Select log groups, and then run a query or choose a sample query.

| Select log group(s) |
| --- |

| JCTemperature ✕ |
| --- |

```
1    fields @timestamp, @message
2    | sort @timestamp desc
3    | limit 20
```

| Run query | Save | History |
| --- | --- | --- |

Figure 8.11 – Log Insights

*Harold*: I suppose we can also subscribe our applications to a log.

*Alex*: What is the subscription thing? I've heard about it several times since I joined TrendyCorp.

*Berta*: It's a common concept when you write applications or systems that communicate. One component could be interested only in some data. For example, look in a log for all entries related to errors. The application can continuously read all information and then filter only the needed data. But this requires lots of I/O, lots of CPU, and probably lots of traffic, and it's a crazy way to get information.

So, a **subscription** is a good solution. If the service provides it, the application can say *I'm interested in this data, but only if it follows some conditions. Every time you have a new record following the given conditions, only then notify me. In the meantime, I'll stop asking*. That means, the client is now subscribed to some data, but not all of it.

*Alex*: I get it. It's like driving my nephews to a resort in my car. During the trip, they always keep asking "*Are we there yet? How much time is left?*" constantly, non-stop. I then try to force them to *subscribe* to my notification service, by constantly saying "*Play now with your consoles, I'll tell you when we're almost there,*" but it doesn't work in this case. They are hardcoded to poll constantly for the entire trip, 500 km, and back.

*Raj*: Fortunately, CloudWatch Logs allow some applications to subscribe to a log in real-time. With a feature called **metric filter**, these applications will be notified only when the specific filtered data is logged. Then, the data can be streamed automatically to another destination. This will probably need a Lambda function.

*Alex*: And what is a Lambda function?

*Raj*: A generic piece of code you write. But I think we can wait for some weeks until we see them; let's now concentrate on the logging itself. One more thing about metric filters: you can connect a metric filter to a CloudWatch alarm; in this way, every time the filtered data is logged, the alarm goes into the ALARM state, and, optionally, you can get notified with Amazon SNS.

*Harold*: Then is there something special about security logs?

*Raj*: Well, yes, security is always *special*. Most of the logs can be related to the security of an application, for example. They can be treated by CloudWatch logs in the same way; for example, applications logging the entries they want.

But there's a special type of log: the one internally generated by every AWS service, every time you attempt an operation, by calling the API. In this case, all calls, no matter whether successful or failing, are sent to a different service called **CloudTrail**. As you mentioned, these audit logs are much more sensitive, and they are separated in this different service. They can be used to analyze access and your company compliance, and you can even create policies based on the attempts logged here.

To protect these logs (which are called **trails**), you can even manage permissions through which you specify who can read which logs. Lastly, based on what we have learned recently, we have to remember that these logs can also be encrypted with AWS KMS.

The team, and especially Berta, are much happier now. They feel they have a complete overview of all monitoring options now that logging has been explained. Berta will be able to complete her work document by adding all these new concepts (security logs, operation logs, and custom logs) as well as the two services used to handle them (CloudWatch and CloudTrail) and the related options to effectively use the information inside the logs, such as log groups, querying with Log Insights, and the possibility to subscribe to specific entries.

# Summary

After a long day, the team has learned how to monitor with CloudWatch. Gloria meets them around the coffee machine to verify what they've learned.

*Gloria*: Well, everyone. What have you found out during the day?

*Alex*: That every service in the cloud can be monitored… and should be monitored. And that we have so many metrics available.

*Harold*: That we can define alarms based on that monitoring and take action immediately.

*Berta*: That we can also have logs for all operations, and even a security audit log.

*Gloria*: Fantastic, and what's your action plan for the next steps?

*Berta*: I'm building a short reference document with all the services we need, CloudWatch and CloudTrail. We'll also build together a comprehensive list to document which metrics will be needed, how frequently to measure and display them, and which alarms to build over them.

*Harold*: I'm also studying how to integrate our old applications and systems with CloudWatch monitoring, including some on-premises servers and maybe also our IoT environment.

*Charles*: I'd like to investigate how to export our monitoring data to other systems. Some other teams might benefit from it. This should be easy, thanks to CloudWatch. And maybe we can also get information in the other direction, importing their data into our monitoring, similar to what Harold mentioned.

*Raj*: And I'm thinking of something more ambitious. We can build a predefined list of likely problems, how to detect them, and how to fix them, automatically. This has to include the original request about obsolete versions of code and many more, as, of course, this will grow with the issues we might find in the future.

Gloria is really happy with the knowledge acquired by her team and their attitude. But she has perceived the most important thing: the team realized the value of monitoring. Living without monitoring seems a very dangerous way to run an IT shop.

# Further reading

- Scientific method: `https://en.wikipedia.org/wiki/Scientific_method`

- CloudWatch: `https://docs.aws.amazon.com/cloudwatch/`

- CloudWatch Metrics: `https://docs.aws.amazon.com/AmazonCloudWatch/latest/monitoring/working_with_metrics.html`

- CloudWatch Alarms: `https://docs.aws.amazon.com/AmazonCloudWatch/latest/monitoring/AlarmThatSendsEmail.html`

- CloudWatch Logs: `https://docs.aws.amazon.com/AmazonCloudWatch/latest/logs/WhatIsCloudWatchLogs.html`

- CloudWatch Events: `https://docs.aws.amazon.com/AmazonCloudWatch/latest/events/WhatIsCloudWatchEvents.html`

- CloudWatch Tutorials: `https://docs.aws.amazon.com/AmazonCloudWatch/latest/monitoring/CloudWatch-tutorials.html`

- CloudTrail: `https://docs.aws.amazon.com/cloudtrail/`

# 9

# Scalability – I Scale to the Moon and Back

The team is feeling more confident as they are progressing steadily with their understanding of the cloud. With monitoring in place, they get lots of data related to the performance, security, and utilization of the system. This data can also help them in planning for future workloads or defining a workload characteristic. Another important question they have in mind is whether to use the flexibility of the cloud infrastructure to handle variable traffic and to design scalable architectures.

Berta enters the office and finds that Alex is already there.

*Berta*: Good morning, Alex. Looks like you have come in early today.

*Alex*: Well, yes, relatively early. I was trying to buy a product from an online flash sale, but I could not complete the purchase. The whole process seems very slow; I thought it was because of my home network, but it is the same in the office too.

*Berta*: Oh. Then it's probably not a network speed issue. Is this flash sale huge in size? I mean, will lots of customers be trying to buy products during this time?

*Alex*: Oh, absolutely. This sale is offering healthcare products at half price, and I guess everyone is buying them in abundance. On regular days, the checkout process is very smooth, but today, after this sale started, it seems so slow.

*Berta*: The seller probably didn't estimate the volume of the traffic correctly and the application didn't scale well. A system with a variable volume of transactions should be designed for scalability.

Harold barges into their conversation.

*Harold*: Good morning, Alex and Berta. Alex, can you try opening this website for me? My daughter wants to buy something from this website, but it is not opening up on her laptop.

He shows a web address on his phone to Alex.

*Alex*: You are not alone, Harold. It seems there is an issue with their systems; I am also trying to buy something from them, and it is taking ages to just search for a product.

*Harold*: Oh. My daughter said that this is a limited-time sale. Their systems are probably not able to scale with the load. Scalability is always a concern in these situations.

*Alex*: This is the second time in a few minutes I am hearing about scalability. I think this is also a concern for our public-facing e-commerce portal, isn't it?

*Harold*: Yes, it is. I remember the last time we had a new product launch and people went crazy buying it. Our systems were not ready for that much load and crashed: not a good thing for a business's reputation at all. I remember being in the office for three straight days and nights before we could fix it.

*Berta*: That's not good at all. I have similar stories from my previous work as a database administrator. Scalability works slightly differently for databases. You need to scale up most databases, not scale out.

They realize that scalability is a crucial factor for an application. In the earlier days of computing, the load on an application was predictable most of the time, as it was probably used by a fixed number of employees within a company. But now, applications are not local anymore; a web application can have users coming from all over the world, at all times, and may get different amounts of traffic and requests. Designing a scalable architecture is crucial for an application's success.

## Scaling – several resources, several types

Alex begins to ask Harold and Berta his questions about scalability.

*Alex*: Isn't scale-up and scale-out the same thing?

*Harold*: No. Let me first tell you about scalability, and then I will go into this difference. **Scalability** is the ability of a system to grow or shrink in a graceful manner. It allows it to function continuously when conditions such as traffic or volume change. Some examples could be how efficiently a system performs when user traffic is increased multifold, how well a database responds to a higher volume of queries, or even how an operating system performs on different types of hardware.

So, a scalable system must perform with the same stability and performance, even if the load on it increases. It can obviously take advantage of increased resources and offer better performance to customers.

And that means the performance of a system is directly related to its scalability possibilities. Performance efficiency is one of the pillars of the **Well-Architected Framework** defined by AWS.

Scalability describes a design or architecture that is growth friendly. And, as someone said, *scalability is a prerequisite for high availability*. If any application stops working when the load increases, it's evidently not highly available.

*Alex*: Got it. By the way, what's that **Well-Architected Framework** you mentioned?

*Berta*: I know about that. It's a comprehensive list of errors, common mistakes to avoid, and of course, their counterpart, or best practices. They are divided into six categories, called **pillars**.

You have to follow those rules to have a well-architected environment, hence its name. You can find all of them on the AWS web page, under the **WAF** acronym.

*Harold*: Thanks, Berta. Now, when it comes to designing a scalable system, there are two approaches: either to *scale up* or *scale out*. For an end user, both may seem to offer the same functionality, but both solve specific problems in different contexts.

In a scale-up approach, you either replace the system with a bigger-sized system or add more resources to the same system. For example, you could scale up your storage by adding more capacity or adding more RAM to the existing system or faster disks.

*Berta*: Or you can replace your old, slow laptop with a newer laptop.

*Harold*: Exactly. But scaling up is a viable solution only up to an extent, as you may hit a limit on how much extra performance a single component can provide. Maybe the operating system has a limit to support only a maximum amount of memory, or a server has a fixed number of slots to add more RAM to it. Scaling up is also to referred as **vertical scaling**.

*Alex*: Got it. What kind of systems will be well suited for this approach?

*Harold*: The most common example is increasing the storage of an existing system. Often, a system may need more storage capacity, and this can be achieved by adding more resources to the existing system.

*Berta*: Also, most commonly, you will find relational databases are scaled up. You either add more capacity, in terms of CPU, RAM, disk, and network, to the existing server or replace the existing server with a bigger server:

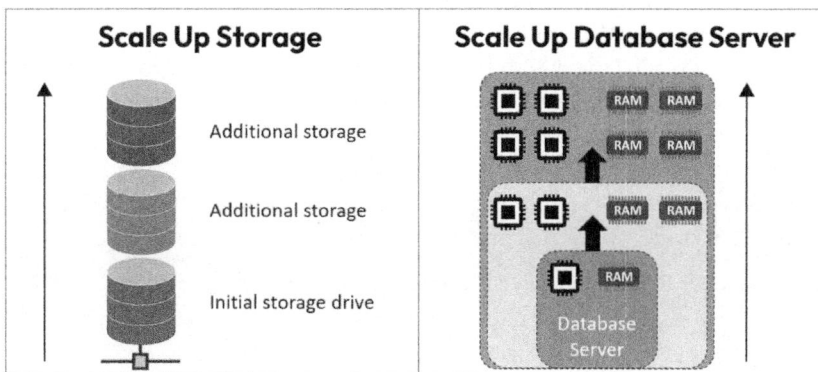

Figure 9.1 – Scale up (bigger resource)

*Harold*: That's a good example, Berta. Let's now talk about the other option. When we scale out a system, we focus on adding more servers to our architecture and spread the workload across these servers. Most of the time, you are creating a logical group (sometimes referred to as a cluster) of resources (**nodes**) that work together as a single unit. When more capacity is needed, you simply add more nodes to the logical group. Scaling out is also referred to as **horizontal scaling**:

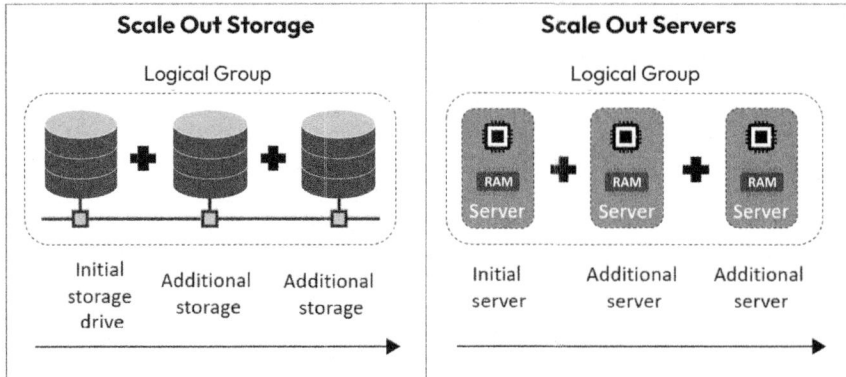

Figure 9.2 – Scale out (more resources)

*Alex*: I understand now. What kind of systems will be well suited for a scale-out approach?

*Harold*: Any system that is distributed, which means most of the more modern technologies. Thinking about the applications running on them, a stateless system would benefit most from it.

*Alex*: A stateless system?

*Harold*: Let me give you an example. When you contact a support center, let's say for your bank account, is it the same agent who responds to you every time?

*Alex*: Nope. Every time, I speak to a different person.

*Harold*: Right, and they always ask you some questions initially, such as your name or account number to pull your details from a central system. They don't memorize all this data. If you are requesting them for something, let's say a replacement card, they will note down all these details. They may also give you a tracking number for further communication. That number is an identifier to find the state (specific data) of your call. If you call again and provide that identifier, the agent will be able to pull details of your request using it, and without asking you the same repeated questions, they may be able to help you faster. Basically, they are operating in a **stateless** manner, not storing anything locally.

*Alex*: I get it now. So, keeping state information in a central place allows a call center to add more agents when needed. The relevant information is not stored locally in only one of the systems, but in a centralized repository, where all can access it.

*Harold*: Exactly; keeping the information in a central system allows you to scale out. Every agent is trained to do the same work.

Similarly, in a scale-out system, each node is able to perform the same tasks. Whichever server receives your request will have access to the same data, and will be able to fulfill the request. This is totally stateless: the server receives each separate request, serves its results, and once done, it will forget about it. In this way, you can quickly add more servers when needed, without the need to maintain or copy local information on them.

*Alex*: This is like an airline check-in desk. I could go to any desk and do my check-in for the flight, and when there are lots of people in the queue, they may open more check-in counters, offering the same service.

*Harold*: Yes, that's a good example of scale-out.

*Berta*: Most non-relational databases, such as Amazon DynamoDB, offer the ability to scale out horizontally, handling huge amounts of data, with a steady performance.

*Harold*: Yes. And when you scale out, you won't hit any individual node limits as the maximum supported memory or physical space to attach disks.

And we have another important difference related to high availability; in a scale-up system, if the node fails, the application will be down, as it has only a single node serving all the requests. But in a scale-out system, if one node fails, only a percentage of the total capacity is lost, as the rest of the nodes can keep the application running.

*Charles*: Are scalability and elasticity the same thing?

Everyone realized that Charles was also listening to their conversation from his desk.

*Harold*: No. They are different. **Elasticity** takes advantage of scalability. Scalability is required for elasticity, but not the other way around. Mostly, elasticity is automatic and reactive to different factors and conditions. As an example, if you're running an e-commerce platform for Christmas decorations, it is expected that you will have a lot of demand in December. And, obviously, you want your e-commerce platform to be scalable in order to handle the seasonal demand. You have to design your platform in a way that it could scale. After Christmas, you won't have the same demand on your platform, and you won't want to pay for the peak utilization when there is no demand. This is where elasticity comes into play. You can reduce your resources to cater to the lower level of demand, and next year at Christmas time, you can again ramp up your resources. In the end, it's saving you money but also guarantees the business runs smoothly when the demand is higher.

*Alex*: I have a very funny example to share with you. Don't laugh. I am sure you all know about a fictional comic and movie character *The Hulk*. This character is most of the time seen as a normal human being (Dr. Bruce Banner), but when he gets emotionally stressed, he transforms into a muscular humanoid with immense physical strength. This is, I would say, a scale-up operation. And on the other hand, there is another character, called Ant-Man, who has a special suit with size-shifting powers, which can make him shrink to the size of an ant or allow him to be a giant. I would say that is elasticity. And yes, please don't judge me, I read lots of comics.

*Harold*: Haha, yes, that's a good example. I would also admit that I also like reading comics. The Hulk becoming a green thing is a scale-up operation, where an individual is increasing their strength to meet the demands, and scale-out would be when all these hero characters come together and form a team.

*Berta*: That's a brilliant example. And sometimes, an actor or actress goes through a rigorous regime to increase or reduce their body weight to meet the need of the film character they are portraying. I would say that is elasticity.

*Harold*: Nice example. I have a more detailed comparison table for it, let me send it to you.

Harold sends the following details in an email. Everyone reads it and gets back to the conversation:

| | Scalability | Elasticity |
|---|---|---|
| **What is it?** | **Scalability** is the ability of a system to uphold its functionality when the size or volume changes | **Elasticity** is the ability to dynamically manage available resources for addressing the size or volume |
| **Use case** | To meet the static increase in the workload | To meet the dynamic increase in the workload |
| **Type** | Strategic operation | Tactical approach |
| **Focuses on** | Design/architecture | Operations |
| **Resource provisioning** | To exceed future demands | To meet the present demand |
| **Consideration** | Medium- and long-term predictions | Short-term demand |
| **Execution by** | Typically scheduled | Typically triggered by automation |

Table 9.1 – Scalability versus elasticity

*Alex*: So, how does AWS handle scalability?

*Harold*: Some of the AWS services offer built-in scalability, such as AWS Lambda. For some services, such as Amazon EC2 or Amazon DynamoDB, you can configure it as required. These services may have one or more scalable dimensions. For example, in DynamoDB, you can auto-scale the read and write capacity of the table. In Amazon EC2, you can auto-scale the number of instances; in Amazon ECS, you can auto-scale the number of tasks, and in Amazon Aurora, you can auto-scale the read replica count.

Be careful with the terms: there's scaling, but also **auto scaling**. Some services will scale automatically based on the load; others can scale, but you have to do it manually.

*Charles*: I was researching some details and found there are three services offered by AWS that can help you with scaling. They are:

- Amazon EC2 Auto Scaling

- AWS Auto Scaling

- AWS Application Auto Scaling

*Berta*: All these services sound similar to me.

*Charles*: Their names may sound similar, but they serve different purposes. Amazon EC2 Auto Scaling focuses only on Amazon EC2 instances. You can configure an **Auto Scaling Group** (**ASG**) by defining a base template, a minimum and maximum configuration, and some conditions for auto scaling. Once configured, the ASG will launch the minimum number of instances, but based on the load and the defined conditions, it will add or remove more instances. It offers different policies to control the adding or removing of instances.

*Berta*: I can imagine the minimum value is used to enforce a minimum guaranteed capacity, and the maximum value will set a cost limit… as you don't want to scale out with no limits, and find a huge bill at the end of the month.

*Charles*: Exactly. Scalability must be performed inside a monitored environment.

*Berta*: That's nice. What about AWS Auto Scaling?

*Charles*: AWS Auto Scaling is a more automated approach for generic resources, not only for Amazon EC2. If you have a three-tier application, where the frontend is on Amazon EC2 and you are using DynamoDB as the database, you can configure unified scaling for multiple resources by following predefined guidance. It also identifies scalable resources powering your application without any manual identification. And through its scaling plan, you can choose to scale for availability, cost, or balance both.

*Berta*: So, it supports both compute and database scaling.

*Harold*: This sounds more like scaling the whole application, so how is AWS Application Auto Scaling any different?

*Charles*: Application Auto Scaling supports a much wider range of services; you can even scale your custom resources. I guess Raj was experimenting with this feature for one of our custom applications. He has created a table regarding the comparisons of different scaling options in AWS. Let me forward it to you.

Charles forwards the table to each of them, and they all check the details.

| | **Amazon EC2 Auto Scaling** <br> **(Launched in 2009)** | **AWS Auto Scaling** <br> **(Launched in 2016)** | **AWS Application Auto Scaling** <br> **(Launched in 2018)** |
|---|---|---|---|
| What? | Focus on Amazon EC2 Instance Auto Scaling | Build scaling plans for application scaling for multiple resources across multiple services | Automatically scale resources for individual AWS services beyond Amazon EC2 |
| How? | Automatically add or remove EC2 instances according to conditions you define in an ASG | Automatically discover scalable resources in your application and configure scaling for all the resources in a single place using predefined guidance or configure it individually | Through a scaling plan, you can track specific CloudWatch metrics and use AWS CloudFormation templates for a custom resource |
| Which? | Amazon EC2 instances | Amazon EC2 <br><br> Amazon EC2 Spot Fleets <br><br> Amazon ECS <br><br> Amazon DynamoDB <br><br> Amazon Aurora | AppStream 2.0 fleets <br><br> Aurora replicas <br><br> DynamoDB tables and global secondary indexes <br><br> Amazon **Elastic Container Service (ECS)** services <br><br> ElastiCache for Redis clusters (replication groups) <br><br> Amazon EMR clusters <br><br> Amazon Keyspaces (for Apache Cassandra) tables <br><br> Lambda function provisioned concurrency <br><br> Amazon Neptune clusters <br><br> SageMaker endpoint variants <br><br> Spot Fleet requests <br><br> Custom resources <br><br> and many more |

Table 9.2 – Several types of scaling

*Harold*: That's interesting. It's a very flexible way to achieve scalability. Now, I think we can have our lunch break and continue the discussion afterward.

The team has started uncovering the various aspects of scaling. With a clear understanding of terms such as scale-up, scale-out, elasticity, and application state, they now know how different components of an application can be finetuned for scalability. Of course, the cloud plays an important role in it as it offers virtually unlimited resources for storage, network, and processing. The AWS offerings related to scalability would make their work much easier because of the ease of use and automation.

## Rules to configure automatic scaling

Everyone comes back from lunch. They very much enjoyed learning about the new cloud concept of scalability that they faced in the morning, and they kept talking about it during their lunch too. Berta didn't join them, as she had decided to start studying the AWS documentation to learn about how the services mentioned before actually work.

*Harold*: I feel I didn't have lunch, but another team meeting instead. Charles, we are too old to keep up with these young colleagues.

*Charles*: Haha, speak for yourself, Harold.

*Alex*: …and I think we just touched the surface, this morning. We discussed scalability, the different types of scalability we can implement, and which kind of services our cloud provider offers to manage all that. But now, we need to understand how the implementation is achieved. I'm pretty sure Berta has already got the information we need to start. Oh, here she is! Berta, how was your lunch?

*Berta*: Well, I would say productive! I quickly ate a sandwich because I was looking for a deep dive into how AWS Auto Scaling works. I got a lot of information that I would like to share with you as quickly as possible. I think we need to seriously reconsider some architectural aspects of what we have built so far; scalability is a critical aspect.

*Harold*: Go ahead, Berta.

*Berta*: Okay. We've already clarified the differences between the three technologies, Amazon EC2 Auto Scaling, AWS Auto Scaling, and AWS Application Auto Scaling. For simplicity, I will refer to them as *auto scaling* in general, especially when referring to EC2 instances. When it is time to implement all of this, we will figure out (using the AWS documentation) which specific technology we will need to use.

*Charles*: Sounds good to me.

*Berta*: One more thing. Earlier, we also talked about vertical versus horizontal scalability. Well, although both ways to scale have pros and cons, generally speaking, the best way to scale is horizontally; that's why we should focus on it a bit more and this is also the way to scale that we should have in mind during today's discussion.

*Alex*: Thanks for making sure everything will be clear, Berta.

*Berta*: Perfect. Let's start then! Following the AWS documentation, I've found out that there are four different ways to scale; let me draw them on the whiteboard:

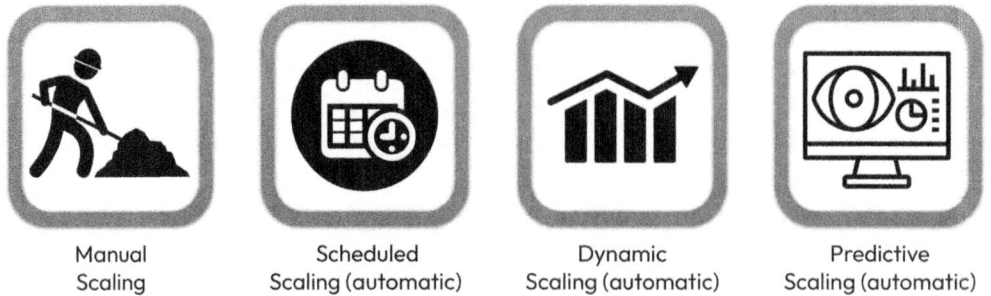

| Manual Scaling | Scheduled Scaling (automatic) | Dynamic Scaling (automatic) | Predictive Scaling (automatic) |

Figure 9.3 – Types of scaling

The first one is manual, as the name says. Evidently, the other three types are automatic—the ones we should consider with more detail.

**Manual scaling** is pretty easy to understand; imagine we have an ASG in place, so a group of a specific number of EC2 instances is up and running, let's say two. Imagine now that the average CPU utilization of the group suddenly increases. We see it because we are monitoring it. Remember, we have CloudWatch.

*Alex*: Yes, monitoring is always in place.

*Berta*: Exactly. It's possible that the CPU increase could be a bad thing. Now, the performance of the whole group is not good anymore. What can we do? We can simply modify the size of the ASG by manually providing a higher value, let's say four. This will trigger the creation of two new EC2 instances; the ASG is now formed by four instances that can easily manage the spike in traffic. Once the spike has gone and the traffic comes back to normal, we can just manually modify the size of the group again, but this time, with a lower value—maybe the original value, two. Easy, right?

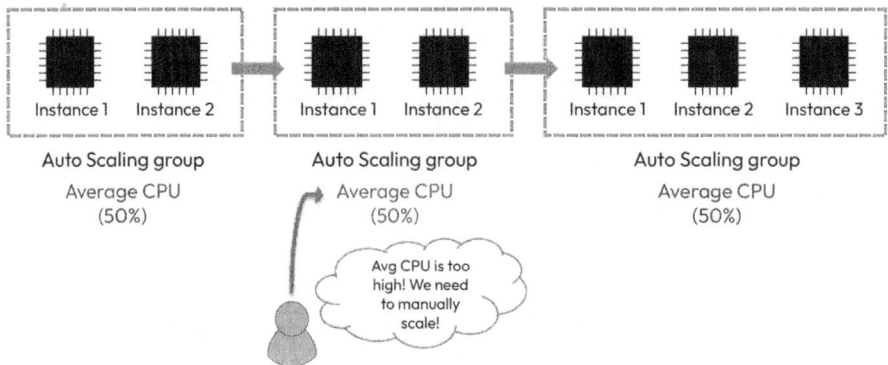

Figure 9.4 – Manual scaling

*Charles*: Yes, it is. So far so good.

*Harold*: It's like what usually happens in a supermarket when suddenly there are more people than expected waiting in a long queue because there is only one cashier line open. The manager may decide to ask another employee in the supermarket to open an additional cash desk; in this way, the two cashiers can now quickly handle all the people in the queue:

Figure 9.5 – Queue at the supermarket

(Source: Photo by Marakero Nai NOOCRPWEO, at https://commons.wikimedia.org/wiki/
File:HK_TKO_%E5%B0%87%E8%BB%8D%E6%BE%B3_Tseung_
Kwan_O_Plaza_%E8%A1%97%E5%B8%82_K-Mart_Fresh_
Market_%E4%BD%B3%E5%AF%B6%E9%A3%9F%E5%93%81%E8%B6%85%
E7%B4%9A%E5%B8%82%E5%A0%B4_Kai_Bo_Food_Supermarket_queue_
check-out_point_August_2022_Px3.jpg, used under Creative
Commons Attribution-Share Alike 4.0 International license.)

*Alex*: Oh yes, true! So, I need to just adjust the minimum value and the ASG will have additional instances to match the value.

*Berta*: There's a better way. There is another parameter in the ASG called **desired capacity**. You want to have more instances right now, but you don't want to change the minimum value. So, if you are adjusting the desired capacity as per your requirement, you are basically using manual scaling:

# Autoscaling Group

Maximum Size

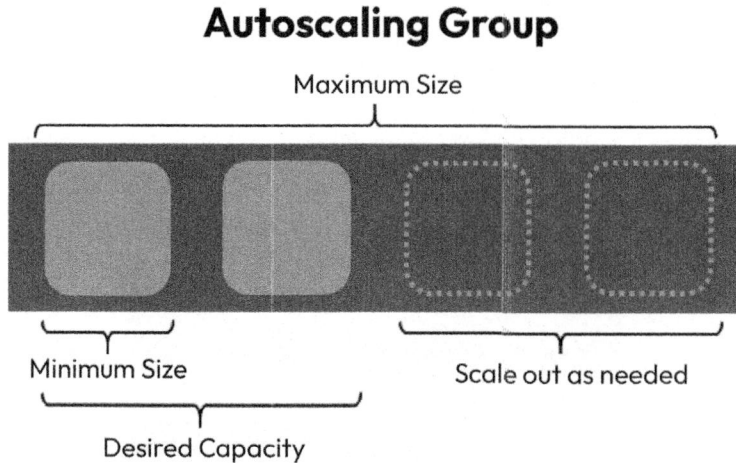

Minimum Size

Scale out as needed

Desired Capacity

Figure 9.6 – Auto scaling group

*Charles*: By the way, it's called manual scaling, but it can be done by a simple script you can run. *Manual* here simply means it's not done automatically by AWS.

*Berta*: True. Cloud providers always suggest to their customers to scale automatically, rather than manually, and there are three ways to do it.

The first one I studied during lunchtime is **scheduled scaling**. You need to create one or more scaling actions, defining when and how to scale. Imagine the same auto scaling I mentioned before, with two servers currently.

Let's assume you know your traffic patterns—when it's lower or higher. For example, traffic is pretty stable most of the time, but between 2 p.m. and 4 p.m., there is a spike in requests. This happens from Monday to Friday; during the weekend, nobody uses the application, and traffic is very low.

In cases like these, it's recommended to automatically scale your group of instances by defining a schedule. In my example, it would be the perfect scenario for two scheduled policies like these:

*Scheduled action #1: set desired capacity to 4 at 2 p·m· on Mon-Fri (scale-out)*

*Scheduled action #2: set desired capacity to 2 at 4 p·m· on Mon-Fri (scale-in)*

Figure 9.7 – Adding capacity by scheduling

*Charles*: That was clear too. I have another example: think about transport in big cities. A long time ago, it was identified when rush hours start and end. During these peak hours, the number of trains or buses increases; meanwhile, it decreases outside these peak hours. Everything is based on a pre-defined schedule.

*Alex*: You are amazing, folks. Everything is so easy to understand. Berta, I would also add one more thing. Based on your previous example, I'd propose adding two additional scheduled actions for the weekend, considering that nobody uses the application:

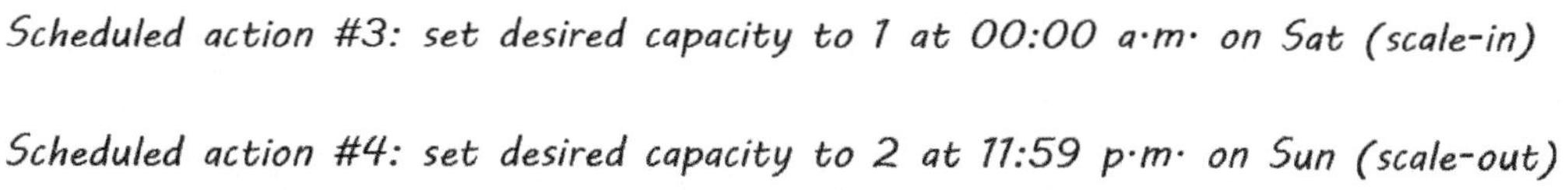

*Scheduled action #3: set desired capacity to 1 at 00:00 a.m. on Sat (scale-in)*

*Scheduled action #4: set desired capacity to 2 at 11:59 p.m. on Sun (scale-out)*

Figure 9.8 – Reducing capacity by scheduling

*Berta*: Awesome, Alex! You are right! So, as I said, scheduled scaling is pretty useful when you know the load your application deals with every day. Like transport in a big city.

*Charles*: I guess there are two other types of scaling, right?

*Berta*: Yes, you are right, Charles. The next one is **dynamic scaling**, which is the most sophisticated. It's still a type of automatic scaling, but it takes place dynamically only when the load requires it, so only when there are *spikes*. The main difference with scheduled scaling is that those spikes are not predictable. In this case, we configure auto scaling to scale only when a spike in load takes place.

*Alex*: But how does auto scaling know when there is a spike in the load?

*Berta*: Well, we learned this recently: by keeping our resources under monitoring! Currently, most of the resources that are part of our environments are monitored, and auto scaling will define some CloudWatch alarms. When the state of a resource changes, or when a performance metric value is over (or under) a certain threshold, those alarms will go into the *ALARM* state. Everyone remembers them, right?

*Alex*: Yes, sure.

*Berta*: So, we can create **auto scaling policies**, where we can specify *how* to scale, and then we attach each of them to specific CloudWatch alarms to specify *when* to scale.

Continuing with my example, we have our ASG that currently has two instances. Suddenly, the CloudWatch alarm used to track the average CPU utilization of the group goes above 90% (our threshold), so that's the moment when a scaling policy will be triggered, and new servers will be added to the group:

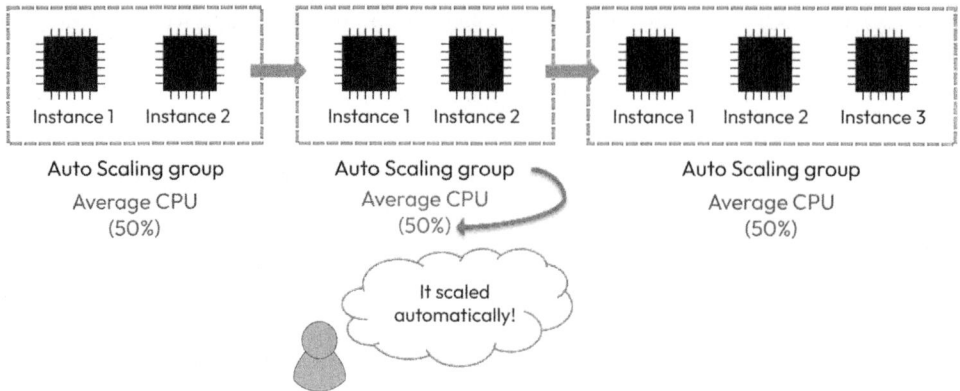

Figure 9.9 – Dynamic scaling

*Alex*: Can you explain it with an example?

*Berta*: Okay, so I know you drive a car. Does your car have a cruise control feature?

*Alex*: Yes, it does.

*Berta*: Can you explain to me in simple terms what it does?

*Alex*: It is an automated feature to help you drive at a constant speed. You can set a desired travel speed, and you don't have to accelerate or slow down your vehicle. You don't have to keep the accelerator pressed, which saves foot fatigue and stress when you have to drive for a long time. Also, it is fuel efficient as you cruise at a consistent speed rather than accelerating sharply, which consumes more fuel.

*Berta*: That's exactly what dynamic scaling can do for your application. Inside a scaling policy, you can set a target. Let's say CPU utilization should not go beyond 60%, and auto scaling will ensure that it is maintained. If, because of a heavy load on your application, the CPU utilization goes beyond the threshold, auto scaling will add more instances to distribute the load. Thus, you will always have a consistent load in all instances.

*Alex*: I get it now.

*Charles*: Another similar example is a thermostat in an air-conditioning unit. It is basically a regulating component that senses the temperature of a room, and if the temperature goes up, it starts the air conditioning to maintain the desired temperature.

*Harold*: Perfect, thanks, Berta and Charles, for all these explanations. I think now it's time for **predictive scaling**. The name scares me a bit; I can imagine there is some kind of artificial intelligence behind that feature—robots are coming and they will take our jobs!

*Berta*: Haha, I don't think we are at this point already, but you are right, Harold. Predictive scaling is a feature that, from what I quickly read from the AWS documentation, leverages **machine learning** (**ML**).

*Charles*: Hmm, interesting. I hope that the ML model used behind the scenes is implemented and maintained by AWS and that we don't have to take care of it.

*Alex*: Hey, wait a second! Machine learning? Model? What are we talking about here?

*Charles*: I'm so sorry. I didn't want to add more complexity and generate confusion. ML is a topic we are not going to cover for the moment. So, please Berta, go ahead.

*Berta*: The predictive scaling that auto scaling provides doesn't require any knowledge about ML, I can confirm that. At least from our side. As the name says, this type of auto scaling can *predict* when a spike in traffic will take place, and then it will scale automatically accordingly. We have to specify *how* and *which* metrics it has to consider for its predictions but then, it works automatically without any other actions from us.

*Harold*: It's still not clear to me how it knows in advance when it's time to scale.

*Berta*: It takes a look at the past! Based on the traffic that took place in the past, more precisely in the last 14 days, auto scaling creates an hourly forecast for the next 48 hours. You need to define a **scaling strategy** through which you specify which is the metric that the feature has to consider in order to scale. It can be CPU utilization or traffic such as *Network In* or *Network Out*.

*Alex*: Amazing! But what about if the traffic suddenly shows unexpected behavior? Predictive scaling will not be able to predict it, or it could predict a scaling activity that could not be useful.

*Berta*: This is true; that's the reason this kind of setting would need a bit of *predictability* or, in other words, *predictable spikes*. But it can be used together with scheduled scaling, for example.

*Charles*: Anyway, folks, these technologies based on ML are getting more precise year after year, so I see a lot of value in them, even now. This policy action is proactive rather than reactive.

*Harold*: Berta, thank you for your explanation and for the effort you put into studying all that stuff. As you said before, we've discussed groups of servers (ASGs), but this logic can be applied to other resources as well, right? This is what we anticipated this morning when we talked about scalability in general.

*Berta*: Yes, absolutely, I can give you some examples. Remember DynamoDB, the non-relational serverless database? Well, with Auto Scaling for DynamoDB, it will automatically scale the performance capacity of the table, rather than manually, by also leveraging CloudWatch alarms. Another one: Auto Scaling for Aurora allows you to scale automatically the number of read replicas. As we have all learned today, scalability is a benefit that you get when in the cloud, especially if this is managed automatically. Technologies like auto scaling seem to provide exactly this. I'm super excited to learn more about it in the next few days.

# Some considerations – how do users interact with a variable number of servers?

After the previous explanations, Harold is thinking about a more philosophical question: how to use the existing applications, which were never designed for the cloud, in the new auto scaling environment. This question will lead to lots of interesting possibilities and many improvements in high availability and security.

*Harold*: Thinking about EC2 auto scaling, I have an important doubt.

*Charles*: Shoot.

*Harold*: Let's imagine a real but simple scenario. We have our company web server, with all those web pages served using HTTPS from EC2 instances. Remember, these are dynamic pages, with our price list, products, catalog, orders, and so on. So, we can't use S3 for them.

*Alex*: Yes, I remember we commented to create a web server in EC2, similar to the one we had on-premises.

*Harold*: Exactly. But now we have defined an EC2 ASG for it. That means we'll have several running instances, following the rules we've set up, with a minimum and a maximum. The group will scale in or out, and we'll have a changing number of instances, depending on the load at the moment.

*Berta*: I can imagine the minimum value is used to enforce a minimum guaranteed capacity, and the maximum value will set a cost limit... as you don't want to scale out with no limits, and find a huge bill at the end of the month.

*Charles*: Right, that's one of the purposes of scalability, to provide enough power depending on changing demand. I seem to remember we set up a minimum of 4 instances, and a maximum of 16. Where's your issue?

*Harold*: You're only thinking as a system administrator. Each one of these instances alone will work perfectly, I'm pretty sure. But how are the clients going to connect to an application that is running on a variable number of instances that could change at any time? Where to connect? We'll have 4 IP addresses, or maybe 5, or up to 16. And think also about the application. Earlier, it was running on a single instance, but now it will run in a variable number of instances. Which one of them is going to keep the user context?

*Charles*: You're right, we have to consider all these points of view. Fortunately, this is a pretty common scenario. I can imagine there are more than a few web servers running applications in the world. Our cloud provider already has a solution for all these reasonable doubts.

*Harold*: Please tell us. For me, it seemed a complex problem, but I can imagine the solution will hide all this complexity from us poor on-premises IT engineers.

*Charles*: Come on, Harold... You already know more about the cloud than many nerdy cloud engineers. Let me explain this.

*Harold*: Great! Please, Charles, go on.

*Charles*: The first problem we have to address is how to send the traffic and IP connectivity to a variable number of servers. Let me start with a scenario: sometimes, you go shopping at a large supermarket and there's only one cashier line open. The management perceives there's a queue growing, so they open another cashier line. Which one to use? In many supermarkets, there's a sign, a display, something to tell you which cashier is free, so you go there.

*Alex*: Something similar to the airport check-in we talked about earlier.

*Charles*: Yes, many systems offer a similar scheme. The number of open cashiers or counters can change, so have you thought about how we decide which one to use? They probably use an electronic display to route you to the next available one. Some companies might use a person instead, to tell you where to go.

*Alex*: So, we can assume there's also a cloud service for this purpose.

*Charles*: Yes, you've got the gist of it. In this case, it is a networking service, called **ELB**, or **Elastic Load Balancer**. It is frequently used with Amazon EC2 instances, so you can find it on the Amazon EC2 menu page.

*Harold*: Cool, we are already using a load balancer for on-premises traffic.

*Charles*: But you'll see there are some differences. First, it has to connect a single endpoint to multiple destinations, so think of a load balancer as an upside-down funnel:

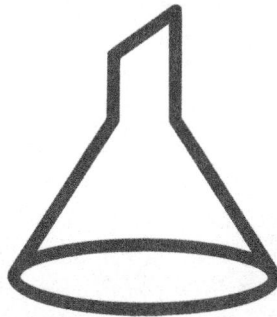

Figure 9.10 – An upside-down funnel

*Alex*: Haha, is there such an *elastic funnel service*?

*Charles*: Well, yes. But remember, it's called ELB. There are several types of balancers, so let's concentrate on the one we need for our web servers, called **ALB** or **application load balancer**. This is specialized in application traffic based on HTTP or HTTPS requests. You go to the console, request one ALB, provide some parameters, and this is what you get.

*Harold*: Okay, it seems to be one entry where everybody connects using HTTP or HTTPS and multiple destinations, each with its own IP address?

*Charles*: Right. On the top, there's a single point of contact, which means a single IP address. But you don't need it because the load balancer instead offers a DNS name, which does not change. That is where all clients will connect. Your web application is visible there, and all traffic from all clients will be sent to this single endpoint, which can use HTTP, HTTPS, or even both.

*Alex*: I get it. As the service is a *load balancer*, it will balance the load amongst all available destinations, which I imagine are the EC2 instances, which should be configured below.

Alex draws a diagram on the whiteboard:

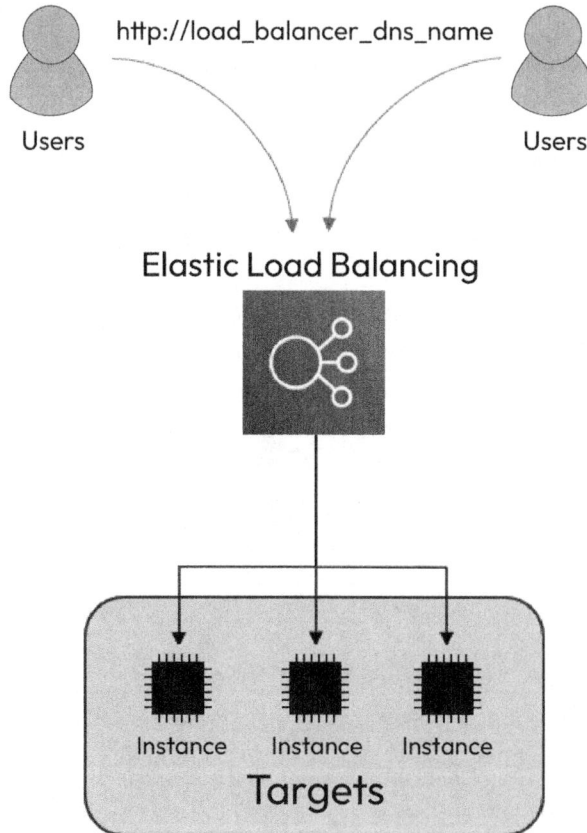

Figure 9.11 – Load balancer as a 1:N relationship

*Charles*: Exactly. At the bottom, there's a variable number of EC2 instances. All of them are known by the load balancer, which will decide where to send the incoming traffic. Of course, the responses from EC2 servers will follow the opposite path.

*Harold*: But the destinations continue to be a variable number of instances; we have the same issues. Do we have to configure these servers?

*Charles*: The destinations, which are called **targets** by the load balancer, will be dynamically discovered and configured. You already have an ASG defined with a name and identifier. You can just register this group to the load balancer, in a **load balancer target group**. This means that every change done to the instances in the ASG will be notified to the load balancer. Everything becomes automatic. This is a very simple step, but don't forget it.

Berta adds some parts to the drawing on the whiteboard:

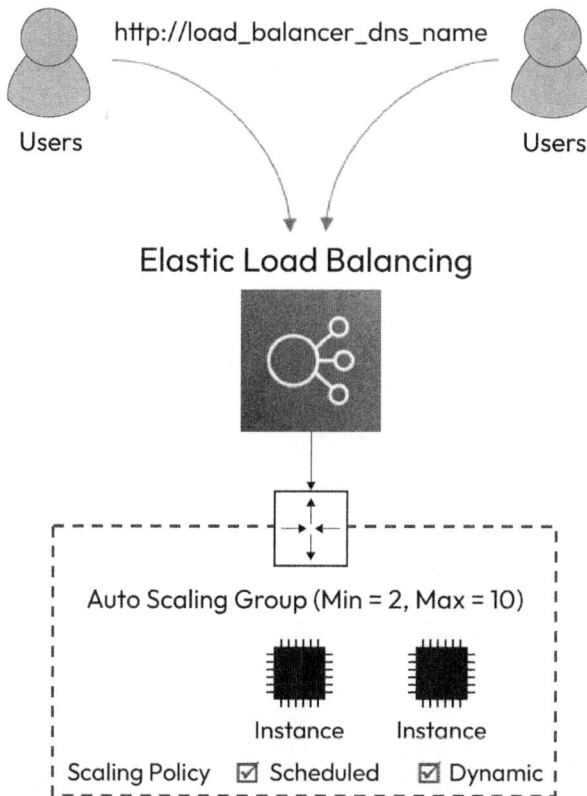

Figure 9.12 – Linking the load balancer to the ASG

*Harold*: Then, every time a new EC2 instance is created or deleted in the group…

*Charles*: …the load balancer will automatically see the change. Remember CloudWatch; it monitors everything, so it is also monitoring this configuration. Apart from checking the servers' health, it will tell EC2 auto scaling when to add or remove instances, based on the metrics you define, remember, inside the scaling policies:

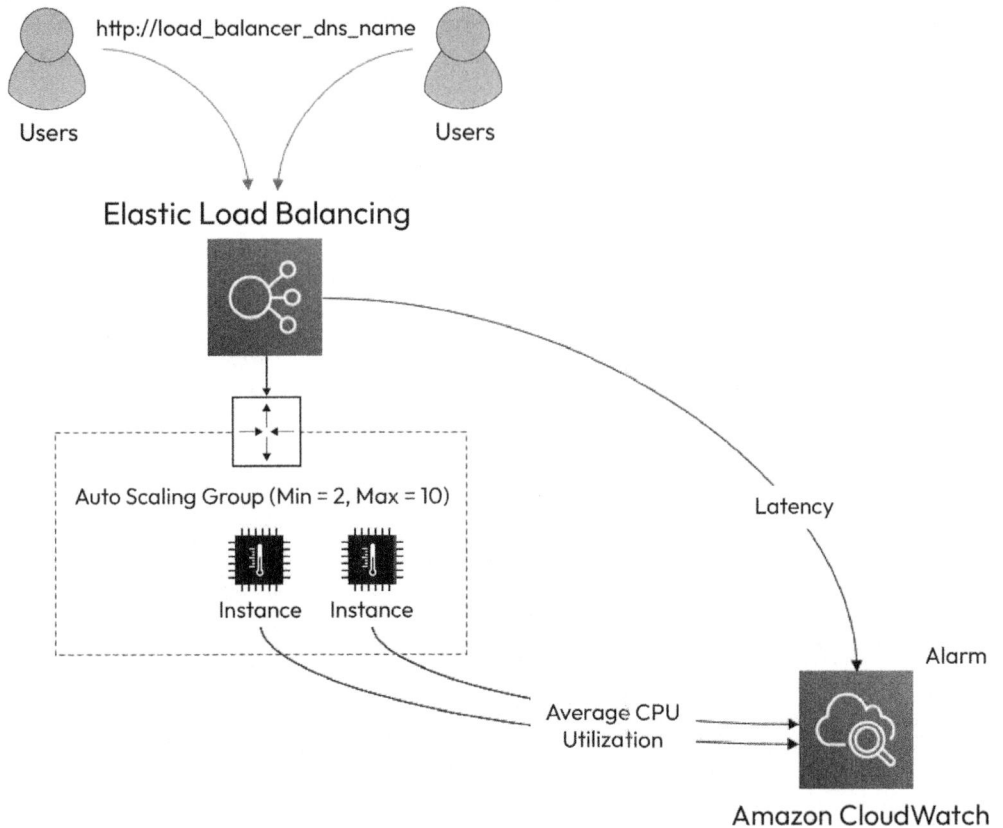

Figure 9.13 – CloudWatch monitoring the configuration

*Harold*: This solves the configuration problem.

*Charles*: And one more thing. Before sending traffic to any instance, the load balancer will perform a **health check** on it. Not just a simple ping; you can configure it to check whether the application is effectively working. For example, checking for a specific page or dynamic results. If any instance fails the health check for any reason, it will be marked as unhealthy, and no more traffic will be sent to it. And, of course, you'll get a notification.

*Alex*: It seems a bit paranoid. Like my younger brother. I'm lending him my car, giving him the keys, but before using it, he keeps asking me for permission and also checking whether the car is in good condition and is full of petrol.

*Harold*: He has probably had a bad experience. But yes, if EC2 creates a healthy instance and tells the ELB to use it, why check again?

*Charles*: Yes, it seems a bit paranoid. But think about your user experience. What would happen if you send your customers or critical applications to a server that is running but has not been properly configured, maybe due to a silly mistake? Better double-check whether the service is effectively working; it is an extra and free check. These checks also provide an extra benefit, which is high availability. If any of the instances fails for any reason, the load balancer will stop using it. But it will also notify the ASG of the fact, and this will generate a new instance, which will substitute the old one. And you can use multiple **Availability Zones (AZs)** for this configuration.

*Alex*: But I see a serious problem with this approach. We can use multiple targets for high availability. But there's a single point of contact, just one load balancer, and that becomes a single point of failure. If the load balancer fails, no one will be able to connect or use the application.

*Charles*: You are imagining the load balancer as a huge router or switch, with a power cord and blinking LEDs, aren't you?

Figure 9.14 – A hardware communication device

*Alex*: What else could it be?

*Harold*: Let me answer this one. The ELB is a service, not just a physical device. As with many other cloud services, it might be implemented using multiple physical devices and be fully redundant.

*Charles*: You got the point perfectly. The service is implemented across multiple AZs. Even if one of them fails totally, the ELB will continue to provide the service. And all the instances in the failing AZ will be created again but in other AZs. Many people use this approach for EC2; instead of creating some separate instances, they create an ASG, spanning several AZs. And this becomes a very frequent configuration – using EC2 Auto Scaling, ELB, and CloudWatch, the three of them collaborating:

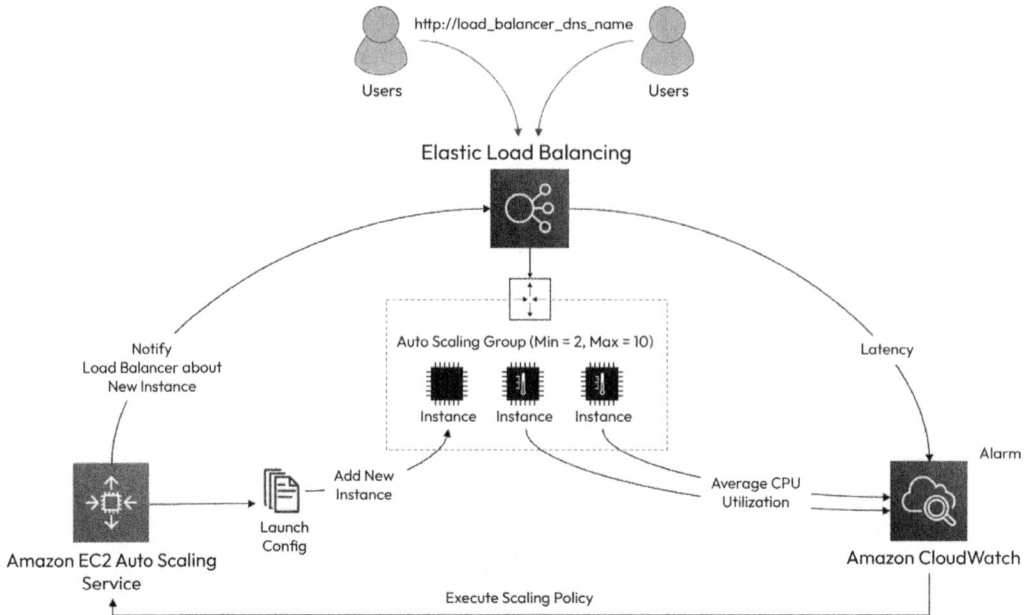

Figure 9.15 – Triad of services

*Charles*: In our supermarket, EC2 would be the open cashiers, ELB would be a single queue where you're told who the next available cashier is, and CloudWatch is the manager who decides to open or close more cashier lines. For example, using a metric as the number of requests, waiting time, or queue length.

*Harold*: What about performance? You can have lots of clients connecting through this single service to many targets, generating lots of traffic.

*Charles*: This is another advantage of using the ELB as a service. The *E* stands for *Elastic*. That means if the traffic grows and grows and grows, the service will allocate enough bandwidth for it, probably using more network devices. It's completely transparent to the users and to us as administrators.

*Berta*: What about IPs? If we use a large ASG, we'll need lots of IP addresses to manage.

*Charles*: That's another important advantage of this approach. IP management gets tremendously simplified. And on the other side, security is highly enhanced. Look, let me draw this on the whiteboard:

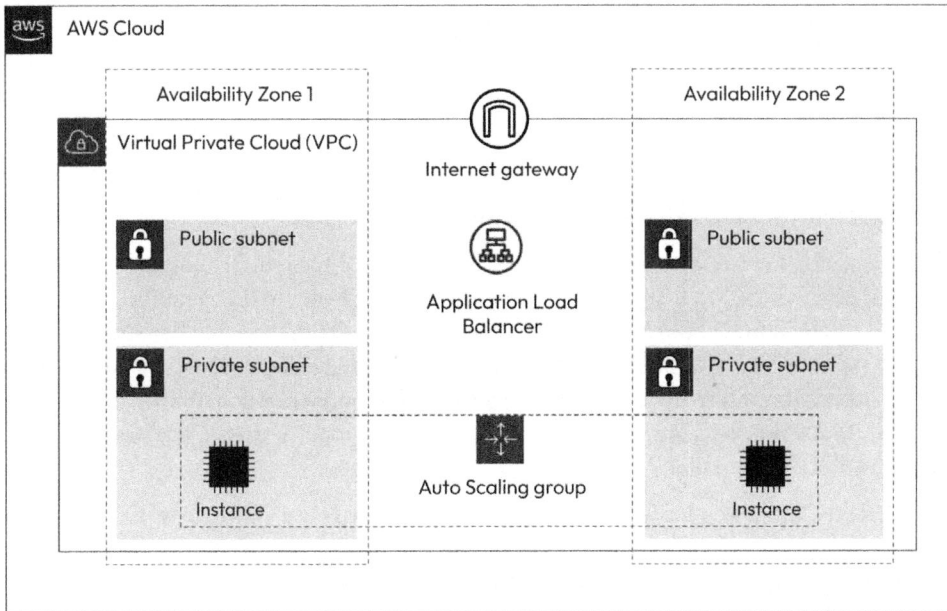

Figure 9.16 – VPC configuration

*Charles*: All this configuration lives in a single region and also inside a VPC.

You see, even if the application is reachable from the internet, we just use one point of contact. Only one DNS name, maybe an alias to make it easier, and one public address or one elastic IP to manage.

The rest of the communication, from the load balancer to the targets, can use the private subnets, so now you have a publicly reachable web server, in an ASG of instances, but all of them are protected inside the private subnets. The only public-facing service is the ELB, and you only open the ports you need (HTTP, HTTPS, or both, but not any other).

Apart from that, you can use the filtering mechanisms we already saw for any VPC.

*Alex*: Security groups and network ACLs?

*Charles*: True. And one more thing. You can also define the ELB as internal, not facing the internet, so you can provide load balancing to your internal groups when the traffic does not arrive from the internet.

*Berta*: This seems really powerful. I'm thinking of some future applications. Soon, we'll have to build some distributed applications in the cloud, and we'll find a similar problem, with many users connected to a distributed system but using a single point of contact. Maybe we could use ELB too. When you use a load balancer, does the target have to be a group of EC2 instances?

*Charles*: Good question. The targets can be EC2 instances, but also containers, or Lambda functions. In fact, everything that has an IP address could potentially be a target. You could specify the IPs manually, but usually, you just register a group of targets, and the balancer will take care of them. You're right, we'll find this again when we start modifying our applications later.

*Harold*: This seems to cover all networking and security aspects. But what about the application state?

*Alex*: Is that the same one you mentioned when talking about horizontal scalability?

*Harold*: Yes. Let me provide an example that relates to our environment. Imagine a web application where you first identify yourself. Then, you begin to do operations like shopping, for example, filling your shopping cart. Every time you click on a page or submit a request, HTTP or HTTPS will transmit it and forget it. It is a stateless protocol. So, someone has to remember all your previous data (that is, the state) for you. Traditionally, web servers store all of this in RAM or on a local disk. But now we have horizontal scalability. What happens when there are several servers?

*Alex*: I see. Maybe you log in with your username and password, and ELB sends you to Server1. After some time, you start to buy something, but now ELB sends you to Server2. This server doesn't know you, so it will request your identity again. Imagine there are 20 servers; it would be a terrible user experience.

*Charles*: Exactly. There are two solutions to this situation. The first one requires some time, as you have to redesign the application for the cloud. This is part of what we call *modernizing the applications*. In fact, it is a simple change. The state cannot be any more in RAM or local disks in a specific server. So, when you add something to the state (login details, cart, or whatever), the application stores it in an external database where all instances will share the information—the centralized source of information we mentioned. Remember the range of databases we saw? It can be DynamoDB, RDS, or even in RAM, using ElastiCache.

*Berta*: It seems an easy change, but yes, it has to be done and tested. What's the other solution?

*Charles*: You can force the ELB to send all traffic coming from a session to the same instance. The application will keep the state in RAM or wherever it was done, being assured that all traffic from a user session will be sent to only this server and not the others. You keep using the old-fashioned application, which does not know there are many other servers. The ELB hides this fact from the application.

*Berta*: Seems like a valid workaround for some applications. What do you call this configuration?

*Charles*: It's called **Sticky Sessions**. You enable it on the ELB, and it will automatically balance the user sessions. It will try to use all available targets, keeping them busy, but now, each separate session will be always sent to the same target.

*Alex*: I use a Sticky Session in my supermarket. Every time I'm paying, I try to go to the same cashier. Even if the manager tries to push me to an idle cashier, I always go to my favorite one.

*Harold*: Maybe someday you'll tell us the reason. I'll call you Sticky Alex from now on.

The team now begins to really understand how sessions work. What's more, they relate the new concepts provided by the cloud with what they already knew about web-based applications. They most like the possibility to run these applications not in a single server, but in a variable number of them, defined by an ASG. Concepts such as **Session State** and **Sticky Sessions** and the role of the **load balancer** and its **health checks** are now clear.

## Summary

Charles and Berta are happy with the whole explanation and how the team understood it. They had the time to cover the relationship between a huge amount of users and a variable number of servers using load balancers. They also described the basic configuration steps and aspects related to high availability, scalability, and security. The relationship to previous concepts such as VPCs, security groups, and network ACLs is also clear. The possible improvements that can be done to the existing applications seem to open a world of possibilities.

The team is currently handling the full environment with automatic scalability on it, and monitoring is also properly performed. Some actions are automatically handled by the cloud provider, but most operations are still done manually. They still don't know it, but the company management will soon require a more automated style.

## Further reading

- Well-Architected Framework: `https://aws.amazon.com/architecture/well-architected`

- Elastic Load Balancing: `https://aws.amazon.com/elasticloadbalancing/`

- AWS Auto Scaling: `https://aws.amazon.com/autoscaling/`

- EC2 Auto Scaling: `https://aws.amazon.com/ec2/autoscaling/`

# Part 3: Application Services

After completing this part, you will understand cloud computing concepts and technologies related to the development area. You will also understand how, in cloud computing, developers can only focus on their applications, without worrying about the underneath infrastructure.

This part has the following chapters:

# 10

# Automation – Look, My Infrastructure Is in Code!

Gloria has attended an important meeting with the board of directors. Because of the latest improvements the company has been implementing, sales are skyrocketing. But this is also putting some pressure on the IT team. So now Gloria has to transmit the new requirements to her team.

*Gloria*: Hello, everyone. I have some new requirements for you and some questions.

*Alex*: Such as: who wants to be invited for coffee today?

*Gloria*: Nice try. But my question is, what do you know about *automation in the cloud*?

*Alex*: I remember from our essentials course there was a tool to automate the creation of environments.

*Berta*: Come on, that was just one of the options. I've read there are many ways to automate multiple types of tasks. But I didn't have the opportunity to try them. Why are you asking, Gloria?

*Gloria*: I was in a meeting with our board of directors. It seems the company is growing very quickly; the number of customers and orders is skyrocketing, and our net benefit with it.

*Alex*: This doesn't exactly sound like bad news. Hehe, I already told you the way we set up those autoscaling groups would be highly appreciated by our customers.

*Gloria*: Yes, you've been doing a fantastic job in migrating our services to the cloud using scalable services, such as the EC2 Autoscaling Groups. I assume that means they are constantly monitored and will scale depending on the load.

*Berta*: Exactly, that is the idea of scalability. Where's the problem? We are able to scale our IT services quickly, even anticipating sudden spikes in demand, and of course to whatever our competitors do and automatically. I'd like to see even more customers.

*Gloria*: You are absolutely right. However, our directors are not worried about the configuration of our cloud services but rather the required operations. It happens every time we have to create a new environment for a project, to migrate or modify it. Once you have analyzed the requirements, you perform all the steps needed. You are doing it fantastically, but it is done manually. This takes some time, and maybe we'll need to be able to grow exponentially. And I quote: *We'll have to do it with the limited resources we already have.* They are also worried about the possible risks of someone making a mistake, especially under pressure.

*Harold*: I don't like when HR calls us employees *resources*. Anyway, I get your point; these repetitive or risky tasks could be automated somehow. This would provide faster answers, free some time for creative tasks, and reduce the risk and our operating costs.

*Gloria*: Completely true. And this should be generalized for all processes. Do you have an idea of how we can proceed? I attended a presentation from our cloud provider, and they are offering multiple options for automation.

*Berta*: I'd propose continuing with our classical approach, which seems to work perfectly. Someone should spend some time investigating and then share this new knowledge with the rest of the team. And then, we'll choose the best tools and begin to automate some selected tasks.

*Gloria*: Good. Alex, take the rest of the week to investigate this. Let's think about which tasks we can automate and in which ways.

*Harold*: I think I can help too. Some time ago, I wrote some scripts with Charles in some classical scripting languages. They were intended to do some configuration and also automate backups on-premises.

*Gloria*: Great. Alex, Harold, and Charles, after this week, I'd like you to meet, maybe with the whole team, to decide how to proceed. After you do your testing, we can comment on all your findings to decide how to use them. One more thing. Someone from the board of directors will probably attend this last meeting, so please prepare a simple explanation, nothing too technical.

*Alex*: Okay, we've got it. We have to prepare a manager speech.

*Harold*: Sure.

*Charles*: I'll try to find and study our existing scripts.

Alex goes home, slightly worried about this new commitment. He'll have to learn something new, coordinate with the more experienced people on the team, especially Harold and Charles, and probably present his findings to some unknown person from the board of directors.

And suddenly, he realizes he can forget his nervous attitude regarding non-technical meetings. He only needs to concentrate on the technical requirements. In the end, cloud technologies are here to help him in his career, as they are fully documented, modular, and easy to understand.

He knows there are several options available, and they should be easy to use, just like every other service they've tried. But he also knows the scope is now broader, as every service in the cloud can be automated.

On his way home, a brilliant idea strikes him. He can share some beers with his old friend John. He has effectively automated many tasks in multiple environments during his long IT career. So, Alex decides to ask for help from a real automation expert.

# Automation – The need

Alex meets his old friend John at his home. He's decided to have a nice evening and also to learn as much as possible about automation.

*John*: Hello, Alex! It has been a long time since we last met. Was it at that beach party?

*Alex*: Yes, exactly, at that fabulous party long ago, but I still remember you love this beer brand. I've brought this 12-pack! We can finish it while we talk about the old times.

*John*: I prefer talking about the present. We're living in interesting times. How's your new job at TrendyCorp?

*Alex*: I was hired to help migrate most of their services to the cloud. We're a small team, but fortunately, we have the time and resources to learn, discuss, plan, and then do the migration. We're having lots of formal and informal training about the cloud.

*John*: You lucky one! TrendyCorp seems like it's one of those companies that believes in the power of training. Uncommon, but very reasonable. A clear win-win situation for everyone.

*Alex*: Yes, they consider training a tool, not a prize. I thought that should be the norm, but it seems it's not. We've been learning a lot about multiple cloud services, and now I've been tasked to start considering cloud automation. I've read a bit about AWS CloudFormation, but I'd love to understand your point of view, which will certainly come from more experience. And, of course, we can drink these beers together.

*John*: **CloudFormation**. This is a practical tool for infrastructure automation operations, but not for all types of automation, and of course, not the only one. There are multiple ways to automate IT. I'm even considering writing a book about them, full of practical examples. But maybe we can start from the beginning.

*Alex*: Opening those beers?

*John*: Exactly. And now, for you, what is automation?

*Alex*: Something like having a script describing which tasks must be done.

*John*: Yes, partially. But you must think in a much more generic way. **Automation,** in any technology, is the approach of running processes in a way that human intervention is minimized. Sometimes, it can be completely unnecessary. *It's a way to make the computer work for humans, performing tasks without them.*

*Alex*: Funny, as what I have seen in other companies is the opposite: humans tied to the mouse, clicking, cutting, copying and pasting, and dragging and dropping for hours. And many of those repetitive tasks could probably be done by computers.

*John*: Many companies are stuck in this strange situation. Copying spreadsheets to reports, in a hurry, after hours, even during weekends. Everybody is tired, unmotivated, even angry, and making mistakes. As you mentioned, it's the opposite of IT; it is humans working for computers.

These companies bought expensive offices, chairs, computers, and desktops, but nothing was spent on learning the right tools.

It's like having a powerful motorbike, like my Harley, but only using the externally visible parts and not the powerful internal engine. That means using it as a classical bicycle, moving just by pedaling. It might take you to the same places, but the effort will exhaust you. People use IT in a similar way; the manual option is enough for them.

*Alex*: And why do we work this way? It seems like a total waste of time.

*John*: It's a real waste of time. And motivation. And money. And it is also the **mother of all risks** (**MOAR**). And, as I always say, the main difference between humans and computers is that humans make mistakes. So, it's very likely these repetitive tasks will end in errors; it could be environments where someone forgot a step, or it was "forgotten" deliberately to go home earlier. Maybe you'll find the errors, or maybe not, but for sure, your customers will find them later when a critical application does not work or provides the wrong information. Bad for business!

Repetitive tasks also kill creativity and motivation. And working manually is an error in itself. If you work in IT, the computers must run the tasks, not you. You'd have more free time for creative tasks, ideas, and applications, the ones that give more value to the business.

*Alex*: But again, do you know why we work this way?

*John*: There are several reasons. The most likely one is people have not been trained in the automation options. Just clicking and that's all. They don't even know automation exists or consider it very difficult to learn. Companies do not invest in automation training, which, in my opinion, is the most productive training. Minimum cost, maximum productivity. But there's the idea that it's enough if you can perform the tasks manually. Why learn a better way? We're too busy:

Figure 10.1 – We're too busy
(Source: Photo by Alan O'Rourke, at https://www.flickr.com/photos/toddle_email_
newsletters/15599597515, used under Attribution 2.0 Generic (CC BY 2.0) license.)

*Alex*: I get your point. And I can detect some sarcasm in your words. Automation is not so difficult.

*John*: Sarcasm is my middle name. Exactly. There are many different ways to automate, and several are really easy. And in all cases, the benefits will far outweigh the cost of learning.

*Alex*: Do you have some practical examples?

*John*: I found one situation where I had to prepare 15 virtual servers for a class. They had to be identical except for their names and IP addresses. We were in a hurry, so I asked two colleagues to join and help. All of us followed exactly the same installation guide, and after three hectic hours, we ended with a mix of lower-case and upper-case names and some other defaults done in different ways, which made some computers completely different from others.

The following time, we did the same process using a script, and the task finished in 10 minutes, leaving a perfectly coherent environment. The script provided exactly the same defaults for everything that was not documented or agreed upon. During those 10 minutes, we had some coffee and chatted, as the script was working for us and not the opposite. And, of course, I have the script ready to reuse the next time.

*Alex*: I see; operating manually has lots of risks.

*John*: If you perform a task manually, all the steps are documented, but only in someone's head. Maybe you'll forget some steps. In a team, each individual will perform the task in subtly different ways, in a different order, with different defaults. It's also very likely you'll have a hard time finding the only person in the company who remembers how to do the task and then find out that they are on holiday. And transmitting this knowledge, maybe to newer employees, completely depends on what you remember and your mood at the time. Totally subjective and dangerous.

*Alex*: But you can document the process in a step-by-step manual.

*John*: Hahaha. Good joke; you can have another beer. The classic *operation manual*. These manuals are typically huge, hard to maintain, and usually wrong. I've seen these manuals with around 800 pages; even the writers admitted they were useless even before finishing them. The instructions immediately become obsolete if something changes, maybe just a minor change in the user interface. And these manuals will never cover all the possible details.

I mentioned that this is also dangerous. The worst thing about these manuals is that people follow them blindly. And if something is missing, incorrect, or obsolete, there is no way to check the results. A sure recipe for failure.

*Alex*: Then the solution is keeping all the steps in a file?

*John*: Yes, in single or multiple files. They are usually called **scripts**, but I'll show you some options. These files can store all the steps needed to perform the task and verify whether you got the exact result or situation you need. Some companies have automated all the generation and maintenance of their environments, troubleshooting, testing state, and performance, finding issues, and fixing them with the right solution. 100% automated. 0% human error.

*Alex*: You mentioned *reusing* a script. What do you mean?

*John*: If you have the same need after some time, you can find the script you wrote some time ago and run it again. Or maybe it was written by someone else. But this requires some expertise in the design. It is very likely you'll need the same tasks but with some differences. Maybe just different S3 bucket names, Regions, the number of computers in an Auto Scaling Group, and so on. If you can anticipate those possible needs in your scripts, you'll write them in a more generic form. You have to be able to define parameters on them and write them modularly so you can reuse only parts of a script, maybe being called from others.

For example, I have functions to upload, download, and delete objects in S3. These functions are generic enough; they can be called from any other script by just passing the right parameters.

You build on what you already have. This gives you a nice feeling of building, of creativity.

*Alex*: I imagine you don't write the scripts alone. I think I can propose a collaborative effort, creating a huge collection of required scripts maintained and used by the whole team.

*John*: Exactly! This is one of the most important aspects of automation: teamwork. If you can convince your team of its importance, you'll start by having some simple scripts, or generic functions, in a shared library. You can, of course, start from the thousands of scripts available on the internet. Now all operations will be defined in a well-known repository, as files, not as crazy ideas in someone's head. Then, whenever you need to perform a task, you head to this library. Some tasks can also be scheduled or run as a consequence of an event; remember, no human intervention when possible.

*Alex*: I can imagine how powerful this can become after some months if everybody collaborates. In the end, you finish with a collection of scripts to do most of your frequent tasks.

*John*: Keep in mind always that *good scripts are like good wine. They can only improve.* If the team uses these scripts, they can be reviewed and improved by any member. Every time there's an improvement made, it will be made to all files, and it will stay forever.

In my previous company, we built a huge, shared library of scripts with versioning. Everybody was trying to improve everything. It became a funny contest. It created lots of teamwork and ideas. As the scripts are permanently in files, everybody can provide new ideas over them and maybe, after some months, create a new version. And we also created an approval process, so you can only run approved pieces of code.

But you have to remember something we learned: always write the files as modularly and generally as possible. You'll build faster, and the results will be coherent, reliable, and self-documented.

*Alex*: I assume the tool you use for automation will define a language you have to learn.

*John*: True. There are several possible languages, some older, but they can be grouped into two categories: **declarative language** and **imperative language**. The language you use defines how to write your scripts and what you can do, but especially how easy it is to learn, create and modify your script files, and always in a reliable way. I'll show you a few of them; let me check on my laptop where I have my script collection.

*Alex*: What is the difference between these two categories of languages?

*John*: Let's imagine I am telling you, *"Alex, I'd like to see the news on TV. It's airing on Channel 6."*

*Alex*: I see, that's declarative language. You just mention the result you want. How would this be phrased in imperative language?

*John*: Something like, *"Alex, find the remote in drawer 1, point it to the TV, click the red button to start it, wait three seconds, check whether it is on, wait until it is, and point again to the TV, then click channel six, leave the remote in drawer 1..."* and I'm probably forgetting some steps or possible situations.

*Alex*: Yes, what if the drawer is closed? But I get the point. You mentioned many different types of tasks. Are all of them considered automation?

*John*: Here's my definition of automation. It is the possibility to perform any task, on any set of servers or services, at any time, repeated any number of times, and launched in any way: scheduled, by another script, by events, or whatever.

*Alex*: So, I imagine my reference to CloudFormation fits only into some of these scenarios.

*John*: Yes. But as CloudFormation is one of the easiest ways to automate in the AWS cloud, we can start with it. But first, open two more beers.

Alex is beginning to realize some of the benefits of automation: reliability, performance, fewer errors, social recognition, teamwork, a sense of creativity and power, and more free time. So, he's planning to dedicate more time to it. But first, he needs to listen to the existing possibilities in the cloud.

# Infrastructure as code

After a short two-beer break, John continues. He thinks the benefits of automation will now be clearer for his friend Alex, so he'll go into a well-known technology, called **infrastructure as code (IaC)**.

*John*: Alex, do you know what IaC means?

*Alex*: No. It seems like a common buzzword nowadays, but I have no clear idea.

*John*: IaC means you describe your environment, the servers, network, services, or whatever you might need in several text files. Whenever you need to create this environment, you ask the system to use the files to do it, and it will just do it for you.

*Alex*: And why that name?

*John*: These files fully describe your infrastructure, as your **virtual private clouds** (**VPCs**), EC2 instances, S3, databases, and most services can be included. And these files are handled in the same way as your code files. You store them in a repository or a version control system; you edit, create versions, review and test them, share them with your team, and request approval for them. These files, handled as code, can create, modify, or destroy the described infrastructure; hence the name IaC.

*Alex*: Are they like the script files we talked about earlier?

*John*: Similar, but even simpler. In this case, we use declarative language. In these files, you just declare what you need in an easy-to-understand language describing the final results you need. You don't specify the steps; you just declare what you want but not how to achieve it. All the details will be handled for you.

*Alex*: Something like a recipe?

*John*: Not exactly. When you need to prepare a complex dish, what do you do before shopping at the supermarket?

*Alex*: I hate forgetting something and having to make two trips. I have always written everything on a shopping list to avoid these mistakes.

*John*: Humans make mistakes, so let's try to avoid them: you need a shopping list; look, this is the first one I used:

- 7 eggs
- Some bread
- Milk
- 144 beers
- Milk
- A Hammer
- One chocolate bar

Figure 10.2 – A shopping list – v1

*John*: You see, it does not tell you how to get the goods. This is the idea; you just state what you need, not how or where they are located.

*Alex*: But your list has some issues. Well, it's better than nothing, of course.

*John*: Yes, I wrote it very quickly. I only tried it once, and I got back nothing at all. Just a handwritten piece of paper with some warnings:

- Seven eggs: We can't sell you seven eggs; they come in six-packs. Do you want 6 or 12?

- Some bread: Which one and how much?

- Milk: Which brand? We provide several brands and different levels of fat.

- 144 beers: Really? 144? Bottled or canned? Which brand? Which size?

- Milk: Again? Do you really need more milk, or is it a cut-and-paste error?

- A hammer: Sorry, we don't sell these.

- The last one is just impossible to read.

*John*: In my original approach, I thought my list should be clear enough, so why were they asking all these questions? Of course, I needed those 12 eggs! But then I realized something important. A shopping list can be terribly ambiguous, error-prone, and maybe can be only understood by the original writer, and in this case, I couldn't even read my own writing.

*Alex*: So you had to write a better one?

*John*: Yes. Now the list is designed so anyone can do the shopping, not just me. I can send it to any supermarket personnel, and they will bring all of these to my home. No matter who reads the list, I want to get the goods I need. Of course, it will be slightly strict to avoid any doubts, but it continues to be simple; I just specify what I need.

Something like this. In this case, I got everything I needed except the hammer:

(Shopping List - v2)

If (eggs are sold by units): seven eggs; else one box. A-quality eggs.

Bread: One loaf of standard baguette.

Milk: One bottle, brand "Happy Cow", no fat, 1L.

Beers: Brand "Frying Pigs", 330 ml can, 144 units.

Milk: Add one extra brick of the previous milk.

Only if in a hardware store: A hammer, 30 cm long, iron, ref: X123456.

A chocolate bar: Brand X, Size XXX, 102% chocolate content.

Figure 10.3 – A better shopping list – v2

*Alex*: And what does this have to do with IaC?

*John*: Well, AWS offers a service called CloudFormation, which gives you the full IaC approach. The one you mentioned before, with files, versions, and approvals.

The key idea behind CloudFormation is similar to the shopping list approach. You simply write the components you need in a file called a **CloudFormation template**. That is your shopping list in AWS. This uses declarative language, where you just declare or write down what you need.

Now you can review the template with your colleagues or managers before making any real changes. And when you are ready, you ask CloudFormation to create the environment based on only what's in the template. It will triple-check the syntax and possible errors, check for missing parameters, analyze possible dependencies, reorder the components, and will finally get all those services for you. That means it creates the full environment.

*Alex*: I would never have considered AWS a supermarket for components.

*John:* It's a useful way to consider CloudFormation. And remember, this service is provided at no additional cost. You only pay for the resources created.

I'm showing you another shopping list similar to a CloudFormation template. With it, everyone could go to the supermarket and always get the same results:

(Shopping List-v3)

- **DAIRY AREA**

    o **Eggs**

        • If (eggs are sold by units): Seven eggs; else on box, A-quality eggs.

    o **Milk**

        • Milk: One bottle, brand "Happy Cow", no fat, 1L.

        • Milk: + one bottle.

            (But keep it separate; it has to be given to a neighbor)

- **DRINK AREA**

    o **Beers**: Brand "Flying Pigs", 330 ml can, 144 units.


- **BAKERY AREA**

    o **Bread**: One loaf of a standard baguette.

        Condition: Buy it if and only if eggs are also bought.

    o **A chocolate bar**: Brand X, Size XXX, 102% chocolate content.


- (Only if in) HARDWARE STORE

    o **A hammer**: 30 cm long, iron, ref: X123456.

Figure 10.4 – A complete shopping list – v3

*Alex:* I can see this list format is much more strict and also more powerful. For example, it includes nested properties; that's properties inside other properties, or conditional buying.

*John:* Exactly. Strictness is the opposite of ambiguity. Let's avoid mistakes. The CloudFormation language uses a nice balance between clearness, strictness, and simplicity. Something like this shopping list. You can also include variables, conditional expressions, and some other language possibilities.

*Alex:* Where can I get real examples and learn about syntax? I'm afraid I'll need it.

*John*: Take a look at the CloudFormation documentation; you'll see lots of examples about the template syntax, tools, and template libraries and examples. You can use several formats; I'm showing you a couple of them:

```yaml
Resources:
  HelloBucket:
    Type: AWS::S3::Bucket
    Properties:
      AccessControl: PublicRead
```

(a)

```json
{
    "Resources": {
        "HelloBucket":
        {
            "Type": "AWS::S3::Bucket",
            "Properties":
            {
                "AccessControl": "PublicRead"
            }
        }
    }
}
```

(b)

Figure 10.5 – A simple CloudFormation template, in YAML and JSON formats

*Alex*: Simple. Just the services you need and some properties. Does the order inside the file matter?

*John*: You can declare your services in any order in a CloudFormation template. The service will create them in the required order. For example, you must create an EC2 instance inside a subnet inside a VPC. But these three can be declared in the file in any order you choose; the implicit dependencies between them will be automatically sorted for you. That means CloudFormation will first create the VPC, then the subnet, and finally the instance, in this exact order. In a classical programming language, you must follow the exact dependency order.

You can also declare **explicit dependencies** if you need a specific order, for example, create an application only when its database is created, and its endpoint is available. The syntax offers the DependsOn keyword to specify these dependencies. If you don't use them, all the creation will be done in parallel as much as possible.

*Alex*: So, we can create a full environment, with no errors, and have coffee while it is created, assuming we have the right template.

*John*: Yes. The environment created by CloudFormation is called a **stack**. A single environment can also be created from multiple templates, maybe created by different teams, such as security, application, databases, and so on. Each partial template will provide a part of the final results:

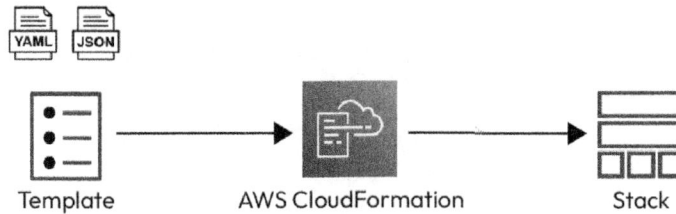

Figure 10.6 – AWS CloudFormation

*Alex*: And I can see the templates are simple enough that even my managers would understand them.

*John*: That's one of the ideas. Maybe your team creates the templates, and the managers review them until they approve the stack creation. Maybe not all the details, but they'll get a bird's eye view of the full environment.

*Alex*: Or we could have some templates tested and ready, so anyone in the team, even some trainees we might hire in the future, would be able to build a coherent environment without errors or any expert teaching them a bunch of steps.

*John*: Exactly. But wait, there's more. You're only thinking about the creation of the environment. CloudFormation can also delete or modify an existing stack. For example, if CloudFormation created something, it can also be deleted by CloudFormation.

*Alex*: Yes, it makes sense. The stack remembers all components that were added.

*John*: And this brings us to an amazing way to experiment. For example, what is that thing called Bitcoin? Let's play with it. I find a free template with all the components; I then ask CloudFormation to create the full stack while I'm having a break. Remember, computers work for humans, not the opposite!

Now the environment is created, and I can use it to mine my bitcoins. And after finishing my experiment (or getting rich, whatever comes first), I can remove everything with a single click. Everything that was created from the template is now destroyed. No leftovers. No money is being spent on forgotten components.

*Alex*: My managers will love this feature when I tell them!

*John*: Wait till you hear the next one. CloudFormation can modify an existing environment, for example, by updating something you forgot on the original template. Updates are incremental; they will not modify other existing components in the current stack. This takes us to something called **detecting configuration drift**.

*Alex*: What's that?

*John*: Imagine you have created an environment, a stack, and it has been running for some time. Then someone performs manual updates or deletes a part of the stack (by mistake or maliciously). Now you have a configuration drift, meaning what you have running in the cloud differs from what you wanted.

CloudFormation will compare the desired configuration, as declared in the template, with the current configuration, the stack running in the cloud. It will report all differences and fix them if you run the creation again; remember the creation is incremental.

*Alex*: Oh, oh, oh. I can't wait to tell my team all of this. By the way, how can we get those templates?

*John*: I'll give you a list of repositories, there are many of them in the AWS documentation or on the internet. There is also a myriad of template editors. My favorite one runs in Visual Studio Code, but there are many others:

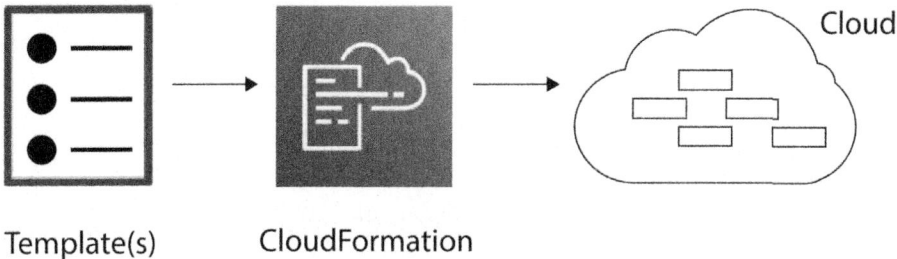

Template(s)    CloudFormation

Figure 10.7 – AWS CloudFormation – from templates to the cloud

*Alex*: Thanks!

*John*: And you can reuse templates as they are in different environments or if you want to tweak them based on the parameters you specify. So, maybe, a template creates a highly available environment when you deploy it in a production environment and just a standard deployment for your test environment and saves you money:

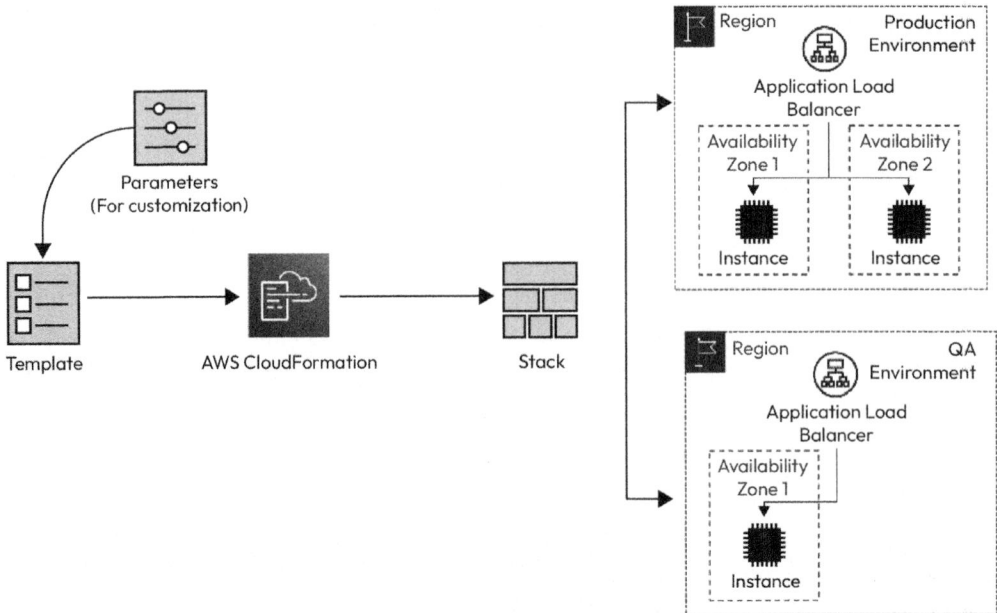

Figure 10.8 – AWS CloudFormation – the reuse of a template

*Alex*: That's very helpful.

*John*: Let's open another beer. We'll need it; there are more options for automation.

*Alex* has compiled a full list of possibilities for CloudFormation. Creating environments is the most evident one, but modifying or deleting existing stacks also seems really powerful. And detecting configuration drift seems to be a critical option for daily operation management.

## Automation using APIs

After a short break, John plans to describe the most powerful way to control the cloud, but maybe also the most complex one. He wants to describe this to Alex so he can get the complete picture, but he also thinks there might be other people on the team who favor a developer approach. He'll describe what an **application programming interface** (**API**) is and where it can be found as a key component in all automation.

*John*: Now we can consider the other extreme of automation. In fact, I wouldn't call it strictly automation but rather a development. In short, you can write a program in any classical programming language to perform the needed cloud operations from it. You can choose a language you might already know, such as Java, C#, Go, Python, or some others. And of course, everything you did on the console should also be possible from this language.

*Alex*: I assume this is like classical programming, using an imperative language in this case. That means you have to specify all instructions, logic, flow, loops, conditions, their order, error handling, and so on.

*John*: Exactly. Most of the available languages are compiled, so in the end, you get an executable program with all the functionality you need. You can embed it in any of your applications and run it as you wish, so this is not human intervention, but it is a program you have to write.

For example, and this is a real one, *find all the servers called "Test\*" or "Demo\*", which have been running for more than two weeks, and are not using the t2 or t3 instance types. If they are not running a process called "setup", stop them.*

This is the sort of logic you can write, far beyond what CloudFormation can do. Which is, remember, only the creation, modification, or deletion of a stack. Building your own programs provides the *maximum power*. You can add your own logic with no limits; there's no restriction on what you can do.

*Alex*: How can these programs interact with the cloud services?

*John*: Every cloud service is designed to provide an API. This is a predefined, standardized way to communicate with every service and request every possible operation or data. Each service provides all its functionality, every option, through its API.

*Alex*: It sounds a bit abstract. Do you have any examples for this?

*John*: Think about your car. When you change your wheels, you can choose which model you prefer, some cheaper, some more expensive. Maybe you use a different set for summer and winter. Or perhaps you have to replace a headlight. Fortunately, you don't have to worry whether they'll fit, or their volts, or their size. The car manufacturer has standardized how these connections must be made. You can think about any other component; each one follows a standard, which forms the collection of all car APIs.

When you use it from your own application, the API for every cloud service is reachable from every programming language by using predefined libraries. Of course, everything is totally documented.

*Alex*: Do you think using this approach is a good idea? These APIs seem really complex, each service has one, and they are probably expensive.

*John*: Talking about the price, you'll like it: all libraries are free. You can download them and get some tools to ease your development, such as add-ons for Visual Studio, Visual Studio Code, and Eclipse, all of them also free. Just choose your favorite language and development environment.

But of course, this method requires a higher development effort and you need some developer experience in at least one programming language. Fortunately, you don't start from scratch and there are many examples available. I'll also get you a list of where to find these tools and examples.

*Alex*: I can imagine there are simpler options. I don't see myself writing programs.

*John*: Yes, we'll see another simpler but more flexible and powerful option soon.

You could find some people in your team who prefer this API approach in their favorite programming language. Remember, it's the less flexible option but the most powerful. Going back to our supermarket, it's like building the instruction manual of the full supermarket. Operations for inventory, providers, sales, prices, discounts, and allergies; every possible operation has to be available and documented.

*Alex*: Yes, I imagine all the operations, requests, and results will be there.

*John*: True. And I'd say this is the most important aspect: you always have to remember that the cloud uses these APIs internally. It's the only way services can communicate among themselves; they use API automation.

Also, when you click on the console, your clicks are translated to API calls, any CloudFormation operation, or a backup you scheduled for an **Elastic Block Storage** (**EBS**) volume. Any task in the cloud ends up calling the API.

And, by the way, have you already learned about CloudTrail? Every time anyone calls an API, the fact is logged. No matter where the call came from. This way, all operations are logged.

*Alex*: Cool, but I need a break. Let's open two more beers.

Alex feels a bit worried about this development approach. Using APIs directly seems far beyond his experience, but he knows this is an important concept, and maybe some people in the team will prefer it. Anyway, he's waiting for the next explanation.

## Automation via scripting

After a short stretch break and two more beers, John is eager to describe his favorite way of delivering automation: scripting. He feels Alex will also like the idea, as it is easier than pure development but offers the same power with much better flexibility.

*John*: Finally, we can have automation in the cloud using classical **scripting**. This is an intermediate approach and very practical. You get lots of flexibility, but you continue to have no limits on what you can do. This makes it my favorite way of delivering automation.

*Alex*: How does it compare to the other options?

*John*: Let's start with the similarities. You write one or multiple files in one scripting language, typically Python, Bash, or PowerShell. Again, we're using imperative languages, where you write your logic and the code flow. You can also use the **command-line interface** or **CLI**.

*Alex*: CLI?

*John*: Yes, that's a program already built, provided by AWS, which allows you to perform every API operation in every service. People call it the CLI, but in fact, it's not the only one, as there are several command-line interfaces. This classical CLI is just a Python script that interprets your parameters as the desired operations to call the API.

*Alex*: And the differences?

*John*: These languages do not need explicit compilation, so you can modify your scripts at any time and run them again. This flexibility allows for creating scripted tasks in seconds or editing an existing script very quickly.

*Alex*: You mentioned CLI, Python, and PowerShell. Which one should we use?

*John*: Choose the free one. Hahaha, all of them are free!

*Alex*: Then?

*John*: It depends on your preferences and previous knowledge. Many people use the CLI as it was the first one to be published, is highly documented, and can run the same scripts, with no modifications, from Windows, Linux, or macOS. But the syntax can be difficult sometimes, as everything is text-based. All the results and commands are text, though sometimes embedded into JSON.

Here, you have an example: get all the contents of an S3 bucket. By the way, the CLI executable is called `aws`, so, run the following code:

```
aws  s3api  list-objects  --bucket jcanalytics
```

*John*: Then you can write your scripts in Python; it seems to be a popular language nowadays. I have an example of how it looks to get the same bucket contents:

```
import boto3
aws = boto3.Session(
        aws_access_key_id=><your_access_keyid>>,
        aws_secret_access_key=><your_secret_accesskey>>)


objs3 = aws.resource('s3')
the_bucket = objs3.Bucket('jcanalytics')
for each_bucket_object in the_bucket.objects.all():
  print(each_bucket_object.key)
```

*Alex*: Boto3? What's that?

*John*: It's a type of dolphin found in the Amazon River, but also the library you need to use in Python to access the AWS API. You have to remember to include them, or your program will not be able to use the API.

*Alex*: Pretty clear. What's next?

*John*: The last one is PowerShell. It is a scripting framework and development environment with its own language. Many people think it's only for Windows, but this is no longer true. For many years now, it has been open source and can also run on Windows, Linux, or macOS. It is fully object-oriented—in fact, everything is an object, even parameters, results, or help.

This is my favorite approach, especially if using multiple clouds. There are commands for every service in every cloud and for many other environments, not only Windows.

Look, I have this example, a one-liner that will stop all Linux EC2 instances in seconds:

```
Get-EC2Instance |
  Select-Object -Expand Instances |
    Where Platform -eq "Windows" |
      Stop-EC2Instance -WhatIf
```

*Alex*: It seems pretty easy to understand and has very clear semantics. And I see it has the option, `WhatIf`, to simulate the operation while testing.

But I can see two errors in your script. First, you're stopping the Windows instances, not the Linux ones. And the other error is more subtle: if an instance is already stopped, it will try again and probably show an error.

*John*: Good catch. Let me edit it, so you can see how easy it is. It takes 10 seconds. What about now? Here, take a look:

```
# Better version, only if Linux and Running
Get-EC2Instance  |
    Select-Object -Expand Instances |
      Where { $_.State.Name -eq "Running" } |
        Where Platform -ne "Windows" |
          Stop-EC2Instance -WhatIf
```

*Alex*: Fantastic; it seems really easy, flexible, and powerful, and loops are implicit.

*John*: Yes. Once you know a few basic concepts, you can control multiple environments with a single language. You can use it with at least three popular cloud providers and from any operating system. Your scripts will run exactly the same in Windows, Linux, or macOS. In the end, you can forget about the OS.

PowerShell is imperative, as any scripting language. You mentioned implicit loops; you can also use explicit ones to make learning or porting easier. But it also offers a declarative language called **desired state configuration** (**DSC**). And it's totally modular: you can create your own functions, maybe named in your human language, and integrate your logic in a more complex workflow. For example, start and stop these instances only at specific times. Autoscaling is great, but here you have total control.

By the way, I'm challenging you to write this same functionality, stopping all the Linux instances but using the CLI. It can be done, of course, but you'll need some more time and lots of patience with case sensitivity and null values. If you manage to do it, I'm buying you another box of beers.

*Alex*: I'll try! I like both options, but this last one seems more expensive.

*John*: You're kidding; everything we've talked about today is free. You'll pay for the services you create or their usage but not for using any of these tools.

*Alex*: In this case, which tool should be used?

*John*: Generally speaking, *use the tool you already know*. If you're an expert in Python, continue to use it. If you write scripts in PowerShell, continue with that.

But if you are not an expert in any of them, *don't go blindly for the first language which seems more fashionable or trendy*. Instead, take some time to investigate all of them, and only then choose the one you feel is best. I can assure you this decision will save you lots of time and make you the automation guy in your company.

*Alex*: Hmm. I don't know any of these. I'll follow your advice and invest some time.

*John*: Okay. Now give me some minutes before we continue with the last option.

In the meantime, Alex is writing on a piece of paper all the options he learned, as he doesn't want to forget any of them. He writes down CLI, Bash, PowerShell, and Python. But he's leaving some space so he can fill every section dedicated to each scripting technology with the links John will provide later.

## Automation using AWS services

After a short break, John wants to end the day by briefly explaining some other options. These are clearly based on AWS services, so they should be easier to manage. Of course, they will require more time later, as they are full-featured powerful services, but at least he wants to give Alex a basic idea of their functionality for completeness, so his team can later investigate them.

*Alex*: Wow! My colleagues were right. There are multiple ways to automate in the cloud.

*John*: Well, most of them were available on-premises a long time ago and are just an evolution, now running in the cloud. But wait, there are still two beers left. Let's drink them while I mention the last few possibilities.

*Alex*: Even more? I mean, yes, let's open those last beers.

*John*: Don't worry, I'll just mention them so you can investigate further later when you need them. These use managed services, so they should be easier to use. They are full-featured products, but I don't want you to forget them; at some point, you should take a look at what they can do for you.

*Alex*: Okay.

*John*: We've used some options to control the AWS services, starting and stopping instances. But what happens when you want to do a different thing, such as running code inside some servers? That is, you need to control tasks running inside the OS and the EC2 instances, not the EC2 service and the instances themselves.

*Alex*: I assume you can copy the script to those servers and ask the OS to run it.

*John*: Yes, but how do you do that distribution task? Again, this can be really tedious and error-prone. Imagine you need to run a script on 100 servers at midnight. Do you want human intervention?

*Alex*: I assume I'd be in charge of them, as I'm the newest employee. What is the automated option?

*John*: Some AWS services are designed to run scripts on a set of computers. The most generic one is **AWS Systems Manager**. It allows you to run any collection of scripts on any collection of computers scheduled at any time.

*Alex*: Cool! How does this work?

*John*: It will first carry out an inventory of all our systems, Linux or Windows, using an agent. These servers can be EC2 instances but also on-premises machines. You will also be able to group them as you wish; then, you'll be able to run any set of scripts on any group of servers at any moment you wish.

*Alex*: What sort of scripts?

*John*: Systems Manager offers a huge collection of predefined tasks called **automation documents**. But you can also use your own scripts in Python, PowerShell, or Bash.

*Alex*: And I assume they can be scheduled?

*John*: Yes, you can control when to run them and how many to run in parallel. And you can control the execution results in a centralized way.

*Alex*: Wow, a generic script scheduler with no limits! What else can it do?

*John*: Many more interesting things, such as inventory, explorer, grouping computers, and also patch management with defined maintenance windows. It is also a change management system. You can also integrate it with CloudWatch alarms and connect to servers remotely. And most basic functionality is also free.

*Alex*: It seems much more powerful and easier, as it is a managed service.

*John*: It is like having a personal assistant. You just tell what to do and when, and it will take care of everything.

*Alex*: And you said it also works with on-premises servers?

*John*: Yes, you simply install an agent on them, and they have to be reachable from the internet. Once there, you have the same functionality. And they can be Windows or Linux, or any combination of them.

*Alex*: What about security? Running scripts on a large number of computers could be risky.

*John*: Of course. Everything we've seen today, CloudFormation, the API, the CLI, PowerShell, Python, and Systems Manager, all require the right permissions, and all integrate with IAM. Only authorized users will be able to perform the tasks.

# Summary

John thinks he has already covered all relevant options: CloudFormation, APIs, scripting with multiple languages, and all AWS services using these, such as Systems Manager. At least he has provided a comprehensive first view of all of them, so Alex can return to his office and compare them. He knows he'll need more information before putting forward a proposal, but lots of help and documentation are available for all the options commented upon.

And they've run out of beer, so they agree to continue the chat soon.

*Alex*: I'm now getting a clear idea of how to start. Thanks, John. I'll phone you soon to tell you how we proceeded and maybe to get more ideas.

*John*: Tell me if you manage to write the CLI challenge I proposed. By the way, I assume you'll leave your car here and walk home.

On his way back, Alex has time to think about the next steps, with many ideas coming to his mind.

The first thing he'll propose is using CloudFormation to create all new environments. This is a straightforward change, especially if they find some useful sample templates already prepared.

And the second proposal will be to create a collection of useful scripts for any other tasks. For that purpose, he'll have to discuss with the rest of the team which scripting languages to use and define some coding standards so everybody can find and reuse them easily.

He will also check all the links provided by John. As there are many available examples, that will help choose the best options.

In the meantime, Harold and Charles have been really busy. They have started to compile a full inventory of all the scripts they're currently using, where they are located, their languages, and specifically, their purpose. In the middle of that process, they realized that most of the inventory could also be done by another script. They finally built a spreadsheet with all this information.

After a short meeting with Alex and Gloria, they decided which scripts they will prioritize for their main cloud tasks, and also which ones to run from Systems Manager, and which ones will run manually. Their next task will be testing and improving them and start building a shared script library.

Finally, everyone on the team presented this spreadsheet to the management. Now, Alex was much more confident as he had a clear picture of the next steps. The spreadsheet immediately became an action plan for all.

Now, most of their daily routine tasks are fully automated, so the team has more time to do more productive tasks. Scripting to the rescue!

# Further reading

- CloudFormation:

  - `https://aws.amazon.com/cloudformation/`

  - `https://docs.aws.amazon.com/AWSCloudFormation/latest/UserGuide/template-reference.html`

- Links for sample templates:

  - `https://docs.aws.amazon.com/AWSCloudFormation/latest/UserGuide/cfn-sample-templates.html`

  - `https://aws.amazon.com/cloudformation/resources/templates/`

  - `https://aws.amazon.com/quickstart/`

  - `https://aws.amazon.com/solutions/`

  - `https://github.com/awslabs/aws-cloudformation-templates`

- Scripting AWS:

  - `https://aws.amazon.com/powershell`

  - `https://docs.aws.amazon.com/powershell/latest/userguide/pstools-using.html`

  - `https://aws.amazon.com/cli`

- Development on AWS:

  - `https://aws.amazon.com/tools`

- All APIs:

  - `https://docs.aws.amazon.com/`

- Multiple samples:

  - `https://github.com/aws`

  - `https://github.com/aws-samples`

  - `https://github.com/awslabs`

- Systems Manager:

  - `https://aws.amazon.com/systems-manager/`

# 11

# Decoupled Architectures – in Space and Time

The team is now happy as they have a consistent way to deploy the required components. The automation approach helped alleviate the burden of many mundane tasks and reduced the risk of human errors. Now they can easily create and scale some components, but they still have a long way to go.

They are beginning to suffer an evident increase in complexity: a standard application architecture may have lots of interconnected services communicating directly with each other. They need a way to independently scale those services while simplifying this potential complexity at the same time. To take full advantage of the cloud services, the application architecture will need a **decoupled architecture**.

Decoupled architectures will allow them to remove those complex integration challenges, scale different layers independently, isolate potential problems, and perform maintenance activities much more efficiently.

## Understanding decoupled architectures

The team is around the coffee machine, discussing the recently decided action plan for automation. Raj is standing near them, at a reasonable distance, as he's talking to someone on the phone.

> *Raj*: Yes, please change the delivery method for my parcel. Please send it instead to the location I mentioned in my mail, and I will collect it from there. Thank you.

He hangs up the phone and heaves a sigh of relief. He talks to himself, but it is loud enough for Berta to hear him.

> *Raj*: I feel better with this decoupled approach.

The word *decoupled* rings a bell in Berta's head.

> *Berta*: Sorry, Raj, I could not help overhearing your conversation, and your last words caught my attention. Did you say *decoupled*?

> *Raj*: Yes.

*Berta*: I know a little bit about decoupled architectures, but what does a package delivery have to do with decoupling?

*Raj*: Oh. It is a nice way to understand decoupling in real life. I learned about this example in one of the training sessions I attended. I am happy to explain it if you have time.

*Berta*: Yes, I am all ears!

*Raj*: Think about a traditional package delivery for something you ordered. You place your order, and the company ships it to you. They can use their own service, or hand over your package to an external delivery company. In either case, that company delivers the parcel to your home. Perhaps they might ask you to sign a proof-of-delivery receipt, which they maintain for their own records.

*Berta*: That's correct. Sometimes I request the parcel to be delivered to other places, such as my parents' home, if I'm not going to be present at my own home.

*Raj*: Yes, many companies require that the receiver has to be present at the time of delivery to sign the proof-of-delivery receipt. If nobody is present, the courier company may try a second delivery attempt or even return the package. In both cases, this will delay the delivery and lots of energy and time will be wasted.

*Berta*: Agreed.

*Raj*: So, courier companies have improved their delivery process. Now they may not require a person to sign the receipt, but they can leave the package on the porch or in the lobby and take a photo to confirm delivery. The delivery will still be complete even if the receiver is not present. When you return home, you will find your package waiting for you.

*Berta*: Right, my grocery vendor started doing the same around the time COVID-19 started, so they just left the parcels at your doorstep, rang the bell, and left, so no direct contact was required. They called it **contact-free delivery**. I am sure this saved lots of time and kept people safe from infection too.

*Raj*: Exactly. The traditional delivery service is an example of a tightly coupled architecture. Both parts in the communication, sender and receiver, have to be simultaneously there for the transaction to complete. However, in a decoupled architecture, the sender will still send the communication without waiting for the receiver to be active. The receiver might get the data at that very moment or maybe later. They'll just need a way to store the data in a safe place until the receiver can get it.

*Charles*: Like a mailbox.

They realize that Charles was also listening to their conversation.

*Charles*: Sorry for eavesdropping. I think a mailbox also follows a similar approach.

*Berta*: Please, tell us more, Charles!

*Charles*: In the past, the mail carrier walked up to your door, knocked, and delivered your mail. This is a type of **synchronous processing**, as both parties have to be present for the exchange, and the communication happens in real time. But nowadays, many houses have installed mailboxes, so the mail carrier just drops the letters inside them:

**Synchronous**
Both sender and receiver must be present

**Asynchronous**
The receiver is not needed to be present

Figure 11.1 – Synchronous versus asynchronous delivery

(Source for the postman's image: Image by pch.vector, at https://www.freepik.com/free-vector/postman-holding-envelope-with-letter-standing-near-mailbox-funny-man-with-bag-cap-uniform-mailman-delivering-postal-package-letterbox-flat-vector-illustration-mail-delivery-concept_21684266.htm)

*Raj*: That's a nice example.

*Charles*: Yes, I use it daily when checking my physical mail. Usually, *synchronous* means that someone has to wait, the mail carrier in this case. And *asynchronous* means there's no need to wait so the whole delivery system is faster. Imagine the mail carrier had to wait for each letter to be delivered in person to each receiver.

*Raj*: That is a certified delivery service, usually done separately by another team.

*Berta*: So, this is a decoupled architecture, as the mailbox acts as the storage mechanism for the letters until somebody picks them up.

*Charles*: Yes. It also has to be secure. My mailbox has a lock, and only I have the key:

Figure 11.2 – A mailbox

*Raj*: Some e-commerce companies also follow the same approach. They offer their customers the option to use a nearby locker. They deliver the item there and then send you a code to open the box and get your item. I prefer this option if I am ordering something of high value, such as a mobile phone. Having it delivered to your porch is not very safe; it could easily be stolen.

Figure 11.3 – A package collection location
(Source: Photo by Tony Webster, at https://www.flickr.com/photos/
diversey/49376513056, used under Attribution 2.0 Generic (CC BY 2.0) license.)

*Raj*: Nice examples. But they only cover one type of decoupling, which is time-based. That means what to do when the sender and the receiver are not present simultaneously. Like the mail carrier and your parcels.

Alex was around and decided to join the conversation.

*Alex*: So, you mean…let me imagine it. Is there also space-based decoupling?

*Raj*: You nailed it. Decoupling can also handle the complexity of systems with multiple components and their relationships, especially when they are constantly changing.

*Alex*: That sounds too theoretical. Do you have any examples?

*Raj*: Yes. Imagine a large apartment block with many neighbors. The mail carrier has to deliver mail to each one of them. Of course, neighbors might change as they relocate to other places and new people come to live in the building. The mail carrier does not personally know all of them but has no problem delivering all the mail. He just goes into the block, looks for the communal mailboxes, reads the name or the apartment number written on them, and inserts each letter in the right mailbox. If a new neighbor comes to live in this block, the mail carrier will also find the right mailbox:

Figure 11.4 – A communal mailbox

(Source: Photo by Bernard Gagnon, at https://commons.wikimedia.org/wiki/File:Community_mailboxes_-_
Canada_Post.jpg, used under Creative Commons Attribution-Share Alike 3.0 Unported license.)

*Alex*: In my block, we have a concierge in charge of that; the mail carrier just gives him the letters, and he distributes them.

*Berta*: So that is a **1:N** relationship. One single mail carrier can deliver to N neighbors, and N is a changing number every time.

*Raj*: It can be even better. Now imagine your mail can be delivered several times a day or week by different mail carriers. It's an **M:N** relationship. Every mail carrier can, of course, deliver mail to every possible neighbor. Again, each mail carrier does not personally know each of the receivers. And the number of senders (i.e., M) and receivers (i.e., N) can change at any time. Every time I find this type of M:N complex communication, I look for a way to simplify it. I call this **decoupling in space**.

*Alex*: This reminds me of a very funny film I saw. There's a car speeding, and a policeman asks the driver to stop immediately. The driver slams on the brakes but the policeman says, *You should have stopped before*. And the driver goes into a nice philosophical discussion about *before in space* versus *before in time*. I had a great laugh at this scene.

*Berta*: I get the idea of decoupling, but how does it work in our application architecture?

*Raj*: Let me explain it. Let's consider a three-tier application; they usually have a web, application, and storage tier. The web tier acts as a frontend and will probably have a user-friendly DNS name where users connect. Then all processing, the business logic, will be passed to the application tier. Finally, the database will permanently store the data in the storage tier. Of course, each tier is separate, and each one can communicate only with the adjacent tier:

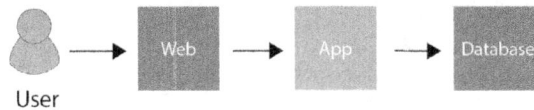

Figure 11.5 – A typical three-tier application

*Raj*: In this model, we have to address two possible problems. The first one is the complexity of a changing number of components. Remember we talked about autoscaling groups; each tier can be formed by a changing number of servers, with a guaranteed minimum and a maximum. So, your three-tier system is likely to be like this:

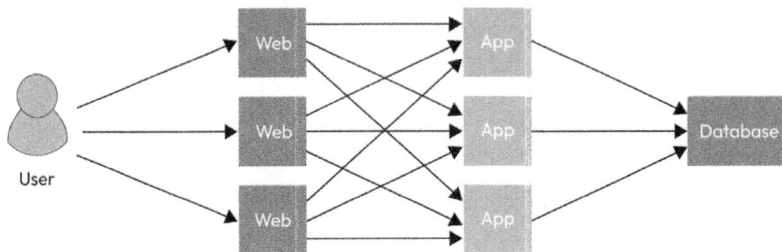

Figure 11.6 – Scaling in a three-tier application

*Berta*: That can surely grow very complex. I can foresee a possible problem; every time you add or remove a server in any layer, you must reconfigure all the components communicating with it. You have to maintain the relationship between the web and the application tier, and additionally, your users must be informed about a new web server being added or removed.

Now Harold joins the conversation after silently listening to them from his desk for a long time.

*Harold*: Exactly. Think about our autoscaling groups, where the number of servers changes with the demand. That would mean that every time there's a single computer added or removed, you would have to store multiple configuration changes: $M$ changes on its left in all senders, and $N$ changes on its right in all destinations. This is pure complexity: just a single addition generates lots of changes. Maybe you need to update a large set of configuration files. The process is not dynamic and is highly error-prone.

*Berta*: And all these additions or removals can happen automatically, at any time, as the result of every scale-out or scale-in activity in every Autoscaling group, with no administrator present.

*Raj*: You got it right. Scary, isn't it? This is a tightly coupled architecture. Now let's try to decouple it.

*Berta*: And that is the *space decoupling* part.

*Raj*: Exactly. And this is a very common scenario in the cloud when every layer can be implemented using an autoscaling group, containers, or Lambda functions. Every time your data moves from one layer to the next, it will find a changing M:N relationship. But we've already seen a way to simplify that; do you remember it?

*Alex*: Having a concierge at the entrance of every block?

*Raj*: Yes, you got it! But in our cloud service world, our concierge is the **Elastic Load Balancer (ELB)**.

Let's add a load balancer in front of the web servers. Now your users are not directly connecting to a changing number of web servers but instead to a single point of contact, your load balancer. Behind it, we can keep an autoscaling group with all the web servers, but users do not need to know about it. For a user, the endpoint of the application always remains the same. And similarly, we can have another load balancer between the web and application tiers.

We have turned an M:N problem into 1:N, which is much easier to handle. Every time there's a change, the load balancer will know about it. By just adding a single service, the ELB, we've removed any tight dependencies; that's decoupling too:

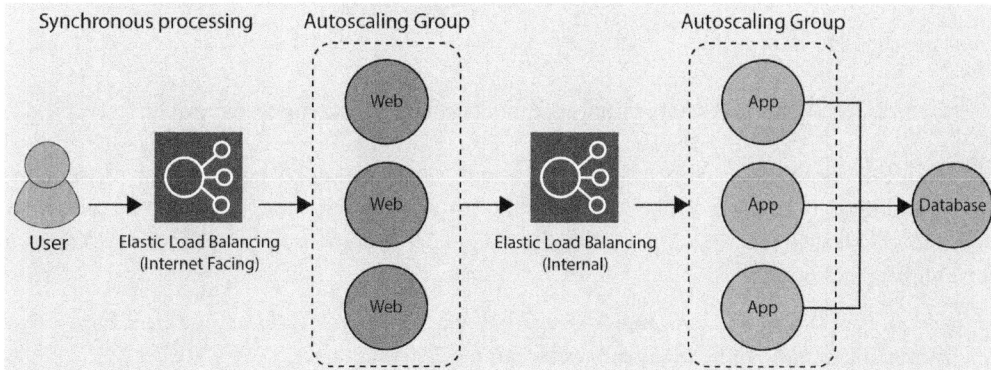

Figure 11.7 – A three-tier application with ELB and Auto Scaling groups

*Charles*: That will simplify the configuration for sure. Now all autoscaling groups will be able to communicate with the load balancer after every scale-in or scale-out operation, and it will also automatically handle the registration or deregistration of different services. But it is still a synchronous process; all the tiers must be running at the same time. If any of them is down, no one will be able to work.

*Raj*: That's right, and that's where *decoupling in time* comes in. This initial architecture is well suited for scaling but still requires all components to be active at all times. If we have to do some maintenance on any tier, the others won't be able to handle the requests. There's also a performance aspect; maybe one tier is slower than the others, fulfilling multiple requests. But the other tiers cannot be affected by this; they cannot be forced to wait.

Fortunately, there is a well-known generic technology designed to introduce asynchronous processing here. Do you know its name?

*Berta*: A **queue**?

*Raj*: Exactly. We can replace the internal load balancer with a queue to store the messages for the application tier. Now the processing of messages between these tiers becomes asynchronous. There's no need to wait; the messages will just be sent to the queue, and the next layer will process them when possible. Something like this:

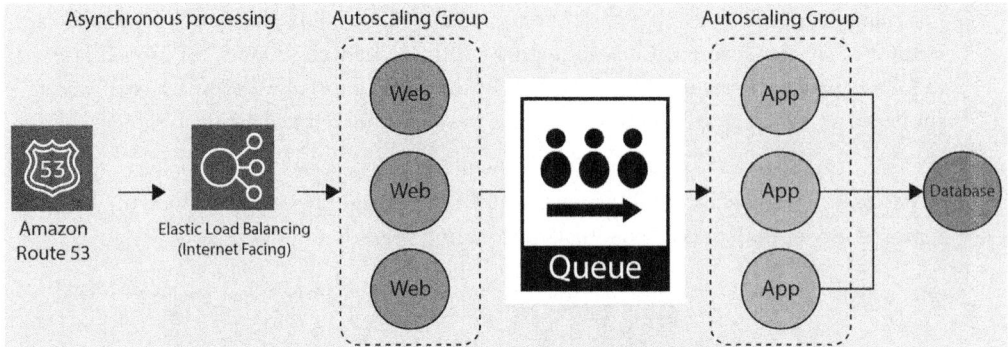

Figure 11.8 – A three-tier application with ELB and a queue service

*Raj*: This means the user experience will be much better, as every transaction will not have to wait for an immediate result from the application or the database; it will just be queued and processed later. And this allows the application to perform multiple tasks in parallel, improving global performance.

*Berta*: I see this model continues to use a 1:N relationship; all transactions are sent to a single point, the queue, where many processes can retrieve them later.

*Charles*: This allows the autoscaling groups to scale with different metrics based on the number of connected users or the number of requests waiting in the queue.

*Raj*: You can even completely stop the application logic for some time, for example, for maintenance. All users can continue to work, as the messages will be safely and persistently stored in the queue until they can be processed. Fully decoupled, now in space, and also in time.

*Alex*: Just as a group of mail carriers delivers lots of letters to multiple houses, to a door-person or some of them. Even if all the neighbors are on holiday for some days.

*Charles*: By the way, you mentioned an *internal* load balancer.

*Raj*: Yes, the first load balancer can be publicly accessible if you wish, so that users can connect to the web servers from anywhere on the internet. But the second load balancer can be defined as internal, as it is only reachable from the web servers. This networking model protects your application logic, or the storage, as nobody can reach them from the internet. And, of course, all of this will be inside a **VPC**, remember, a **Virtual Private Cloud**, with all its private networks, security groups, and **network access control lists (netACLs)**. You can filter which protocols will go through.

And the best thing: even if you use hundreds of computers, you only need one public IP address for the whole solution, for the whole three-tier application. Only the public load balancer will require a public IP address, seen through a public DNS name. All computers need only internal IP addresses, even the ones for the web servers. Great for management and its associated cost.

*Berta*: I can imagine AWS offers several options for queues. Do you have any information on them?

*Raj*: Yes, but it's a bit late, and I'm really hungry. If you'd like, let's have lunch together in the canteen, and we can talk about these in the afternoon. But I have a single rule: no talking about work during lunch. Let's see if we can find Gloria, I heard about an important cloud event and would like to know about it.

During the lunch break, the team is happy. They have realized all their three-tier applications can be easily handled by the cloud using this model, and the migration seems easy. In fact, they are starting to think about modernizing some of their old applications to split them into smaller tiers to fit in this model. Or maybe going to a simpler one for some applications by just using two layers but with all the advantages provided by autoscaling, load balancing, and queuing. But they still have to learn about how these queues work.

# Let's queue

After a lunch break with no references to work, the team continues.

*Alex*: I am eager to hear more about how queues are implemented in AWS.

*Raj*: Happy to explain. There's a service called **Amazon Simple Queue Service (Amazon SQS)**. In fact, this is one of the oldest services offered by AWS. But oldest doesn't mean that no new features are being added to it; I mean to say that it has been around for a long time.

*Alex*: Nice.

*Raj*: Amazon SQS is a fully managed service. AWS operates and maintains the backend powering the queues. You just define your queue, select some settings, and use it for various purposes. You can choose to set up a **standard queue** or a **FIFO queue**.

*Harold*: **FIFO** means **first-in, first-out**?

*Raj*: Yes, that one.

*Berta*: But aren't all queues working in a FIFO fashion?

*Raj*: Not necessarily. FIFO queues were introduced a few years ago into SQS, as initially, it was just a standard queue. You may have an architecture where the order is not important. Let me give you an example. Suppose you go to your favorite fast-food restaurant and order a standard meal from them, and the person just before you ordered a customized meal. Who do you think will get served first?

*Berta*: I guess there is a higher chance of the standard meal order being delivered first.

*Raj*: Another example: you go to your grocery store to buy some items from your shopping list, milk, bread, coffee, potatoes, and cheese. It doesn't matter what you put first in your shopping basket, your potatoes or your bread. And the person at the cash counter will scan them in sequence but in another different order. The order is not important here.

*Harold*: Or the emergency entry at a hospital. They treat the patients not by arrival order but depending on how critical they are. FIFO would not be the best possible order.

*Berta*: Now evident.

*Raj*: Many applications don't require a strict order either. For example, if you want to process the comments received on your product, every comment is independent, so they can be processed without any specific order. Standard queues try to follow a best-effort ordering, but they don't guarantee that the strict order of arrival will always be kept.

*Berta*: Interesting. I always thought all queues had to be FIFO.

*Raj*: You have to consider there are two types of actors in a queue: the producer (someone sending messages to the queue) and the consumer (someone receiving or processing these messages). Producers can generate messages in any order, and consumers may process them in a different order. Every consumer polls the queue to see whether there's a message ready and then pulls it from there:

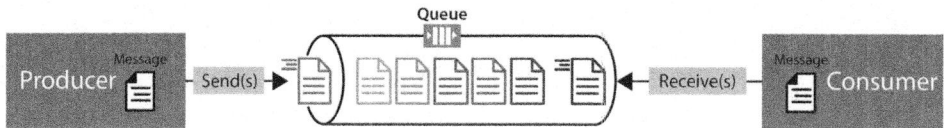

Figure 11.9 – Producers and consumers

*Alex*: One question. I understand the messages are a way to communicate, but can you give me some specific examples of an application architecture using them?

*Raj*: Sure. Let's assume you have created a web application where users can upload their photos into an Amazon S3 bucket. Your program, running on an Amazon EC2 instance, processes those photos, maybe beautifies them, or corrects some coloring issues. When each photo is uploaded, the bucket will generate an event after the upload. All information about the photo can be passed into a queue as a message. Now the queue holds information about every uploaded photo; the application will poll the queue to get the information about each uploaded photo and process it, one at a time:

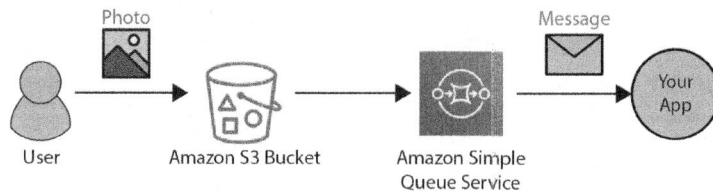

Figure 11.10 – A photo processing application

*Alex*: Okay. So, each message contains only the information about the object in S3, not the full object. Right?

*Raj*: Exactly. SQS has a limit; the maximum message size is 256 KiB, and I am sure most photos are larger. Once your code reads the message – in fact, we say it consumes the message – it will just know a reference for where the file is located and then get the photo from the S3 bucket.

*Alex*: Okay.

Alex was still feeling a little confused, and Raj realized it.

*Raj*: Let me extend your example. Your mailbox has a finite size. If you receive a package that the mail carrier can't drop into it, of course, they won't even try. Instead, you'll get a note saying that your parcel was too big to fit in the mailbox and will be kept at the local post office. That note is a message for you, and you can then act on it by going to collect your parcel at a convenient time:

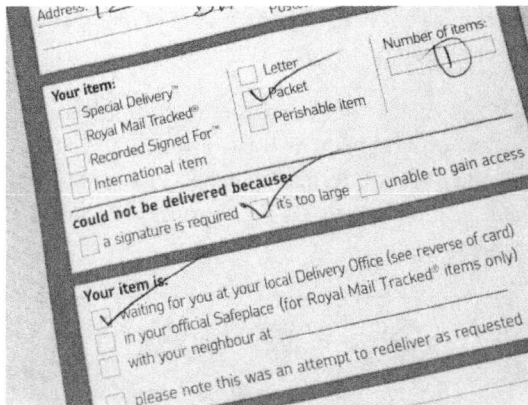

Figure 11.11 – A delivery message

*Alex*: That was a great example.

*Raj*: Thanks.

*Berta*: What happens to the message after its consumption?

*Raj*: Let me ask you a question to answer your question. If you open your mailbox and find lots of letters in it, what do you do next?

*Berta*: I go through those letters, in any order, keep the important ones, and discard any junk mail.

*Raj*: You said you consume those letters in no specific order, right?

*Berta*: Yes.

*Raj*: Does *no specific order* ring a bell?

*Berta*: Oh, I get it, another example of best-effort ordering.

*Raj*: Yes. And as a consumer, you emptied the mailbox, right?

*Berta*: Yes.

*Raj*: It is a consumer's responsibility to delete every message from the queue, but only after it is consumed. There is no limit on the number of messages that a queue can hold, but there is a configurable retention period that could go up to 14 days.

*Harold*: What if a consumer fails while processing the message? Will that message be lost?

*Raj*: No. SQS uses a timeout mechanism for this situation called **visibility timeout**. When a consumer reads a message from SQS, it has a maximum time to process it and then delete it. During this time, the message becomes invisible in the queue, so other consumers won't process it twice. But if the consumer fails while processing, the timer will expire, and the message will appear again in the queue, so another consumer can process it. So, a message has to be processed by one consumer only.

*Harold*: Okay.

*Raj*: Talking about the order of things, standard queues offer **at-least-once delivery**.

*Harold*: Did you say, *at least*?

*Raj*: Yes, *at least*. SQS internally stores messages on multiple servers to provide redundancy. Because of its best-effort ordering and at-least-once delivery, it can deliver nearly unlimited **transactions per second** (**TPS**). But there may be a chance that occasionally more than one copy of the same message is delivered. It is the consumer's responsibility to check for duplicate messages and not process them:

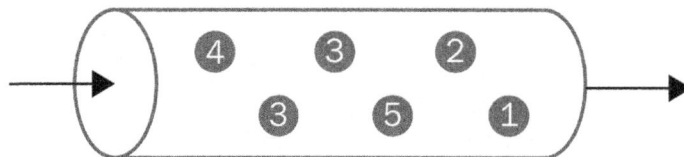

Figure 11.12 – A standard queue

*Charles*: What happens if a message can't be processed successfully due to some error in the message itself or the producer or consumer application?

*Raj*: Glad you asked. You can isolate these unconsumed messages in another queue, called a **dead letter queue** (**DLQ**). Technically, it is just another queue created in SQS, used for your debugging. But SQS doesn't automatically create a DLQ; you must do it.

*Charles*: Got it.

*Alex*: You mentioned we can also have FIFO queues.

*Raj*: Sure. FIFO is a relatively new offering in SQS. Of course, it is used for an application architecture where the sequence is important, as FIFO queues strictly preserve the order in which messages are sent and received. They also ensure that no duplicate messages are present in the queue, so they provide exactly-once processing. Apart from that, a FIFO queue has more or less the same configurable parameters as a standard queue for retention and visibility timeout.

*Alex*: Can you give us an example?

*Raj*: Imagine you want to run commands sent by a user to be executed on a system in a sequence, following an exact order. Or you want your users to register themselves first in your application before buying a product. Or applying multiple price changes to a product in the right order.

*Charles*: Or sending a message to the buyer after shipping the product, but not before.

*Raj*: Exactly. There are a lot of architectures that can achieve decoupling using FIFO queues. One thing here to be aware of is performance. As FIFO queues implement additional processing for correct ordering and exactly-once processing, their throughput is not unlimited as in standard queues. Using the default configuration, you can achieve up to 300 TPS. You could group some messages together, which is called **batching**. In this case, you can achieve a throughput of up to 3,000 TPS, but not beyond it.

*Alex*: Thanks, Raj. I now have a better understanding of queues.

*Berta*: I have noted down the key differences as a table. Check your emails!

Berta shares the following table with everyone:

|  | SQS Standard Queue | SQS FIFO Queue |
|---|---|---|
| Message Order | Not 100% guarunteed, but best-effort order provided | FIFO order is guarunteed. (First-in-first-out) |
| Delivery | Messages are delivered at least once. Consumers have to handle possible duplicates. | Messages are delivered exactly once. |
| Throughput | Pratically unlimited | Limited to around 300 messages per second. (Can be up to 3000/s if batching |

Table 11.1 – Standard queues versus FIFO queues

*Raj*: Thanks, Berta. This will be very helpful to everyone. I will talk about another AWS service that can be really helpful in architecting a decoupled application. But let's have a break first and gather back in 10 minutes. Sound good?

*Alex*: Oh yes, and everyone, please follow a FIFO order at the coffee machine; no jumping the line.

Everyone laughs and leaves the room for a quick break. Alex was still thinking about how technology can be easily explained and understood using daily examples. After all, technology has not come from outer space; it is basically a refined version of our common activities.

The team has now taken a complete look at queues and their features: message ordering and delivery type, maximum message size, retention of old messages, consumers and producers, visibility options, and the maximum possible performance. But another type of queue, Amazon **Simple Notification Service** (**SNS**), will appear in their lives pretty soon.

## Let's notify

The team is returning from their break. It has been an exhausting day (like many others in the recent past), but at the same time, they are happy because they are constantly learning something new, which is extremely useful for their job and makes their lives easier.

*Harold*: Oh, I'm too old for this cloud thing, haha.

*Charles*: Hehe, you keep saying that, Harold, but everyone is seeing the extraordinary enthusiasm you are bringing to this project; you really like it, but you will never admit it!

*Harold*: From what I understood, Raj, we still have to talk about one last but important topic, am I right?

*Raj*: Correct; we need to talk about how we can implement *notifications* in the cloud. I like that you mentioned the word *topic*.

*Charles*: Is this related to what we have discussed so far today? I mean, decoupling and the different types of communication between processes?

*Raj*: Yes, definitely. Highly related. Sometimes an entity, which can be a process, service, or user, needs to send a notification to another one. There's a separate service called SNS, used to manage notifications between entities within a system.

*Alex*: Exactly, I remember it from the course we did.

*Berta*: Me too. If I remember correctly, it is a service to decouple your architecture, allowing you to send asynchronous notifications. In the course, there was a lab where we used SNS to send an email once a certain process was completed, or something like that.

*Raj*: Do not forget that it is serverless; this is another important characteristic of the service.

*Alex*: But how does SNS differ from SQS? I mean, if I understood, SQS can be used to allow resources to *talk to each other*. Earlier, we spoke about a service that sends *messages* by putting them into a queue. But now we are talking about a service that sends *notifications* to another one; there isn't a queue, but it's still asynchronous. I'm a little confused.

*Berta*: It seems SNS is designed to send notifications to humans, as I can see email and SMS messages as possible destinations.

*Raj*: Well, that was a long time ago. Nowadays, SNS is much more generic; it can also send notifications to processes or even other queues. So, that means SQS and SNS are now similar in some characteristics.

*Charles*: So what is the difference? It makes no sense to keep two different services doing the same thing.

*Raj*: I've found a table in the AWS documentation comparing both. Let me write their differences on the whiteboard; the main one is their usage paradigm:

| Features | Amazon SNS | Amazon SQS |
|---|---|---|
| Message persistence | No | Yes |
| Delivery mechanism | Push | Pull |
| Producer and consumer | Publisher and subscriber | Send and receive |
| Distrubution model | 1:M  (One to many) | 1:1  (One to one) |

Table 11.2 – Amazon SNS and Amazon SQS

*Alex*: Paradigm? Now we speak Greek?

*Charles*: Okay, let's say *how they behave* and *how we have to use them*.

*Raj*: Exactly. You remember SQS; we talked for a long time about how to read from a queue. Producers write messages into the queue, and they will stay there until a consumer checks it to find whether there's a message to process. Technically, the consumer *polls* the queue at the desired intervals and reads one message if present. That action is called **polling**.

This pattern is called **producer-and-consumer** or, sometimes, **sender-receiver**. The SQS service implements the producer-and-consumer paradigm. Every time you check your mailbox to see whether there is an email that you are waiting for, you are polling your mailbox.

*Alex*: I'm curious to hear what the paradigm used by SNS is.

*Raj*: SNS implements the **publisher-subscriber** (or simply **publish-subscribe**) paradigm, which works differently: you define a *topic* and configure which entities are *subscribed* to that topic. When anyone sends a message to the topic, all its subscribers will be automatically notified, and all of them will receive the message that was sent. In this case, the receivers – better if we call them subscribers – don't need to perform any polling or type of active task. Instead, the message – well, the notification – is *pushed* into the destination, usually a mail or SMS message, a piece of code that will be run, or another queue that will receive it. The whole process is always asynchronous.

*Berta*: So that means a single notification can be sent to multiple subscribers?

*Raj*: Yes, that's a very powerful feature of SNS. We'll comment on the possibilities later.

*Alex*: When you install a mobile app, it usually asks you to enable or disable its push notifications. That uses the same mechanism, I suppose?

*Raj*: Correct! Your phone gets notified by the application about software updates. The publisher here is the backend of your application, which is running somewhere, and the subscriber is your phone.

*Berta*: Alex, your example is clear, but the subscription phase is missing. I think it is just transparent for the mobile user. I have another one; please correct me if I'm wrong: we have installed the same chat app on our company phones and everyone is part of a chat group. For example, all of us, including Gloria, are members of our well-known cloud team group.

*Alex*: Okay, go on…

*Berta*: When you decided to join the chat group, you subscribed to a topic—using the right terminology. Every time someone writes a message in the chat group, everyone is *notified* about that message:

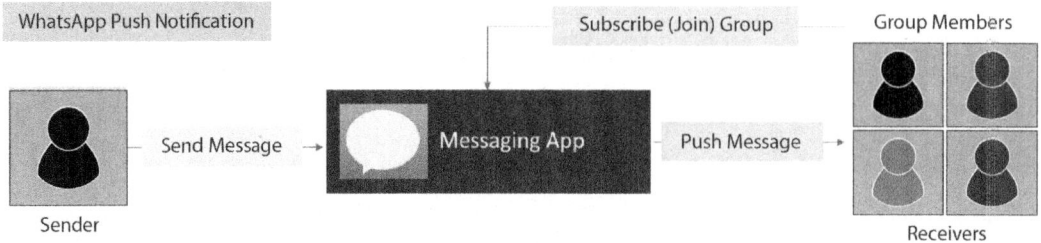

WhatsApp Push Notification   Subscribe (Join) Group   Group Members

Send Message →   Messaging App   Push Message →

Sender   Receivers

Figure 11.13 – Chat group in an instant messaging app

*Raj*: Very good example, Berta. The other main difference between the two services is message persistence. In SQS, the receiver will get the message after some undetermined time, so the queue must provide durable storage where the message will persist until then. In SNS, we don't need persistence, as the message is published and sent to the subscribers, so there's no need to have it stored somewhere.

*Harold*: Hmm, I don't think the SQS service will allow you to store the message forever.

*Raj*: You are right, Harold. There is a parameter that you can configure for your queue by which you specify the *retention* of the messages produced. According to the documentation, the maximum is two weeks.

*Harold*: But what happens in SNS if a notification is pushed and no one receives it?

*Raj*: When you define an SNS subscriber, you can configure a **delivery policy**, determining the behavior of the SNS in case the subscriber is not available. Basically, we are talking about a retry mechanism, so SNS will retry to push the notification a certain number of times until it will *give up*, and only in that case does the notification expire.

*Harold*: Clear. Thanks, Raj, but do you remember whether SNS also supports a DLQ mechanism?

*Raj*: Yes, it does, with a little help from its friends. If the number of retries in SNS reaches the maximum you specified, the message can be sent to a DLQ you set up for that purpose, which is in SQS. At any time, you can take a look at the queue, see the information in the message, and understand why it wasn't sent.

*Berta*: It seems that SNS is a very useful service, one we can use in our architecture for many use cases. I remember, weeks ago, when we talked about monitoring, and we mentioned one of the CloudWatch features, **CloudWatch Alarms** (in *Chapter 8*). We defined several alarms for our applications currently in the cloud. I have an idea: if some of them go into the **ALARM** state, we can now get notified by SNS via email or SMS.

*Harold*: I have another one: with **EventBridge**, another service we studied when we talked about monitoring (in *Chapter 8*), you can *catch* events when they happen. Now we know that we can catch certain events (for example, the creation of a new resource or when a resource goes down) and then get automatically notified by SNS, as Berta said, through an email or an SMS.

*Raj*: Absolutely, folks, you are both right. But we don't have to rely only on emails and SMS. We need to consider a more generic type of notification, as SNS supports several subscriber types. Let me show you the list I've found in the official SNS documentation. The available subscriber types are as follows:

| Email |
| --- |
| SMS |
| Apps on mobile devices |
| SQS |
| HTTP/HTTPS |
| AWS Lambda |
| Amazon Kinesis Firehose |

Table 11.3 – Available subscriber types

*Alex*: It's interesting to find SQS in that list, so that means SQS and SNS are not mutually exclusive services, but they can be used together?

*Raj*: Good catch! That's true. In SQS, only one process can handle each message. But by using it together with SNS, you can build very interesting solutions. As SNS can have multiple subscribers, they can be SQS queues, meaning you can send one task to SNS, which will send the message to multiple SQS queues for different processing in parallel. We call this **fan-out**.

I can think of a use case for some of our applications. For example, the main server, now running in EC2, receives customer data; for each new record, we must process it but at the same time we need to be notified about it. We could use both SQS and SNS to achieve this:

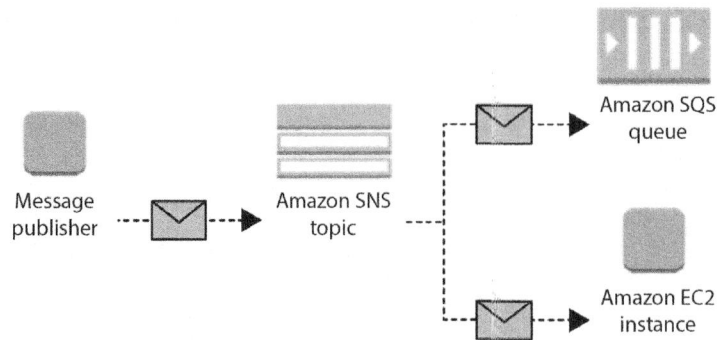

Figure 11.14 – A fan-out use case

*Berta*: This is highly decoupled!

*Harold*: Your list shows another interesting point. I can see we can use SNS to trigger actions as well. For example, instead of notifying a person, we can *notify* a Lambda function, and it will be executed. Another possibility is having that piece of code on a server, fronted by an API we can call with the REST or the HTTP/HTTPS protocols. It seems very powerful to me.

*Alex*: What is Lambda?

*Harold*: Oh, sorry, I was reading a bit about this technology. In a very simplified way, it's a piece of code you provide as a function. Well, many functions if you wish. The Lambda service will keep all the code for you and execute it only when requested. Totally serverless!

*Raj*: You mean we could go into a pure serverless solution for that application, removing all those EC2 servers and just using SQS, SNS, and Lambda?

*Harold*: Probably, yes. We will have to investigate this option; let's spend some time on it now that we know all the decoupling concepts. But I think that's enough for today. We need to relax; let our brains process what we have learned. Then, after the weekend, we can start thinking about using these technologies in our current or future applications' architectures.

*Berta*: Very cool! I'm collecting all the ideas we discussed today in a file. We talked about postal workers, mailboxes, and package collection locations. Then I'm thinking about a specific example: when you order some products online, the package arrives at the destination (maybe at our concierge or in a collection location). Together with the package, you also get an SMS notification that tells us that the package has arrived. Super clear now!

*Alex*: I agree! Thanks, everyone, it was another amazing day.

## Summary

*Gloria*: Hello, everyone. Sorry to interrupt you. Well, I was waiting for you to finish your technical explanations. Amazing.

*Alex*: Hello, Gloria. Welcome to our meeting. Any news?

*Gloria*: Yes. I've been talking with other managers, and we have agreed that your efforts are going in the right direction. That means everybody is happy with how applications are running. Autoscaling and monitoring are helping us avoid problems. Everything seems to run like a charm. So, we have agreed to send you to a technical convention about the cloud, which starts in a few days. All of you. So, pack your bags, and our travel agency will send you the hotel and location details.

*Alex*: WOW!!! One week in a convention center!

*Gloria*: Yes, but remember you'll have to learn a lot so we can use that knowledge later. Have fun, but don't drink and autoscale!

*Berta*: Yeah! That's a good one.

The team now understands all the possible risks related to a tightly coupled architecture. They have studied the available possibilities to create a decoupled solution and, of course, the advantages of using this model. For that purpose, they are considering starting to use some of the services provided by the AWS cloud, such as ELB, SQS, and SNS.

Now a new idea has emerged: running the code serverless, not inside EC2 servers. The team will investigate this possibility, as it seems to offer many advantages.

But first, they will attend the technical convention about the cloud as they know it will be a fast way to learn many new concepts and ideas.

# Further reading

- Three-tier application model: `https://docs.aws.amazon.com/whitepapers/latest/serverless-multi-tier-architectures-api-gateway-lambda/three-tier-architecture-overview.html`

- Generic autoscaling: `https://aws.amazon.com/autoscaling/`

- EC2 autoscaling: `https://aws.amazon.com/ec2/autoscaling/`

- ELB: `https://aws.amazon.com/elasticloadbalancing/`

- Queuing: `https://aws.amazon.com/sqs/`

- Notifications: `https://aws.amazon.com/sns/`

- EventBridge: `https://aws.amazon.com/eventbridge/`

# 12
# Containers – Contain Yourself and Ship Some Containers

The team is in a different city, attending a three-day yearly event hosted by AWS. They expect a highly technical event, where they can learn a lot of details about the services they are already using, but also about new services, ideas, and possibilities.

Gloria was able to allocate some budget for the IT team's travel as she had promised. She could not attend due to some personal commitments but is very hopeful that her team will use this opportunity to the fullest and learn more about the various cloud technologies.

Berta was the first to arrive at the hotel as she used public transport rather than taking a cab. The rest of the team is still stuck somewhere in the traffic of the evening rush hour. They have decided to meet early in the morning at the hotel breakfast lounge and plan for the first day of the event.

The next morning, Berta is the last person to arrive at the breakfast lounge while everyone else has already started their breakfast. She joins the group and their conversation.

*Berta*: Good morning, all! I see everybody has arrived.

*Raj*: Welcome, Berta! Hope you slept well. Try the avocado sandwich – it's really tasty.

*Alex*: And the pastries too. They are yummy.

*Berta*: It's fantastic to be here! I have always considered attending this event, but I never thought it would happen so soon.

She joined the discussion and realized that David, the consultant from CloudXperts, was also sitting at the same table as her team.

*David*: Good morning, Berta. So, I can add at least one person to my session's audience.

*Berta*: Good morning, David. Good to see you here. Are you presenting at the event?

*David*: Yes, I am. And I am lobbying to get more attendees for my session on **Microservices on Containers**.

*Berta*: Oh, you are presenting that one. You're not going to convince me… as that session is already on my list. But can you give me some details?

*David*: Sure. In brief, it is going to be a short history of enterprise architectures. How code was built and distributed in a monolithic way, and then how it evolved to something more modular.

*Berta*: Interesting. I've always loved the history of computing. Tell me more.

*David*: In the early days of computing, applications were written only in a single way: every application had to be designed and built to fit into a single executable.

*Berta*: Yes, I saw some practical examples of that coding style at my previous company – monolithic applications. It was hard to check, to distribute…

*David*: Yes. Monoliths served their purpose well for a long time, but the internet began to be used exhaustively, the demand and the applications started to grow, now serving thousands of simultaneous users, and monoliths could not cope with the faster deployment cycles needed.

*Berta*: You call them monoliths?

*David*: Yes, it's a practical way to refer to those monolithic applications. The term was coined a long time ago, but the idea remains the same.

*Berta*: So I can assume some solutions appeared for this problem, as all companies faced it at the same time.

*David*: Exactly. At that time, some intermediate options appeared, all of them based on splitting applications into smaller components. But that componentization introduced many new problems, especially because each one of the possible solutions used its own standards – too many of them, in fact. And at the same time, application usage continued to grow, now serving millions of simultaneous users – the magic of the internet.

*Berta*: How interesting! What happened then?

*David*: Fortunately, container technology paved the way for a more robust and standard approach to building components and allowing them to communicate. This microservices-based approach became the shining beacon of hope. Applications become more agile and decentralized, as they can now be divided into smaller services. These services can be built, scaled, and monitored separately, and complex architectures can now be decoupled and highly simplified.

*Berta*: Divide and conquer, as someone said a long time ago. So, your session will be based on these containers?

*David*: Containers, of course, in the cloud. And also the microservices approach, using these containers to build applications.

*Berta*: Amazing. Count on me being there. I'm not a developer but I imagine everybody should know a bit about these options.

*David*: I totally agree. It will be in Arena 2, Hall 6. See you there. Let me also catch up with some of the other customers; luckily, they are also staying at the same hotel.

David leaves and Berta finds out that the whole team will be attending this session. After breakfast, they all leave for the venue. Once there, they realize the convention center is buzzing with activity. It is so good to see so many like-minded people attending a technical event with the intention of learning, sharing, and networking. Everyone goes in different directions to attend the sessions they chose and agrees to meet again at David's session.

# From monoliths to microservices

At the given time, they all meet in the designated room, settle down in the chairs, and wait for the presentation to begin. David starts, and after the formal introduction, he shows a picture of a hammer and some nails:

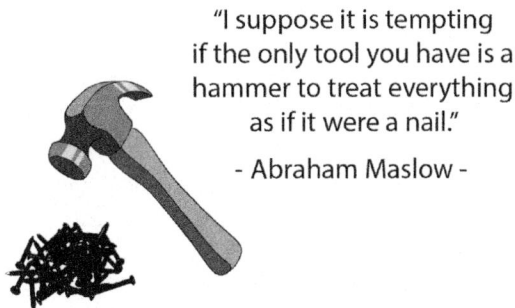

"I suppose it is tempting if the only tool you have is a hammer to treat everything as if it were a nail."

- Abraham Maslow -

Figure 12.1 – Hammer and nails

*David*: When the only tool you have is a hammer, every problem looks like a nail.

The audience roars with laughter.

*David*: This was so true in our approach to application design when the only option we had was building a monolith. I will first explain to you about them and then we'll talk about how microservices are a better solution. But let's first hear what a monolith is by comparing it to a taco stand:

Figure 12.2 – A taco stand

(Source: Photo by bradleyolin, at https://commons.wikimedia.org/wiki/File:Taco_

stand.jpg, used under Creative Commons Attribution 2.0 Generic license.)

*David*: We can see our stand is a one-person operation, where one person is responsible for everything related to selling tacos. This person takes care of sourcing all ingredients, cooking, customer service, accounting, sales, marketing, taxes, quality control, and so on.

Monolithic code does the same. Usually, one monolith is running on a large computer system and is probably built from one single code base. It is designed as a single and indivisible unit, without having any modularity. It is deployed all at once, and each part of the code depends heavily on the others to work. The user interface, business logic, and data access layer are bundled together into one application, and it will probably use a single database to persist the data:

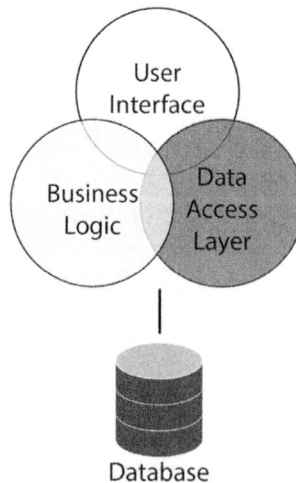

Figure 12.3 – A monolithic application

*David*: This model served well in the past and is not extinct yet. But modern application architectures may not be well suited for this approach. Monoliths are a barrier to adopting new technologies. Somebody decided years ago to use a specific language and a specific database and just kept on adding more and more application logic over it. Maybe that was the best choice at that time, but nowadays this might be not so efficient, or might even be impossible to manage. Can you find skilled Cobol programmers? How long does it take before they understand what that huge application is doing and all the possible consequences of a change? Making radical changes in a monolithic application is kind of impossible.

David can sense that the audience is following the conversation; they are nodding to some of the challenges he is talking about. He continues.

*David*: Monolithic code was also designed to be deployed all at once, as a single entity. That meant that all testing activities had to be repeated with every new deployment. This worked, more or less, as the deployment of a new version of an application was done infrequently – maybe monthly, quarterly, or even yearly. But today's application development is much more agile. Some enterprises may deploy their changes much faster – even hundreds of times in a single week. And this is not a suitable approach for a monolith.

Another difficulty is scaling. When you need to scale an application to support more users, you can just add hardware capacity such as CPUs, memory, disks, or networks. That will affect the whole application. In this case, you can soon hit the physical limitations of a server, for example, how many CPUs or RAM it can support.

Now, imagine you need to scale only an individual functionality of your application, for example, the user registration to support this event. This is just not possible.

David takes a quick look at the TrendyCorp team. They are all listening very carefully.

*David*: After some time, your code will become too complex and too difficult to maintain. Even a simple issue or bug could disrupt the whole application because of its tight dependency. Troubleshooting, auditing, monitoring, performance optimization – all these activities get more difficult day by day and steal most of your time and efforts.

So, what could be the solution? Here come microservices. But let me explain this concept first by using an example.

He shows another picture:

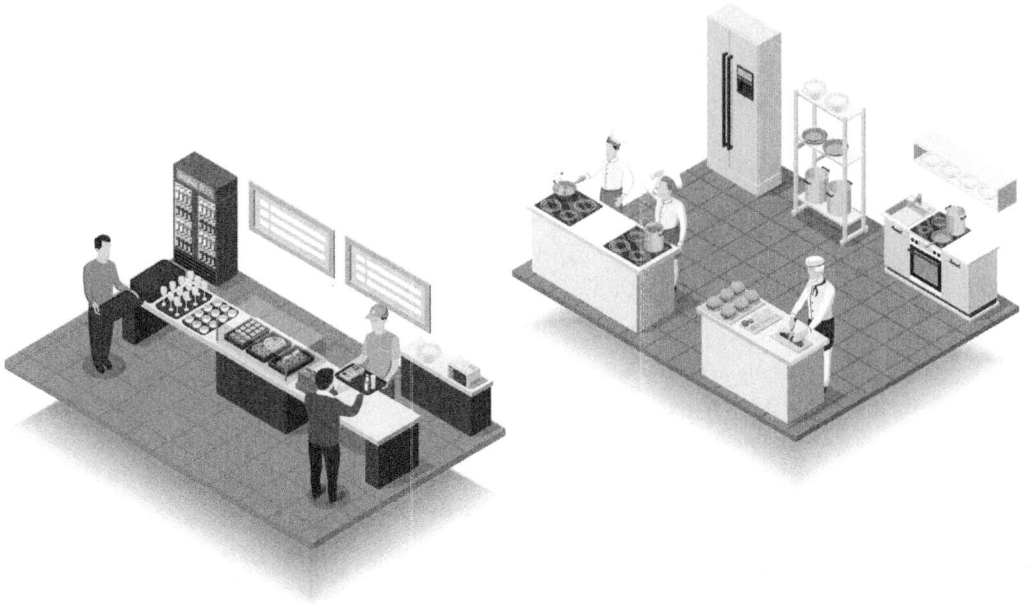

Figure 12.4 – A pizza shop

*David*: This pizza shop is also serving food, like our taco stand. But you'll notice there are three people working on it. One person is taking the orders and getting the bills. Another one is focusing on baking the pizza, and also taking care of ingredients. The third one is delivering the orders to the customers' tables, and maybe taking care of cleaning the tables too.

They all are working together for a single purpose, but they have different responsibilities. And most certainly they have a communication mechanism in place allowing them to work efficiently. The person who is delivering the pizza to the customers' tables may not know whether the customer has paid by cash or card. The person who is accepting the payments may not know how much cheese to add to a large pizza. But the whole business is efficient in the one thing they are doing, serving hot pizza.

If you take this example to a large scale and think about a fine-dining restaurant, there are also a lot of people working together to offer a fine-dining service, but they all are probably doing one thing at a time efficiently:

Figure 12.5 – A fine-dining restaurant
(Source: Photo by star5112, at https://www.flickr.com/photos/johnjoh/4863621966,
used under Attribution-ShareAlike 2.0 Generic (CC BY-SA 2.0) license.)

David realizes that everyone is following his conversation and can relate things to their daily life.

*David*: Microservices also follow a similar approach. A microservice-based application is composed of multiple independent services. Each one of them is designed to efficiently perform a single task at a time. Maybe just sending emails, performing credit card checks, verifying stock, or storing data – you name it.

Now, every individual team in your company can own these microservices. They can define their own roadmap and take their own separate decisions, selecting the technology stack that best suits the purpose. Each team will control and improve its part, which includes release cycles, monitoring, maintenance, and all optimization activities. This may also include the use of a purpose-built database rather than using a standard database for all types of data.

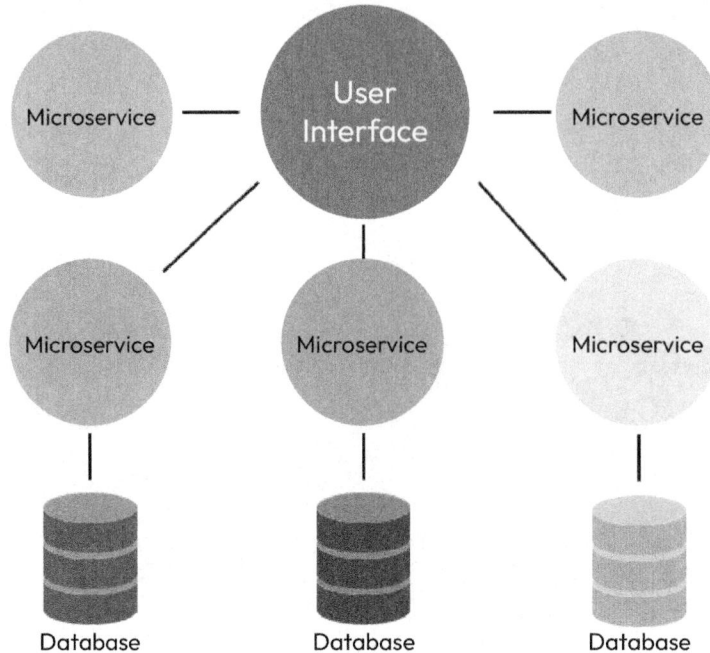

Figure 12.6 – A microservice architecture

David sees that someone in the audience has raised her hand to ask a question. Before he can ask for it, the support team has rushed over and hands over a cordless microphone.

*Audience member 1*: So, I can decide to use one language – let's say Java, and another microservice may use a different language – let's say Python. Then how will these services communicate?

*David*: Great question. These different services communicate over well-defined APIs. An **API** is an **Application Programming Interface**. APIs provide interaction points for services to communicate. So whatever language you write your code in, the API interface remains the same. The internal details are hidden, but the service offers a sort of **black box** to the user of the microservice.

*Audience member 1*: Sorry, a black box? Like the ones in airplanes?

*David*: Not exactly. **Black box** is a term that represents a service, where some parts of it are hidden. The APIs ensure that you don't have to worry about their internal details. Think of a drive-through restaurant; you have a well-defined process to follow to get your food: you order through a sound box, pay for the order, and collect it. Do you know the internal details, such as which fryers they use? Or how many employees are working inside at that very moment? Or when their shifts end? Probably not. You just need a service and it is delivered to you efficiently, without you worrying about any internal details. That's a black box, and the API, the interface, is the window where you request and collect what you need.

*Audience member 1*: That's helpful. Thank you.

*David*: Another benefit of this approach is that a relatively small team can maintain a microservice. As the team is not very big and there are fewer dependencies, decision making is much faster. They have to build the service, but also ensure that it runs smoothly.

Let's see some of the challenges present in monolithic applications, and how microservices can solve these issues. Now let me give you a little glimpse of how applications have evolved up to this point.

He shares the following slide and gives the audience a little time to understand how applications have evolved over recent decades:

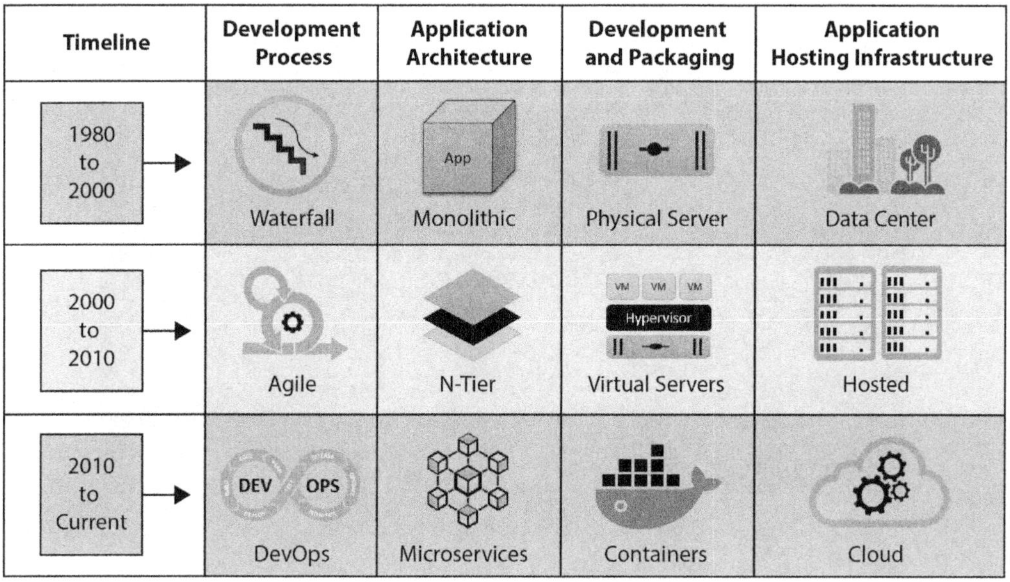

| Timeline | Development Process | Application Architecture | Development and Packaging | Application Hosting Infrastructure |
|---|---|---|---|---|
| 1980 to 2000 | Waterfall | Monolithic | Physical Server | Data Center |
| 2000 to 2010 | Agile | N-Tier | Virtual Servers | Hosted |
| 2010 to Current | DevOps | Microservices | Containers | Cloud |

Figure 12.7 – How applications have evolved

*David*: If you look at the bottom row, most of the enterprise application development is now following a DevOps approach, using a microservices architecture. Applications are packaged and run as containers, and now they are hosted in the cloud, not on your physical servers.

David takes a short break so everybody can have some time to assimilate the concepts in the image. Some people take photos with their mobile phones. Up to this moment, he has defined the old monolithic approach for writing code, its possible problems, and the start of the evolutionary process leading to the usage of microservices. But now he needs a real implementation, so he will need to formally define what a container is.

# What is a container?

After this short break, David starts again.

> *David*: Okay, folks, it's now time to talk about the second topic of this session: **containers**. What is a container in IT? But before giving you the answer, let us consider shipping containers.

David displays his next image:

Figure 12.8 – Shipping before containers
(Source: Photo by Buonasera, at https://commons.wikimedia.org/wiki/File:Hafenarbeiter_
bei_der_Verladung_von_Sackgut_-_MS_Rothenstein_NDL,_Port_Sudan_1960.png,
used under Creative Commons Attribution-Share Alike 3.0 Unported license.)

You can see here how people used to ship goods, of any size and shape, many years ago. We all can imagine how tough it would be to move those goods around, and how challenging it would be to bring them onto ships. Let's focus on a specific moment: when goods arrive at the destination. They must be unloaded from the ships, put on some kind of vehicle, and transported.

With this scenario in mind, let me ask you some questions: at the destination port, how can you know in advance how many goods will arrive? How many people or vehicles will be needed to transport those goods, considering all of them have different sizes and shapes?

At that time, there were two problems to be solved: **the lack of a standard**, and **the lack of abstraction**. The standard that was invented (and that is still in use today) was shipping containers:

Figure 12.9 – Shipping with containers
(Source: Photo by Glenn Langhorst, at https://www.pexels.com/
photo/shipping-containers-at-a-cargo-port-9211513/)

Every shipping container has a standard size, shape, and maximum weight. It can contain many different goods but will stay sealed until it reaches its final destination. During its transit, all stakeholders have relevant information, such as the number of containers to be transported. Everyone knows the standard size of a single container. That means all transport can be planned in advance, so people are prepared with the right means. Every part of the process of loading and unloading containers is perfectly adapted to the standard structure. Even the hooks used to lift a container are standardized.

David stops talking for a few seconds – just a quick pause to see his audience's faces and to understand whether they are still following him.

*David*: I also said there is another problem to solve, a **lack of abstraction**. Well, shipping containers solved that too. From the point of view of the people who work in a port, loading and unloading ships, it doesn't matter how many goods are inside a single container, nor their individual sizes, shapes, or weight. The only thing that matters is the shipping containers – in particular, the number of them – because the structure is standard, and everyone who works there knows it. **Goods' characteristics are abstracted**, which means **hidden**. And, in this way, they can be managed much more easily.

The closure of the story generates a positive *Oooh* effect among all the people new to this information. It is a good sign for David about the audience's feelings. He continues.

*David*: In IT, we had to deal with a similar problem too: many IT companies had the challenge of running and maintaining multiple different applications across multiple physical environments. Because each application has its own specific needs (for example, running on a specific operating system, or having some libraries installed and configured), IT companies struggled to manage different applications in the same physical environment or, to avoid that complexity, they used isolated physical environments and, as a consequence, they saw their hardware multiply:

Different apps running on the
same physical server

| App A | App B | App C |
|-------|-------|-------|
| Libraries | | |
| Operating system (OS) | | |
| Server hardware (HW) | | |

Challenge: apps incompatibilities

Different apps running on
separated physical servers

| App A | App B | App C |
|-------|-------|-------|
| Libraries | Libraries | Libraries |
| OS | OS | OS |
| HW | HW | HW |

Challenge: multiplicity of hardware

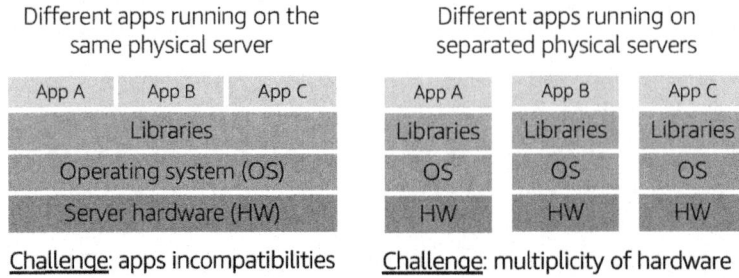

Figure 12.10 – Maintaining multiple technology stacks across multiple environments

*David*: It is difficult to run multiple different applications on the same physical server with no standards or abstraction. For the same reason, it was difficult managing separate goods on a ship.

Just as the shipping industry got revolutionized by the use of shipping containers, similarly, packaging your code in a container can remove a lot of the heavy lifting required to create, distribute, and run an application.

Another hand is raised from the audience.

*Audience member 2*: What about virtualization? By using it, many IT companies have already solved the challenges you just mentioned.

*David*: Yes, absolutely! That's correct. You just anticipated me introducing the last step that was taken just before IT containers: **virtualization**. It is possible **to virtualize physical servers** by using a piece of software called a **hypervisor**. You can use them to create multiple virtual servers from a physical server. These virtual servers really seem like full servers, with all their resources, such as RAM and disks and CPUs, from the application's point of view. The application does not know whether the server is physical or virtual. But, under the hood, these virtual servers are just processes that run on a large physical server, usually called the **host**:

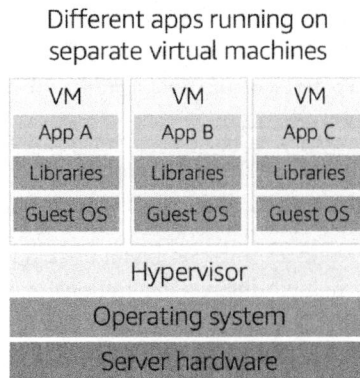

Different apps running on
separate virtual machines

| VM | VM | VM |
|-------|-------|-------|
| App A | App B | App C |
| Libraries | Libraries | Libraries |
| Guest OS | Guest OS | Guest OS |

| Hypervisor |
|------------|
| Operating system |
| Server hardware |

Figure 12.11 – Virtual machines on a hypervisor

Just as abstractions help increase agility in the physical world of shipping containers, they also help remove difficulties and inconsistencies in the virtual world. In the past, it was difficult to consistently and efficiently deliver goods before shipping containers. Similarly, in the virtual world, it is difficult to consistently and efficiently deliver applications with bare-metal servers, especially when all virtual machines or processes compete for scarce resources such as RAM.

Did we solve the challenges I mentioned before? Well, yes, because IT companies can now keep the number of their physical servers lower, every application is now isolated, and virtual servers are much easier to manage than their physical counterparts. For example, you can automate their creation or destruction – something you cannot do with physical servers. If you destroy a physical computer every week, you're surely fired. If you do the same with a virtual computer, probably you'll get a promotion.

*Audience member 2*: Interesting idea! And thank you for the clarification!

*David*: You're welcome. Unfortunately, the challenges didn't finish here. The downside to **virtual machines**, or **VMs**, is that the virtualization layer is a heavy consumer of resources. Each virtual machine needs its own **Operating System (OS)**. This causes higher use of the host CPU and RAM, reducing efficiency and performance. If you have many VMs on the same host, you'll need lots of RAM on it to guarantee that all of them will provide the right performance at all times. You'll also have many processes running inside each VM that you probably don't need. Having an individual OS for each VM also means more licenses, more patching, more updates, and more space being taken up on the physical host. There's also significant redundancy: you've potentially installed the same OS four times and the same library three times.

David stops for a moment to drink a bit of water. Then he continues.

*David*: So, I can finally answer my initial question: what is a container in IT? A **container** is a **portable application environment**. It could contain an entire application but, more often, it usually represents a service in a microservices architecture. A container is much lighter than a VM because it contains the application code, its libraries, configuration files, and some hooks to the underlying operating system. But it does not contain the entire OS, its graphical interface, or any unneeded processes or services.

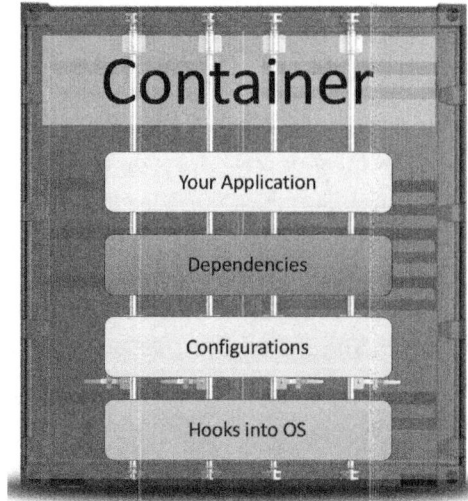

Figure 12.12 – What is a container?

Containers help us solve the problems I mentioned about running entire applications across virtual servers and managing those servers: they generate less overhead, they are more portable, they scale better, and applications implemented with them can be deployed much faster.

The technology you use to create, deploy, and manage them is called a **container platform** (or **containerization platform** or **container runtime environment**):

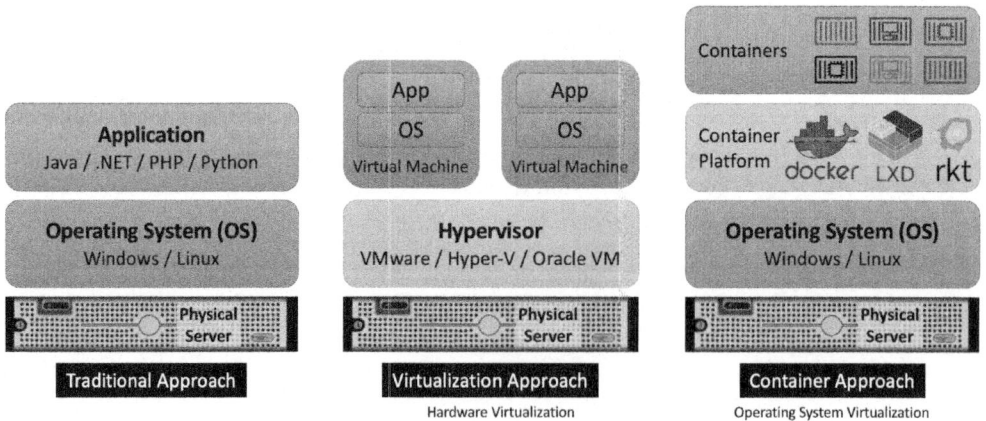

Figure 12.13 – How containers run

You can use containers with any operating system that supports the containerization platform. You can also run different application versions with different dependencies and different libraries simultaneously. This is similar to transporting shipping containers consistently on trucks, trains, ships, and other means of transport, without needing to change the container at all!

With virtualization, we abstract physical servers; with containers, we abstract the whole OS and the application space.

Another hand is raised by the same person who asked the previous question.

*Audience member 2*: What are the most popular containerization platforms we could use?

*David*: Now that we finally know what a container is, we can mention some well-known technologies used to implement them. **Docker** and **ContainerD** are probably the ones that come to people's minds. The first one probably deserves some more details. Docker is an open platform for developing, deploying, and running containers. It supports different operating systems and it can run in multiple configurations (on a single server or on a cluster of servers). Once an application or a service is developed, by using the powerful command-line tool **Docker**, it's possible to define a file called a **Dockerfile** that contains all the commands that Docker needs to execute in order to create (the right term is *build*) the **container image**, which includes the application code and everything else that the piece of code will need to run (libraries, configuration files, and hooks to the operating system):

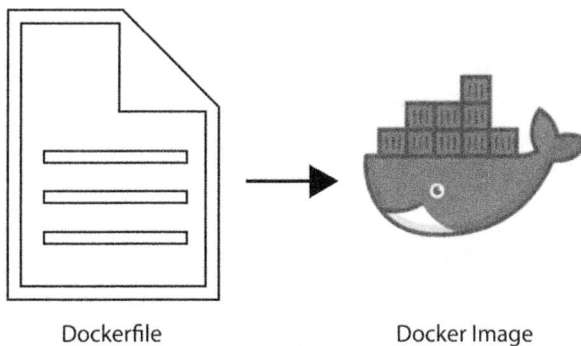

Dockerfile                              Docker Image

Figure 12.14 – Docker's main elements

The container image we have built can now be *tagged* and, finally, *pushed* to a location called a **container registry**.

David now shows a slide with a simple sequence of the Docker commands he just mentioned:

```
#The myapp folder is the one that contains all the files that
will be part of the container image; it also contains the
Docker file, here not visible
cd ./myapp
```

```
docker build --tag=myapp .
docker tag mytag
docker push mytag
```

As you can see from the commands in the slide, now the `myapp` application is stored in the container registry, ready to be *run* on your servers.

David stops for a second to see that everyone is following what he is saying and then continues.

> *David*: Now imagine you're a developer. You have created your perfect application and tested it exhaustively until it seems error-free. Then you deploy it in your company. If you have 100 computers and 100 users trying it, you'll get around 50 calls on the first day saying, "*It doesn't work on my computer.*" 50 or more, actually...

Everybody laughs.

> *David*: The application could be perfect but has been tested in the developer's environment. Maybe every computer has a different setup, so you have to guarantee it will work in all of them, and that needs exhaustive testing for a long time. It is really time- and money-consuming. Maybe you never finish as there could be many unknown scenarios, libraries, incompatibilities, and so on. However, if the application is built inside containers, it can be copied to all environments, and it will just work. You only need to have the Docker runtime running on them.

Finally, David takes a breath and prepares to close the session.

> *David*: Let me finish with a question. Let's imagine you're an administrator and have decided to use containers in an environment such as Docker. What are the challenges you'll have to deal with? It's evident you now have to install and manage the containerization platforms on different servers, no matter whether they are physical or virtual. Containers are easy to manage, yes, but the infrastructure underneath is still there, waiting to be maintained...

David stops talking, looking toward the audience with a big smile on his face.

> *David*: ...and that's the reason you should come to my second session I will deliver this afternoon, still in Arena 2 but in a different hall – this time no. 2. The session's title is *Running containers on AWS*; you can't miss it! Thanks, everyone, for listening; it was a real pleasure. Enjoy the rest of the day and see you later.

David's session ends with long applause from the audience. Everyone is happy about what they've learned, and our friends are no exception. Now they have a better understanding of containerization technologies, especially Docker and its advantages, as opposed to using monolithic applications or virtual machines.

There is still plenty of time before David's next session, so it's time for a quick break just before attending the other sessions they have on their agendas.

# Running containers on AWS

It's only the afternoon of the first day at the AWS event, but our friends Raj, Alex, and Berta have already learned a lot of new things about cloud computing on AWS and they are obviously super excited about the sessions they have attended so far.

The three of them are now in front of one of the conference center coffee booths, taking a break and having a drink before attending the next session.

*Berta*: Oh, I would like to stay here learning new things forever! The event is amazing!

*Raj*: I totally agree. I also want to add that the organization is incredible – with the mobile app they asked us to download before the event, it's very easy to find the list of available sessions, the topics covered, and where exactly they take place.

*Alex*: Don't you feel a bit tired? The only downside of having the event in a such big venue is that at the end of the day, you have probably walked for several kilometers!

*Berta*: Hehe, true. I feel tired too. By the way, which session are you going to attend now?

*Raj*: David's session, *Running Containers on AWS*.

*Alex*: Me too!

*Berta*: Okay, then let's go there! It's going to start in 15 minutes, but I would like to reach the room as soon as possible, so we can sit in the front seats and ask David questions this time.

Raj, Alex, and Berta are in the room. David is already onstage and he starts his presentation.

*David*: Good afternoon to everyone, welcome, and thank you for attending this session. This morning, in my previous session, I talked about containers. Now we'll discuss how to make them run on AWS.

As I explained at the end of that session, microservices applications implemented with containers provide you with multiple benefits, but it's also true that they increase the complexity of your architectures. There are different challenges that we will discuss this evening, but let's start with the first one: the complexity of managing the infrastructure behind.

No matter whether your servers are physical or virtual, they still need to be maintained once provisioned. You have to configure, upgrade, and patch them. And managing a medium-sized Docker cluster can be tedious from the operational point of view – it could take weeks to get it ready in a physical environment.

It's likely you already know about Amazon **Elastic Compute Cloud** or **EC2**, the AWS service used to create virtual servers. You can install and configure your Docker cluster on EC2, so you will not have to manage the hardware underneath and it will take less time to create it, but you still have to manage every single aspect within each server. This approach may be suitable if you need to have control of the OS of the instance.

An audience member raises their hand.

*Audience member 3*: Any use cases where this approach could be useful?

*David*: Maybe you need to install monitoring or security software on these instances. Or you want exactly the same experience as your on-premises environment.

*Audience member 3*: Got it. Thanks.

*David*: So, as you may have already imagined, AWS provides you with a range of managed services to smoothly run your container workloads without worrying about the servers behind. At a high level, you could divide these services into two categories. The first one is where to store your containers, that is, storage for your container images. The second one is a compute platform where you run your containers.

Let's start with the first one. The storage for your container images is also referred to as a **Container Registry**. The Amazon **Elastic Container Registry** (**ECR**) service can help you store and distribute your container images.

*Audience member 2*: Is this the same as Docker Hub?

*David*: Somewhat similar. In order to store, share, and distribute your container images you need a central place, the **container registry**. Your developers can push updated container images into it, either manually or through your deployment pipeline. Then those images can be pulled by your users, customers, other developers, or test engineers for further use. Based on your requirements, you may make the registry public or keep it private:

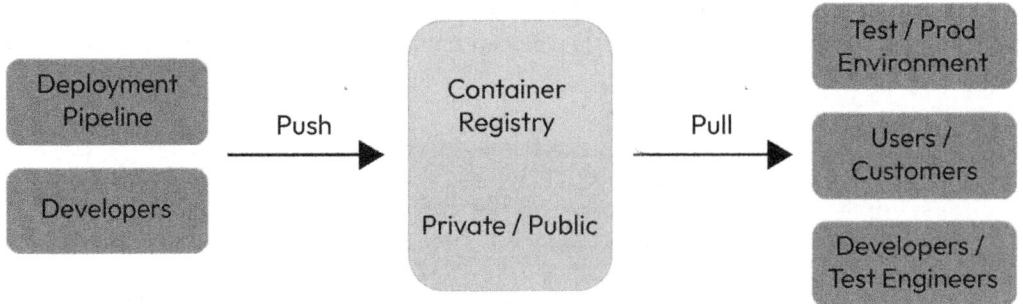

Figure 12.15 – Container registry

*David*: Apart from the durability Amazon ECR provides, you can take advantage of its tight integration with AWS IAM for authentication and authorization. This allows you to access your images easily from other AWS services. You can use it to store, manage, and encrypt your container images. Also, there are two more notable benefits of using Amazon ECR. First, you can enable immutable image tags, so images can't be modified after they have been pushed to ensure their integrity. Second, you can scan your images for common vulnerabilities, ensuring they are safe. You can create multiple repositories in Amazon ECR and store your container images in them:

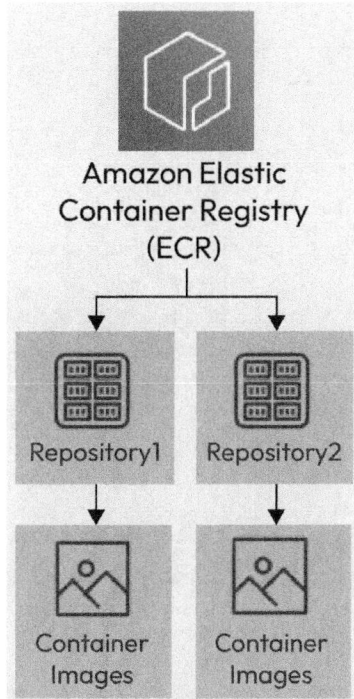

Figure 12.16 – Amazon Elastic Container Registry (Amazon ECR)

*David*: Once you have safely stored your container images, you have to decide where you want to run them, that is, provide the compute resources to launch your containerized applications.

AWS provides a container web service called Amazon **Elastic Container Service** or, simply, **ECS**. ECS is a fully managed version of Docker Compose, hiding all its complexity. With ECS, you work with clusters and with your container images:

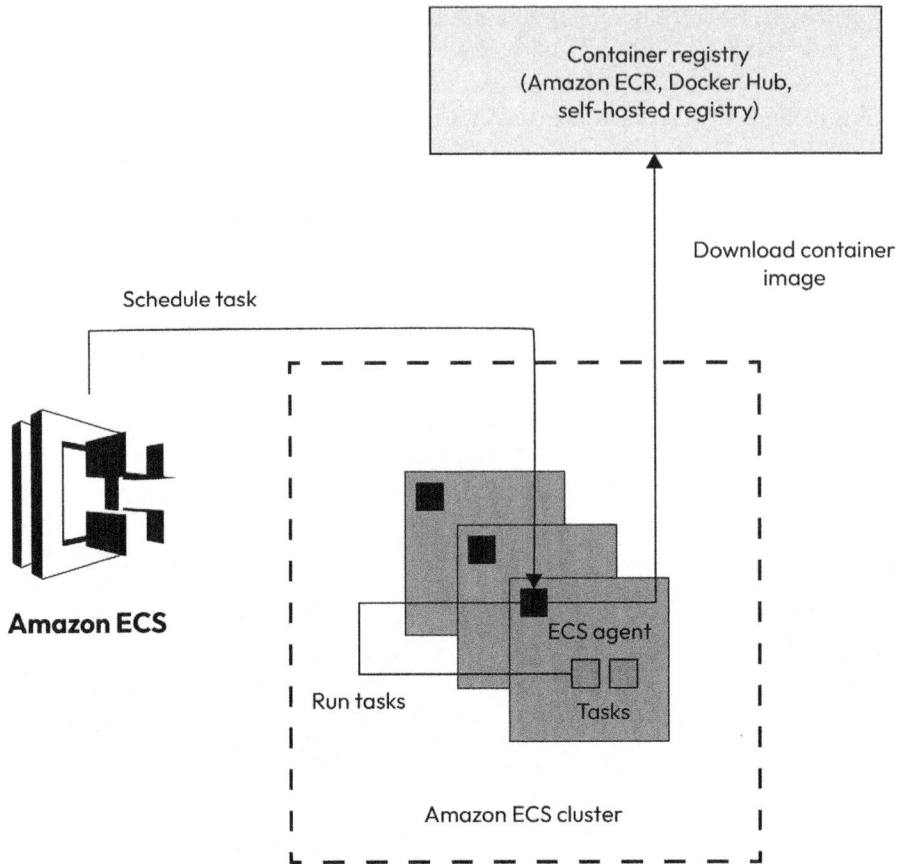

Figure 12.17 – Amazon ECS cluster

*David*: An **ECS cluster** is built from Amazon EC2 instances, here called **ECS container instances**. It can be created in a few minutes because AWS takes care of the preparation of each node, including the installation of the Docker agent on them. One nice feature: the cluster can scale automatically based on the load, because of Amazon **EC2 Auto Scaling**. Once your container images are published and ready to be used, you can deploy and manage your Docker containers through the ECS API, using the commands that ECS provides. You can use most of the Docker syntax you might already know.

David decides to stop talking for a few seconds, just to help people absorb what he has just said, and, in the meantime, he drinks a sip of water. He then continues.

*David*: The next thing we have to do is orchestrate our containers. Does anybody in the audience know what that means? Please raise your hands.

Only a few hands are up.

*David*: Let me explain an **orchestration service** with an example. You have seen a musical orchestra performing, and surely have noticed a person in front of it, using a baton or hands to guide the performance of the musicians. Of course, I'm talking about the conductor or music director. Based on the director's gestures, musicians will adapt their music, either to go to a high pitch, increase their tempo, pause, or resume. This person is not playing any instrument but providing a unified vision of the music to the audience, managing the performance as a whole.

Figure 12.18 – A conductor or music director
(Source: Photo from https://www.peakpx.com/579311/orchestra-
conductor, used under Creative Commons Zero - CC0 license.)

*David*: Similarly, a container orchestrator is a process, managing the operations required for running containerized services in large, dynamic environments. It automates all the common tasks needed in an environment with containerized workloads. That includes provisioning, redundancy, availability, upgrades, scaling, resource allocation, health monitoring, and load balancing.

This is a common challenge that impacts development and operation teams. An IT company may have hundreds of microservices applications, each of them potentially implemented by several containers. So, it might be possible that the company has to manage hundreds or even thousands of containers. In this case, you need an orchestrator:

**Managing a single container is easy**          **Managing a fleet is difficult**

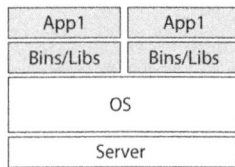

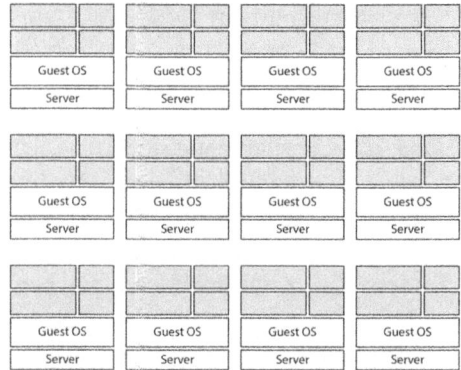

Figure 12.19 – Managing fleets

*David*: Kubernetes, Docker Swarm, OpenShift, and Apache Mesos are some popular container orchestration environments. But if you just need an out-of-the-box orchestrator, or you don't want too much complexity, ECS offers this orchestration functionality too. You can orchestrate your containers with ECS, even if you have only a couple of them.

*Audience member 3*: What about Kubernetes?

*David*: This takes me to the next service, thanks! Let me ask you: please, raise your hand if you know **Kubernetes**!

Most of the people in the room know that technology and raise their hands; only a few people do not, and among them are Alex and Berta. They feel a bit embarrassed, especially when they see their colleague Raj raising his hand quickly with determination. David takes a look at the audience and then he continues.

*David*: Okay, perfect – as expected. **Kubernetes** has now become very popular. Kubernetes, also referred to by the acronym **k8s**, is another open source technology that is meant to solve one of the container challenges – I mean managing them at scale.

It is the most popular container orchestrator and is widely used by many companies to run and manage their microservices applications implemented with containers. Kubernetes allows you to manage Docker but also other container platforms.

But again, you still have to manage clusters of servers, physical or virtual. Also, Kubernetes architecture is much more complex than Docker, because in fact, you have two clusters to manage: the **control plane**, a sort of coordinator, and the **data plane**, where your containers actually run.

So, what can we do to make our life easier when we work with Kubernetes clusters? Of course, we can use a fully managed version of Kubernetes in the AWS cloud. This is called Amazon **Elastic Kubernetes Service**, or **EKS**. It reduces the number of maintenance tasks needed extremely.

David shows a slide representing a high-level EKS architecture:

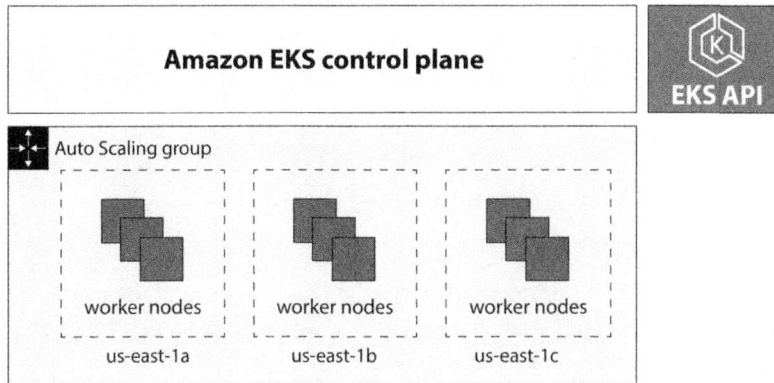

Figure 12.20 – Amazon EKS cluster

At this point, Raj decides to raise his hand. He knew that the presentation would arrive at this point, and he has been waiting for this moment since the morning. Someone from the staff immediately provides a microphone to Raj, who starts asking his question.

*Raj*: I wanted to ask you, David: if a company decides to move its containerized application to the AWS cloud, based on what you said, it has three options: running it on EC2, on ECS, or on EKS. It's clear what the advantages are of managing everything on EC2, but when should I use ECS and when should I use EKS?

*David*: Well, Raj, as a cloud consultant, the best answer I can give you is *It depends*. Hehe. It depends on which containerization platform you already know, your previous experience, and whether you have already built something on-premises and you want to build the same thing in the cloud. If you start from scratch, I would suggest you take an in-depth look at Kubernetes and analyze whether it matches your needs and your knowledge. If the answer is no, I would recommend you think about ECS.

Suddenly, Berta finds some courage and decides to raise her hand too for a question. She gets the microphone directly from Raj.

*Berta*: David, I'm far from being an expert on Kubernetes but just looking at the EKS architecture, it seems much more complex than ECS. Why should I go for that complexity?

*David*: I totally understand the point, Berta, but having a higher complexity could be just the price to pay for having something extra. EKS provides many more features than ECS, especially because the technology used – Kubernetes – has one of the most active open source communities in the IT world. They are always releasing new tools or features that help you manage your Kubernetes cluster better; most of these tools and features are available on EKS pretty quickly too. EKS is also more flexible because, as I said before, it allows you to orchestrate different types of containers, not only the ones based on Docker. Yes, Kubernetes is more complex but more powerful in the end.

Both solutions may be able to offer you similar functionality and you should select a solution that is most aligned with your application requirements and your operation preferences. You may also have to look at the simplicity, flexibility, pricing, security, portability, and support for both offerings.

Berta was very satisfied with the answers she got from David.

*Berta*: Okay, thank you, David!

*David*: You're welcome! For those who had the chance to attend my morning session, you probably remember I mentioned the taco stand, pizza shop, and fancy restaurant. A taco stand may be considered very simple compared to a pizza shop. It's a similar case if we compare the pizza shop with a five-star restaurant, operating on two floors with two different kitchens working in parallel. Sometimes, we just want simplicity if we just want to eat a taco; sometimes we prefer eating while sitting at a table and being served in a proper way, maybe eating food that we can choose from a very sophisticated menu. As I said before, it depends!

David now feels a bit tired; this is his second speech, and the day was pretty long. He knows he's close to the end, so he just drinks some water quickly and he continues.

*David*: Let me now close this session with two more things. The first one is just a map, with all the services you can use:

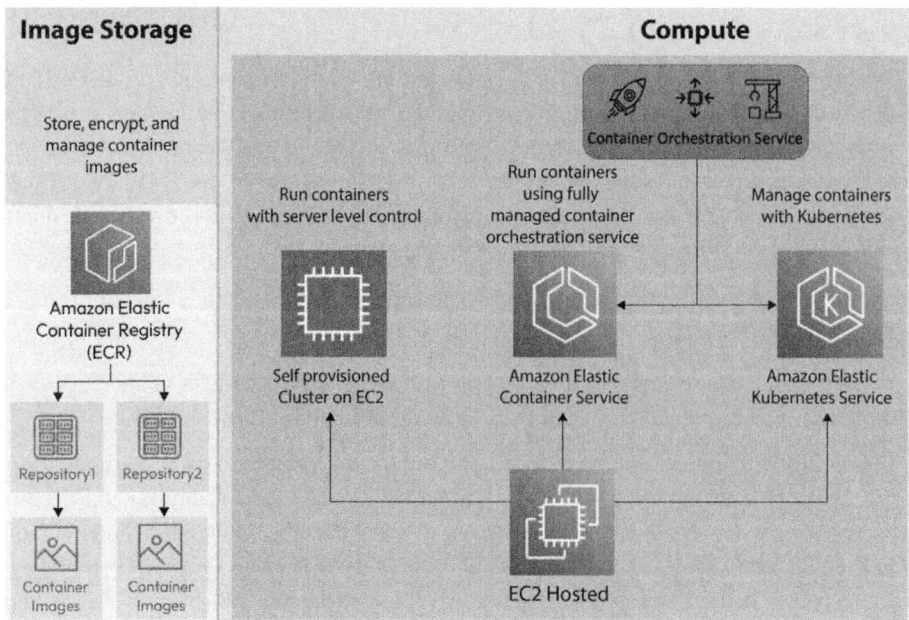

Figure 12.21 – Running containers on AWS

*David*: The last topic I'd like to share with you, and I promise we'll finish with this, is **Serverless Computing**. This is a bit of advertising for my next session, tomorrow. Haha.

In this session, we talked about running your code, but we spent some time, as we had to, considering servers. ECS or EKS are fully managed, but in the end, they use servers, RAM, CPUs, disks, and so on to run your container's code.

But now let's imagine an even better world. What would happen if you just provided your code and it ran… but without any server? And, as you don't use servers, you don't manage them and you don't pay for them when your code is not running.

So, if you are interested, look for my sessions tomorrow. One is focused on **AWS Fargate**, and the other on **Amazon Lambda**. I'm pretty sure you'll remember the names and you'll enjoy them.

David notes that his session time is almost up. After answering a few more questions from the audience, he wraps up his session.

*Alex*: Thanks. I will be joining your session tomorrow.

The TrendyCorp team stays in the hall to catch up with David and ask some more questions. Afterward, they all disperse in different directions and get lost in the crowd.

## Summary

After attending a few more sessions, they all gather in the evening for dinner and discuss the various sessions they have attended and the people they have met. Everyone feels this is a great opportunity to learn about the latest innovations and also enjoy a break away from the office. They are also eagerly waiting for the session on **serverless computing**, which they believe will be as informative as the session about containers.

The TrendyCorp IT team has thoroughly enjoyed the sessions and thinking about how to best leverage containers for running their workloads. They are already building plans to get started with a proof-of-concept for an upcoming project.

## Further reading

- Containers: `https://aws.amazon.com/containers/`
- Containers: `https://aws.amazon.com/blogs/containers`
- ECR: `https://aws.amazon.com/ecr/`
- ECS: `https://aws.amazon.com/ecs/`
- EKS: `https://aws.amazon.com/eks/`
- Docker: `https://www.docker.com/`
- Kubernetes: `https://kubernetes.io/`

# 13
# Serverless – So, Where Are My Servers?

It's the second day of the cloud event our friends are attending. They already have had the chance to attend several sessions and, through them, have learned a lot of new things.

It's lunchtime; every member of the team is going around the conference center pretty hungry, looking for some food. Some of them are attending sessions in groups, others are walking alone, like our friend Harold. He finally finds a comfortable place, sits down, and begins to write something on a small piece of paper. Raj also arrives at the same table.

*Raj*: Hello, Harold. Time for lunch!

*Harold*: Hello, Raj! Just give me one second; let me finish my lists.

*Raj*: Sure, take your time. May I ask what you're writing so carefully?

*Harold*: Yes, the first list is my lunch menu, so I'm sure what to order in these machines with so many options. The second one is my session list: which technologies or sessions I have already attended, and which sessions I want to attend today, so I don't repeat any. Look, maybe you can reuse my list:

    ✓    Applications : Monolithic to Microservices
    ✓    Containers : ECS (maybe with ECR) and EKS
    ✓    Fargate

    ✓    Serverless Architectures
    +    Lambda
    +    Step Functions

Figure 13.1 – Harold's checklist

Raj: Good idea! That will be very practical to choose your next sessions, and also to create a service map when we go back to the office. I assume you have already attended the first ones. I also plan to attend the last ones, so we'll be able to discuss Lambda and Step Functions later in more detail.

Harold: Exactly. We'll have to see what all this *Lambda* is about.

## Going serverless

Harold goes to a kiosk and orders his lunch, selects the table service option, grabs a locator token (with a table number sign), and enters its number while ordering:

Figure 13.2 – Lunch kiosk – ordering
(Source: Photo by LMgamer36, at https://commons.wikimedia.org/wiki/File:McDonald%27s_
Self-Service_Kiosk_in_Petron_SLEX_Southbound,_San_Pedro,_PH_%282_14_22%29.
jpg, used under Creative Commons Attribution-Share Alike 4.0 International license.)

He goes back to their table and places the number sign in a visible location and waits for his order to be served. Raj starts doing the same:

Figure 13.3 – Lunch kiosk – waiting for food

Harold likes the idea of this service, as now he doesn't need to stand in the queue for collection, listen to the staff, monitor the screen for his order number, and then look for a place to sit. Once his order is ready, the staff will find him according to his number and deliver the food to his table, while he can sit back and talk to Raj. As they are waiting, they notice Gloria and Charles are also looking for a place to sit.

*Harold*: Hey, Gloria and Charles! Join us here. We were planning to offer these seats to the highest bidder, but we can make an exception for our colleagues.

*Gloria*: Hi both, thanks. How are you doing? We were thinking about eating something before our next session starts.

*Charles*: Yes, you need a lot of energy to attend as many sessions as you can.

*Raj*: I agree. The sheer number of sessions and spread of the venue are overwhelming. By the way, which sessions have you attended today so far?

*Gloria*: I attended a session on blockchain.

*Charles*: Nice. I ended up in a session related to serverless technologies; it was a level 100, that is, a basic session – exactly what I needed.

*Harold*: I attended the same one, I think. But somehow the term **serverless** always sounded like a misnomer to me. There are still servers, and ironically probably a lot more servers, but the benefit is that you don't have to manage them. If I could rename it, I would have called it *management-less servers*. But I am impressed by the benefits they offer.

*Charles*: Haha, I like the idea. Yes, they offer lots of benefits.

*Gloria*: If you don't mind, could you please explain it to me while we wait for our food?

*Harold*: Sure, Gloria. Let's comment on the same example the presenter used. I am not sure whether you will relate to it or not, but I could completely relate to it per my experience.

*Gloria*: Try me.

*Harold*: Let's go back in time. In the good old days, if you wanted to watch a movie at home, you had to go off to a video store. Once there, you selected the movie, checked whether it was currently available or somebody else was renting it, and then made sure you selected the right format (VHS, Video8, Hi8, or Digital8). Finally, you brought it home, and played it on your video player.

Figure 13.4 – At the video store

(Source: Photo by Joseph Mischyshyn, at https://commons.wikimedia.org/wiki/
File:Douglas_-_Strand_Street_-_Duke_Video_store_interior_-_geograph.org.uk_-_1714873.
jpg, used under Creative Commons Attribution-Share Alike 2.0 Generic license.)

*Gloria*: Yes, I remember those struggles. And probably you had to wait hours rewinding the whole movie to start from the beginning.

*Charles*: Sometimes if a movie title was very popular, the tape might have worn out because of constant usage, and the quality was far from perfect.

*Harold*: And don't forget all the complex setup – all the connectors and cables from your TV to the video player and the sound system. It was like solving a complex puzzle.

Figure 13.5 – Video player and system audio setup

(Source: Photo by TStudios, at https://www.pexels.com/photo/close-up-of-cables-8071904/)

Charles and Gloria both nod. Harold continues.

*Harold*: But in today's world, with all the smart TVs and streaming services, you just switch on the TV, search for the movie, and just play – it's serverless! Or, specifically, hardware-less.

*Gloria*: That's a nice explanation, thanks!

*Raj*: Simple as that. You just get what you need – your film – without worrying about all the complex cabling or visiting the video store.

*Charles*: And the streaming provider will take care of scaling, no matter whether it's one or one million viewers.

*Harold*: Exactly, not like the old days when you had to pre-book and wait for popular movie cassettes.

*Gloria*: I understand it now. But a streaming provider usually charges me a monthly fee, even if I don't watch any films.

*Harold*: It might, but think about a streaming provider that charges you only when you watch a movie.

*Gloria*: Sounds good.

*Charles*: And consider that this provider will charge you only for the minutes you watch the movie.

*Gloria*: Even better. If you don't watch the full film for any reason…

*Harold*: You can take it to the limit; maybe they can charge you only for the milliseconds seen.

*Gloria*: Better. Maybe not for films, but I can imagine other services where this makes sense.

*Harold*: Exactly. That's exactly how most serverless technologies are priced.

*Charles*: And the service provider will take care of all scaling, availability, patching, upgrading, maintenance, and security for you.

*Gloria*: That's interesting. So, serverless technologies remove the burden of server management. There are still servers, but as an application builder, I no longer have to think about them… and the underlying maintenance complications.

*Harold*: That's the point. The cloud provider gives you what you need, but no more than that. All other details are abstracted away.

*Raj*: Let me share one more example. My neighbor occasionally invites me to a backyard barbeque party she hosts. She calls it **bring your own drinks** or **BYOD**. She takes care of everything else – food, tables, cutlery, sitting arrangements, music, cleaning up at the end – you name it. You just need to show up, bring your own drinks, and enjoy the party.

*Gloria*: That's nice.

*Raj*: Now think of serverless as **bring your own code** or **BYOC**. The cloud provider will take care of everything else – servers, hardware, OS, runtime, scaling, and so on. *You just bring the code you want to run.* Serverless architectures can be an approach to various services. You may get storage, networking, compute, messaging, email, machine learning, data analytics, and many more services in this way.

*Gloria*: That would save a lot of time and effort.

*Harold*: And money too.

*Charles*: Definitely.

While they are engaged in conversation, their food gets delivered almost simultaneously.

*Gloria*: That was fast. I was thinking it might take some time because of the peak hour.

*Harold*: I would say this restaurant is operating in a highly scalable manner. Probably, they have more people on this shift because of this event. When the event is over, they will probably scale it down.

*Gloria*: And I would consider this place a serverless offering too.

*Charles*: How?

*Gloria*: If I had to make this burger at home, I would need to go to different grocery stores to source the ingredients. I might also have to rely on an alternate spice if the exact one was not available. Then I would have to follow a recipe (which I always find difficult), prepare the burger, cook it, and finally eat it. It's like a small project for me. But here I just ordered what I wanted, customized some options to suit my taste, paid for it, and just got it delivered to my table. Completely serverless.

*Harold*: Let's call it a kitchen-less way of getting your food.

*Gloria*: Exactly. And if I had made it at home, it probably would not have tasted the same because of my limited cooking skills.

*Charles*: And probably you would not get it in a cost-effective manner, as this restaurant may have sourced the ingredients in the most efficient and economical manner, rather than us buying them from a small grocery shop.

*Harold*: Economies of scale, isn't it?

*Gloria*: Yes. And they can serve one burger or thousands of them because they know how to scale.

*Charles*: And as you don't manage the kitchen, there are no dishes to wash at the end. I hate that part the most.

*Gloria*: And they are not only making burgers in a serverless way; their table service is also serverless. You don't worry about who will bring your order to the table, and the person who is delivering the food to the table doesn't have to worry about who actually requested it and how they paid for it.

*Harold*: That's nice. But now let's eat, I am starving. Luckily, there is no *foodless meal*. I would probably not like it.

Everyone laughs and starts eating their lunch. But in the meantime, all of them are thinking about the serverless concept. They can find many examples in real life, but when it comes down to IT, it seems like a really interesting idea to explore, and something they could use in most of their projects.

But it also seems intriguing, as for them it is still too generic a concept. They still don't know how to implement it or which services to use. So, everybody is checking their agendas to see which sessions will cover it. It seems AWS Lambda is the way to go.

## Splitting your code even further

Alex is also taking a short break in the middle of all his sessions. He has found a quiet room in the convention center, where only a few guys are connecting their laptops or phones to the shared Wi-Fi. He sits at an empty table and starts to sip his cup of coffee. Suddenly, a young man comes by.

*Thomas*: Hey, Alex! What are you doing here?

*Alex*: Oh! Hello, Thomas! What a surprise! Well, trying to learn as much as possible about cloud technologies. I began working at TrendyCorp and we're moving most of our services to the cloud, so some training is needed. What about you?

*Thomas*: Well, after I finished my two-year course on development, I began to work for a services company. I started writing and adapting lots of their applications, but this week they've sent me to this event so I can learn more technical details about the cloud.

*Alex*: Yes, many concepts are similar to on-premises, but some others are completely different and require some training.

*Thomas*: True. Which sessions are you enjoying the most?

*Alex*: Yesterday, it was about containers, and today, I'm planning to attend something related to serverless computing.

*Thomas*: Interesting topics, but I already know them pretty well. I've been working with containers and serverless for the last year. Though maybe I could check whether there were some new features recently released, especially about AWS Lambda.

*Alex*: Cool! Can you give me an idea of what these Lambda functions are? I still have to decide whether I really need to learn about them or not.

*Thomas*: Sure. What do you know about traditional, monolithic code?

*Alex*: I learned about it just yesterday. There were many problems associated with having an application built into a single, huge piece of code. So, the solution is splitting it into smaller parts, for example, into microservices. And launching those inside containers, so an OS is not needed for every component.

*Thomas*: That's a simplified view but highly accurate. Now imagine you are a developer and you are required to split your code even further.

*Alex*: Smaller than a container? Maybe just a single process?

*Thomas*: Even smaller. Imagine you have a sequence of operations to do, as long or as short as you need. You just put those lines of code together, store them, and give them a name. That is a **Lambda function**. Let me show you an example on this piece of paper; let's write a function to do a backup of some important files:

```
Function BackupTheFiles
{
    $SourceB="SourceBucket"; $DestB="DestBucket"
    $Files = Get-S3Object -BucketName $SourceB
    Foreach ($File in $Files)
    {
        Copy-S3Object -BucketName $SourceB           `
                      -Key $File.Key                 `
                      -DestinationKey $File.Key       `
                      -DestinationBucket $DestB
    }
    Publish-SNSMessage -Message "Finished" -TopicARN
$SomeTopic
}
```

*Alex*: Interesting. Only the code, without a server or even an OS?

*Thomas*: Exactly. This is pure serverless. You don't need any server at all to run this, just the S3 buckets and the function itself. This function is just defined and available to run when you need it.

*Alex*: Wow! I assume you can have many functions ready, all stored in the cloud, and available to use for many different tasks. How are they organized?

*Thomas*: Each function has a different name to identify it. All of them are stored in the cloud, ready to be used. Of course, you can also provide parameters to them. And you can also have different versions of each function, while you're testing and improving them.

*Alex*: And what can be done inside those functions?

*Thomas*: Well, it is your own code. No limits – you can do whatever you need. And obviously, you can call any service on the cloud. There are also tools to monitor them and coordinate their execution and group them into different applications.

*Alex*: Can I schedule them?

*Thomas*: Yes. These functions can be invoked directly, associated with an event or an alarm, or scheduled. When the event is triggered, the function runs; this allows functions to be called automatically. For example, it can run every time a new file is added, a server is started, or a threshold is reached. Inside a function, you can run whatever you want – in the end, it is your code. And you can run any function whenever you need it, using the method that best suits your needs.

*Alex*: Highly interesting and useful. Now I'm pretty sure I will attend that session on AWS Lambda. Please, let me ask you a final question: first, we had monolithic code; then we were told to split it into microservices, maybe in containers; and now we should split it even more, into functions. What will be next? Maybe I should wait for another, even smaller component, and only then learn about it?

*Thomas*: Well… it seems a Lambda function is the smallest piece of code, so that should be the limit. Nobody can be sure these days, but I'd recommend you learn about them. It will be a good investment of time. If you attend that session, you'll also see how Lambda functions save you money.

*Alex*: Thanks, Thomas! It's a bit late – I think it's time to go to our sessions. I'll follow your advice. Maybe we can meet again when we're back from this event.

*Thomas*: Sure! It has been a pleasure to see you again. Let's run or we'll be late.

Both friends head for their respective sessions, but now Alex is thinking about his next session in a different way. He now has a general idea of what a Lambda function is, and he can imagine some applications split as a collection of Lambda functions stored in the cloud. He has decided he'll attend the next session on AWS Lambda to learn about the implementation details.

# AWS Lambda functions

At the last minute, Alex arrives at his next session. There are only a few seats in the front row, so he sits there. He realizes David is the speaker again. He nods at him slightly before he starts his talk.

*David*: Welcome, everybody. This is the session on AWS Lambda functions, so please check you are in the right room. The one about how to get rich with cryptocurrencies is in the next room. Haha. Before we start, who attended my session yesterday on containers?

Many hands are raised in the crowd.

*David*: Okay, let's make it slightly more interactive today. I'll start with some questions. The first one to answer will win some goodies! First question: think about your favorite old, monolithic applications. Any of them, but please do not mention any language starting with COB. How can we split this application?

Many hands are raised again. Some people shout *Containers, ECS, EKS*.

*David*: Great! But now imagine you need to split your code even further. What do you do then?

The crowd stays silent now, except Alex who seems to have a valid answer that he recently learned.

*Alex*: Use functions!

*David*: True! We have a winner in the first row. But let's elaborate on this a little. In AWS, we can split and run our code using **AWS Lambda functions**. A **Lambda function** is just a piece of code you write, performing whatever you might need, and it has to have a name.

The most important concept is that a Lambda function is the smallest piece of code you can provide. Not a process, not a task, not a container, not a full OS. Just a function; you won't find anything smaller. Some lines of code, and you can choose in which language you write them.

*Audience member 1*: Does it mean that if I split my application into multiple functions, maybe I'll end with several hundred of them?

*David*: True. You have to split the application into smaller pieces. If your application is complex, you'll end up, of course, with more functions. Then the AWS Lambda service will store all of them, each one with a different name, all ready to be called when needed. Here's the good news about this: storing functions is free; you'll only pay when you invoke them.

*Audience member 2*: You mean, you then pay for their execution?

*David*: Generally speaking, yes. You pay only when your code is running. It has to be cheap: the first million invocations, every month, are free. If you need more, it will cost only cents, again per million operations. You have to invest some effort in splitting your code, but once it's done, you'll realize it is much cheaper in the long term. Cheaper, modular, easy to maintain, and effective.

*Audience member 2*: Sorry to insist on this. Are you saying that you don't pay if the function is just stored but nobody needs it for some time?

*David*: Correct. Some functions are only used at specific moments. Backups, translation, reports – you pay only if you run them.

*Audience member 3*: Is AWS Lambda serverless?

*David*: Totally. You just provide your functions and your code as text. You don't handle any processes, tasks, OS, servers, or hardware. Your code will just run, as AWS provides whatever is needed to run it. There are no visible servers. That also means you don't pay for them; remember, you just pay for the execution of the function.

Now your code is going to be much more modular, as all your functions can be built, tested, distributed, and improved separately, maybe in different languages and by different teams. No more looking for a developer who knew an old, arcane programming language. And of course, you can download existing, prebuilt functions from well-known repositories.

*Audience member 4*: If every function is written in a different language, how does Lambda know how to run it?

*David*: Good question. When you create every function, you provide its name and declare its code. But you must also provide a couple of configuration parameters. One of them is which runtime or language is used. Java, Go, Python, C#, PowerShell, Node.js, and Ruby are the ones currently supported. With this information, the Lambda service will load the needed runtime before running the function. You also have to specify how much memory the function needs:

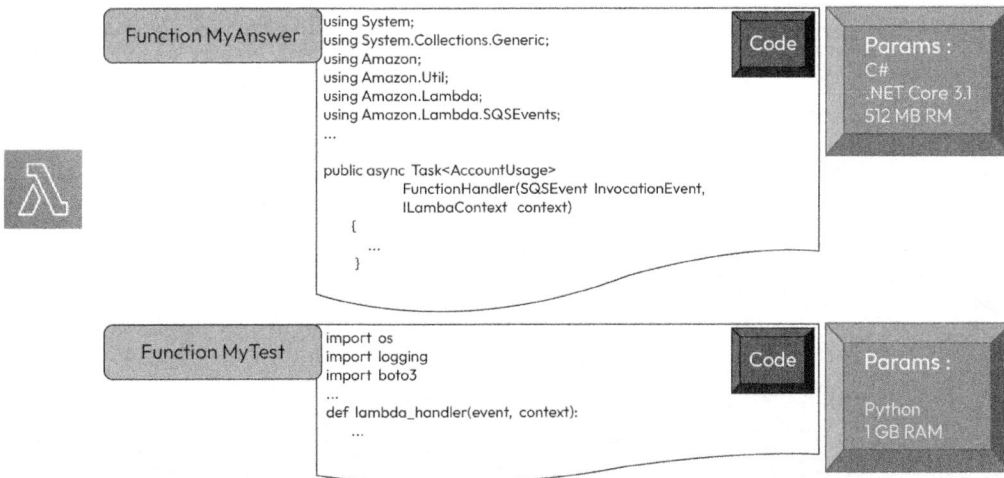

Figure 13.6 – Two Lambda functions

*Audience member 5*: You said Lambda is serverless, but then you have to specify RAM?

*David*: Yes. Virtual memory, not RAM. You provide just a single parameter – the amount of memory that every function will require to run. And this will also assign a proportional amount of CPU and network resources.

*Audience member 6*: Once I have created and stored my functions, how can I run them?

*David*: Every Lambda function is invoked by an **event**. This allows them to run automatically, with no user intervention. Every AWS service can generate events, for example, EC2 Launch, Stop, Terminate, any CloudWatch alarm, or many others.

You can also schedule your functions, or run them manually, maybe by clicking an icon on your desktop or any other application.

*Audience member 7*: Can I run multiple functions at the same time?

*David*: That's one of the main advantages of Lambda functions, their extreme concurrency. Yes, you can run maybe one or several thousands of simultaneous invocations. Imagine a large project with lots of customers or processes, for example, saving and processing separate files in S3. Each file upload started by each user will generate an event; this event will then invoke a Lambda function to process each file separately. Lambda will handle the resources needed to run thousands of simultaneous functions concurrently. And this solution is serverless, fully managed, and can scale the needed resources to these limits.

David takes a small break to drink a glass of water.

*David*: Now, an important point. You can create many functions, doing whatever they have to, but every Lambda function has a time limit. *The light that burns twice as bright burns half as long.* They can only run for a maximum time of 15 minutes.

David hears some murmurs from the audience.

*David*: Yes, you heard right – 15 minutes. You might think it's too short for your application but, honestly, 15 minutes is a long time in IT.

*Audience member 8*: But my application processes a large log, and it usually takes longer than that. Does it mean I cannot use Lambda functions?

*David*: It means you have to split your application into smaller pieces, processing your log in different parts, and maybe in parallel. The 15-minute limitation applies to every single Lambda function, not to the whole application.

Having this maximum time might be initially perceived as a limitation but it is not. It's a good design decision, as it will force you to properly redesign your application into smaller pieces. That means you will probably have to redesign the code to also consider its execution duration. Again, smaller and more modular in both space and time. If you need to do something in more than 15 minutes, that means you have to split your code, or use a different approach, maybe using SQS queues.

*Audience member 8*: So, I have to rebuild my application, making it more based on events and parallelism?

*David*: Probably, yes. Some applications are much easier to split. You can also use **AWS Step Functions** to help you. This is another AWS service, a serverless workflow orchestration service, which allows you to build applications as workflows. You can build them by using a nice editor that uses a simple drag-and-drop interface, where you coordinate all the Lambda functions along with other supported AWS Services, in which order or sequence to run them, loops, conditions, and so on. You can also use queues or other synchronization mechanisms. Of course, the full application doesn't have any time limitations.

In the end, you'll end up with better code, as programmers will try to optimize the function code so that it finishes early:

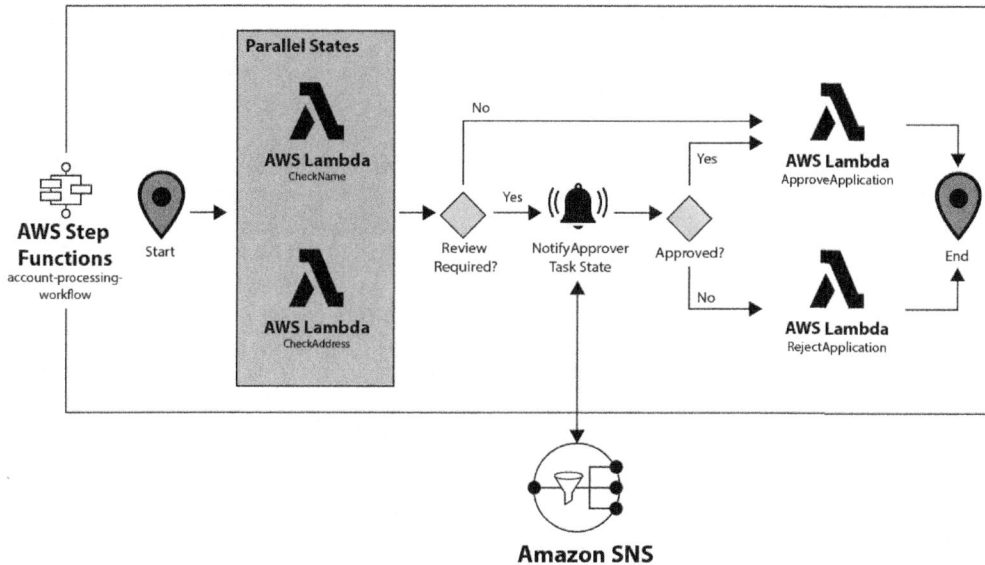

Figure 13.7 – Step Functions workflow

*David*: We're almost at the end of our time slot. We have time for one extra question.

Alex raises his hand.

*Alex*: Something came into my mind while you were explaining that we can invoke functions written in multiple programming languages. Loading some runtimes can take the same amount of time, maybe more than running the function itself.

*David*: Yes, that is called a **Cold Start**. The runtime is only loaded once, on the first invocation of each function. Once there, it will be cached in memory, ready for all subsequent invocations.

*Alex*: The first invocation will be slower then. Am I right?

*David*: Yes, that was a problem that people used to face some time ago; now it is fixed. You can choose to load the runtime in advance – we call it **pre-warming**. The first invocation will also find the runtime already there, so no need to wait. Please, take a look at the AWS documentation, and search for **Provisioned Concurrency**. Also, be sure to look for a language that offers a modular runtime, so you can load only the parts you need.

The session ends as the room is needed for the next session. Everybody runs to find their room for their next session.

Alex is sitting outside with a piece of paper, trying to summarize everything that was commented on. He wants to write down every key idea so nothing is forgotten. He has learned about the difference between having separate functions in AWS Lambda and a full application using Step Functions. He has also learned about how to invoke these functions, how to configure the resources they need, the possible languages they can be written with, and, especially, the pricing model. Finally, he recalls the 15-minute time limitation imposed on each function, and the possibility to use Step Functions to build complex applications without that time limitation.

## Serverless architectures

The cloud event is close to its end, but there are still some sessions in progress. In some rooms of the conference center, the cloud provider that is hosting the event is leading some lab sessions. These special sessions allow people to sit down and use their own laptops to connect to a dedicated AWS account and follow some instructions to build a full solution from scratch.

Berta and Raj didn't want to lose the opportunity to get some practice with some of the AWS services they have learned about so far during the event. They decided to join the lab session about serverless architectures.

The speaker, an AWS technical trainer, is introducing herself and the lab: expectations, pre-requisites, how to get access to the initial environment, and a quick description of the final serverless architecture they will build:

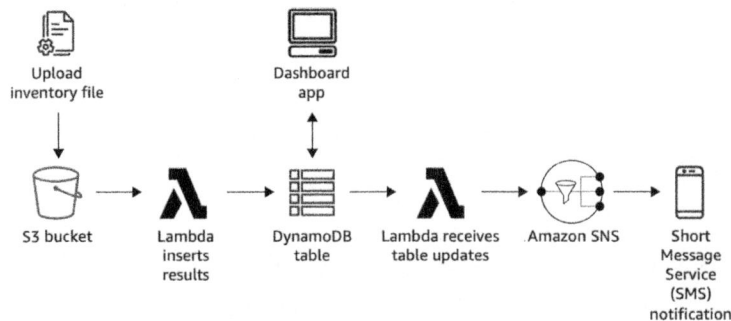

Figure 13.8 – Example of a serverless architecture on AWS

*Berta*: I'm so excited, Raj! I have to admit that I'm a bit tired but, at the same time, I was looking for an opportunity like this. I hope it's fine for you if we do the lab together.

*Raj*: Sure… this way, we can discuss immediately how we can apply the serverless paradigm to our infrastructure. In the recent past, we studied and used already-serverless services, but I like this lab because it puts some of them together into a completely serverless architecture.

Our two friends start the lab. They open a web page showing them the instructions, and then they click a button that opens the AWS Management Console they will use. Lab instructions are organized into tasks, some of them required and some optional – the latter are called challenges.

*Berta*: The challenges are pretty cool! They give you only a few hints, and then you have to figure out the right steps to do by yourself.

*Raj*: Yes, definitely!

Berta and Raj almost completed the lab. It took them around 30 minutes to do so when the time available was 45 minutes.

*Berta*: Okay, great, I think we have completed it. As you can see, we are using the **Simple Notification Service** (**SNS**). I've got those SNS notifications on my mobile phone, so that means everything is working. We still have 15 minutes left though.

*Raj*: We can spend that time discussing what we have built. The challenging question that I would like to ask myself is *Why didn't we build this architecture by using EC2 instances?* I think the answer will lead us to the benefits of serverless architecture.

*Berta*: Let me start. I think most of the services we used could potentially be replaced by EC2 instances, not only the Lambda functions. With serverless services, you really only pay for what you use. Now we don't have servers that we have to pay for every second they are running; if the application is not used, you just pay a minimum amount of money for the data storage on S3 and DynamoDB. If no compute capacity is consumed, you don't pay.

*Raj*: Exactly. If nobody adds inventory files to the S3 bucket or nobody takes a look at the dashboard, costs are extremely low. This is a great benefit, especially, but not only, for all those applications that are not used 24 hours a day but only for a few hours a day or just during business hours.

*Berta*: Anything else that comes to your mind?

*Raj*: Well, without servers, maintenance tasks are extremely reduced. In this architecture, no one has to provision any servers, and no one has to maintain them. Patching, upgrades, and OS misconfigurations to fix are all activities that are not needed anymore because the cloud provider manages them for you.

*Berta*: Yes, and think about **high availability**. What about if one of the servers goes down? Someone has to set up monitoring and alerting, and then someone has to fix the issue. In a serverless architecture, there aren't servers to manage or fix. Of course, you could find some errors at the application level. For example, sending an SMS message could fail on the first attempt. Even then, the services themselves offer mechanisms to help you deal with those situations. If SNS can't send a message for any reason, it will retry several times. Or if a Lambda function fails its execution, you can configure it to retry automatically before alerting someone.

*Raj*: Another issue I see in a server-based architecture is its lack of scalability.

*Berta*: In what terms?

*Raj*: Take a look at our serverless infrastructure and imagine what is happening now, when the traffic is low: not many files are uploaded to S3, and no one is looking at the dashboard. That also implies not too much activity on the underlying DynamoDB table.

*Berta*: Okay, then?

*Raj*: Now imagine that there is a sudden spike in the workload: a lot of files are now uploaded to S3, and that also generates a very high number of read operations against DynamoDB. Lambda functions will be triggered more often and more users will get their SMS messages. The question is: do you need to do something special to manage this spike?

*Berta*: Hmm, EC2 instances need to be properly set up, with the right instance type and size. To avoid problems, you can configure powerful instances from the very beginning.

*Raj*: That's right, but this means wasting money when traffic is low.

*Berta*: But there is **EC2 Auto Scaling**!

Suddenly, people in the room hear a loud shushing sound coming from a person sitting not too far from Berta and Raj. Our two friends realized they were raising the volume of their voices, and that they were still in the room even after completing the lab. The moderators around the room glared at Raj and Berta, who now started to whisper.

*Raj*: Hehe, seems we need to keep our enthusiasm down. About what you said, yes, you can use EC2 Auto Scaling, but you have to configure it properly. You need time and knowledge to set up the right instance types, and the minimum and maximum limits. And there is still the risk of setting them up in the wrong way.

*Berta*: Okay, got it. Before we leave, I would like to add one more benefit I noticed while analyzing that serverless architecture: I'm pretty sure that whoever implemented that solution didn't take too much time. Think about the time it takes to create an S3 bucket or a DynamoDB table; you can do it in seconds! We've begun to learn about AWS Lambda just today, but in the lab, it was clear that once you developed your code, it took seconds to put it into a Lambda function. Same thing for SNS: it took us a minute to set it up in the lab.

*Raj*: Absolutely, yes, not only is the time spent on maintenance tasks reduced but also the time spent on the provisioning ones – totally agree.

*Berta*: You know… While we were doing the lab, I was thinking about my favorite cinema, near my home. It is a good example of another serverless architecture.

*Raj*: Yes, there are many components running there: selling tickets, checking access to the screen, projecting the films, and cleaning. But as a final user, you just pay for your session. No other task is to be performed other than sitting, relaxing, and watching.

*Berta*: Exactly. What I find interesting about all these components are their relationships. How people queue at the entrance but then are sent to the right screen. Also, how many films are projected in parallel, and they will probably end at different times. Lots of things have to be perfectly coordinated. And especially how they scale; how much personnel is needed if there are only a few customers at late-night sessions, or at a peak hour when all screens are running at full capacity?

*Raj*: I think we've learned a lot from this lab about serverless architectures. Let's leave now.

*Berta*: Yes! Let me just end the lab and provide feedback.

# Summary

The event has finished and all attendees are preparing for their trip back home. Lots of trolleys are now seen.

The team is refreshed and filled with new ideas that they'll use in their code. They have learned about serverless architectures and how to split their code even further into Lambda functions or step functions. They know now how to build a fully serverless architecture, using these and other services, such as SNS, SQS, and many others, but no virtual servers in any form. They now look forward to the possibilities and limitations they will find.

As soon as they return to the office, they'll start to split some of their code into functions. Some backups and reports are the first candidates.

But once there, they will also face a new, important issue. Some of their critical applications are not fast enough for their growing needs. They will need to investigate a way to make them faster by using several of the caching technologies available in the cloud.

# Further reading

- Lambda functions:

  - `https://aws.amazon.com/lambda/`

  - `https://docs.aws.amazon.com/lambda/latest/dg/best-practices.html`

  - `https://aws.amazon.com/blogs/compute/operating-lambda-performance-optimization-part-1/`

  - `https://aws.amazon.com/blogs/compute/new-for-aws-lambda-predictable-start-up-times-with-provisioned-concurrency/`

- Lambda samples:

  - `https://github.com/awsdocs/aws-lambda-developer-guide/tree/main/sample-apps`

- Serverless in general:

  - `https://www.serverless.com`

  - `https://www.serverlessland.com`

  - `https://serverlessland.com/reinvent2021/serverlesspresso`

# 14

# Caching – Microseconds Latency: Why Are We Always in a Rush?

The team has returned to the office after the cloud event. They attended multiple sessions and they've learned a lot, but now it's time to return to work at TrendyCorp. The knowledge gained has given them new ideas to experiment with, and they are eager to start as soon as possible with them.

Once at their desks, they begin to empty their mailboxes. But one email seems more important than the others: Gloria is asking them to meet at her desk, as they need to talk about a new issue – the performance of their critical applications:

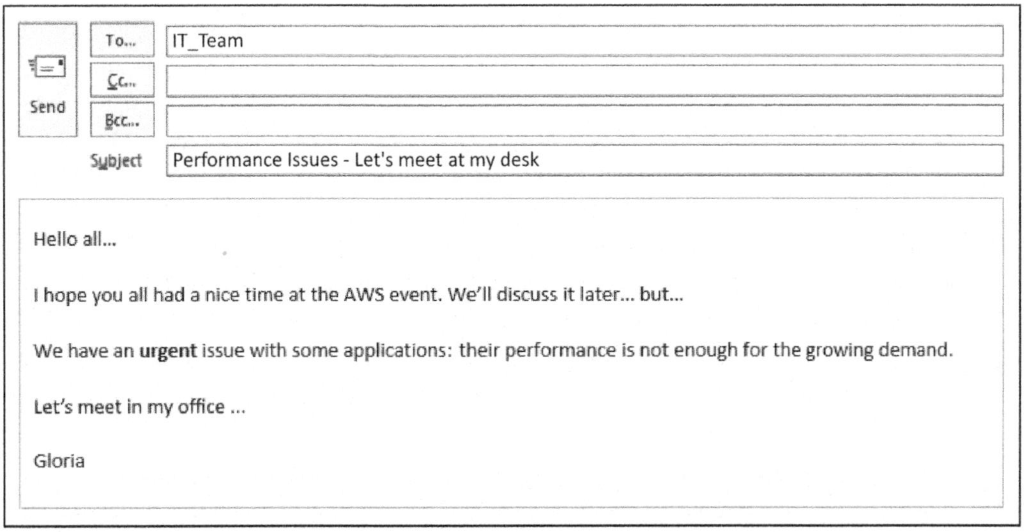

| | To... | IT_Team |
|---|---|---|
| Send | Cc... | |
| | Bcc... | |
| | Subject | Performance Issues - Let's meet at my desk |

Hello all...

I hope you all had a nice time at the AWS event. We'll discuss it later... but...

We have an **urgent** issue with some applications: their performance is not enough for the growing demand.

Let's meet in my office ...

Gloria

Figure 14.1 – Gloria is reporting a new problem

The team members meet early at Gloria's office.

*Gloria*: How was your cloud event? I can see many happy faces today.

*Alex*: Amazing. I learned a lot about containers, and then serverless, and Lambda! I also had the opportunity to talk with an old friend I met there.

*Berta*: I also attended similar sessions but I decided to swap one of them to learn about something different that interested me, blockchain technologies.

*Gloria*: Good to hear. From what I've heard from our management, I assume we'll also need to deal with that technology too, but not immediately.

*Harold*: I understood that by making some changes in our applications we could save lots of headaches, and maybe money too. I'd propose starting a new project to modernize some of our simpler tasks, starting with backups, for example, and then maybe proceeding later with other more complex tasks.

*Gloria*: It seems a fantastic idea to me. But you have probably read my email. We have something to do first, something more important and also more urgent. We have some news coming from our monitoring team.

*Alex*: I hope nothing is on fire.

*Gloria*: Not really, but we have an opportunity for improvement here. And you probably already have all the knowledge to address this. They are telling us that some of our business applications that have been migrated to the cloud may not be fast enough for the increasing rate of requests.

*Harold*: Those applications were running perfectly before we went to the event, weren't they? Who has broken them?

*Gloria*: No, you got it wrong. The issue is that those applications are so fantastically good, that now everybody wants to use them. Our internal departments, sales, marketing, finance—all of them; and of course, the number of customers also continues to grow, as we mentioned in a previous meeting. More users mean more load on the servers and worse performance. Fortunately, there are no user complaints… yet. But there will be in the near future if we don't do something soon.

*Alex*: I don't think this is a serious problem. We know how to provide more power to our applications, even automatically by using **auto scaling**. Let's tune some parameters in our auto scaling policies, just increasing the maximum number of servers.

*Gloria*: This could be a possible solution, but maybe we also need to follow a different approach. Moreover, we now have more offices and customers in new locations, where their internet connectivity is not so good. We have to consider all of them.

*Berta*: Well, that's a new problem. But I'm sure this is not a strange problem only we happen to have. It seems a common issue, for which our cloud provider probably has a solution already; we just have to find it.

*Harold*: I'm pretty sure that those problems could be solved by **caching**. We faced similar challenges years ago, in our on-premises environment, but I can imagine the idea should be the same in the cloud.

*Alex*: Caching? What does that mean?

*Harold*: Our data is persistently stored somewhere in disk subsystems, maybe as files or in databases. **Caching** means that if some of this data is accessed frequently, it's a best practice to keep a copy of it somewhere else, in a much faster system, most likely in memory. You need to bear some extra cost, but the performance benefits are huge.

*Berta*: I was also thinking about network performance: we have the data in our systems, but it is only stored in the regions we have chosen in the cloud. Maybe we'd need to also store a copy in a location that is nearer the users, if they are located elsewhere.

*Harold*: Yes, it's a different need, but in the end, it uses the same idea – that is, storing the most frequently used data in a place where users or processes can retrieve it faster. Nearer in space and also in time.

*Alex*: I get that caching can improve performance, but can you give me some simple examples, please?

*Charles*: Alex, I have an example for you: let's imagine you want to cook an omelet. That means you go to the supermarket, and you buy an egg and some oil. Then, you go home and prepare it:

Figure 14.2 – Cooking an omelet. I need a supermarket!

*Alex*: You're spying on me! That's exactly what I did yesterday for dinner. I'm a great cook and I like very elaborate food. Unfortunately, I forgot to add salt, and it burnt a bit.

*Berta*: Haha, do you really think an omelet is *elaborate*?

*Charles*: Think about it: what happens if you cook that meal frequently? Would you go to the supermarket every day to buy a single egg?

*Alex*: Well, I don't go to the supermarket every day. I usually buy a dozen eggs and keep the extra ones in the refrigerator in my kitchen.

*Charles*: Do you remember what happened some months ago, when you relocated to that flat, and you didn't have a refrigerator yet? It took you two months to decide which model to buy.

*Alex*: Yes, I had to spend a terrible amount of time going to the supermarket every day, walking for six blocks and back, waiting in the queue with other customers just to pay…

*Charles*: Exactly. It took you two hours to cook an omelet because you had to buy a single egg from a faraway place. Not a good performance… But if you can keep some eggs in your refrigerator, then the process is accelerated, taking only a few minutes. Your refrigerator becomes your **cache**, where you keep some frequent articles nearer you. But you need to have a refrigerator, which represents an additional cost, and probably a big one.

*Harold*: Hmm. Now I understand the technical reasons why I'm keeping two dozen beer cans at home instead of going to the supermarket every time. Please don't take me too seriously; I'm just joking.

*Charles*: You can find caching at your home, your refrigerator, and maybe your toolbox also. But also in many other common places. Think about fast food!

*Harold*: Did you realize, folks, how frequently we talk about food? Is it because our meetings take place before or after lunch? Sorry, I'm joking again.

*Gloria*: Fast food, Charles?

*Charles*: Yes, a fast food outlet is a place where you can *eat* fast. But it can also be a place where you *get* food fast. For those who work there, products such as hamburgers are classified in two ways: the ones that customers buy frequently, and the ones that are rarely requested.

Figure 14.3 – Hamburgers at the fast food outlet

*Charles*: The hamburgers that are frequently requested are prepared in advance, so people can get them very quickly. You get your hamburgers fast but only if you ask for the popular ones because you find them in the cache. Sometimes, you can see them there, prepared in a row, ready to be dispatched.

*Alex*: That's true! This is not my case; I always have to wait when I ask for mine.

*Charles*: We humans don't like to spend too much on some tasks, especially if we have to wait.

*Harold*: True. In IT, a **cache** is usually a faster system with plenty of memory, or maybe a system with good networking connectivity, strategically located near the end user or application that needs data. In all cases, you need to add some more resources, but the main benefit you get is better performance.

*Gloria*: Cool! Then it seems we could have a solution to our performance problems, by using a cache?

*Charles*: I just wanted to add one more thing about this topic, if we have the time.

*Gloria*: Sure, Charles, please continue.

*Charles*: As we have already said, the main benefit that caching provides is **better performance**, but there are **cost benefits** too. Though having a cache has a cost, once deployed, it will help you reduce the burden on your backend for repetitive requests. If something can be read from the cache, it will not be read again from the database. That means you won't need a huge database server to handle repetitive queries. As cloud providers charge you for the read and write operations you perform on your databases, caching can help you reduce costs.

*Gloria*: Oh, that's great. Management will appreciate that! Could you folks please investigate our specific performance issues, check what our cloud provider offers in terms of services, and see whether you can find a solution that could fit our current architectures? Again, organize yourself as you feel convenient.

The problem is not totally defined yet, but the team members already know they'll have to investigate two types of solutions, both related to caching. Some of the performance problems seem related to the network: the data is not near the final users, and the network latency can be the issue. Other issues seem related to the application itself, accessing data that is on disk, especially at peak hours, when many users are requesting data at the same time.

In both cases, adding a cache seems to alleviate the problem, even if that leads to adding another service to the solution.

The team members start looking at the documentation. The initial approach is simple: look for **cache** or **caching** keywords in the cloud provider documentation. They will also talk with the monitoring team to see their specific metrics and understand the exact problem in each application.

They decide to meet again after some time to comment on their findings.

# Caching data using Amazon ElastiCache

Once the team members gather in the meeting room, everyone seems eager to discuss the solution they want to propose. Berta goes first.

*Berta*: I think I've found two interesting services that can be used to implement data caching. Let's consider a typical three-tier application, with and without a cache.

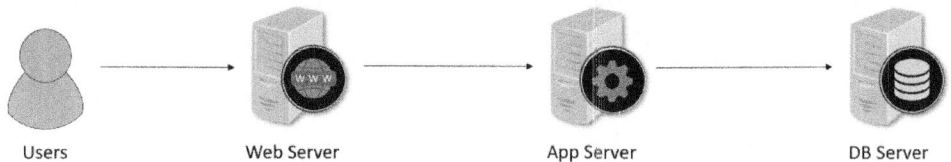

Berta draws the following on the whiteboard:

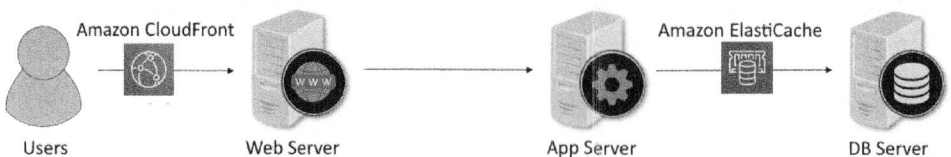

Figure 14.4 – A typical three-tier application with and without a cache

*Alex*: Is it just me, or can anyone else see two new services in your drawing?

*Berta*: Yes, **Amazon CloudFront** and **Amazon ElastiCache**. They are two commonly used caching services for workloads running on the AWS platform. They are intended for different types of requests.

*Alex*: Can we discuss Amazon ElastiCache first?

*Berta*: Yes. Conceptually, it is pretty simple: in the end, it's a bunch of servers with lots of memory, configured together as a cluster, and serving the data. It is fast, as data retrieved from RAM is thousands of times faster than retrieving it from disk.

*Alex*: Is this service serverless, like AWS Lambda? I assume we only need the memory.

*Berta*: Not exactly, this one is server-based. But this is a fully managed service, so you don't have to worry about the operations overhead.

*Alex*: So, we have to learn a new language to communicate with ElastiCache?

*Berta*: AWS offers this in-memory caching service using well-known open source technologies, widely used by several companies. You can choose between two caching engines, **Redis** or **Memcached**. Many developers are already using them on-premises, so they are proven, robust, stable, and well-known technologies, which means you don't have to learn something new if you need to use this type of caching in the cloud.

*Raj*: Please don't reinvent the wheel. If there's already a memory management-proven application, let's use it instead of creating it again.

*Harold*: Yes. AWS offers this functionality inside ElastiCache, simply choosing Redis or Memcached, exactly as it is used on-premises. You specify the number of nodes you need in your cluster, with the required size; the larger the servers, the more memory they have. These servers are then fully managed by AWS.

*Alex*: What is not 100% clear to me is why Amazon ElastiCache is referred to as a **NoSQL database**. Is it a caching service or a NoSQL database?

*Berta*: I can explain this to you, Alex. I like databases, as you probably know. In the recent past (*Chapter 6*), we discussed the existence of SQL (or relational) databases and NoSQL (or non-relational) databases. We are currently using some of them in our architecture. For sure, you remember that there are several NoSQL database types, and one of them is labeled as an "in-memory database."

*Alex*: Yes, I remember it. Ah, we're talking about this one. Its main benefit is that it is very fast.

*Berta*: Super-fast, I would say. We can retrieve data with microseconds latency. ElastiCache can be used in two ways: as a database or as a cache. In the first case, you will end up with a database that will store data for your application, like any other database. The second use case is the one that Harold and Charles described minutes ago, where it is used as a cache, to store and serve data you access frequently.

*Alex*: Thank you, Berta, now it's clear. I seem to remember you have to store your data as key-value pairs in memory – that is, each one containing both a key and a value. Correct?

*Berta*: Yes. Remember, ElastiCache is a service for developers, so they can improve the performance of their applications. In-memory database solutions just provide the storage, but developers still have to write the code to decide how to use it as a cache. If you have properly defined your caching strategy, you'll get more **cache hits** and fewer **cache misses**.

Alex is confused about cache hits and misses. Harold realizes it, stands up, and, once in front of the whiteboard, starts drawing something:

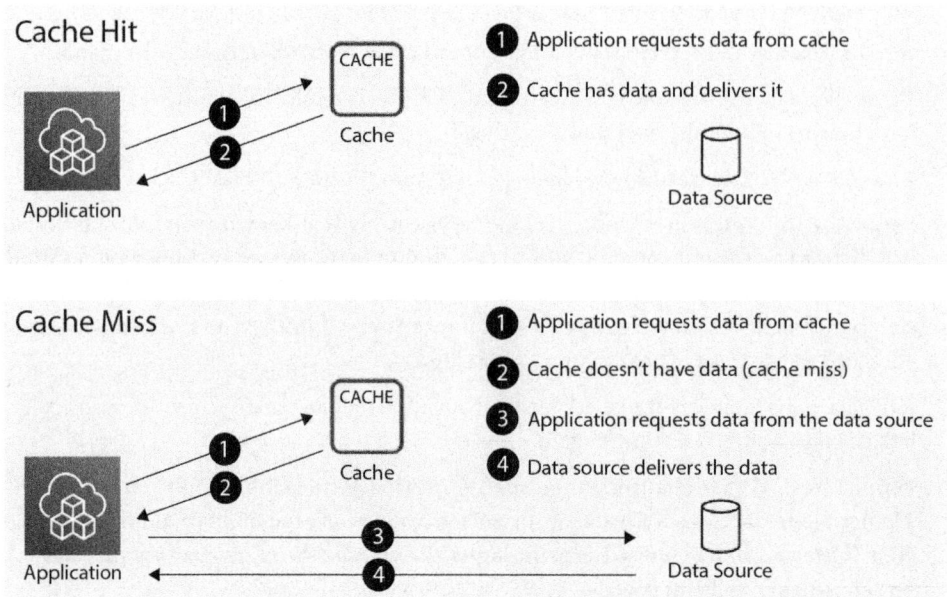

Figure 14.5 – Caching: cache hit and cache miss

*Harold*: Let me explain to you what a cache hit and a cache miss are. If your application requests data and it is found in the cache, it is a cache hit. If the data is not found in the cache, it will be a cache miss. In the latter case, your application will have to retrieve the data from the original database.

*Berta*: Okay, that's the basic approach, and then there are different ways, or strategies, to decide what to store in the cache, and when to read or write on it. The logic beneath all of this lies in the fact that reading from memory is much faster than reading from disk, even in the cloud.

*Charles*: How can a developer read data from the cache?

*Berta*: Once ElastiCache is configured, your application can use the right command or supported API calls. For example, in Redis, you use something like this, which is an example in PowerShell. Notice the Get-RedisKey or Add-RedisKey commands. You will have something equivalent in your favorite programming language:

```
$EPAdd,$EpPort = ReadEndpointConfigurationParams
$ConnectionString =
"$($EPAdd):$($EPPort),abortConnect=false,Connect
Timeout=100"
Connect-Redis -ConnectionString $ConnectionString
```

```
Add-RedisKey -Key "Customer001" -Value "Data for
Customer001"
$Data = Get-Rediskey -Key "Customer001"
Get-RediskeyDetails -Key "Customer001"
```

*Charles*: Why are there two technologies? Which one should we choose?

*Harold*: AWS offers both options so you can choose which one is best for your development. Memcached, if you want a short description of it, is simpler and, for certain use cases, even faster. You just choose some nodes, and how much memory is in each, and you have that total amount of memory to store your data. This is the simplest approach and could be useful for many projects that require a simple technology to use as a cache.

*Alex*: Does that mean if we request 4 nodes with 2 GiB each, we get in total 8 GiB for caching our data?

*Harold*: Exactly. You get all the memory offered and managed together in a single entity called a **cluster**. There's no redundancy in Memcached, so that's what you get: all memory added together. Well, there's a minor overhead, as some memory is needed for the OS.

*Alex*: Good. Can we assume that the other option, Redis, is more powerful, and Amazon ElastiCache offers this option for whoever is looking for a more sophisticated engine?

*Berta*: Well, yes, Redis is feature-rich, offering many more functionalities; the decision does not depend on the developer's ability but on the application's needs.

*Alex*: Then, what can you do with Redis?

*Harold*: Redis offers lots of extra features. You can create a cluster with multiple nodes offering data redundancy, where one node is the *primary* and the others, asynchronously replicated, are the *replica(s)*. This provides high availability because if the writer fails, there will be an automatic failover and one of the replicas will become the new primary.

*Alex*: Amazon ElastiCache for Redis seems really powerful. Anything else?

*Harold*: Yes, it provides persistence. The data can also be saved to disk. This provides a backup functionality that allows you to store the content of your cache on S3 and then, if needed, restore it or even create another cluster using the stored data elsewhere, maybe in another region.

*Berta*: And it supports complex data types and publish-subscribe logic; probably some other stuff as well that I don't remember now, haha. That's the main reason many developers prefer Redis to Memcached.

*Harold*: I just want to insist that it depends on the requirements. You always have to use the technology that best fits your needs: Memcached is used mostly for its simplicity, and Redis is used for all the features it provides and the level of scalability and high availability provided.

*Berta*: Let me forward you a quick comparison table.

Berta forwards the following table:

| Feature | Redis | Memcached |
|---|:---:|:---:|
| Stores key-value pairs in memory | ✓ | ✓ |
| Open source | ✓ | ✓ |
| Supports different data types natively | ✓ | ✗ |
| Supports native persistence | ✓ | ✗ |
| Replication | ✓ | ✗ |
| Clustering | ✓ | ✗ |
| Supports multithreading | ✓ | ✓ |

Figure 14.6 – Redis versus Memcached

Our friends have discussed the first of the caching technologies offered by the cloud provider, Amazon ElastiCache. They have found out the two standards that can be used inside it: **Redis** and **Memcached**. They have also compared the available features in each one, so they can decide which one to use in each project.

The main concept seems clear now, but some doubts are still floating in the air. As they will have to discuss caching with the programmers at TrendyCorp, they feel some more details are needed.

## Caching strategies

After a short break, Alex returns with some more questions. He has understood the principles behind ElastiCache, and he's now considering how to use it in the TrendyCorp projects.

*Alex*: It's evident that ElastiCache is a technology for developers. Are there any common approaches we should compile to tell our developer team?

*Berta*: There are a couple of basic design possibilities, or I should say **caching strategies**. Obviously, you can build your own based on them. In the end, it's your code. But the key principles remain the same.

The first one is called **lazy loading**:

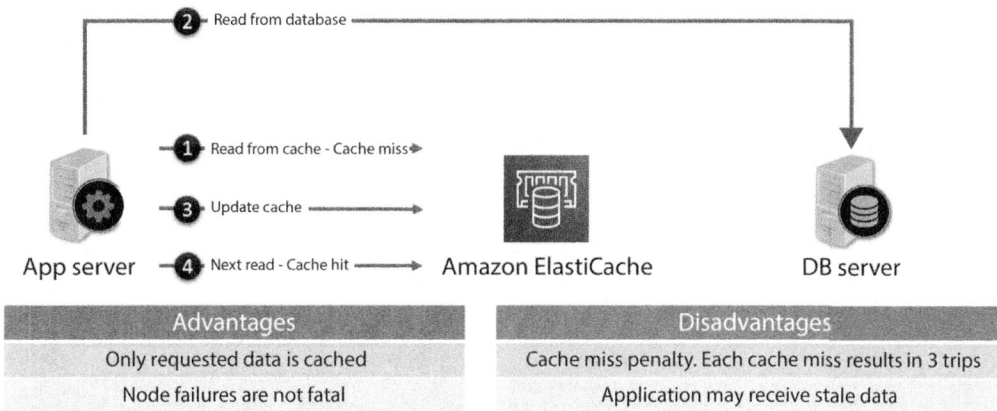

Figure 14.7 – Lazy loading caching strategy

*Berta*: In this strategy, the cache is initially empty. That means that when the data is requested for the first time, the cache won't have it. It will be a **cache miss**.

Now, the application has to read the data from the database, deliver it to the requester, and also write it in the cache. Now, all subsequent requests for the same data will be fulfilled by the cache; it will be a **cache hit** for all of them.

In the end, the main benefit is that only the requested data will be stored in the cache. It allows you to have a big database but only a fraction of it cached, saving costs.

*Alex*: Okay, I've got it. It's like having my refrigerator empty at the beginning of each week. The first time I prepare my dinner, I get a cache miss because I don't have the ingredients, so I have to go to the supermarket first to refill; after this, I have some food that I can use for the next few days if I want to prepare the same dishes.

*Berta*: More or less, true. Then there's another caching strategy, called **write-through**:

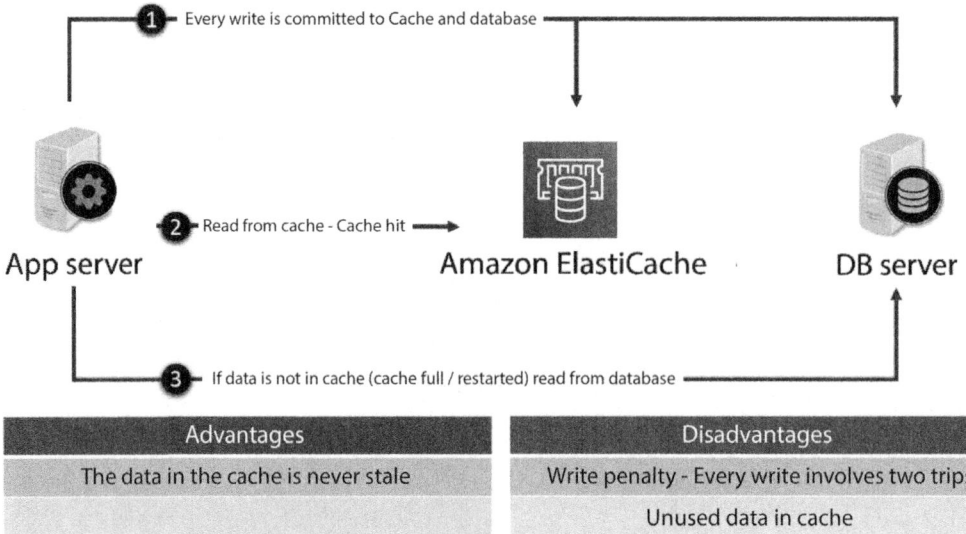

Figure 14.8 – Write-through caching strategy

*Berta*: With this approach, you pre-populate the entire cache in advance. Usually, you copy all the information from the database, or at least the part of it you know you'll need later.

*Alex*: That is, you fill your refrigerator in advance with food for many different meals, even if you are not sure whether you are going to cook all of those meals, but in case you do, you know everything will be there.

*Berta*: That's right. No cache misses, and no first-usage victim; but that assumes you'll probably need a larger cache, which means a larger ElastiCache cluster. This is the likely approach when used by microservices, where each one uses a potentially smaller database and its own cache.

*Harold*: But this model has a drawback. If the application makes any updates to the data, it has to do it twice: first, to the database, and second, to the cached data. That's why it's called **write-through**. Fortunately, both writes can be done in parallel, so if the application code is properly optimized, the user shouldn't perceive any performance penalty.

*Raj*: What happens if the cache gets full and maybe there's more data to be stored inside it? I can assume the database could be much bigger than the amount of memory allocated to the cache.

*Berta*: Good question. Let me…

*Alex*: Maybe we can automatically remove the oldest data in the cache?

*Berta*: Thanks, Alex. Well, almost, but not always. The best approach will be to let the cache remove the **least recently used** data automatically: I'm talking about the **LRU** algorithm. It removes the data that has not been requested in a long time. That's slightly different! If some data is old but users continue to request it, it will not be removed.

*Alex*: Ah, okay. Like the rotten piece of ham I found at the back of my refrigerator. It's like the **never used** algorithm. I completely forgot about it for months. It would have been great if the refrigerator had disposed of it automatically. It turned blue with white mushrooms and a strong smell.

*Harold*: A good idea for your omelet!

*Raj*: Eeekkk. Please stop!

*Berta*: The decision about which stale data should be removed depends on its usage. Only after that is evaluated is the age of the data inside the cache used. Frequently used data should be kept in the cache, even if it is there for a long time.

Let me give you an example: think about your mobile's last dialed number list. It is a form of cache for recently dialed numbers. Your phonebook (i.e., source data) may have hundreds of numbers stored, but the last dialed number list is small (i.e., cache). If you have recently dialed a number, it will be at the top of the last dialed number list. As the list keeps on filling up, the least recently used number will be evicted from the list. But if a number is about to be evicted and you dial it again, it will come to the top and will stay in the cache. So, only the LRU data gets automatically evicted.

*Alex*: I get it. Thanks, Berta and Harold. I have a better understanding of the Amazon ElastiCache service now.

Now the team understands the in-memory caching technologies. They already knew the options offered by ElastiCache, but now they have realized that the cache in memory can be smaller than the available data on disk. So, some strategies are needed to decide how to populate the cache, what to store, and when to do it. For that purpose, **lazy loading** and **write-through** seem to provide a good base for their developers to use. Finally, they discussed the options to automatically remove stale items from it and the LRU algorithm.

# Using Amazon CloudFront to cache data on edge locations

At the same time that Berta and Harold were investigating caching in memory, Raj and Charles did the same with the options to cache in the network. Now, they have some time to explain their findings.

*Raj*: While you were investigating ElastiCache, we've been checking some possibilities for our other problem: customers in remote locations. This is much more related to internet connectivity rather than an application issue, so maybe we'll have to coordinate this with our network team. The solution is also based on caching part of the data.

*Charles*: Yes, let me explain the basics. What happens if our customers are not physically near an AWS Region? Some countries have one or several Regions nearby but others might not. Take a look at the Region map provided by AWS, and look at where we have set up our applications.

*Alex*: Maybe these customers could use a better internet connection?

*Charles*: Maybe, yes, but not always. They can even use satellites, by the way, as there's a service for them. But they provide connectivity, not performance. In certain cases, the application needs better performance, and delivering the data in a remote region might not be fast enough.

*Alex*: Yes, they need a large refrigerator nearer to them!

*Charles*: Exactly! Well, not a physical refrigerator, but another type of cache. In this case, we can offer cached copies of the data they might need, physically, near the client's location. We're talking about physical distance, how many kilometers to the data.

*Alex*: But how is this done?

*Charles*: With a little help from my friends. AWS has its main global network, connecting all Regions with their own cabling and fiber optics, and highly redundant, of course. We spoke about this a long time ago (*Chapter 2*). But there is also another part of this layered network, offering physical connectivity in many other major cities across the globe, where a lot of the population lives.

*Alex*: So, having it near highly populated areas will address the requests coming from this large customer base?

*Charles*: Yes. So, AWS has collaborated with trusted partners and set up the required infrastructure in these cities. These centers are physically connected to the AWS global network. These locations are called **edge locations** or **point-of-presence** (**PoP**), and they form what's called the **global edge network**:

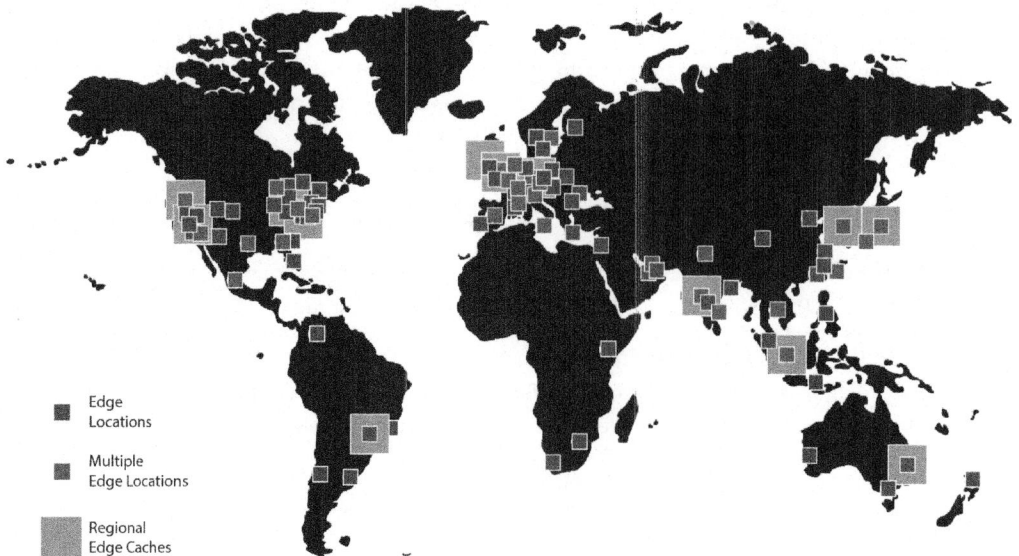

Figure 14.9 – AWS edge locations

*Raj*: You can take a look at the full map; you'll see there are more edge locations than Regions.

*Charles*: AWS keeps on expanding its global edge network and you can leverage it when you use specific AWS services. One of them is called Amazon **CloudFront**. It is used to build what we call a **content delivery network**, or **CDN**. You can use CloudFront to cache content, nearer to your users. You create what are called **distributions**, which, in the end, is caching a copy of the specified data you have on the Region, but now physically nearer to the requester.

*Raj*: In a CloudFront distribution, you can store a copy of the content your users request, which is retrieved from the source. The source is called the **origin**, and this is a configuration property you have to define for each distribution. A CloudFront distribution supports data retrieval over the HTTP and HTTPS protocols:

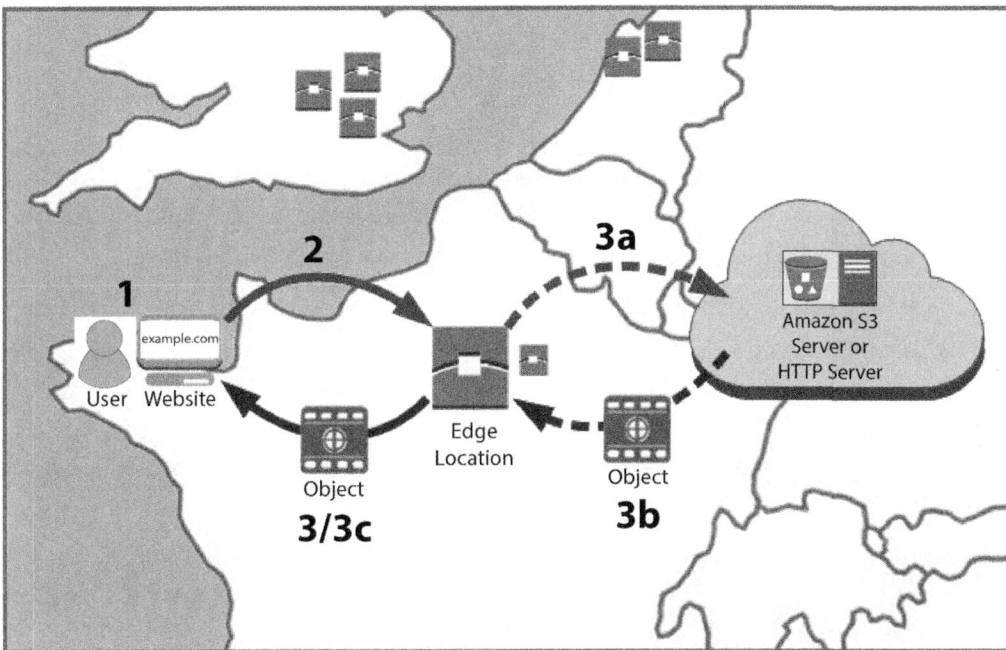

Figure 14.10 – Content delivery using Amazon CloudFront

*Alex*: Sorry, Raj, I don't understand: is the user redirected to the origin server over the AWS global network?

*Raj*: The user will use the CloudFront distribution URL, and the distribution will provide the cached data. If it is not there, there will be again a cache miss. CloudFront will then fetch the data from the origin, using the same relative path, obviously by using the AWS global network. Finally, data will be stored in the cache for the next users:

# HTTP Request - www.example.com/image.jpg

Figure 14.11 – Content delivery using Amazon CloudFront

*Charles*: You can easily cache data stored in an Amazon S3 bucket, but don't get the impression that only static data can be cached. If your web application is hosted on-premises or maybe on an Amazon EC2 instance, which generates dynamic data, you can also cache it by using CloudFront.

*Raj*: And that leads to an important aspect. For how long do we cache the files?

*Alex*: I assume it should be a configurable setting. Maybe some data is worth being cached forever.

*Raj*: Yes, that could be valid for some files, such as your company logo, or some pages that never change. But let's imagine you have to cache a price list, where prices change every night.

*Charles*: It could be a serious issue; customers would get stale price information, which is not good for a financial transaction. For that reason, you can configure CloudFront to store different types of content with different **time-to-live** (**TTL**) values.

*Alex*: I think I saw that James Bond movie.

*Charles*: Haha! Separate TTLs mean you can store every object in the cache, specifying how long it must be there. After that time, CloudFront will automatically remove it. So, you can't forget to do it, and there's no need to write a process to clean; it will be automatically removed from every location.

*Berta*: I assume you can use multiple possible values for each TTL, ranging from a few seconds to many days.

*Charles*: Or even an infinite TTL for static content, which will never expire.

*Berta*: But then what happens if you set the wrong TTL or forget to set it, or you just change your mind? Will the file stay there forever?

*Charles*: You also have an option that allows you to invalidate objects inside the cache. You select which specific content you want to invalidate, and they will be deleted from all the edge locations. This is considered your last resort, usually, as it takes some time and is not free.

*Harold*: I can imagine. We have to decide which data from our applications has to be cached in CloudFront, which files, and with which TTL values; and CloudFront will probably need IAM permissions to access them from the origin. Seems the place for an IAM role we'll have to create.

*Raj*: Exactly. Just a final comment I'd like to add: AWS provides other services that allow you to get benefits from edge locations. For example, you can apply DDoS protection mechanisms, invoke Lambda functions, accelerate S3 uploads, and so on. But maybe this is enough for the moment, hehe.

The team has now discovered the other option for caching: in the network. They have learned a lot of terms, such as point of presence, edge location, content delivery network, and edge network. The main service running on them is CloudFront; distributions and origins are the critical concepts they'll have to configure. Finally, they also found out the importance of setting the right TTLs to avoid stale data being served to the users.

## Other services offering caching

The team has planned to have some drinks together. Just a quick meeting, as it's late and they're tired, but they have some goodies that they got at their cloud event and they'd like to share them with others. They are about to fetch their things and move out, but Berta stops them.

*Berta*: Hey guys. Do we have an extra 5 minutes before we leave? I'd like to add one more thing about caching – in particular, about database caching. There's more.

*Alex*: More caching?

*Berta*: Yes, developers can use ElastiCache to have entire control over the caching process, by deciding what, how, and when to cache the result of certain operations. But besides that, most of the databases already offer their own cache.

*Harold*: For example?

*Berta*: Most databases cache the result of your queries in memory: Oracle, SQL Server, MySQL, PostgreSQL, MariaDB, for example – all of them are supported by RDS. Think also about Aurora, which caches a lot of stuff in its fast, highly available, and redundant store, not only in its instances.

*Raj*: Do we need to modify our code to use that cache?

*Berta*: Sometimes yes, but usually you don't need that complexity. The cache is used transparently, so your queries do not have to be modified. It might happen that database administrators or developers want to change some parameters at the database level, to modify the size or the behavior of the cache slightly. It's part of their performance and tuning activities.

Lastly, some engines allow you to specify **hints**, or labels, that you can use to influence how a query is run in a database. For example, whether the query has to take benefit from caching or not. Something like this:

```
SELECT sql_no_cache * FROM Table WHERE...
```

*Harold*: So, this seems a very easy change to do in some SQL queries – that is, keeping compatible SQL language but using the cache at your own will.

*Berta*: AWS gives you all the options, and then you decide based on your requirements. With ElastiCache, if used to cache your database data, you get a cache that is *decoupled* from the database, giving you the ability to manage and scale it independently from the database behind. But if you don't need this, you can simply leverage the caching features that databases provided internally.

By the way, there is also **DynamoDB**, which offers its own caching feature; in this case, it needs a separate service, called **DynamoDB Accelerator**, or simply, **DAX**:

## Amazon VPC Virtual private cloud

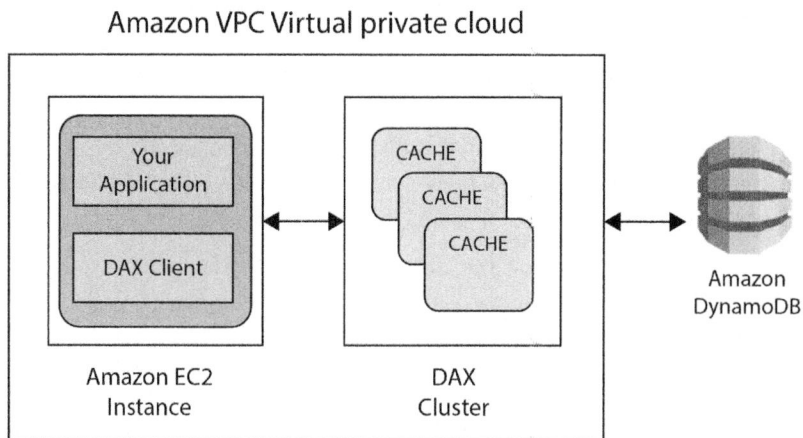

Figure 14.12 – Caching with DynamoDB: DAX

*Berta*: This is another example of a decoupled cache, but that works only for DynamoDB. Developers who are working with DynamoDB and want to speed up their queries to microseconds can use this feature, and they don't have to change the code too much. The DAX cluster (yes, another cluster) is managed by AWS; you just decide the size and the number of nodes.

*Alex*: I'm going to take note of all of these technologies we covered. ElastiCache, CloudFront, DAX, and so on. I'm going down to floor 1, to the supplies room, to get a pen and a notebook. Do you need something from there?

*Harold*: You don't need to go downstairs; you can get these from our local material room, behind the printers.

*Alex*: Oops. Some more caching to the rescue!

This was another option of caching that nobody but Berta considered. Databases can perform their own caching, by themselves, or with some external service, such as DAX. This option has also been taken into account as it can simplify some of the proposed solutions. Of course, the database administrators will also have to be considered in the meeting they'll have with the developers.

## Summary

Now, all options for caching are covered: caching in memory (with ElastiCache), caching in the edge locations (with CloudFront), and caching performed by some databases. Each one of them uses a different set of services. Decoupling the services continues to be an important feature, as they can be managed and scaled separately. In all cases, there's one main goal: improving performance.

The team is considering using both services, ElastiCache and CloudFront, to improve the performance of their systems. One project will involve the developers using Redis in ElastiCache, instead of accessing the data directly, as it is being done now. This will be led by Harold, and they will probably invite the database administrators too.

The second project is more network-focused and will be led by Raj. They'll configure CloudFront distributions for some of their public web applications.

The rest of the team will coordinate their efforts and will have the responsibility of measuring the performance improvements. Remember, they need metrics, or objective numbers, to measure their level of success.

Berta also mentioned that she attended a session on blockchain, something they will need very soon. There's a completely new, different request coming along, so this will prove very useful.

## Further reading

- Caching overview: https://aws.amazon.com/caching/

- Amazon ElastiCache: https://aws.amazon.com/elasticache/

- Amazon ElastiCache for Memcached: https://aws.amazon.com/elasticache/memcached/

- Amazon ElastiCache for Redis: https://aws.amazon.com/elasticache/redis/

- Caching strategies: https://docs.aws.amazon.com/AmazonElastiCache/latest/mem-ug/Strategies.html

- Networking on AWS: https://aws.amazon.com/products/networking/

- AWS Global Infrastructure: https://aws.amazon.com/about-aws/global-infrastructure/

- CDN and edge locations: https://aws.amazon.com/edge/

- CDN and edge locations: `https://aws.amazon.com/cloudfront/features/`
- Amazon CloudFront: `https://aws.amazon.com/cloudfront/`
- Database caching: `https://aws.amazon.com/caching/database-caching/`

# Blockchain – Who
# Watches the Watchmen?

The holidays are approaching and the team is beginning to prepare for them. After the recent changes performed on the environment, all applications are running smoothly and automatically and are perfectly monitored. However, there is still one serious task they don't know about yet but that they'll have to perform soon.

Gloria summons everyone into a meeting room and mysteriously locks the door:

*Gloria*: Hello, all. How are you doing?

*Alex*: Great. I can imagine everybody is planning their holidays.

*Gloria*: Good to know, but we have a last-moment requirement. And this one seems to be more serious, as it comes from our legal department.

*Alex*: Maybe I need a lawyer. They've realized I filled my refrigerator beyond the maximum load allowed.

*Gloria*: I'll never get used to your sense of humor. Especially with refrigerators. No, this is something that could take some more time to fix than yours.

*Berta*: Please tell us! Such terrible suspense!

*Gloria*: Yes, let me explain the problem in a simplified manner. We have some legal contracts with various vendors we work with; most of them are stored in a database in digital form. These show some financial facts, sales, and several customers – all standard information. But because of a new compliance requirement, our legal department needs a way to verify that these contracts are not altered after they have been signed. And they want us to ensure that every change that happens afterward is tracked and the integrity of the documents is maintained.

*Harold*: Should be easy, I guess. We can remove all permissions to edit the documents once they are stored and track all changes if anyone modifies them.

*Gloria*: Wouldn't that create a new issue when we actually have to modify the contract?

*Harold*: I guess we could maintain another copy of the contract as a separate entity.

*Raj*: No, Harold. I'm getting an idea of the real problem. My cousin is a cybercrime lawyer and we talked about this recently. Every piece of data you extract from an electronic system can be manipulated. Maybe the administrator changed some records, or someone destroyed part of them, or just modified the final report. Everybody with permissions could do any sort of unwanted, even illegal, manipulations during the process and remove all logs and any proof of what happened.

*Gloria*: Exactly, you nailed it. We have to show the data but also prove that it was not manipulated by anyone, not even us.

*Harold*: But anyone who is an administrator could modify the data, all the logs, without anybody ever noticing. And of course, we need some administrators. I don't see any technical solution to this.

*Alex*: Hmm. I think there could be a technical solution. Berta commented something about blockchain during our last day at our cloud event. While flying back from our event, I read a magazine on the plane, and there was an article about it. Nice coincidence. This could be our solution.

*Berta*: Sure. Maybe you can explain what you learned and I can provide elaboration based on what was talked about in my session.

*Harold*: Blockchain? This is something related to cryptocurrencies?

*Alex*: Yes, the article mentioned crypto coins. But there are many other possible uses. Let me explain a bit about it and we can then decide whether that's our solution. Berta, correct me if I'm terribly wrong.

*Berta*: Take it for granted; I'll show no mercy!

## Blockchain technologies

Everyone gathers in a meeting room and Alex starts his explanation:

*Alex*: On a very high level, people consider blockchain just a special database, but it is not exactly that. A **blockchain** is a kind of digital shared archive of information that can be accessed only by authorized people (a network of people). A typical database stores data inside tables, but a blockchain stores data together in groups known as **blocks**. These blocks have a fixed storage capacity; when one block is filled, a new one is created for the remaining data, and it is linked to the previous block, thus forming a **chain**.

*Harold*: So, it is a chain of blocks and that's why it is called blockchain. That's evident.

*Alex*: Yes, exactly. All data gets chained in chronological order. Think of it as a block that is set in stone; it can't be modified once stored. It becomes part of a timeline and is given an exact timestamp when added to the chain.

*Harold*: What kind of information can be stored inside a block?

*Alex*: It could be anything, as long as it fits inside a block. Most commonly, it's transactions. If you are using blockchain for financial transactions, a block will probably contain the transaction ID, sender and receiver information, amount, currency, and maybe additional metadata. All data is stored sequentially, as new blocks can only be added to the end of the chain. Every block stores its own hash, along with the hash of the previous block. If any modification is attempted anywhere along the chain, the value of the hash will also change and that would break the chain, making evident any attempt of modification:

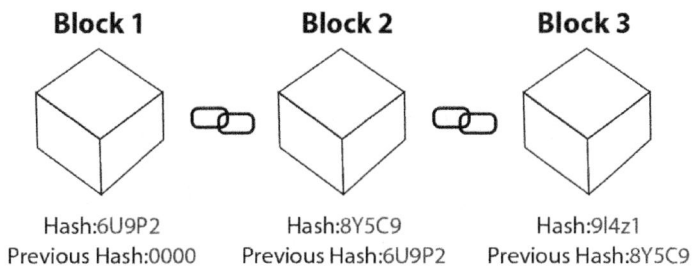

| **Block 1** | **Block 2** | **Block 3** |
|---|---|---|
| Hash:6U9P2 | Hash:8Y5C9 | Hash:9l4z1 |
| Previous Hash:0000 | Previous Hash:6U9P2 | Previous Hash:8Y5C9 |

Figure 15.1 – Information chained in blocks

There is also another characteristic that makes a blockchain secure, and that is its *decentralization*. Instead of using a centralized entity to manage the entire chain, a blockchain uses a peer-to-peer network that everyone can access and join. Whoever joins this network becomes a node and obtains a complete copy of the blockchain.

When someone creates a new block, it is sent to all participant nodes, who will verify the integrity of the whole chain. If it is successfully verified, all nodes will receive an acknowledgement and will store the new block locally. But if one or more blocks were corrupted or tampered with, then the modification will be rejected by all:

Figure 15.2 – A peer-to-peer network in a blockchain system

Raj: Can you give me any practical examples of where this technology is being used?

Alex: The most common example that people relate to is Bitcoin or, similarly, crypto coins. All of them use blockchain to record a ledger of payments. But there are many more scenarios, as the immutable nature of blockchain can help in various projects where you want to rule out any fraudulent attempt to compromise a system, such as voting, tracking, financial transactions, storing property records, patient information, and so on. According to one magazine I read, a company is using it to track the distribution journey of their food products. If necessary, they can track a product to not only the origin but also anything else it may have come into contact with.

Raj: I knew about crypto coins, but I see it's much more generic.

Harold: So, Bitcoin does not mean blockchain and vice versa?

Alex: No. Bitcoin and blockchain are not the same. Bitcoins are built on the foundation laid out by blockchain. Bitcoin uses blockchain technology to record all transactions.

Raj: Think of blockchain as a runtime or framework, which can support and run many applications on it.

*Harold*: That's clear now.

*Raj*: Does it require or use any proprietary software?

*Alex*: Most of the blockchain software is entirely open source so that everyone can review all code if needed, especially auditors. From a business perspective, it is a type of next-generation business process improvement software. Blockchain provides a ledger, which uses strong encryption algorithms and advanced security protocols. Maybe some legislation will soon be passed on how to use this technology and whether it's possible to use it as proof in courts. The article mentioned that some countries were beginning to consider it.

*Harold*: You used the word *ledger*. I only know about financial ledgers. What is a ledger in blockchain terminology?

*Alex*: A financial ledger is used to record each and every financial transaction carried out by a company or person. Similarly, a **ledger** in blockchain records each and every operation and transaction that is carried out. In the case of blockchain, this ledger is **immutable**.

*Harold*: That is clear.

Alex has impressed everyone with his knowledge of such a complex topic. He has also answered all the questions the team has and seems to have done a lot of research on blockchain technology. He takes a quick look at Berta to see whether he has forgotten something:

*Berta*: Fantastic explanation, Alex! I didn't think about all the possibilities. Now, a new world opens up to us!

*Alex*: Thanks, Berta. But I studied the theory behind blockchain. Let's go into its practical usage. I assume there's a managed service in AWS that offers blockchain.

*Berta*: Yes. It is called **AWS Managed Blockchain**. This one was easy to guess. We had a nice session about it at the event.

*Harold*: I can imagine it's a group of servers, totally managed by AWS, with all the blockchain software pre-installed. As in any managed service, we don't have to worry about the operational and implementation aspects.

*Berta*: Yes, it will take care of everything – nodes, their availability, certificates, and anything that is needed. You can create your own blockchain network with your nodes but also join other existing networks. Let's consider these possibilities and the service.

Alex has done a fantastic job in compiling all the information about blockchain with its many possibilities. At the same time, Berta has studied the specific AWS service providing them, AWS Managed Blockchain. The concept is now much clearer to the team, but they still have to dig into the details or maybe other possibilities.

# Quantum ledger databases

After a short break, they return to the room, with a much more decided attitude. They feel they already have the solution to their problem:

*Berta*: Okay, everyone, do all of us agree to use AWS Managed Blockchain for this immutability requirement? Let's begin to read about its implementation details.

*Alex*: Not so fast. I also spent some time reading about Managed Blockchain, and I can definitely say that these are not the droids we're looking for… I mean, this is not the technology we should use for our use case, as I've found something more suitable.

*Berta*: I hope that *suitable* means also *easier*. Hehe!

*Alex*: Well, I would say, yes! Blockchain technology seems far too complex for what we would like to achieve because it is a technology designed for a *decentralized scenario*, but ours is, well, a completely *centralized scenario*.

*Harold*: Could you please, Alex, clarify for us the two terms? You mentioned decentralization before, but could you please compare the two?

*Alex*: Sure! First of all, what I'm talking about is *ownership*. In a *decentralized scenario*, as we saw quickly earlier when I talked about blockchain systems, we have some members, and each one will hold a full copy of all data – the full database. This way, each node can independently verify the transactions and every data change in the chain:

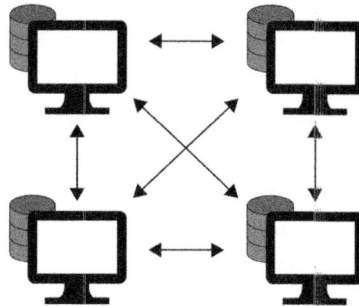

Figure 15.3 – Decentralized ownership

*Alex*: Is there anyone who has played bingo at least once?

*Berta*: Oh yes, I usually play with my parents and relatives at the end of each year. I think it is a boring game.

Alex: Well, many people like it. Anyway, if you have played bingo, you know how it works. Every player has a card with a random list of numbers printed on it. Numbers ranging from 1 to 100 are extracted at random, one by one. There's a person in charge of that, who extracts and publicly announces the number to everyone. Every time a number is announced, each player checks their own card, and updates it by putting a mark on the number if they happen to have it. "Bingo" is called out when a player gets all the numbers on their card marked:

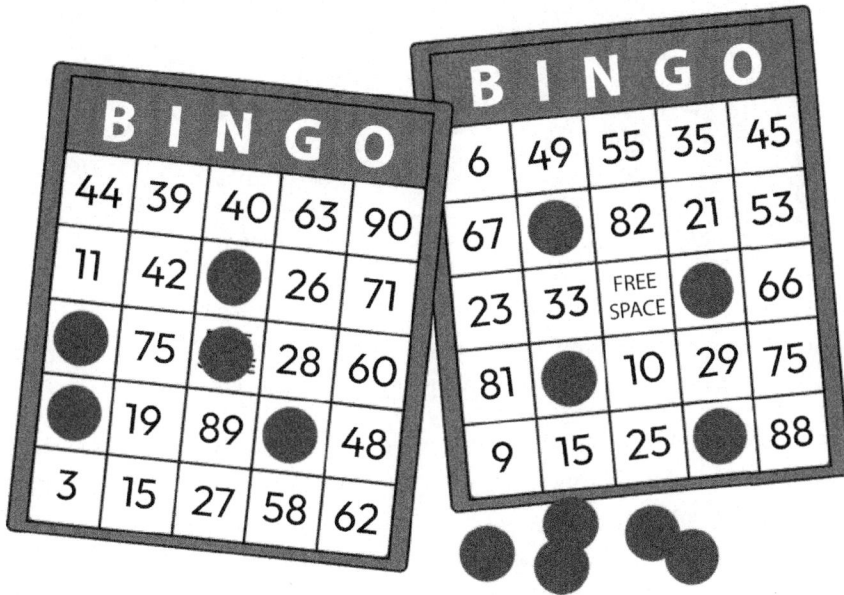

Figure 15.4 – Bingo cards

Harold: I see that each one of the players is playing alone, responsible for their own data card, with no coordination with others. A decentralized system.

Berta: But you can always cheat or maybe, by mistake, mark out the wrong number.

Alex: Yes, but in a decentralized ownership scenario, there will always be some system to verify that data wasn't altered or, in the case of bingo, that someone altered their own card in the wrong way:

Figure 15.5 – Playing bingo – an example of a decentralized ownership scenario

(Source: Photo by istolethetv, at https://commons.wikimedia.org/wiki/File:Bingo_%284579844255%29.
jpg, used under Creative Commons Attribution 2.0 Generic license.)

*Alex*: On the other hand, in a centralized ownership scenario, there is a single database owned by a central entity. Multiple members can read or modify the data from this unique location. Coordination is simpler:

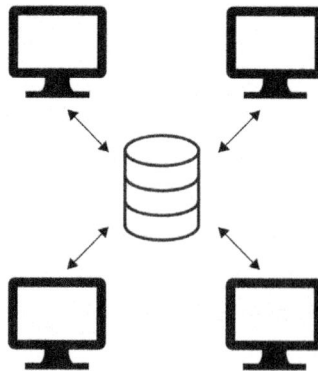

Figure 15.6 – Centralized ownership

*Alex*: An example of centralized ownership can be found with cars.

*Berta*: I didn't know you liked cars, Alex. Hehe!

*Alex*: Well, not particularly, but I read about this example and found it useful. Some car manufacturers, to give a better experience to their customers, provide a mobile app together with a car. This application allows drivers to keep track of all changes carried out, like a passport full of visa stamps, with the full history log. In this case, this "car passport" stores all maintenance tasks performed on the car – revisions, oil changes, diagnostics, car washes, tire changes, and so on.

All this data is tracked in a centralized place, and now all interested parties can take a look at it, including insurance companies, government agencies, repair shops, and, obviously, the car owner or a potential buyer.

Figure 15.7 – The car's "passport" – an example of centralized ownership

*Alex*: In a scenario like this, the best database you would like to have is a ledger, a database that has a journal – you can think about it as database transaction logs, where all transactions are recorded in a time sequence, which is *immutable* and *cryptographically verifiable*.

*Berta*: Oh, Alex, you said it was an easier technology! There are so many new terms!

*Alex*: Haha, don't worry, Berta. I'm going to explain these terms. As I said earlier, ledger databases use some concepts from the blockchain world, but there are also some differences. Yes, there are some new concepts to deal with, but I can promise they will be easy.

First of all, the journal is *immutable*. This doesn't mean that the database is read-only or something like that; of course, you can modify the data at any time, or that would render the database useless. But the history of all changes done or, to be more precise, all the transactions that modified the data… well, these can't be modified by anyone, including the database owner! There's no way to modify this history.

To help you understand, think about hospitals and the medical records related to their patients:

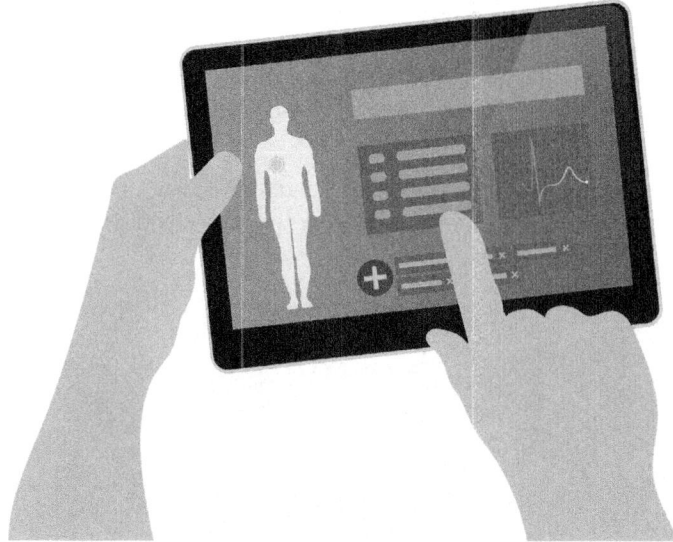

Figure 15.8 – Medical records – an example of immutable data

*Alex*: When a person is at a hospital, their medical history is recorded somewhere in the hospital's databases. Doctors, through the applications they use, can always add new medical records (maybe because the person received fresh treatment) or modify existing ones (maybe because someone entered a mistake). But the history of all those additions or updates can't be modified, so it's always possible to take a look at the medical history of a patient, and what changes were made.

*Berta*: Interesting. If someone makes a mistake, it also gets recorded. No way to hide it. In the end, this should be a good thing for the health system.

*Harold*: What surprises me is the fact that the database owner can't modify the history of the changes under the hood. How is this possible?

*Alex*: This is because the information about the history of all the changes is stored within blocks that are encrypted and strictly related one to another in order to make a chain so… a chain of blocks, the same blockchain concept we talked about earlier:

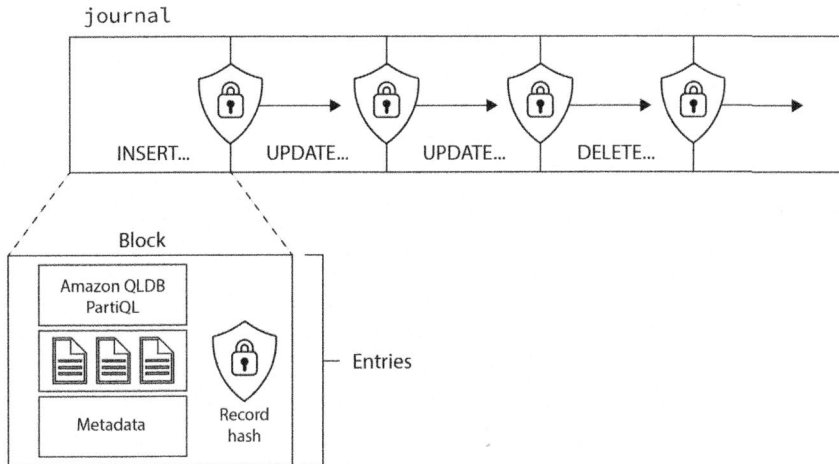

Figure 15.9 – Medical records – an example of immutable data

*Alex*: Data can't be altered but… imagine that there could be a way. So, a ledger database also offers a feature allowing the verification of all of the chain. This cryptographical process…

*Berta*: Hmm, Alex, before you go ahead, I'm a bit uncomfortable with these *crypto* terms…

*Alex*: Sure, Berta, no problem. By **cryptography**, we refer, generally speaking, to the practice and study of the techniques to secure communications, especially when there is a third *malicious* actor that wants to read or see what is not supposed to be read or seen. In the recent past, Berta, when we talked about the AWS KMS service, we talked a lot about **encryption**. Well, encryption is just the name of a process that belongs to cryptography, so, one of its practices.

*Berta*: Okay! Got it! Please, continue.

*Alex*: Sure, you're welcome. So, I was saying that the cryptographical process recalculates the entire chain of blocks and compares it to the current one, which means you can always verify whether someone altered the history of changes. And that feature is available to everyone, not just to the database owner. That's the reason ledger databases are said to be *cryptographically verifiable*. I won't go into detail right now; we can check the related documentation later.

*Harold*: Very interesting. Any other use cases for which a ledger database could be used?

*Alex*: Let me think about it. Hmm. Okay, I got it! I have this other use case about prescription medication; currently, there is significant effort involved in tracing the path of a single lot or batch of medication as it leaves a manufacturing plant and eventually reaches a patient. Each organization along the way, such as a distributor, hospital, and pharmacy, currently has separate and distinct processes for managing data about the batch of medication. By using a centralized ledger database that immutably records data output from each organization's applications, the doctors, pharmacists, and government officials could quickly identify discrepancies in production, distribution, and usage or track down a batch that was impacted by recalls or other safety concerns:

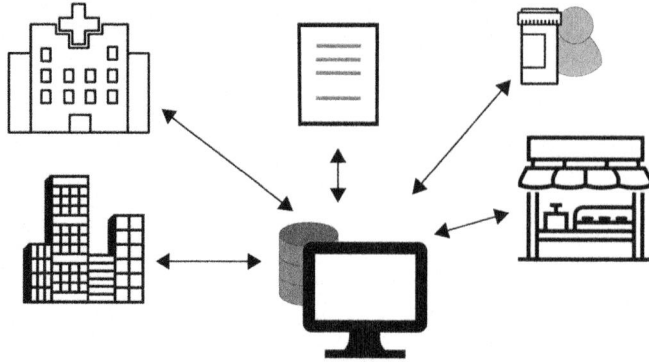

Figure 15.10 – A use case – prescription medications

*Harold*: Does AWS provide a ledger database service?

*Alex*: Here we are! The answer is yes! AWS provides a database service called **Amazon Quantum Database Ledger** or, simply, **Amazon QLDB**. I've taken a look at its documentation over the last 2 days; it's a very interesting service.

*Berta*: Is it a SQL or a NoSQL database? Which data model does it implement?

*Alex*: It's a NoSQL database, Berta, where you store documents. In this case, they are stored as Amazon ION documents, very similar to JSON but enriched with some features, such as data type information and allowing us to add comments. JSON is a standard format we frequently use that has a very simple structure, a collection of keys and values. ION is similar; let me show you an example. In this case, we have a document nested inside another one; look at the Specs key:

```
/* Ion supports comments. */
vehicle = {
        VIN   : "KM12XY34ZWF010234",
        MfgDate : 2023-01-11T,
        Type  : "Truck",
        Mfgr  : "Ford",
        Model : "F150",
        Color : "Black",
        Specs : {
         EngSize: 3.4 (decimal),
         CurbWeight: 4800 (int),
         HP: 330 (int),
```

```
        BatterySize: NULL.int
        }
    }
}
```

Alex: QLDB comes also with a SQL-like language, *PartiQL*, which is an open source project started by AWS. Here, you have an example of a simple query based on the previous document. As you can see, it uses dot notation to access properties inside nested documents. Again, note the `Specs` property:

```
SELECT
    VIN,
    Specs.EngSize,
    Specs.HP
FROM vehicles
WHERE type = 'Truck'
```

Berta: That's cool! I didn't know about this QLDB service, but it could be more related to our needs. Thanks, Alex, for all of this information. I think we need to study its data model a bit more to know more details and to understand the type of statements this language, PartiQL, can run.

Harold: Is QLDB a fully managed service? This is another important aspect we should know from the very beginning.

Alex: Hey, hey! One at a time – too many questions! So, in response to Berta's question – with QLDB you create a database, and within it you create *tables*. You can also add *indexes* to speed up your queries. Each row within a table is an Amazon ION document, as I said earlier. PartiQL is a pretty robust language; you can query your documents by using SELECT statements, you can join tables, and you can obviously insert new documents and modify or delete the existing ones. It's very similar to SQL, so we won't have to learn a completely different language.

In response to your question, Harold – QLDB is a *serverless* service, so there isn't any infrastructure to manage. You create a ledger database in a few minutes and then you are ready to create tables and store data in there:

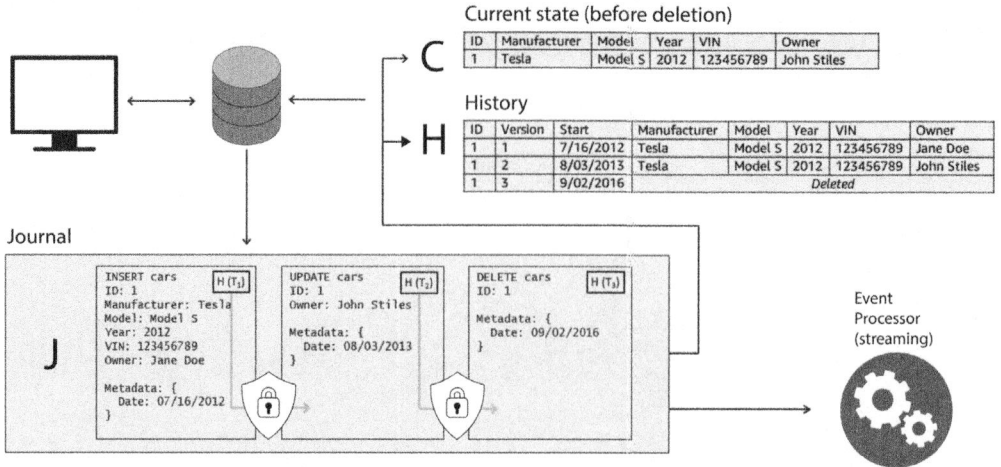

Figure 15.11 – Amazon QLDB high-level architecture

Data (together with some metadata) is stored in the journal, and when you run your queries, QLDB retrieves the data directly from it. The results of your queries represent the *current state or view* of your data; whenever you want, you can get the *history view* of your tables, to retrieve all (or some of) the transactions that were run against those tables.

*Raj*: I assume QLDB is also cryptographically verifiable? I can assume we'll frequently get requests for these verifications.

*Alex*: Good catch. No, it cannot be verified.

*Raj*: But then…

*Alex*: Come on, Raj! Is that a serious question or are you trying to pull a fast one on me? Of course, QLDB can be cryptographically verified! Otherwise, we could not prove the integrity of its contents. Yes, the process uses what is called a **digest**. We can give permission to the legal department so they can run their own digests instead of asking us, or we can automate one digest every week.

*Raj*: Haha, you got me! I was sure you couldn't have gotten mad so easily.

*Berta*: Awesome! This means we only need to study a bit more about how the service works, define the database schema, and that's it! The ledger database will be created in a few minutes. It's not different from other database services we have used so far – for example, Amazon DynamoDB. I love those serverless technologies!

The team has realized that QLDB is going to be a much simpler and better solution than any blockchain. Everybody thanks Alex for his investigation and the exhaustive explanation he provided. All of them are happy to see how he took this initiative.

# Summary

The team immediately discarded the Managed Blockchain option in favor of QLDB. They immediately start a proof of concept by cloning some of the existing customer tables into QLDB and writing some PartiQL queries to get the required information easily. Once this is done, they begin to prepare a process to run digests, both manually and automatically.

Now, it seems all the services needed in TrendyCorp are fully covered. In the next, and final, chapter, they will see how all their consolidated efforts have been perceived by the rest of the company, and some new ideas will arise for the future.

# Further reading

- Blockchain on AWS: `https://aws.amazon.com/blockchain/`
- Amazon Managed Blockchain: `https://aws.amazon.com/managed-blockchain/`
- Amazon QLDB: `https://aws.amazon.com/qldb/`
- PartiQL: `https://partiql.org/`
- PartiQL: `https://aws.amazon.com/blogs/opensource/announcing-partiql-one-query-language-for-all-your-data/`
- Amazon QLDB PartiQL reference: `https://docs.aws.amazon.com/qldb/latest/developerguide/ql-reference.html`

# 16
# What the Future Holds

The holiday season is now approaching. It's a time for celebrations, travel preparation, chats, and a less stressed atmosphere.

The team is far more relaxed now. All their tasks have been accomplished and on time. All the required services are now running in the cloud: databases, web servers, backups, Lambda functions responding to issues and automatically fixing them, and many more. Most tasks are now automated, auto-scaling whenever possible, and continuously monitored, with notifications sent to the relevant parties. Of course, the team will continue to learn and try new features, but all business functionality was delivered without any issues.

They also managed to fulfill all recent urgent requests on time, which was a bit worrying as any delay could have affected their holidays. But in the end, they managed to improve the system performance by using caching. The monitoring team has already perceived a notable performance improvement, and the number of users continues to grow with no waiting or complaints about slow applications.

And the Immutable Database project, which is what they have named it, is currently about to begin. It will need more time to consolidate, but the ledger database is already in place and all testing has proved successful.

## It's time for some company updates

Our team is happy, and everyone is carrying out their holiday preparations, but there is one final task to complete – an important one: all the personnel at TrendyCorp has been invited to a company gala dinner in a stylish restaurant.

All of them are seated at the same table: Gloria, Berta, Charles, Harold, Alex, and Raj. They are enjoying the food, the drinks, and the jokes. Well, only the good jokes.

*Alex*: Great food and drinks! And probably music soon. Nice place. But the best thing about this event is Gloria's rule: no one is allowed to talk about work, or even about IT.

*Gloria*: Yes, that's a rule I have always enforced at these events since long ago. The first one who speaks about work pays for all the drinks.

*Harold*: That is a nice habit we should adopt every day at all our lunches, not only today.

*Gloria*: Unfortunately, I won't be able to follow my own rule tonight. I've been requested by Eva to present what we, as a team, have been doing during the last period; not too technical, but it will be work-related.

*Alex*: Ooohh! This event is a trap! Lots of drinks, now I'm feeling a bit dizzy and I won't be able to escape from a long presentation full of business numbers I will not understand!

*Gloria*: Don't worry, I've negotiated this with Eva. It will be short, and not too boring, I hope. All the numbers have already been sent to management by mail, but maybe there will be some surprises for you.

*Alex*: Really mysterious! I don't really know whether I like surprises at work. Just in case, can I have another glass of that fantastic wine?

A short time after all desserts are served, Eva goes up to the stage, taps on a microphone to see whether it's on, waits for everyone's attention, and begins her speech. We won't reproduce all its contents here, but you can imagine her talking about benefits, effort, commitment, inclusion, sales going up, what a great team we are, and all those classic corporate messages. But everything she says suggests a positive corporate atmosphere. Finally, she ends with:

*Eva*: I'd like to finish my speech by telling you that most of these successful results are because of Gloria's team. I would explain it, but probably would get it wrong, so I think it will be much better if Gloria can tell us a bit about it. Gloria, the floor is yours.

*Gloria*: Thanks, Eva. Yes, I'd like to steal you from your drinks for only 10 minutes. I'll try to keep it short and non-technical.

A murmur goes across the audience. Gloria waits for silence.

*Gloria*: You've seen some changes in the last months. Our applications run more smoothly and quickly and offer more options. But what is the purpose of our applications? Yes, probably you've also seen that now we have far more customers using them, the number of complaints has plummeted, and our sales are skyrocketing.

All the sales personnel shout crazily.

*Gloria*: But that's only the part you can see – the tip of the iceberg. I can tell you how we evolved from our previous situation. Do you remember our previous dinner, one year ago? There was nothing to celebrate then.

She pauses to look at the audience's faces.

*Gloria*: Now all our services are running in the cloud. Everything is running smoothly, monitored, and with auto-scaling. No surprises! No more working after hours; no more of those long weekends fixing a system because of a broken disk. Everything is documented. We have automated many tasks. We don't have to dedicate resources to routine tasks, you know, configuring servers or doing those boring backups. That means the team has more time to dedicate to our business applications. And to you as users.

A round of applause goes through the room.

*Gloria*: And talking about the team: the cloud team that made this possible, you can see all of them sitting at that table. Please, folks, stand up.

They stand up. Everybody looks at them, so they try to find a discrete position to hide, slightly embarrassed by the attention that has come upon them.

*Gloria*: I'd like to announce here, with HR's permission, that all of you are going to get a deserved promotion, for all the effort you dedicated to learning, understanding, analyzing, and finally implementing all the required solutions. Every business need we laid out has been met.

Harold, Raj, Berta, Alex, and Charles look at each other, beaming with happiness and pride.

*Gloria*: And, after this holiday break, we'll be starting some new projects, related to machine learning and data analytics. We need to get more business insights from the growing amount of data. Remember, we still have some really active competitors in our market. So, here comes my second announcement, again, with HR's permission: we're going to hire some more people for the cloud team! We need to grow. In fact, I have already received a couple of resumes from people currently working with our competitors. Haha.

The room joins in the laughter.

*Gloria*: I promised this would be short. I'd like to thank everyone. Please, if you have any business suggestions, come to us and we'll evaluate them. Now we have more time for it, as we're no longer putting out fires! Only one request: do it after the holidays. And now, cheers!

She comes back to her table, where the team is staring at her.

*Harold*: Thanks, Gloria. It was a fantastic speech, and what fantastic news!

*Alex*: Thanks, Gloria, but you broke your own rule, you've been talking about our jobs, and for a long time. You have to pay for the drinks.

*Gloria*: Okay, Alex, go to the bar that has just opened at the end of this room – everything is paid. And please, bring me an orange juice.

*Berta*: Another one for me, please, Alex!

*Harold*: Some soda for me, Alex! With ice, please.

*Raj*: Another one for me too, Alex!

*Charles*: And I want two liters of water – I'm dry! Please, Alex!

*Alex*: Do you think I'm your waiter? Is there no caching system nearby? Okay, okay, I'll go. I probably deserved this. Haha.

Our cloud team parties into the night, happy that their hard work has paid off successfully.

## One final word from our authors

Well, that's all. It took some time to put all of this together, but here it is.

First, thanks for reading. As Alex would say, *"But is there anyone reading up to the Conclusion chapter?"*

We hope you enjoyed all chapters. We tried to keep a reasonable balance between concepts and analogies, and we expect all of them may have provided an interesting read for you.

We've tried to cover most of the foundational services you can find in the AWS cloud: Amazon EC2, Amazon EBS, Amazon RDS, Amazon DynamoDB, and many others. And of course, more generic concepts about the service model, infrastructure, virtualization, containerization, or application modernization, maybe using serverless architectures. We won't detail all of them here, as you can find them in the book's index.

But there are also topics we didn't cover. AWS currently offers around 200 different services, and the list is constantly growing. This book has a limited extent, and we didn't want to add more complexity, as in more powerful services, to an introductory course. That means we'll probably consider writing a continuation of this book in the near future, adding more advanced topics, such as big data (or data analytics), machine learning, and databases in the cloud.

There's another project running in parallel, but using the same style and characters, some sort of a continuation. It will be focused on automation, providing lots of ideas and real examples of how to automate the most frequent tasks in AWS: *Automating the AWS Cloud Using PowerShell Scripts*. Stay tuned.

Technology evolves fast. Probably some new features of every service will appear after this book is published. We are constantly imagining new analogies. Depending on the book's popularity, we might continue with new editions. It will depend on you, readers.

We also hope you liked our jokes (most of them from Alex's mouth) and found all of them appropriate. If you didn't like any of them, apologies. Different cultures have different humor and references. Of course, no offense was intended at all.

We'd like to thank all Packt personnel for all support, ideas, corrections, language, and cultural improvements, and their always positive feedback and attitude. They made it easy. If you ever plan to write a technical book, they're the way to go.

We'd like to end this book with a cliffhanger for its continuation. Imagine a huge collection of CSV text files, constantly growing, not in a database, but you need to make SQL queries on them – immediately and completely serverless. Or, translate their contents to a different language…

*And now we're sure you'll look at your refrigerator in a different way.*

# Index

# ‹packt›

Subscribe to our online digital library for full access to over 7,000 books and videos, as well as industry leading tools to help you plan your personal development and advance your career. For more information, please visit our website.

## Why subscribe?

- Spend less time learning and more time coding with practical eBooks and Videos from over 4,000 industry professionals

- Improve your learning with Skill Plans built especially for you

- Get a free eBook or video every month

- Fully searchable for easy access to vital information

- Copy and paste, print, and bookmark content

Did you know that Packt offers eBook versions of every book published, with PDF and ePub files available? You can upgrade to the eBook version at www.packtpub.com and as a print book customer, you are entitled to a discount on the eBook copy. Get in touch with us at customercare@packtpub.com for more details.

At www.packtpub.com, you can also read a collection of free technical articles, sign up for a range of free newsletters, and receive exclusive discounts and offers on Packt books and eBooks.

# Other Books You May Enjoy

If you enjoyed this book, you may be interested in these other books by Packt:

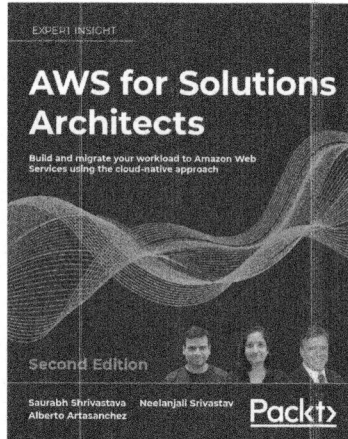

**AWS for Solutions Architects - Second Edition**

Saurabh Shrivastava, Neelanjali Srivastav, Alberto Artasanchez

ISBN: 9781803238951

- Optimize your AWS cloud workload for performance, reliability, high availability, operation, cost, and sustainability using AWS well-architected framework
- Become familiar with the AWS cloud adoption framework and methods to migrate your workload to AWS
- Apply cloud automation at various layers of application workload
- Discover deep networking to build a landing zone in AWS and hybrid cloud
- Identify common business scenarios and select the right reference architectures for them
- Explore the soft skills needed to become an efficient AWS solutions architect

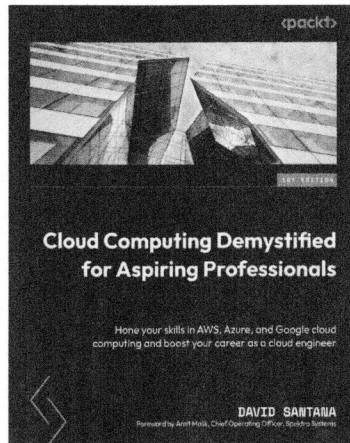

**Cloud Computing Demystified for Aspiring Professionals**

David Santana

ISBN: 9781803243313

- Gain insights into cloud computing essentials and public, private, hybrid, and multi-cloud deployment models
- Explore core cloud computing services such as IaaS, PaaS, and SaaS
- Discover major public cloud providers such as AWS, Microsoft, and Google
- Unlock the power of IaaS, PaaS, and SaaS with AWS, Azure, and GCP
- Create secure networks, containers, Kubernetes, compute, databases, and API services on cloud
- Develop industry-based cloud solutions using real-world examples
- Get recommendations on exam preparation for cloud accreditations

## Packt is searching for authors like you

If you're interested in becoming an author for Packt, please visit `authors.packtpub.com` and apply today. We have worked with thousands of developers and tech professionals, just like you, to help them share their insight with the global tech community. You can make a general application, apply for a specific hot topic that we are recruiting an author for, or submit your own idea.

## Share your thoughts

Now you've finished *AWS Cloud Computing Concepts and Tech Analogies*, we'd love to hear your thoughts! Scan the QR code below to go straight to the Amazon review page for this book and share your feedback or leave a review on the site that you purchased it from.

`https://packt.link/r/1804611425`

Your review is important to us and the tech community and will help us make sure we're delivering excellent quality content.

# Download a free PDF copy of this book

Thanks for purchasing this book!

Do you like to read on the go but are unable to carry your print books everywhere?

Is your eBook purchase not compatible with the device of your choice?

Don't worry, now with every Packt book you get a DRM-free PDF version of that book at no cost.

Read anywhere, any place, on any device. Search, copy, and paste code from your favorite technical books directly into your application.

The perks don't stop there, you can get exclusive access to discounts, newsletters, and great free content in your inbox daily

Follow these simple steps to get the benefits:

1. Scan the QR code or visit the link below

https://packt.link/free-ebook/9781804611425

2. Submit your proof of purchase
3. That's it! We'll send your free PDF and other benefits to your email directly

Printed in Great Britain
by Amazon